Hieroglyphs

Hieroglyphs

unlocking ancient Egypt

Edited by Ilona Regulski

The British Museum

Published to accompany the exhibition *Hieroglyphs: unlocking ancient Egypt* at the British Museum from 13 October 2022 to 19 February 2023

Supported by bp

This exhibition has been made possible as a result of the Government Indemnity Scheme. The British Museum would like to thank HM Government for providing Government Indemnity, and the Department for Digital, Culture, Media and Sport and Arts Council England for arranging the indemnity.

First published in the United Kingdom in 2022 by The British Museum Press

A division of The British Museum Company Ltd
The British Museum
Great Russell Street
London WC1B 3DG
britishmuseum.org/publishing

A catalogue record for this book is available from the British Library.

ISBN 978 07141 9128 7 HB
ISBN 978 07141 9129 4 PB

Designed by Catherine Bankhurst
Hieroglyphs typeset in the Cleo font, designed by Cleo Huggins. Additional signs provided by the Johannes Gutenberg University of Mainz.
Colour reproduction by Altaimage, London
Printed in Poland by Drukarnia Dimograf

Further information about the British Museum and its collection can be found at britishmuseum.org

Cover images: Temple lintel of king Amenemhat III, Hawara, Egypt, 12th Dynasty, 1855–1808 BCE. Limestone, H. 89 cm, W. 239 cm, D. 12 cm. British Museum, EA1072. Fragment of the Book of the Dead of Nedjmet, Egypt, 21st Dynasty, *c.* 1070 BCE. Papyrus, H. 34 cm, W. 416 cm, D. 0.2 cm. British Museum, EA10541. Donated by King Edward VII.

Frontispiece: King list from the temple of Ramesses II, Abydos, Egypt, 19th Dynasty, *c.* 1250 BCE. Limestone, H. 140 cm, W. 376 cm, D. 25 cm. British Museum, EA117.

Contents

Sponsor's foreword

The British Museum was founded in 1753. We don't go back quite as far at bp, only to 1909. But that still means we have been investing in Britain for over a century in many different ways, large and small. These range from producing home-grown energy to supporting our educational and cultural institutions. And I am a firm believer that exhibitions like this one, quite apart from just being fascinating to explore, are vital for inspiring future generations – scientists as well as historians, engineers as well as archaeologists.

The story of how the secrets of a lost language and the everyday lives of ancient Egyptians were deciphered is remarkable, revealed thanks to the ingenuity and persistence of the Rosetta Stone codebreakers.

We are proud to support the British Museum to help many thousands of people enjoy this truly extraordinary exhibition. I hope you enjoy it and find it as inspiring as I do. As always, the team at the British Museum has done a spectacular job and we congratulate them on curating this wonderful exhibition.

Louise Kingham, CBE
Senior vice president, Europe & head of country UK, bp

bp

Director's foreword

The decipherment of Egyptian hieroglyphs in 1822 is often seen as one of the most ingenious achievements of Egyptology, offering previously unattainable insights into an ancient world. *Hieroglyphs: unlocking ancient Egypt* celebrates the bicentenary of this groundbreaking feat by presenting new ideas about the early history and culture of writing, and about the Rosetta Stone, the key to this discovery. Today it is the Museum's most visited object and a symbol for all attempts to unlock the ancient past.

The history of the Rosetta Stone is intimately linked to the story of collecting on the eastern frontier of European imperialism. The Egyptian objects seized from Napoleon's legion by the British army were effectively the first large-scale collection to be given to the British Museum in 1802. In this exhibition, the Rosetta Stone's temporary redisplay allows visitors to fully appreciate its impact on the Museum, modern Egyptology and our understanding of ancient Egypt.

Building on the unprecedented international collaboration that contributed to the decipherment, this exhibition highlights dialogues between generations and cultures, and between Egypt and Europe. Egyptology continues to be a developing field of research and the Museum is proud of its innovative partnerships with institutions in Egypt and around the world.

Significant loans from the Musée du Louvre, France, and the Museo Egizio, Italy, who share similar collection histories with the British Museum, underpin a commitment to exploring the layered stories of objects, including their acquisition, reuse and reception. Collaboration with colleagues in Egypt reveals contemporary perceptions of the impact of ancient Egypt on modern society. Vignettes of personal stories dotted through the publication bring ancient voices to life and allow readers to make their own meaningful connections with the past.

The legacy of decipherment is presented through the rich collection of written sources from the British Museum, many of which are displayed in this exhibition for the first time. Several loans transport us back to when scholars first engaged with hieroglyphs. A rare Coptic alchemical papyrus, borrowed from the Bodleian Library, England, illustrates the medieval Arab interest in the magical powers of hieroglyphs. An original fragment of the Montecitorio obelisk from the Museo Archeologico Nazionale di Napoli, Italy, and the oldest surviving copy of Horapollo's *Hieroglyphica* from the Biblioteca Medicea Laurenziana, Italy, helped trigger the Renaissance revival of Egypt.

The national libraries of France and Britain hold the original correspondence of the story's protagonists, Jean-François Champollion and Thomas Young. What remains of these handwritten notes reveals their thoughts and aspirations, and the trial and error that usually accompanies such pioneering work. Champollion's initial struggles to translate the hieroglyphic text on the Rosetta Stone shifted his attention to the spectacular *Book of Breathing*, now in the collection of the Huis van het boek, the Netherlands, and displayed in the UK for the first time. The remarkable casts and drawings currently kept in the Thorvaldsens Museum, Denmark, provided crucial material for scholars at a time when original source materials and accurate copies of inscriptions were difficult to obtain. The warm correspondence between Champollion and colleagues in Newcastle, England, regarding the cartonnage of Baketenhor, testifies to their collegiate relationship and offers a different perspective to the popular narrative of rivalry between the British and the French. To this day, the collaborative spirit embraced by these early scholars continues to transform our understanding of ancient Egypt.

We are sincerely grateful to our colleagues in institutions across the UK and Europe who have contributed to this exhibition through their generous loans.

Finally, I would like to thank our long-term exhibition partner, bp. Without their support, *Hieroglyphs: unlocking ancient Egypt* would not have been possible.

Hartwig Fischer
Director, British Museum

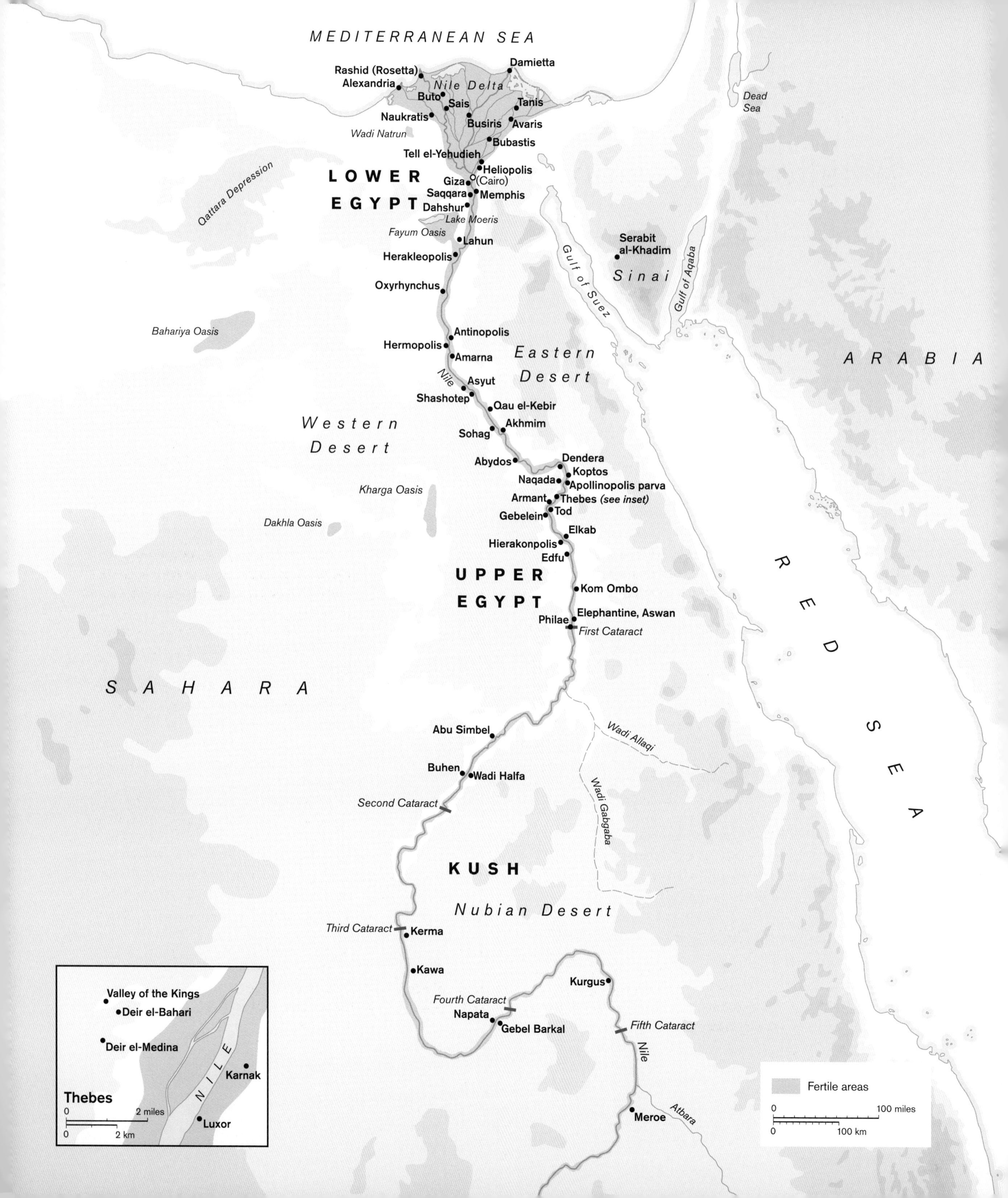
MEDITERRANEAN SEA
Rashid (Rosetta)
Damietta
Alexandria
Nile Delta
Buto
Sais
Tanis
Naukratis
Busiris
Avaris
Dead Sea
Wadi Natrun
Bubastis
Tell el-Yehudieh
Heliopolis
Qattara Depression
LOWER EGYPT
Giza
(Cairo)
Saqqara
Memphis
Dahshur
Lake Moeris
Fayum Oasis
Lahun
Serabit al-Khadim
Herakleopolis
Gulf of Suez
Sinai
Gulf of Aqaba
Oxyrhynchus
Bahariya Oasis
Antinopolis
Hermopolis
Amarna
Eastern Desert
ARABIA
Nile
Asyut
Shashotep
Qau el-Kebir
Western Desert
Akhmim
Sohag
Abydos
Dendera
Koptos
Naqada
Apollinopolis parva
Kharga Oasis
Armant
Thebes (see inset)
Tod
Gebelein
Dakhla Oasis
Elkab
Hierakonpolis
Edfu
UPPER EGYPT
RED SEA
Kom Ombo
Elephantine, Aswan
Philae
First Cataract
SAHARA
Wadi Allaqi
Abu Simbel
Buhen
Wadi Halfa
Wadi Gabgaba
Second Cataract
KUSH
Nubian Desert
Third Cataract
Kerma
Kawa
Kurgus
Fourth Cataract
Napata
Gebel Barkal
Fifth Cataract
Nile
Atbara
Meroe
Valley of the Kings
Deir el-Bahari
Deir el-Medina
NILE
Karnak
Thebes
Luxor
0 2 miles
0 2 km
Fertile areas
0 100 miles
0 100 km

Timeline of decipherment

3250 BCE	Egyptian writing is invented in Upper (southern) Egypt; the earliest evidence comes from the site of Abydos.
2690 BCE	The earliest known complete sentence in the Egyptian language is written down.
644 BCE	The (northern) demotic script is introduced to the south of Egypt and employed across the entire country.
332 BCE	Alexander the Great conquers Egypt, after which the Greek language becomes increasingly dominant in the country's administration.
31 BCE	Octavian (the future Emperor Augustus) brings two obelisks from Egypt to Rome, Italy, after his victory over Antony and Cleopatra.
30 BCE	Egypt becomes part of the Roman Empire.
311 CE	The Edict of Toleration legitimises Christianity.
357	The Roman emperor Constantius II has two obelisks removed from Karnak Temple and transported down the Nile to Alexandria, and one onwards to Rome to decorate the Circus Maximus.
380	Christianity becomes Egypt's state religion.
394	The last hieroglyphic inscription is created on the temple at Philae, near present-day Aswan.
395	Division of the Roman Empire into eastern and western halves; Egypt becomes part of the Eastern Empire (capital at Constantinople, modern Istanbul, Turkey).
451	Council of Chalcedon, where Christian leaders gathered with the aim of unifying Christendom. The disputes there eventually lead to the separation of an Egyptian ('Coptic') Church.
452, 11 Dec	The last demotic text is inscribed in Philae.
456/457	Cults at Philae, the last functioning ancient Egyptian temple, cease.
640	'Amr ibn al-'Āṣ defeats the Byzantine garrison at Babylon, Cairo, completing the Arab conquest of Egypt. The local language was to be replaced gradually by Arabic.
706	Use of Greek as the administrative language in Egypt is abolished.
850s	The Abbasid caliph al-Mutawakkil orders a fort to be built in Rashid (Rosetta).
970 or 972	Al-Azhar University, the oldest surviving university in the world, is founded in Cairo.
***c.* 1000**	Arabic is introduced as a language for the public performance of church ceremonies in the Coptic Church. Ecclesiastical manuscripts are increasingly bilingual, with juxtaposed columns of Coptic and Arabic.
1200s	Egyptian scholar al-Idrisi suggests that Coptic was linked to ancient Egyptian, calling the latter 'the first Coptic language'.
1419	Horapollo's dictionary, the *Hieroglyphica,* is rediscovered on the island of Andros, Greece.
***c.* 1479**	Sultan Qait Bey reconstructs the fort at Rashid (Rosetta).
1517	The Ottomans defeat the Mameluke sultan and Egypt becomes part of the Ottoman Empire.
1587–9	Pope Sixtus V starts a programme of restoring and re-erecting Egyptian obelisks brought to Rome by previous emperors.
1615–16	Coptic manuscripts containing grammars and vocabularies are brought to the West by Pietro della Valle.
1635	Athanasius Kircher sets out to translate the hieroglyphic inscriptions on obelisks in Rome.
1753	An Act of Parliament creates the world's first free, national, public museum: the British Museum opens its doors to 'all studious and curious persons' in 1759.
1764	Excavations at Pompeii in Italy reveal a temple of Isis.
1798, 1 July	Napoleon Bonaparte lands in Egypt with 40,000 troops.
1799, mid-July	Discovery of the Rosetta Stone.
1801, 31 Aug	Capitulation of Alexandria by the French to the British.

1802 Thomas Young is appointed Foreign Secretary of the Royal Society, the UK's national academy of sciences.

1802, Feb The Rosetta Stone arrives at Portsmouth, England.

1802, 27 Mar The Peace of Amiens is signed, and hostilities between France and England temporarily cease.

1805 The Albanian Ottoman governor Muhammed Ali Pasha becomes the de facto ruler of Egypt (until 1848).

1807, Sept Champollion arrives in Paris, France, and installs himself at rue de l'Échelle, a vestige of the medieval city. He has a first serious look at a copy of the Rosetta Stone during 1808.

1810 The Swedish diplomat Johan David Åkerblad writes an important manuscript on the Coptic names of the towns and villages of Egypt.

1812, 12 Nov Champollion submerges an ancient alabaster jar (a canopic jar) in a pot of boiling water in an attempt to loosen the thick, hard substance inside.

1813, 11 Feb Champollion separates a handful of hieroglyphs he characterises as 'alphabetical'.

1814, July Thomas Young begins investigating the Rosetta Stone's inscriptions in Worthing, England, as an 'amusement of a few leisure hours'.

1814, 10 Nov Champollion requests 'a plaster cast from a mould made on the original artefact [the Rosetta Stone]' from the Royal Society.

1815, spring Young realises that the demotic signs are 'imitations of the hieroglyphs, adopted as monograms or verbal characters, and mixed with the letters of the alphabet'.

1815, 1 June Champollion, holed up at city hall with a handful of fellow pro-Napoleon dissidents, issues a proclamation against the menacing coalition of monarchy and church.

1815, 18 June Defeat of Napoleon at the Battle of Waterloo.

1815, 20 July Silvestre de Sacy, Champollion's influential teacher, warns Young about Champollion's claims to have 'discovered many words in the Rosetta Egyptian inscription'.

1815, Nov The explorer William John Bankes discovers and studies an obelisk with the names of Ptolemy VIII and his consort Cleopatra III on the island of Philae, near Aswan.

1817, 16 Oct Giovanni Belzoni discovers the tomb of Sety I in Thebes, present-day Luxor.

1818, 19 Apr Champollion writes to his brother that he has discovered the article ('the', 'a' or 'an'), the formation of plurals, and some conjunctions (linguistic elements linking two or more words, phrases or clauses).

1818, 24 July Champollion identifies the letter 'f' on the Rosetta Stone.

1818, Oct Belzoni removes an obelisk and its pedestal from Philae on Bankes's instruction. The obelisk leaves Egypt in May 1821.

1819 Thomas Young publishes his groundbreaking article 'Egypt' in the *Encyclopædia Britannica*, in which he discusses how phonetics might work in the reading of Greco-Roman royal names.

1821, 27 Aug Champollion admits the existence of phonetics in Greco-Roman names during a lecture at the Académie des inscriptions et belles-lettres, Paris.

1821, Sept The Zodiac of Dendera arrives in Paris.

1821, Sept The alabaster sarcophagus of Sety I arrives in the London docks. Rejected by the British Museum as too expensive, it was instead purchased by Sir John Soane.

1821, Nov The inscriptions on the Philae obelisk removed from Egypt by Bankes are published.

1821, 23 Dec On his birthday, Champollion notes that each hieroglyph cannot alone express an idea, since on the Rosetta Stone there are 1,419 hieroglyphic signs to render only 486 Greek words.

1822, Jan Champollion receives a copy of the Philae obelisk containing the cartouche of queen Cleopatra.

1822, 14 Sept Champollion collapses, probably after discovering phonetic elements in the cartouche of two pharaohs of the New Kingdom: Thutmose and Ramesses.

1822, 27 Sept Champollion reads his *Lettre à M. Dacier* at the Académie des inscriptions et belles-lettres.

1823 Publication of Young's *Hieroglyphics*, in which he outlines his readings of the royal names.

1824 Publication of the *Précis du système hiéroglyphique des anciens Égyptiens,* in which Champollion details his decipherment

	of the hieroglyphic script, demonstrating the values of its phonetic and ideographic signs.
1824, spring	Champollion's biographer Hartleben reports a trip to London to see the Rosetta Stone, but this trip is not confirmed.
1824, 7 June	Champollion arrives in Turin to document the newly delivered Drovetti collection. He stays in Italy until 1825.
1826, 4 Mar–30 Oct	During a second trip to Italy, Champollion visits Turin, Livorno, Rome, Naples, Florence, Bologna, Venice and Domodossola.
1826, Feb	The Louvre, Paris, acquires the second Salt collection at Livorno (the first was purchased by the British Museum).
1826, 15 May	Champollion becomes the first curator of the Department of Egyptian Monuments at the Museum Charles X, later the Louvre.
1826, 16 Oct	The second Drovetti collection is delivered to the Museum Charles X/the Louvre.
1827, Apr	The Duke of Wellington lays the foundation stone for the Philae obelisk at Kingston Lacy, Bankes's home in Dorset, England.
1827, 15 Dec	Opening of the new Egyptian galleries of the Museum Charles X/the Louvre, of which Champollion was keeper.
1828, 18 Aug	Champollion arrives at Alexandria with Ippolito Rosellini for his journey along the Nile; the Franco-Tuscan Expedition to Egypt continues until March 1830.
1828, 17 Nov	Champollion enters the temples of Dendera and finds the remaining cartouches of the Zodiac empty.
1829, May	Champollion visits the tomb of Sety I, the most famous tomb in the Valley of the Kings, Thebes (present-day Luxor), and reports on its poor state of preservation.
1830, Oct	The Philae obelisk is installed at Kingston Lacy, England.
1831	Champollion becomes the first Professor of Egyptology at the Collège de France.
1832, 4 Mar	Champollion dies in Paris at the age of forty-one, probably of a stroke.
1841	The first ancient Egyptian dictionary, written by Champollion, is published after his death.
1842	The German scholar Karl Richard Lepsius publishes a Ptolemaic funerary text on papyrus and calls it a 'Book of the Dead', a designation that has remained in use ever since.
1852	The birth of literary studies in Egyptology, as the first known Egyptian tale on the Papyrus d'Orbiney is published.
1858	The first Egyptian Museum in Egypt is founded near Cairo's port in Būlāq.
1866	Karl Richard Lepsius studies another trilingual decree found at Tanis and confirms Champollion's system.
1880	Discovery of the first hieroglyphic texts on the walls of pyramids at Saqqara.
1884	A hieroglyphic copy of the Rosetta Stone is discovered at Nobeira in the Delta.
1902	The Egyptian Museum is moved to its current location in downtown Cairo.
1903–23	Ahmed Kamal Pasha prepares the first ancient Egyptian dictionary in Arabic.
1907–8	A copy of the Rosetta Stone in hieroglyphs, demotic and Greek is discovered at Elephantine, near Aswan.
1922	Discovery of the tomb of Tutankhamun.
1923	A Greek copy of the Rosetta Stone is discovered at Leontopolis, near Alexandria.
1927	Sir Alan Henderson Gardiner publishes his *Egyptian Grammar: Being an Introduction to the Study of Hieroglyphs*, considered to be the most thorough textbook of the Egyptian language in existence.
1945	Discovery of a significant collection of early Christian and Gnostic texts in the Coptic language, including the *Corpus Hermeticum*, near the Upper Egyptian town of Nag Hammadi.
1955	The British Museum's Department of Egyptian and Assyrian Antiquities is split into the Department of Ancient Egypt and Sudan (now Department of Egypt and Sudan) and the Middle East Department.
2005	A new hieratic copy of the Teaching of Kaires, and the first one including the name of the author, is discovered in a tomb at Asyut in Middle Egypt.
2011	The earliest known written Egyptian papyri (2500 BCE) are discovered on the shore of the Red Sea, 119 km south of Suez.
2017	The Digital Rosetta Stone project is launched at Leipzig University, Germany.

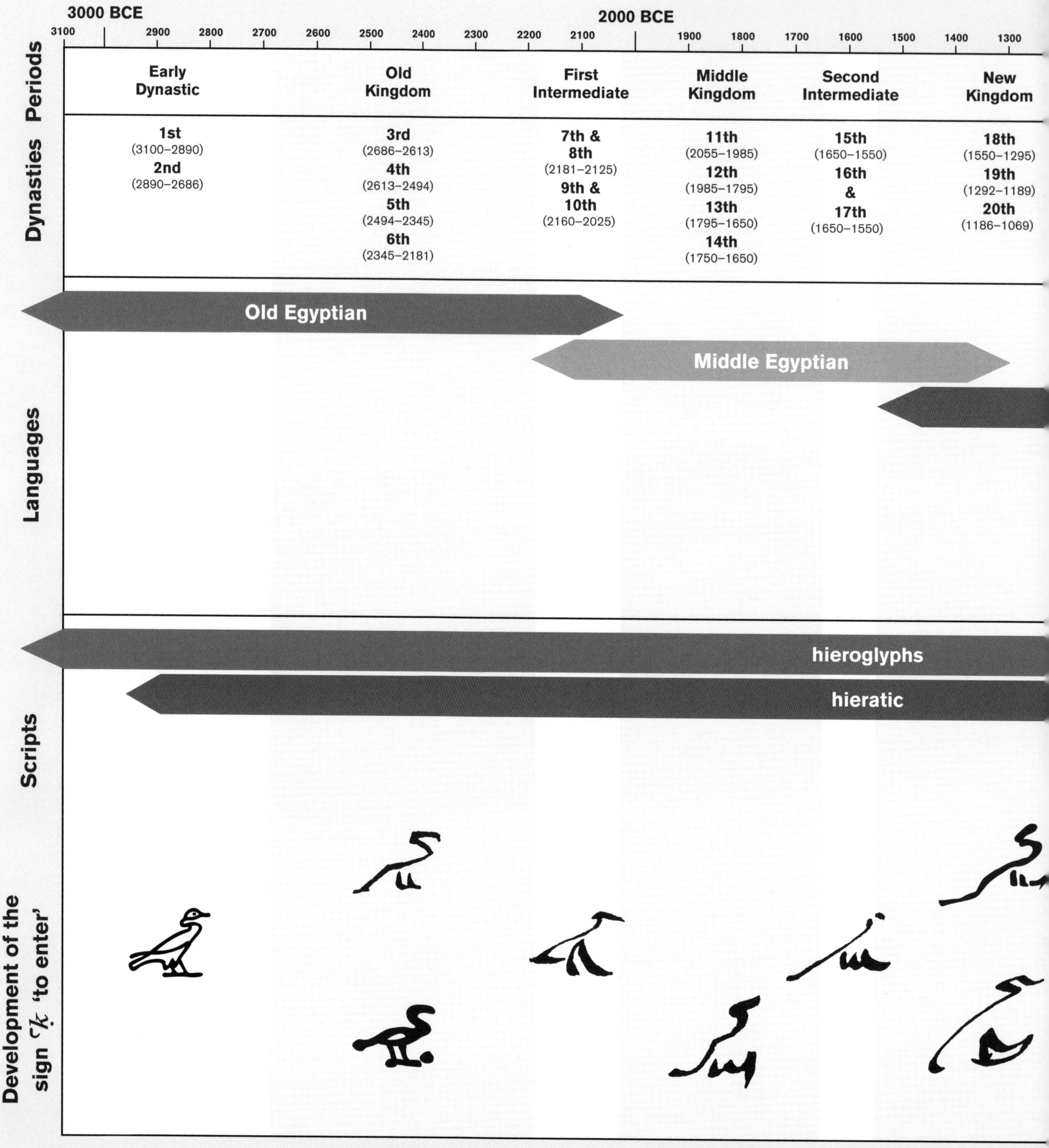
3000 BCE
2000 BCE
3100
2900
2800
2700
2600
2500
2400
2300
2200
2100
1900
1800
1700
1600
1500
1400
1300
Periods
Early Dynastic
Old Kingdom
First Intermediate
Middle Kingdom
Second Intermediate
New Kingdom
Dynasties
1st (3100–2890)
2nd (2890–2686)
3rd (2686–2613)
4th (2613–2494)
5th (2494–2345)
6th (2345–2181)
7th & 8th (2181–2125)
9th & 10th (2160–2025)
11th (2055–1985)
12th (1985–1795)
13th (1795–1650)
14th (1750–1650)
15th (1650–1550)
16th & 17th (1650–1550)
18th (1550–1295)
19th (1292–1189)
20th (1186–1069)
Languages
Old Egyptian
Middle Egyptian
Scripts
hieroglyphs
hieratic
Development of the sign ꜥḳ 'to enter'

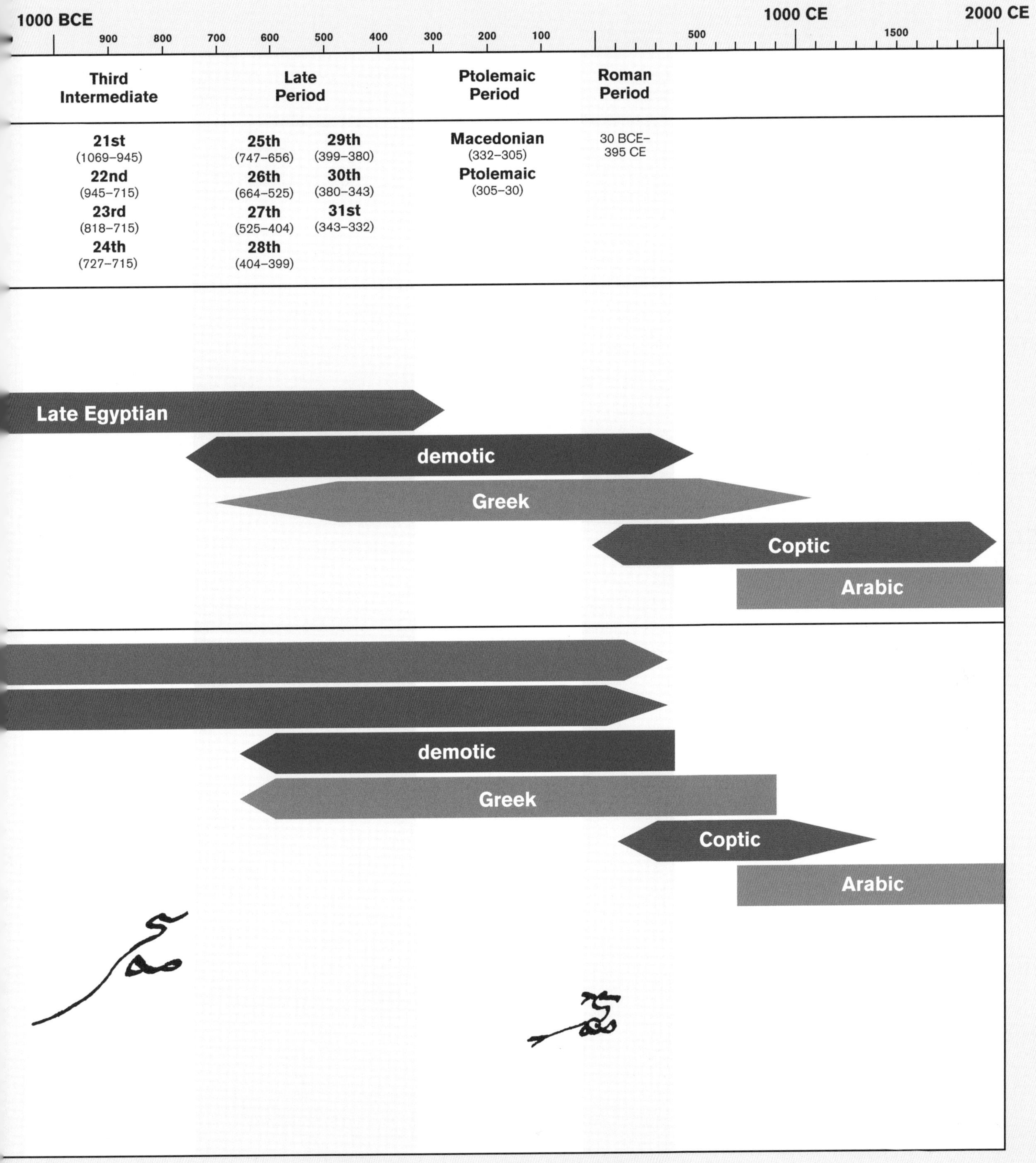
1000 BCE
900
800
700
600
500
400
300
200
100
500
1000 CE
1500
2000 CE
Third Intermediate
Late Period
Ptolemaic Period
Roman Period
21st (1069–945)
22nd (945–715)
23rd (818–715)
24th (727–715)
25th (747–656)
26th (664–525)
27th (525–404)
28th (404–399)
29th (399–380)
30th (380–343)
31st (343–332)
Macedonian (332–305)
Ptolemaic (305–30)
30 BCE–395 CE
Late Egyptian
demotic
Greek
Coptic
Arabic
demotic
Greek
Coptic
Arabic

Introduction

INTRODUCTION

Ilona Regulski

Writing is one of humanity's greatest inventions. By giving a material form to spoken language, it enabled people to store and transmit information across space and time. It was the first information technology and it was groundbreaking. In trying to reconstruct the history of writing, we often turn to sources from ancient Egypt (fig. 1). Every aspect of ancient Egyptian culture, its religious practice, monumental buildings and bureaucratic minutiae, relied on a system of writing developed around 3250 BCE. The earliest known complete sentence written in Egyptian has been dated to about 2690 BCE.[1] The spoken language was used until the fifteenth century CE, making it one of history's longest-surviving recorded languages. But following the conquest of Alexander the Great in 332 BCE, the ancient scripts slowly fell out of use in Egypt and a new alphabet to record the spoken language became more widespread. The last known hieroglyphic text was written at

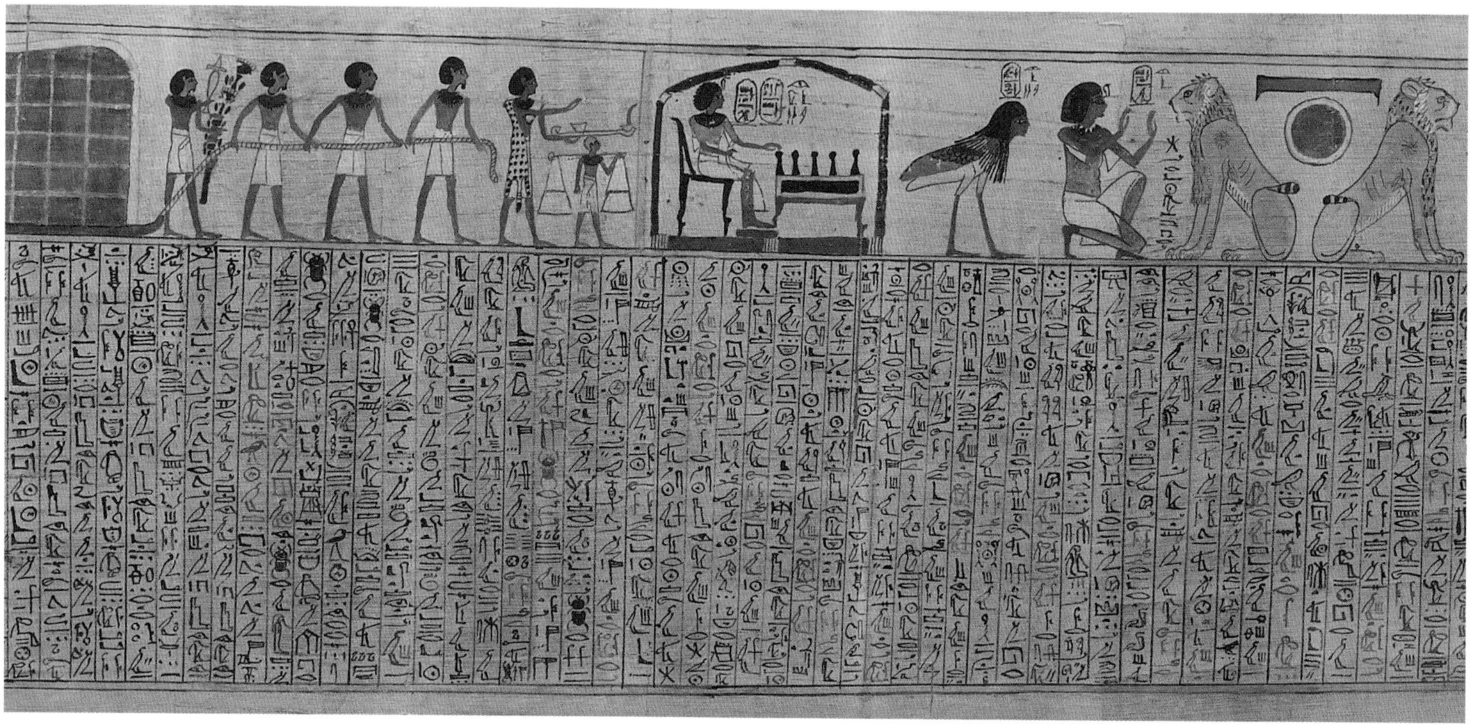

1
Detail of the Book of the Dead of Nedjmet, wife of king Herihor
Egypt, 21st Dynasty, *c.* 1070 BCE
Papyrus, H. 34 cm, W. 416 cm, D. 0.2 cm (entire fragment)
British Museum, EA10541
Donated by King Edward VII

the Temple of Isis at Philae in 394 CE and the last text written in demotic (a cursive form of hieroglyphs) was inscribed there on 11 December 452 CE.[2] Roman and Greek authors, who could not read hieroglyphs, believed them to be symbolic rather than linked to the sound of spoken language, a belief that went unquestioned and effectively obstructed decipherment for centuries.

In the Middle Ages and early modern times, Arab and European scholars attempted to explain Egyptian hieroglyphs, acknowledging that they may have had a phonetic component (that is, reflected the sounds of speech, at least in part). But the discovery of the Rosetta Stone in 1799 provided the decisive key to unlocking the meaning of the mysterious characters (see p. 67). The Rosetta Stone is inscribed with a priestly decree in three different scripts: hieroglyphic, demotic and Greek. Based on the Stone's own declaration that the text is identical in all three cases, the Greek version would eventually lead to the decipherment of the hieroglyphic and demotic text. Recognised as the last remnant of ancient Egyptian, the Coptic language served as an initial reference to give sound to the hieroglyphs. This was only partly successful and it would take another two decades for the code to be cracked.

The Egyptian writing system was deciphered in the early nineteenth century through the work of several scholars, culminating in a final race between Jean-François Champollion (1790–1832) and Thomas Young (1773–1829). Champollion's famous *Lettre à M. Dacier* of 27 September 1822, describing a method for translating hieroglyphs, is usually considered the foundational document of Egyptology. His extraordinary achievement allowed us for the first time to understand the way ancient Egyptians lived and experienced the world, and to read the letters they exchanged with one another, the shopping lists they wrote and the poetry they enjoyed.

The story of decipherment and the consequential birth of Egyptology has often been told,[3] but the ingenious work of Champollion and his peers marked the turning point in a study that is still progressing. Building on 200 years of continuous work by scholars around the globe, the bicentenary of the decipherment celebrates new research carried out in a spirit of international cooperation. The field of Egyptology is as active as ever in seeking to provide access to the ancient world. More diverse, more interdisciplinary and more technologically advanced, Egyptology continues to deepen our knowledge of an ancient civilisation that has ignited our collective imagination and widened our view of the human enterprise as a whole.

Egyptologists continue to shape our dialogue with the past, embracing a broader approach to Egyptian heritage, including its entanglement with Western imperialism. The decipherment of hieroglyphs is also a story of antiquities collection in the age of Empire and the cultural competition between two colonial powers, Britain and France. After the British victory over Napoleon's forces in Egypt in 1801, the antiquities transferred from French ownership helped transform the British Museum into a genuinely public institution, renowned for its collections. The Rosetta Stone's fascination comes not from its visual form or even its content, but from what it represents. More than any other Egyptian artefact, it changed our understanding of the ancient world.

A WRITTEN LANGUAGE

Hieroglyph, meaning 'sacred carving', is a Greek translation of the Egyptian phrase 'the god's word', which was used at the time of early Greek contact with Egypt to distinguish the older pictorial script from the handwriting of the day (demotic). The ancient Egyptian writing system is famous for its use of hieroglyphs depicting animals, plants, humans and objects from the real world (fig. 2). The pictorial nature of the script tended to obscure the fact that it represented a spoken language, and that misapprehension delayed its decipherment for centuries. Like the Roman alphabet used to write English, hieroglyphs largely stood for sounds in the Egyptian language, supplemented with signs to classify their meaning. In ancient Egyptian society, most people would have experienced writing through oral performances of texts, such as the reading of a letter or decree, the singing of poetry or the reciting of religious texts.

Ancient Egyptian belongs to the Afro-Asiatic language family (also known as Hamito-Semitic), attested in northern Africa, the eastern Mediterranean and western Asia. Egyptian resembles Akkadian, Arabic and Hebrew, and differs from such Indo-European languages as English, French and German. The spoken language evolved at a steady rate until it was gradually replaced by Arabic after the Arab conquest of Egypt in 640 CE. Five stages of the ancient Egyptian language are now recognised: Old Egyptian, Middle (or classical) Egyptian, Late Egyptian, demotic and Coptic. They were written in four different scripts: hieroglyphs, hieratic, demotic and Coptic (see pp. 12–13).

Because Egyptian is recorded for over 4,000 years, the archaic and late stages of the language are separated by the same amount of time that divides Old Latin from Modern Italian. Significant phonetic changes must have occurred during that long period. These changes gradually penetrated written forms and certain text genres were more susceptible to alterations than others. For example, religious texts retained a fossilised form of classical Middle Egyptian for centuries, while personal letters tended to mirror the conversation of the time. The hieroglyphic section of the Rosetta Stone was

2
Temple lintel of king Amenemhat III. The hieroglyphs yielding the king's titles are arranged in vertical columns oriented towards his name in the centre.
Hawara, 12th Dynasty, 1855–1808 BCE
Limestone, H. 89 cm, W. 239 cm, D. 12 cm
British Museum, EA1072

written in Neo-Middle Egyptian, which was around a thousand years old when the Stone was created, whereas the demotic represented the language of the moment. The changes between early and later Egyptian affected vocabulary, word order and grammar. For example, the word order in verbal sentences changed from verb + subject + object ('hears he a bird') to subject + verb + object ('he hears a bird') around 1200 BCE.

Only a tiny proportion of ancient Egyptians could read, perhaps 1 per cent. Even among that minority, literacy in everyday cursive scripts and in sacred hieroglyphs differed sharply; most of the literate could probably only read the former. Very few individuals would have been able to read and write the hieroglyphs that were reserved for formal and religious monuments.

ANCIENT HANDWRITING – HIERATIC AND DEMOTIC

The use of a brush or reed pen and ink, as opposed to carving in hard stone, led to a progressive development in cursive writing called 'hieratic' (fig. 3). Painted versions of hieroglyphs began to appear at a very early date, but only around 2700 BCE did the increasing simplification and abbreviation typical of hieratic script become visible.[4] In hieratic, the pictorial aspect of the writing was considerably reduced, and two or more characters could be joined into 'ligatures'. There was a general preference for an orientation in which the script was read from right to left, in contrast to hieroglyphic texts

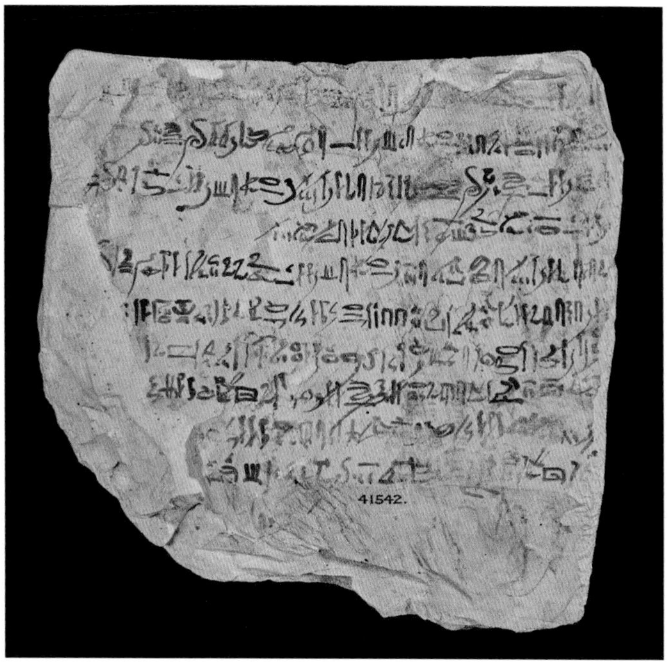

where there was more flexibility in reading orientation. Complex hieroglyphs could be replaced by simpler versions. For example, in hieroglyphs 'cat' was written or classified with the sign depicting a cat , while in hieratic, this was replaced with an abridged sign depicting an animal skin .

The scope and cultural hierarchy of cursive scripts changed over time. Hieratic was used for daily correspondence and literature during the Middle Kingdom (2055–1650 BCE), but 2,000 years later, when Egypt was under the control of the Ptolemaic dynasty, it was used exclusively for priestly purposes, while the more cursive demotic became the everyday script for letters and documents (fig. 4). The late hieratic used in the north developed into demotic during the eighth and seventh centuries BCE.

Champollion introduced the term 'demotic' to modern literature to refer to this later form of cursive script. He was following classical Greek sources which named the 'popular' script (δημοτικά) as demotic, in contrast to 'sacred' or 'priestly' writing (hieroglyphs). Thomas Young instead employed the term 'enchorial', a direct translation of the Rosetta Stone's Greek, which he interpreted simply as the vernacular 'of the country'.[5] The Egyptians themselves referred to demotic as 'letter script', in contrast to the hieroglyphic and hieratic scripts which were called 'script of the House of Life' (Canopus decree, see p. 231) or 'script of the word of god' (Rosetta Stone).

3 (above left)
Limestone sherd (ostracon) inscribed with a hymn to a goddess, possibly Seshat, in hieratic
Thebes, 19th Dynasty, 1295–1186 BCE
Limestone, H. 27.5 cm, W. 27.8 cm, D. 5 cm
British Museum, EA41542

4 (above right)
Ceramic sherd (ostracon) with a demotic text recording the theft of a *ḳbꜣ*-cloth and other items from a tomb
Gebelein, Ptolemaic Period, 100–88 BCE
Ceramic, H. 7.8 cm, W. 10.5 cm, D. 0.6 cm
British Museum, EA29703

Demotic script was used for texts in a phase developed out of the Late Egyptian language. These texts are mostly documentary, such as notary acts, letters and receipts, but also include literature and diverse sorts of lists used in everyday life. After the conquest of Egypt by Alexander the Great in 332 BCE, the Greek language became increasingly dominant in the country's administration, but also in literary texts and day-to-day exchanges. The country gradually grew bilingual.

In the Roman period, after 30 BCE, demotic was replaced by Greek for official contracts and increasingly relegated to inner-temple affairs.[6] Nonetheless, demotic literature thrived for several more centuries. The script used more alphabetic spellings than in earlier periods. Owing to the Roman government's policies disfavouring the native elite, demotic declined from the second century CE onwards. It is no coincidence that its last testimonies are temple graffiti, texts with a very personal message from the faithful to the deity.

TOWARDS ALPHABETIC WRITING IN EGYPT – COPTIC

At the beginning of Roman rule, there was a desire to continue reciting traditional formulae and literature even though the language they were written in was considered archaic. Correct pronunciation was, however, crucial; the idea that what is spoken becomes real is central to ancient Egyptian beliefs.[7] At first these texts were therefore transcribed entirely into demotic one-letter signs to ease pronunciation. Later, a system of pronunciation aids was used, written above the words that needed explaining (glosses), often to indicate vowels precisely. As the Greek language became increasingly dominant in daily communication, a glossing system rendered all the sounds of Egyptian words in the Greek alphabet. Egyptian names and other words were also written in Greek letters. Later, this process came to include demotic signs in order to adequately express sounds of the Egyptian language that did not exist in Greek (sh, f, h, j, ti and the ayn).

This 'new' system of writing must have emerged in an Egyptian religious milieu, since by that time only priests would have had the requisite knowledge of demotic writing to devise the additional demotic-based letters. At around 100 CE a fully functioning system for rendering Egyptian by means of Greek letters and additional signs derived from demotic was in place in different parts of Egypt, with local variants in how these signs were rendered. What we now know as the 'standard' Coptic alphabet grew out of one of these systems, most likely the one used in northern Middle Egypt.

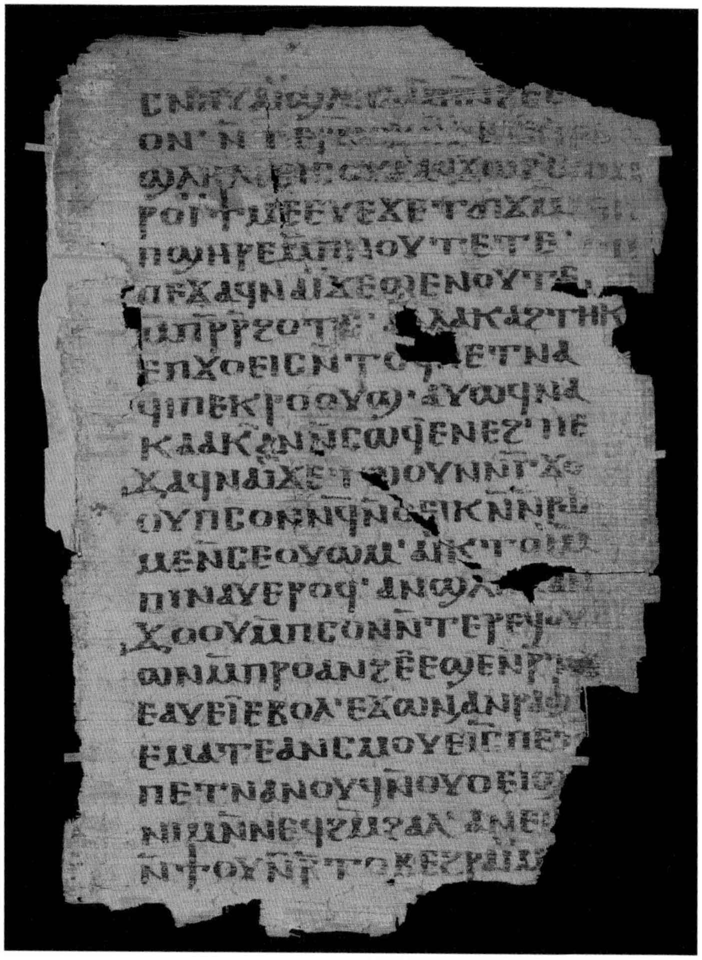

5
Papyrus codex leaf with a narration of miracles attributed to Shenute, the abbot of the White Monastery, near Sohag, in Sahidic Coptic
Egypt, 7th century CE
Papyrus, H. 20.2 cm, W. 14.2 cm, D. 0.2 cm
British Museum, EA71005,6
Donated by Messrs Rutter & Marchant

'Coptic' is an adaptation of the Greek term for the indigenous people of Egypt, *Aigýptios* (Αἰγύπτιος). The ancient Greek term derives from Middle Egyptian *Hut-ka-Ptah*, 'estate of the ka [spirit double] of Ptah', the name of the temple complex of the god Ptah in the city of Memphis. The Coptic language comprises ten different dialects and subdialects; Bohairic, the last and most widely used, was adopted as the official liturgical language of the orthodox Coptic (Christian) church in the eleventh century.[8] Literary attestations of other dialects were initially rare outside Egypt, but it was known that Sahidic, spoken in Upper (southern) Egypt, was the standard dialect by the ninth century (fig. 5). A fully functional alphabetic writing system was therefore in place without the influence of Christianity. Even in the context of polytheism, hieratic and demotic writing would have eroded away, in favour of a writing system based on Greek, the language of the ruling elite.

HOW DOES THE EGYPTIAN WRITING SYSTEM WORK?

Pascal Vernus

Almost all hieroglyphs are pictures. To write words and phrases in the Egyptian language, the writing system uses two main strategies, the 'ideographic' and the 'phonetic' (both are explained below). The two strategies are often combined in the same word or phrase. Hieroglyphic text can be read top to bottom, right to left, or left to right, with the correct orientation often indicated by images of birds, which almost always face towards the start of the text.

Note on transliteration: For ease of writing, reading and pronunciation, hieroglyphs are often written out by students and scholars using mostly letters of the modern alphabet, in an approximation of the sounds of the ancient Egyptian language. This process is called 'transliteration' and it is used widely by Egyptologists. Because many of the precise sounds of the Egyptian language are not known (including the vowels, which are never recorded in hieroglyphic writing), transliterations are only ever approximations, based on evidence from Coptic and other sources.

THE IDEOGRAPHIC STRATEGY: WRITING A CONCEPT

When used ideographically, a hieroglyph basically represents an idea. This could be an object, an action or a category to which the word belongs.

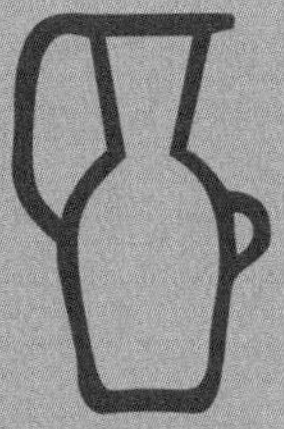

Within ideographic signs, there are two subgroups: logograms and determinatives. When it functions as a logogram, a sign represents a word, or different words, that can be pronounced in the ancient Egyptian language. When used as a determinative, the sign conveys meaning, but not a sound that can be spoken aloud.

LOGOGRAMS

The first type of logogram means a word that is directly related to the object it depicts, and corresponds to a specific set of sounds in ancient Egyptian. For example:

means 'jar', pronounced *ẖnm*

When the word is a noun, this is sometimes, but not always, clarified by the addition of a stroke:

rd (foot); *ḫtm* (seal)

In ancient Egyptian, all nouns have a gender, either masculine, feminine or neutral. Feminine words have a *t*-ending marked by the sign ; e.g. *mḏꜣ.t* 'book'.

In the hieroglyphic system, a logogram can also be combined with other hieroglyphs to create related words and meanings. In the following example, the logogram functions as the root of multiple other words:

The hieroglyph depicting a seal functions as a logogram in *ḫtm* (the verb to seal); *ḫtm.t* (contract); *ḫtm.w* (seal bearer); *mḫtm.t* (sealed chest).

All these words involve the basic idea of 'seal' and employ the consonants of the root, *ḫ+t+m.* They are distinguished from each other by different pronunciations and affixes (*-t*, *-w* and *m-*).

A hieroglyph can also function as a logogram in words built on different roots but sharing a related meaning:

The hieroglyph depicting the folds of the intestine functions as a logogram in the spelling of *ḳꜣb* (intestine); *wḏb* (fold over); *pẖr* (turn around); *dbn* (go round).

WHAT A LOGOGRAM DEPICTS AND WHAT IT MEANS

Since a hieroglyph is a picture, when it is used as a logogram it involves a relationship between what it depicts and what it means. In *ẖnm* (jar), and in *ḫtm* (seal), this relationship is clear: the hieroglyph means the thing that it depicts.

Often, however, it is much less straightforward. The meaning frequently deviates from what the picture intuitively suggests (this is known as a trope). For example:

> A picture of a tool can mean an activity: a hoe excavating means *grg* (establish) and not a hoe excavating.
>
> A picture of an effect can mean a cause: a sail puffed up means *ṯȝw* (wind).
>
> A picture of a cause can mean an effect: a sunshade means *šw.t* (shadow).
>
> Some pictures may, by extension, represent abstract concepts: a cow suckling a calf means *ȝmś* (to take care of).
>
> Some pictures spring from elements of Egyptian culture: , a ship with a sail, means *ḫntj* (sail upstream). The Nile flows south to north, so boats going north can use the current, but sailing upstream, i.e. southwards, requires the north wind.

DETERMINATIVES

Placed at the end of a word, a determinative indicates the semantic category to which that word belongs, but does not correspond to any spoken sound. A good example is the name of the sun god Ra, in Egyptian *rʿ*. The determinative of the falcon on a standard indicates a deity.

It can follow Ra's logographic spelling , resulting in ; or it can follow its phonetic spelling , resulting in . In either of these spellings, the determinative indicates to readers that this name belongs to the category of supreme beings or deities, but it has no phonetic value; that is, it is not pronounced.

Some other determinatives, following the same principle:

at the end of the word indicates motion: e.g. (fold over), (turn around), (go round).

shows that a word belongs to the category of plants and flowers: e.g. (herbs).

shows that a word belongs to the category of buildings: e.g. (office).

THE PHONETIC STRATEGY: WRITING SOUNDS

Contrary to common belief, the hieroglyphic system is widely phonetic (sound-based) and many hieroglyphs function as phonograms (sound signs). In this case, the pictures convey a sound or a set of sounds, but no inherent meaning. Their phonetic values are based on the principle of a 'rebus': a sign is used for its sound value only, regardless of what it depicts. For instance, in an English rebus, a picture of a saw could be used for the sound of a completely different sense of 'saw': 'I saw a bird'.

Egyptian phonograms function in a similar way, with a slight difference: only the consonants and semi-consonants (letters that look like vowels to English readers) are taken into account. For instance, the hieroglyph depicts a kid, whose name is *j+vowel+b* in Egyptian. When it is used as a phonogram, only the semi-consonant *j* and the consonant *b* are read. In Egyptian, meaning is conveyed by consonantal roots while different vocalisations and affixes help readers work out the different words in which a root may be used. As in the Hebrew and Arabic scripts, it is left to readers to figure out the vowels, drawing on their mastery of the language.

A single phonogram can signify up to a total of four consonant sounds:

Quadriliteral (four-letter) phonograms combine four consonants: e.g. ∩∩∩ combines *m*+ꜥ+*b*+ꜣ (thirty).

Triliteral (three-letter) phonograms combine three consonants: e.g. combines *s*+*n*+*ḏ* (roast goose or fear).

Biliteral (two-letter) phonograms combine two consonants: e.g. combines *m*+*t* (vessel (of the body)).

Uniliteral (one-letter) phonograms signify one consonant. They are usually termed 'alphabetic signs': e.g. and , seen in previous examples, signify the consonants *r* and ꜥ.

For each of the twenty-four basic sounds of the Egyptian language, an alphabetic sign is available (fig. 6).

USES OF THE PHONOGRAMS

Phonograms can be used in various ways:

To code all the consonants in a word e.g. the alphabetic signs and can code the consonants *r* and ꜥ in *r*ꜥ, or *Ra*, the name of the sun god.

To code some of the consonants in a word, while the others are coded by logograms; e.g. in *ẖtm.w* (seal bearer), the logogram codes the root meaning 'seal' and the consonantal pattern bound to it, *ẖ*+*t*+*m*; the alphabetic sign *w* codes the suffix -*w*.

Sounds that are familiar to English speakers		Sounds rarely used in English or not represented by one-letter signs			
𓃀	*b*	𓄿	*ꜣ**	*a* as in *ah*; the most obscure letter as it probably originally had a very different sound	E.g. *mꜣꜣ* meaning 'to see', pronounced 'MAH-ah'
𓊪	*p*	𓇋	*j*	*ee* as in *meet*; originally may not have had a sound of its own but indicated that a syllable began or ended with a vowel	E.g. *bjt* meaning 'bee', pronounced 'beet'
𓆑	*f*	𓇋𓇋	*y**	*ee* as in *meet*	E.g. *ky* meaning 'other', pronounced 'kee'
𓅓	*m*	𓂝	*ꜥ**	*a* as in *ah*; originally a sound deep in the throat, known as 'ayin' in Arabic and Hebrew	E.g. *mꜣꜥt* meaning 'order', pronounced 'MAH-aht'
𓈖	*n*	𓅱 𓏲	*w**	like an English *w* when used at the beginning of a word; otherwise mostly *oo* as in *too*	E.g. *wj* meaning 'me', pronounced 'wee'; *tw* meaning 'you', pronounced 'too'
𓂋	*r*	𓎛	*ḥ*	like an English *h* but originally deeper in the throat	E.g. *ḥwj* meaning 'hit', pronounced 'HOO-ee'
𓋴	*s*	𓐍	*ḫ*	like *ch* in German *ach* or Scottish *loch*	E.g. *ḫꜥw* meaning 'appearance', pronounced 'KHAH-oo'
𓎡 𓎡	*k*	𓄡	*ẖ*	*ḫ* followed by an English *y*	E.g. *ẖꜣy* meaning 'thwart', pronounced 'KHYAH-ee'
𓎼 𓎼	*g*	𓊃	*z*	like an English *z* or *s*	E.g. *zj* meaning 'man', pronounced 'zee' or 'see'
𓏏	*t*	𓈙 𓈙	*š*	like an English *sh*	E.g. *šj* meaning 'lake', pronounced 'shee'
𓂧	*d*	𓈎	*q*	like an English *k*; originally as deep in the throat as possible	E.g. *qꜣꜣw* meaning 'hill', pronounced 'KAH-ah-oo'
		𓍿	*ṯ*	like an English *ch*	E.g. *ṯꜣw* meaning 'wind', pronounced 'CHAH-oo'
		𓆓	*ḏ*	like an English *j*	E.g. *ḏꜣj* meaning 'to cross', pronounced 'JAH-ee'

Letters marked with an asterisk (*) are known as semi-consonants in Egyptian.

Because hieroglyphs do not yield vowels, Egyptologists normally put a short *e* (as in the English word *met*) where necessary between one-letter signs other than *ꜣ*, *j*, *y*, and *w*. Here is a short sentence in transliteration, showing how most Egyptologists would pronounce it:

ink	*sḏm.w*	*r*	*wn*	*mꜣꜥ*	*tm*	*dj*	*nmꜥ*	*n*	*nb*	*ḏbꜣw*
EE-nek	SEJ-em-oo	er	wen	MAH-ah	tem	dee	NEM-ah	en	neb	jeb-AH-oo

The sentence, from a Middle Egyptian autobiographical inscription, means 'I am a proper judge [literally: one who listens to the truth], who does not give preference to the one who can pay.'

6 (facing page)
Table of one-letter (alphabetic) signs and pronunciations

For clarification or reinforcement; e.g. to clarify some (or all) of the consonants of a logogram or phonogram. In *wḏb* (fold over), the two-letter phonogram *w+ḏ* and the alphabetic sign *b* clarify the consonantal pattern involved in the logogram *wḏb*, and the determinative indicates that the word belongs to the category of movement.

ORGANISING THE TWO STRATEGIES

No systematic rules organise the way in which the ideographic and phonetic strategies are implemented to spell words in the Egyptian language. Usages, customs and traditions vary according to the genre of the text and the period in which it was written. Three main kinds of spellings can be distinguished:

Purely logographic spellings, sometimes including determinatives.

Purely phonetic spellings, sometimes including determinatives.

Mixed logographic and phonetic spellings, sometimes including determinatives.

For example, the different spellings of the name of the sun god Ra demonstrate the great variety and flexibility of the hieroglyphic writing system over time:

Purely logographic spellings: , , , , ,

Purely phonetic spellings:

Mixed logographic and phonetic spellings: , , , , ,

Such flexibility in spelling makes the achievements of the pioneers of decipherment even more extraordinary and continues to present challenges to Egyptologists today.

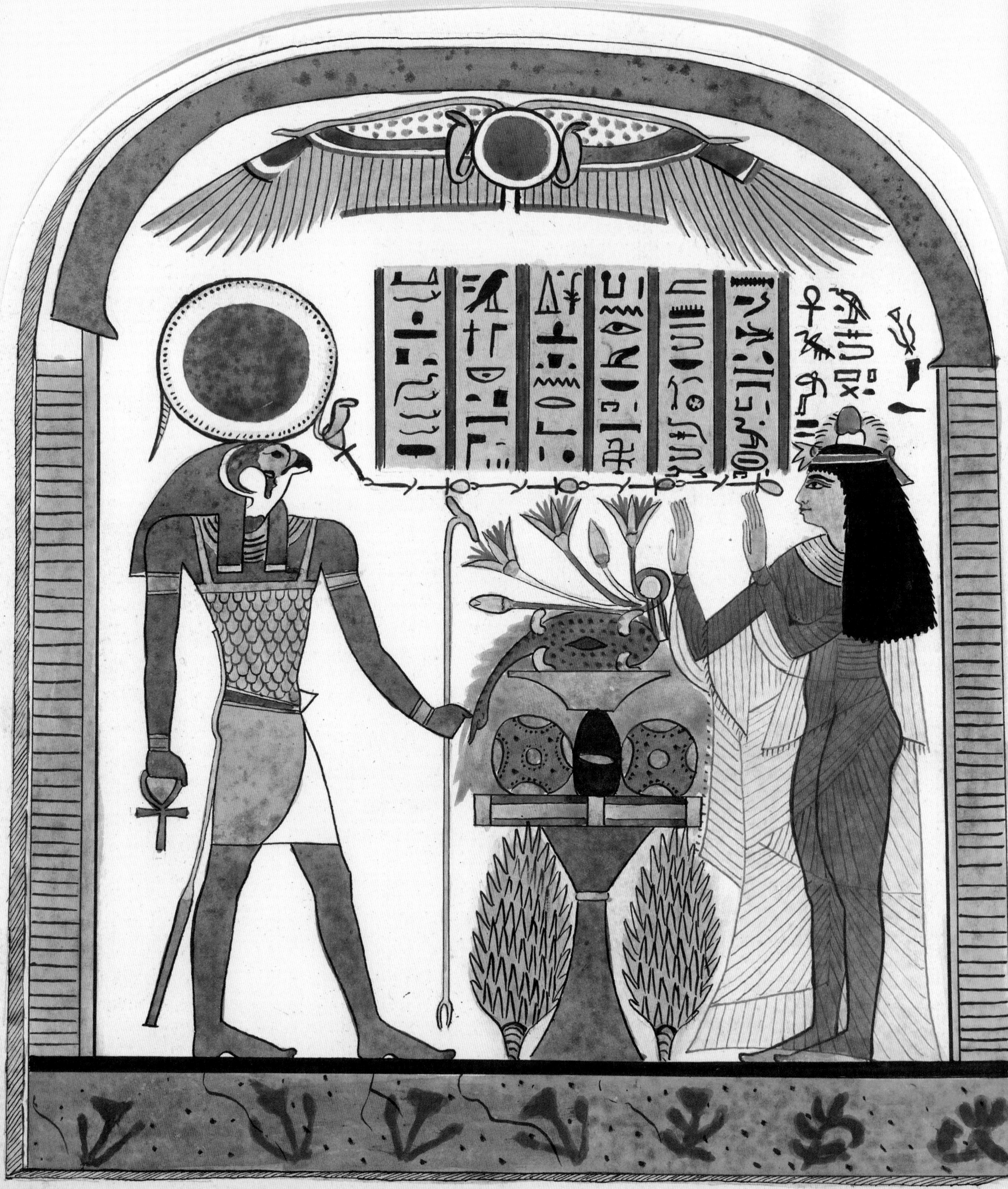

CHAPTER 1 The truth in translation

THE TRUTH IN TRANSLATION: THE JOURNEY TO UNDERSTANDING EGYPTIAN HIEROGLYPHS

Ilona Regulski

> To represent knowledge, they draw an ant. For if a man should hide something safely, this animal would know it.
>
> *Horapollo the Younger on Egyptian hieroglyphs, fifth century* CE[1]

Understanding hieroglyphs was a journey fraught with conjecture and misconceptions, occasionally illuminated by insight and fuelled by an unwavering appetite for knowledge of the ancients. Vibrant, vividly hued hieroglyphs ignited the imagination of medieval Islamic scholars in their explorations of ancient temples and tombs, leading to far-fetched speculation as to their intended meaning. Likewise, Western scholars contributed to the misunderstanding of ancient Egypt owing to their tendency to view the culture through the lens of classical and biblical sources. The writing system

7
Sarcophagus of Hapmen, associated with magical powers since the late 900s and in the 1600s known as the 'lovers' fountain' and believed to relieve visitors of torments of the heart. Echoing this history, in 1902 the British built a hospital on its findspot (still called *al-Ḥawḍ al-Marṣūd*, 'the enchanted basin') dedicated to treating venereal disease, where registered sex workers reported for annual medical examinations.
Cairo, 26th Dynasty, *c.* 600 BCE
Black granite, H. 119.4 cm, W. 274.4 cm, D. 139.7 cm
British Museum, EA23
Donated by King George III

remained a mystery until 1799, when the discovery of the Rosetta Stone provided the vital key. Over the subsequent two decades, the language of the ancients was fully deciphered by European scholars, notably Jean-François Champollion and Thomas Young. Only then would the centuries-long quest to unravel the workings of Egyptian civilisation finally begin in earnest.

INSPIRED GUESSWORK: MEDIEVAL ISLAMIC INTERPRETATIONS OF ANCIENT EGYPTIAN WRITING

Ilona Regulski

The Middle Ages in Europe was a dark period in the history of Egyptology. The ancient script could not be read, and the hints regarding its nature found in classical and early Christian literature were obscure and selective, such as: 'when Egyptians wish to indicate "earth" with hieroglyphic letters, they put the image of a bull'.[2] The writings of the Greek philosopher Plato and his successors, who saw hieroglyphs as symbolic and mystical, were not yet well known in the West, but Egyptian writing was already associated with magic (fig. 7).[3] The most accessible and authoritative sources concerning ancient Egypt were the Bible and other Christian texts.

During the eighth to fourteenth centuries CE knowledge of Egypt stagnated in Europe, but the Islamic world, which stretched across North Africa and into central Asia, experienced a golden age of cultural, economic and scientific florescence. Greek and Latin manuscripts were translated into either Arabic or Syriac, and sometimes Aramaic and Persian as well. Studies of ancient Egyptian monuments were composed and cited frequently in Arabic literature from the tenth century onwards. Perhaps influenced by philosophers such as Plotinus (204/5–269/70 CE) and Clement of Alexandria (150–211/15 CE), some Arab scholars perceived that Egyptian hieroglyphs had phonetic (sound) as well as ideographic (representational or symbolic) value, and were the script of the kings, whereas the less formal demotic script was 'the script of the commoners' and hieratic 'the script of the elite which is the cursive one of the priests'.[4] Surrounded by the imposing ruins of ancient Egyptian civilisation, Arab scholars sought to explain their original functions

[illegible]

ثم ظهر الطعام ... الطعام ... ان شا الله

وبعد ذلك ان شا الله ... البشنسية

[illegible]

والطعام ... ان شا الله ...

[illegible]

وبعد ... ان شا الله ...

[illegible]

and possible hidden meanings. In Arabic, obelisks were called the 'needles of the pharaoh' and hieroglyphs the 'letters of the birds'.

Arab travellers visiting Egypt at the end of the tenth century, 400 years after the Arab conquest, noted that 'the customs of the Copts prevail' and that people were still conversing in Coptic, the vernacular language of Egypt.[5] As Arabic gained ascendancy, concerned Copts ensured the survival of their language by producing grammar books in Arabic, and Coptic/Arabic dictionaries, often with Greek translations.[6] Medieval Arabs consequently had access to Coptic in more than one script and language. Coptic monks were believed to be the keepers of the wisdom of their ancestors and were often consulted for translations when an ancient text was found. The Egyptian scholars al-Idrisi (d. 1251) and al-Qalqashandi (1355–1418) were among the first to acknowledge that Coptic was linked to ancient Egyptian, calling the latter 'the first Coptic language'.[7] They specified that 'the first Copts' had thirty-two to thirty-six letters in their alphabet.

Connoisseurs of the occult sciences, the Arabs were attracted to the esoteric quality of the Egyptian script. Perhaps influenced by the Greeks, they believed the hieroglyphs contained the secrets of alchemy, the study of mystical chemistry and philosophy (fig. 8, see p. 248). But the Arabs needed no prompting when it came to imagining the magical properties of the arresting hieroglyphs that covered ancient temples, which they viewed as alchemical laboratories (fig. 9). Arab scholars believed that the writing concealed treasured knowledge that, when translated, would grant the power to understand and alter the laws of nature.[8]

Little is known of the tenth-century Iraqi alchemist and historian Ahmad Ibn Waḥshīyah, whose books on the decipherment of ancient scripts were considered authoritative and often consulted (fig. 10). His near contemporary, al-Nadim, claimed to have seen a manuscript 'in Ibn Waḥshīyah's own handwriting' that contained the letters used to 'gain the ancient sciences of Barabi (Egyptian temples)' (fig. 11).[9] Ibn Waḥshīyah referred to several scripts: one that he called 'Letters of the Copts(?)', another called 'Letters of the Alphabet' or 'Letters of South Arabia or hieroglyphs' (a Greek word referring to ancient 'sacred writings'), and a third that, he suggested, were letters that served as keys to decode the other two scripts. His novel idea, that a known language could provide the key to an unknown one, became the principle on which the later decipherment of Egyptian scripts was based. Original manuscripts by Ibn Waḥshīyah are rare, but his work enjoyed enduring and widespread popularity, as evidenced by medieval Spanish and later translations.[10]

The temples and tombs of the pharaohs, their walls covered in enticingly graphic hieroglyphs, provided a limitless source of illustrations for medieval

8 (facing page)
Coptic alchemical manuscript with symbols for words (sun = gold). The presence of Arabic vocabulary suggests it was translated from an Arabic text. Only four such alchemical texts are known.
Egypt, 11th century CE
Papyrus, H. 86 cm, W. 40.3 cm, D. 3.5 cm (framed)
Bodleian Libraries, MS. Copt. a. 2

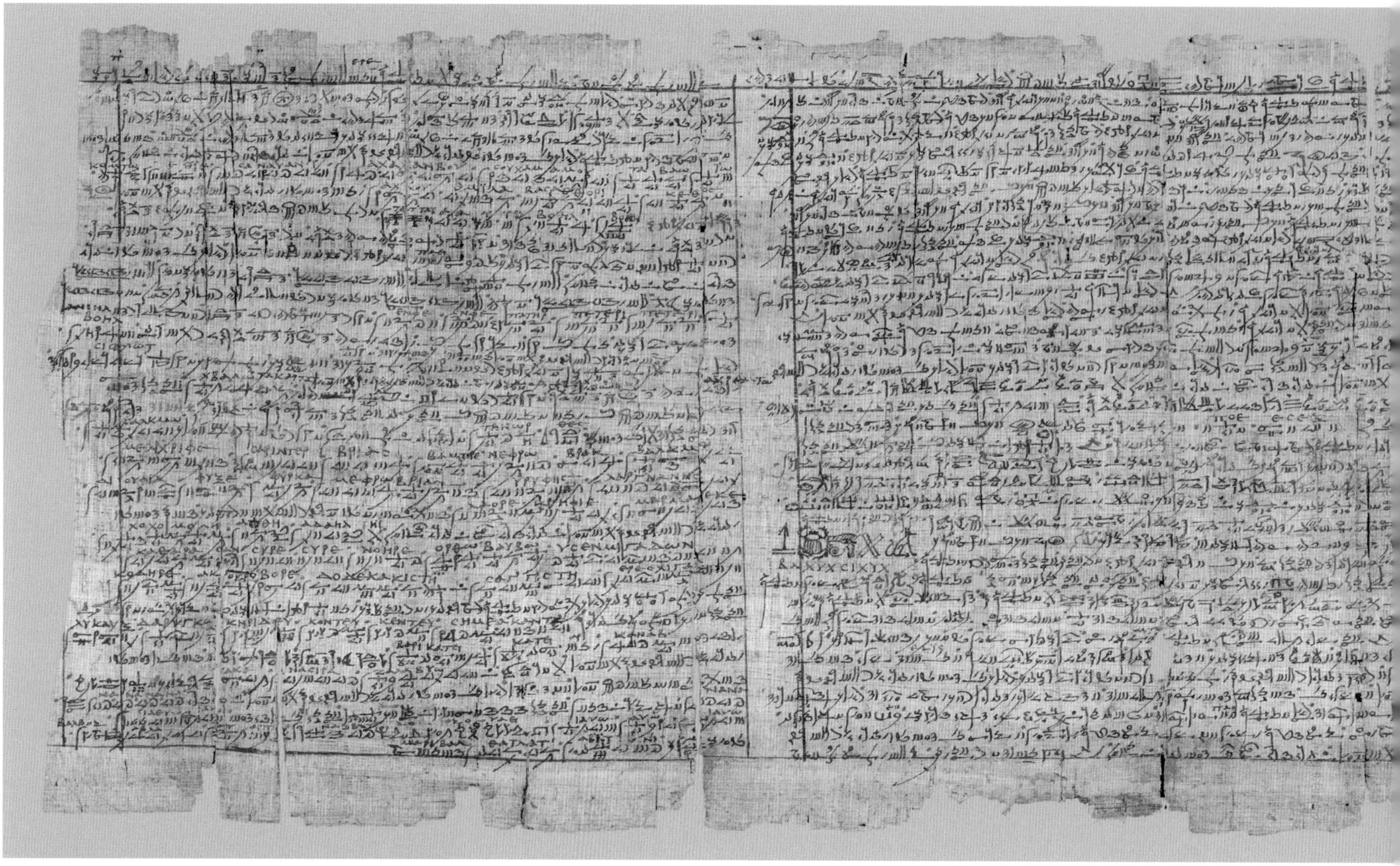

9 (above)
The London Magical Papyrus, with demotic spells and recipes, contains glosses in demotic, Old Coptic and Greek. Spells for healing, conjuring love and counteracting poisons (recto) are combined with prescriptions and invocations (verso). Magical names must be recited by the practitioner wishing to channel their power.

> Lines 6–8 read: 'If you put frankincense up in front of the lamp and look at the lamp, you see the god near the lamp. You sleep on a reed mat without having spoken to anyone on earth, and he tells you the answer in a dream. […] FORMULAE: Here is the writing which you should write on the wick of the lamp: Bakhukhsikhukh'

Thebes, Roman Period, 3rd century CE
Papyrus, H. 24.3 cm, W. 85.7 cm, D. 0.2 cm
British Museum, EA10070,2

10 (left)
Mummy section of the original manuscript of Ibn Waḥshīyah. In a list of Egyptian signs indicating materials, organised into groups such as fruits, herbs and minerals, Ibn Waḥshīyah included *mummia*, written with a human upper body, probably in reference to the substance. In his day, it was known that *mummia* was extracted from mummified cadavers for pharmaceutical purposes.
Provenance unknown, 1751
Paper, H. 21 cm, W. 15 cm, D. 2.5 cm
Bibliothèque nationale de France, Département des Manuscrits, Ms Arabe 6805

11 (right)
Joseph von Hammer-Purgstall's translation of Ibn Waḥshīyah's Arabic *Ancient Alphabets and Hieroglyphic Characters Explained*
London, England, 1806
Paper, H. 21 cm, W. 29.5 cm, D. 2.5 cm
British Library, 66.b.24

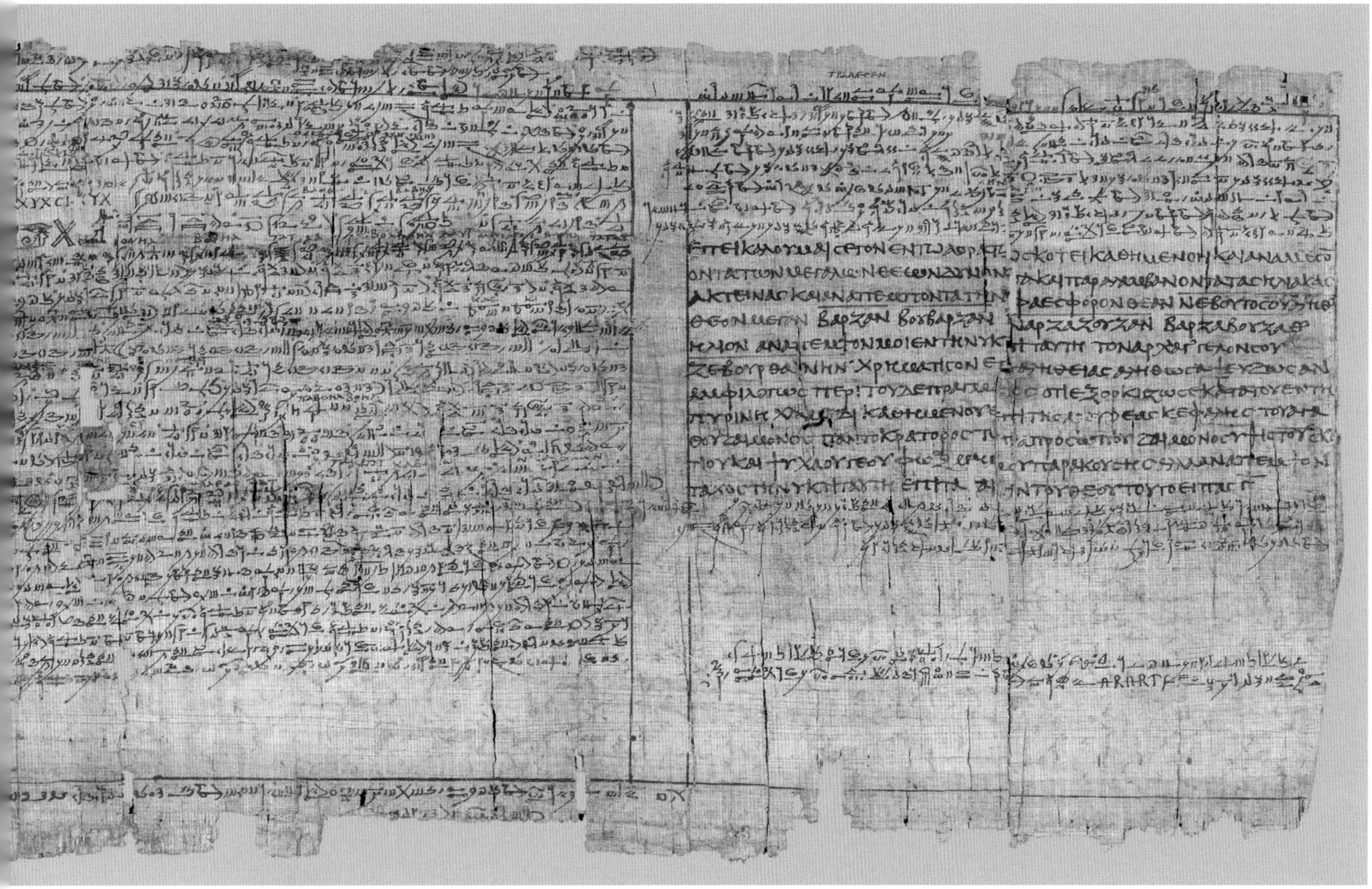

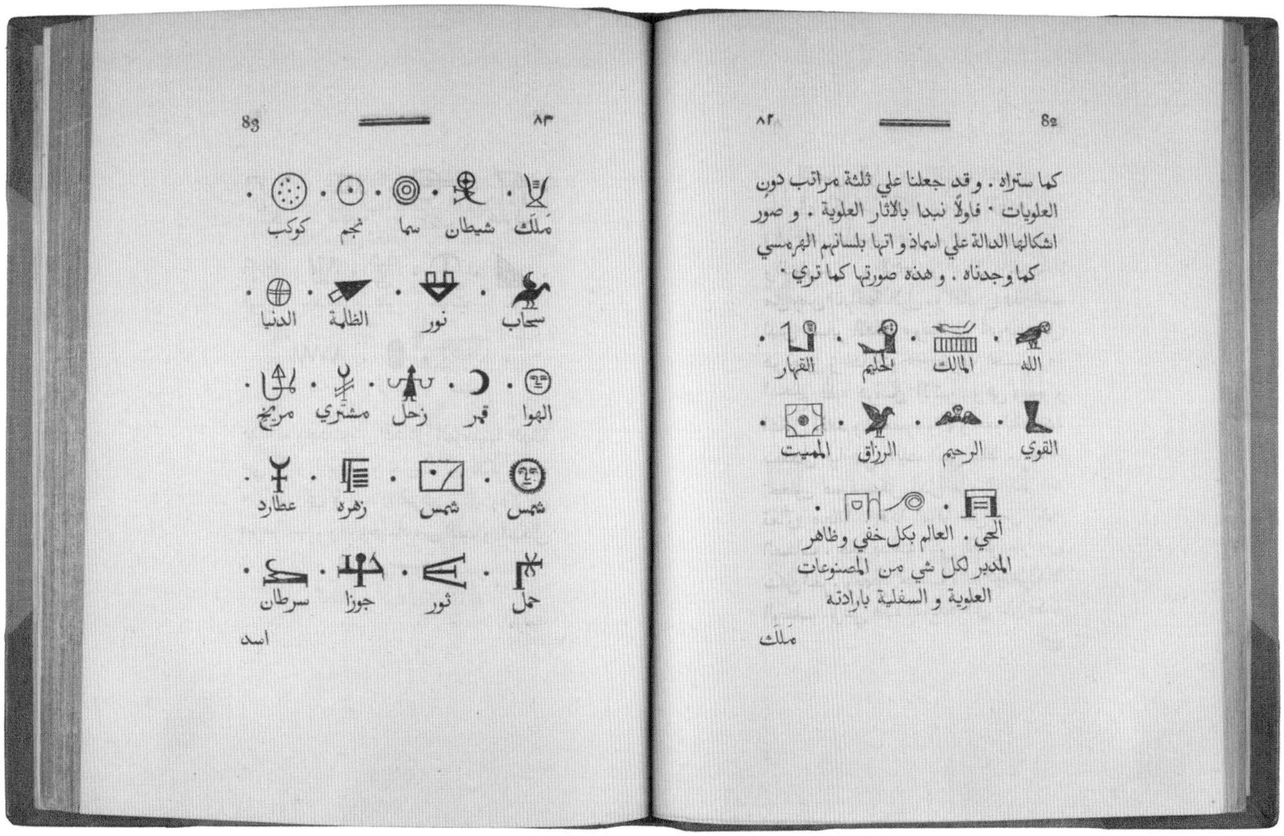
83 ٨٣
مَلك شيطان سما نجم كوكب
سحاب نور الظالمة الدنيا
الهوا قمر زحل مشتري مريخ
شمس شمس زهره عطارد
حمل ثور جوزا سرطان
اسد
٨٢ 82
كما ستراه . وقد جعلنا علي ثلثة مراتب دون
العلويات · فاولاً نبدا بالاثار العلوية . و صور
اشكالها الدالة علي اسماذ واتها بلسانهم الهرمسي
كما وجدناه . وهذه صورتها كما تري ·
الله المالك الحليم القهار
القوي الرحيم الرزاق المميت
الحي . العالم بكل خفي وظاهر
المدبر لكل شي من المصنوعات
العلوية و السفلية بارادته
مَلك

12
Medieval Arabic manual on talisman making, exploring the magical and medical properties of jewels, plants and animals. The book also discusses Hermes Trismegistus, the Greek equivalent of the ancient Egyptian god of writing.
Provenance unknown,
probably 14th century CE
Paper, H. 23.7 cm, W. 34.5 cm
Bodleian Libraries, MS. Arab. d. 221, fols 48b and 49a

treatises (fig. 12). Many hieroglyphs are, however, difficult to recognise in these works since they were not accurately copied, and served instead as the basis of secret codes developed for the twenty-eight letters of the Arabic alphabet. Scholars used such codes in their own writings and to decipher messages left by others who had adopted them.

Author of widely circulated manuscripts, the alchemist Abū al-Qāsim Muḥammad ibn Aḥmad al-ʿIrāqī (d. 1341) was known as al-Sīmāwī, 'the practitioner of natural or white magic'. His *Book of the Seven Climes* is the earliest known treatise focused on careful illustrations of purportedly alchemical hieroglyphic texts (fig. 13).[11] Al-ʿIrāqī states that the text in his *Book of Seven Climes* was copied from a 'Hidden Book' attributed to the legendary Hermes Trismegistus. Hermes was the Greek name for the Egyptian god of knowledge and writing, Thoth, while Trismegistus or

13 (above)
Copy of a drawing in Abū al-Qāsim al-ʿIrāqī's *The Book of the Seven Climes* (*Kitāb al-aqālīm al-ṣabʿah*) depicting a lost stela of Amenemhat II (12th Dynasty, c. 1922 BCE) with hieroglyphic inscriptions
Egypt (?), 18th century
Paper, H. 31 cm, W. 36 cm (opened)
British Library, MS Add 25724, f. 50v

'thrice-great' was an epithet borrowed from an ancient Egyptian title for Thoth used in the Ptolemaic period (305–30 BCE), 'greatest and greatest great god' (fig. 14).[12] The teachings of Hermes had been transmitted through the ages in the works of Aristotle and Apollonius of Tyana, philosophers the Arabs translated and held in high esteem.[13] In keeping with Greek tradition, the Arabs saw Hermes as the founder of sciences including medicine, astronomy and alchemy, and the inventor of the alphabet, who recorded his wisdom in hieroglyphs on the walls of temples and tombs.[14] Guided by the legend of Hermes, al-ʿIrāqī explained hieroglyphic texts in an alchemical vein.

While literature regarding Hermes Trismegistus led the Arabs astray about the meaning of ancient texts, their extensive alchemical investigations laid the foundations for modern chemistry and yielded significant discoveries, such as methods for fabricating cheap ink and ceramic glazes, for refining metals and waterproofing cloth.

Although its meaning was misconstrued, the inclusion of an authentic hieroglyphic text in the *Book of the Seven Climes* is testimony to the care some medieval Arabic scholars took in replicating earlier manuscripts. Just as the Greeks influenced the Arabs' understanding of ancient Egypt, so the translation of numerous Arabic treatises into Latin, which began in the late tenth century and peaked in the twelfth and the thirteenth centuries, shaped the Western perception of Egypt. Alongside Egypt's historical reputation as the land of science, wisdom and mysticism, Egyptian writing was increasingly characterised as occult.[15]

14 (right)
Mould and cast showing the Egyptian Hermes (Trismegistus) seated, writing on a papyrus roll lying across his knees
Egypt, Ptolemaic Period, 3rd century BCE
Plaster, H. 17.3 cm, W. 15.6 cm
British Museum, EA51804

RENAISSANCE CONFABULATIONS: HIEROGLYPHS SEEN THROUGH A CLASSICAL LENS

Ilona Regulski

By the fifteenth and sixteenth centuries, Europe had access to a quantity of written material related to ancient Egypt. In these ancient and contemporary sources, Renaissance readers encountered a land of prodigious kings who built splendid monuments to honour their gods.[16] Attention turned to material remains, direct testimonies to Egypt's former greatness, such as the hieroglyph-inscribed obelisks, statues and other artefacts brought to Rome as trophies of Octavian's conquest of Egypt, and Roman-made tokens of devotion to the popular cults of Egyptian gods (fig. 15). Pilgrims and other medieval travellers had remarked on Egypt's monuments, but the memory of their origins was lost; the obelisks were praised as marvels of the ancient Romans.[17] Many monuments had fallen into ruin until their 'rediscovery' during the fifteenth and sixteenth centuries. Italian humanists began to study them, along with a growing corpus of ancient inscriptions, from a more historical perspective, as sources of 'authentic' texts that had survived from antiquity.

The obelisks were impressive but they could no longer speak, since knowledge of hieroglyphic script had long since vanished. Renaissance scholars turned to classical authors for their accounts of Egypt's monuments, collecting, copying and 'correcting' manuscripts by Greek authors Herodotus, Diodorus Siculus, Plutarch and Strabo, and by Latin authors Apuleius, Pliny the Elder and Ammianus Marcellinus. Influenced by the Neoplatonic belief that a single principle is both the creative source of the universe and determines the purpose of all existing things, the scholars decided that hieroglyphs represented things as symbols corresponding to their essential natures, rather than constituting a written language.

According to this Greek misconception, hieroglyphs were not phonetic (sound-based) and in no way formed a normal language obeying rules of grammar and syntax. Rather, as signs directly connected to the ideal realm, they required a symbolic reading. The catalyst for this interpretation was the rediscovery and transportation to Florence, Italy, of two manuscripts: Horapollo's *Hieroglyphica* in 1419 and the dialogues of Hermes Trismegistus in 1460–2.

15
Etching of the Piazza di Montecitorio in Rome by Francesco Barbazza
Italy, 1789
Paper, H. 62.5 cm, W. 47 cm
Thorvaldsens Museum, ThM E1327

16
Horapollo's *Hieroglyphica*, an early hieroglyphic dictionary
Andros, Greece, 1301–1400 CE
Paper, H. 28.5 cm, W. 22.5 cm, D. 4 cm (closed)
Biblioteca Medicea Laurenziana, MS Plut. 69.27 (fol. 69v)

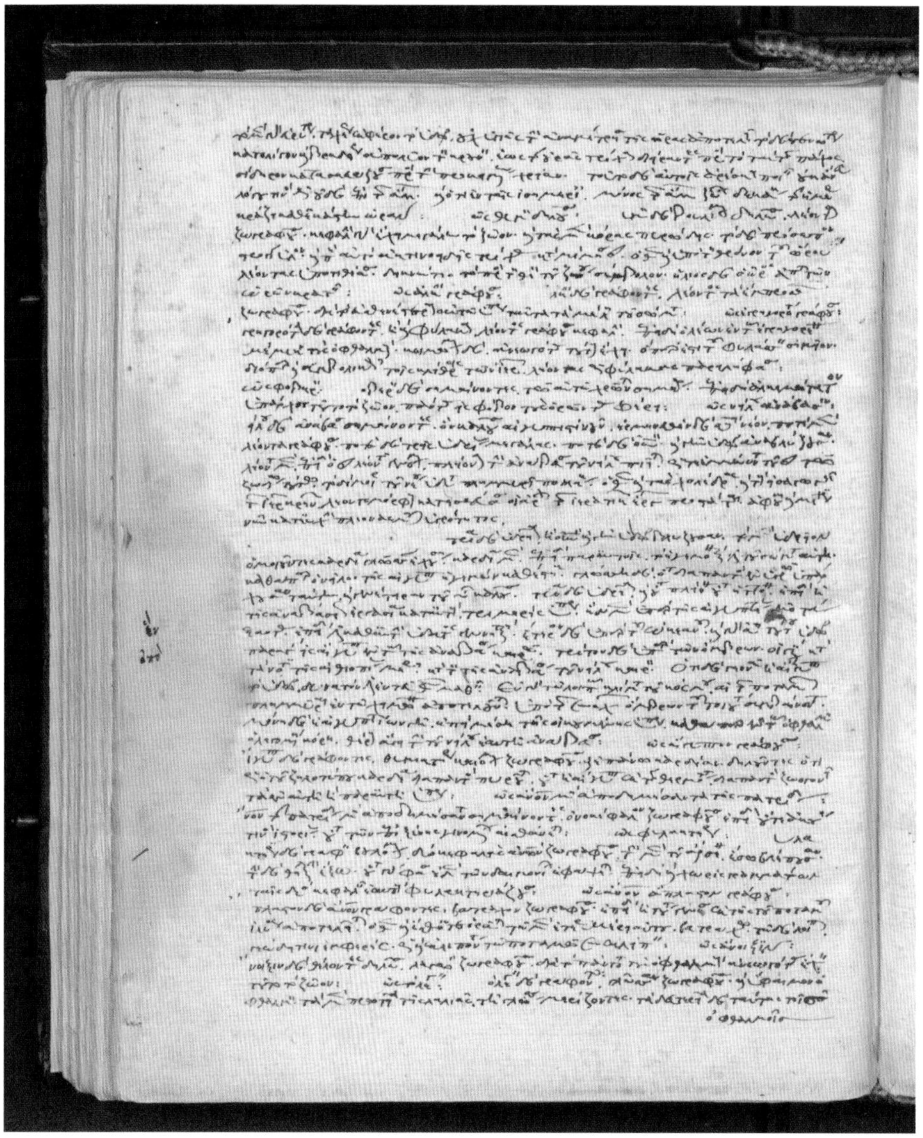

The *Hieroglyphica* is a hieroglyphic dictionary attributed to the fifth-century Alexandrian priest Horapollo the Younger and providing descriptions and symbolic interpretations in Greek of some 189 signs (fig. 16).[18] A few were correctly identified, such as the bee  for kingship and the hare  to express the idea of opening. As we now know, the hare sign starts a sequence of consonants (*wn*) required to write the word 'open' in ancient Egyptian. Despite scattered accuracies, Horapollo's methodology reflected the late antique view of hieroglyphs as allegorical image-signs and was essentially wrong.[19] Unfamiliar with the mechanisms of the writing system, Horapollo turned to naturalistic or apparently logical explanations: for example, the hare was appropriate 'for this animal always keeps its eyes open' (fig. 17).[20]

The *Corpus Hermeticum* is a collection of religious and philosophical discourses assembled from the first to the third centuries CE and presented as translations into Greek of the work of anonymous sages in Roman Egypt. The principal character is Hermes. By the time the *Hermetica* were being composed, only allegorical explanations of Egyptian script survived in cultural memory.[21] Like the *Hieroglyphica*, the *Corpus Hermeticum* represented a Neoplatonic and nostalgic conception of Egypt as a land of ancient and increasingly remote wisdom.

The Latin version of one of the most 'prophetic' hermetic dialogues, the *Asclepius*, was well known in the West at a time when Hermes was believed to be a pagan contemporary of biblical Moses. That Hermes Trismegistus had somehow anticipated important aspects of Christian doctrine, including the decline of paganism and the advent of the 'son of God', appealed to Church authorities. The idea that ancient Egypt was a point of origin for 'Western' civilisation was consequently embedded in both classical and biblical tradition and would persist in various forms for centuries.

Translated from Greek into Latin and other languages, both the *Hieroglyphica* and the *Hermetica* profoundly influenced European understanding of hieroglyphs and symbolism in general. Renaissance scholars were searching for a universal language and Egyptian hieroglyphs seemed to express ideas more immediately than the phonetic alphabets of their own times.[22]

A leading figure of this movement, architect and polymath Leon Battista Alberti (1404–1472), interpreted hieroglyphs as a system of allegorical image-signs whose meanings were derived from knowledge of the essential nature of the depicted things. Like their alchemist predecessors, Alberti and his fellow humanists believed that secrets of the highest order were entombed in the stone-carved texts, awaiting resurrection.[23] Alberti maintained that 'Egyptian letters' were the basis of all representational art and monumental inscriptions, and consequently held the promise of a universal, image-based language that could transcend the limitations of ordinary speech. Just as medieval Arabs had made symbolic interpretations of hieroglyphs related to alchemy, so the signs provided a vehicle for the quirky inventions of the Renaissance.

Alberti became the father of the 'neo-hieroglyphic' tradition, reinventing hieroglyphs by merging together ancient iconographic elements in new combinations. The winged eye, combining the eye of Horus with a wing,

17
Amulet in the form of a hare, with a suspension ring behind the ears
Egypt, 26th Dynasty, 664–525 BCE
Glazed composition, H. 2.9 cm, W. 4.4 cm, D. 1.3 cm
British Museum, EA20853
Donated by the Egypt Exploration Fund

18
Medal of Leon Battista Alberti
Italy, 1446–50 CE
Bronze, D. 0.5 cm, diam. 9 cm
British Museum, G3,IP.1
Donated by King George IV

became his personal icon (fig. 18). As the first neo-hieroglyph, formulated in 1432, the winged eye is emblematic of fifteenth-century scholars' fascination with an idealised concept of ancient Egypt, as essayed by the likes of Plato and Plotinus.[24] By the end of the fifteenth century the exalted status of the Egyptians as founders of the arts and sciences had set the stage for an outbreak of 'Egyptomania' in the visual arts.

At the turn of the sixteenth century artists and scholars began taking a more critical and monument-centred approach to archaeological study, and documentation of hieroglyphs became more precise.[25] The sketchbooks and albums of artist-antiquarians included drawings and engravings of Egyptian monuments and copies of hieroglyphic inscriptions.

During the papacy of Sixtus V (1585–90), Vatican-initiated projects for Rome's urban renewal were designed to signal continuity with the past, folding Egyptian pharaohs, Roman emperors and Catholic popes into a single illustrious tradition.[26] Under the direction of a small, distinguished group of artists with close ties to the papal court, the Eternal City was adorned with renovated Egyptian obelisks. Rome's obelisks were the prime object of scrutiny for Renaissance Egyptologists. They produced some of the earliest drawings of hieroglyphic inscriptions that might be called epigraphically accurate.

The Vatican palace and the homes of great families such as the Medicis were, meanwhile, filled with imagery reflecting the renewed interest in Rome's Egyptian heritage. The most famous 'Egyptian' artefact in Renaissance Europe was the Mensa Isiaca, also known as the Bembine tablet after its first owner, the Venetian poet and future cardinal Pietro Bembo (1470–1547) (fig. 19).[27] The inlaid bronze tablet, covered in Egyptian cult scenes and inscriptions centred on the figure of Isis, provided a visual databank that triggered fresh studies. Modern Egyptologists consider the tablet to be an Egyptianised product of imperial Rome rather than a genuine Egyptian artefact, though it was probably used in a temple dedicated to Isis. Its images of Egyptian gods and accurately written, but literally meaningless, hieroglyphic inscriptions were the subject of many studies of the Renaissance and subsequent periods.

The humanist belief that hieroglyphs represented ideas governed most theories expressed during the latter part of the sixteenth century and the whole of the seventeenth century. It was a matter of looking at an inscription, fitting meanings to the symbols, conjecturing necessary verbs, adverbs, adjectives, prepositions and conjunctions, and if the reading was occult enough, publishing it as a translation.

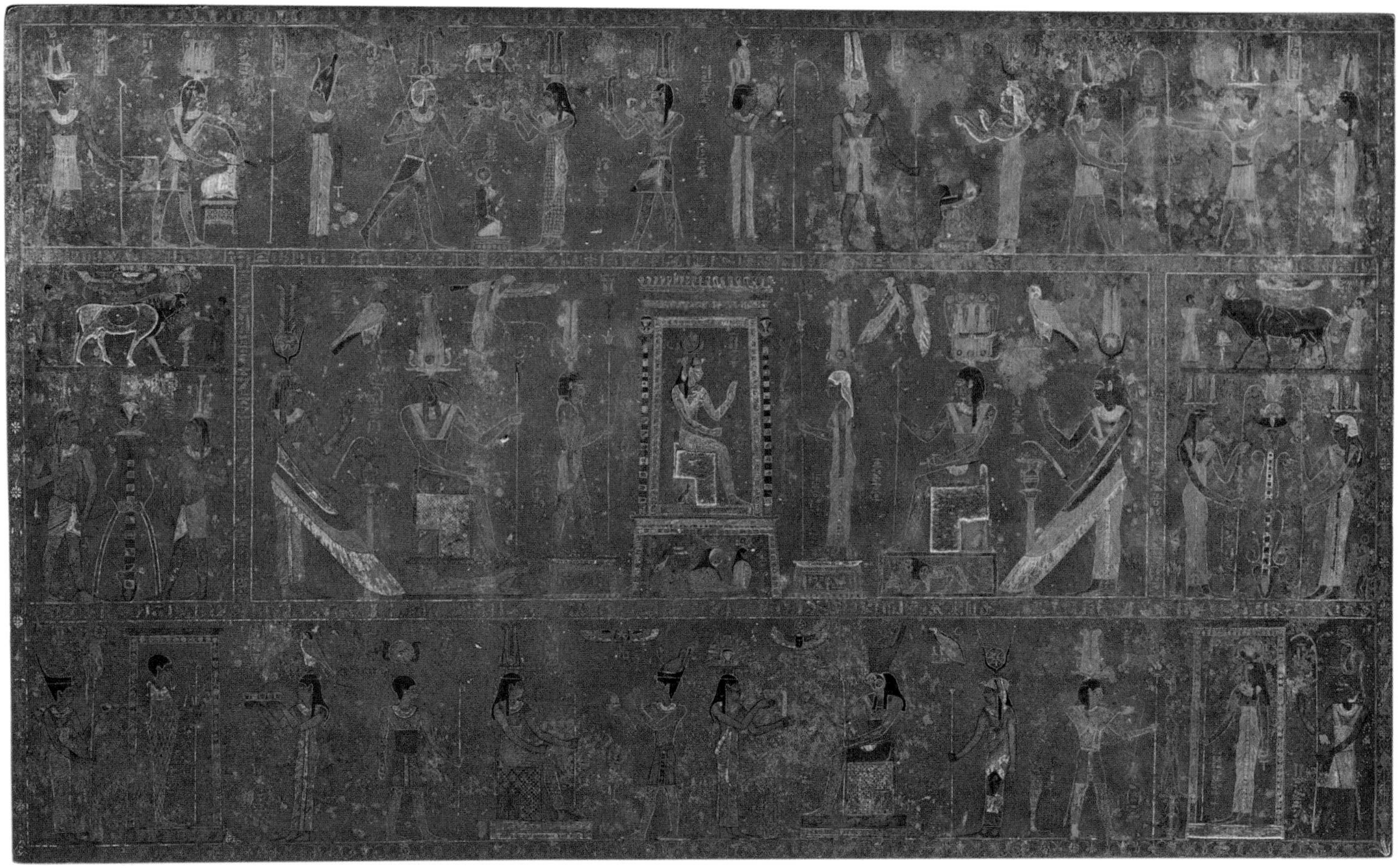

19
The Mensa Isiaca
Italy, 30–395 CE (?)
Bronze with inlays of other metal alloys,
H. 75.5 cm, W. 125.5 cm, D. 5.5 cm
Museo Egizio, Cat. 7155

DOCUMENTATION, MISSTEPS AND ADVANCEMENTS

Ilona Regulski

Progress in deciphering hieroglyphs and understanding ancient Egypt depended largely on the material available for study. The quantity of artefacts imported to Europe greatly increased by the seventeenth century, when the royal fashion for assembling 'cabinets of curiosities' was adopted by well-to-do merchants, clergymen and travellers. These personal and 'scientific' collections, displayed in glass-fronted cases sometimes occupying an entire room, comprised all things that were (to a European eye) strange and marvellous: samples of rare plants, animals, minerals, items of fine local artistry and foreign objects of interest.[28] Mummies and mummy cases, canopic jars (see pp. 181–3), small objects from tombs, inscribed stones and papyri were purchased or excavated and carried across the Mediterranean. Cabinet owners occasionally hosted mummy unwrappings, a sought-after form of entertainment. At these events, the wrappings were cut into pieces and distributed to attendees as souvenirs, the inscribed strips of cloth being the most coveted.

One of the earliest such events was the 1698 unwrapping of the mummy of Aberuait from Saqqara, as described by the French consul in Egypt at the time, Benoit de Maillet.[29] Fragments from unwrappings were mostly held in cabinets of curiosities through the seventeenth and eighteenth centuries until they were acquired by newly established state museums or royal collections. Individual pieces of Aberuait's mummy linen can be identified in hand-drawn illustrations in eighteenth- and early nineteenth-century publications. The best known of these is the so-called 'Calendrier Egyptien', named by its first publisher Bernard de Montfaucon in 1724 because he misinterpreted its content (Book of the Dead spell 149) as depictions of an ancient Egyptian calendar (fig. 20). While few specimens of mummy bandages were known or seen during those early days, they played an important role in the early history of decipherment, especially in the decipherment of hieratic (fig. 21).

The cabinets typically contained small, easily acquired objects. The sistrum (see fig. 195), for example, a rattle-like musical instrument traditionally used in the worship of the Egyptian goddesses Hathor and Isis, was subject to detailed analysis and lively discussions in antiquarian and early museological circles. Models of ancient objects (some dating to

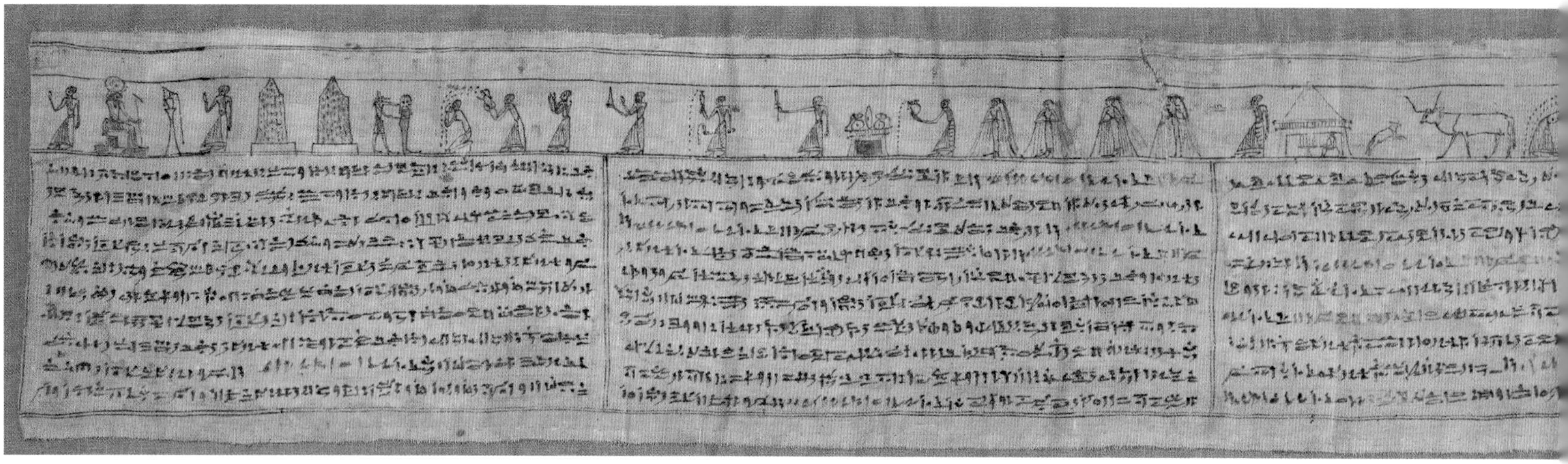

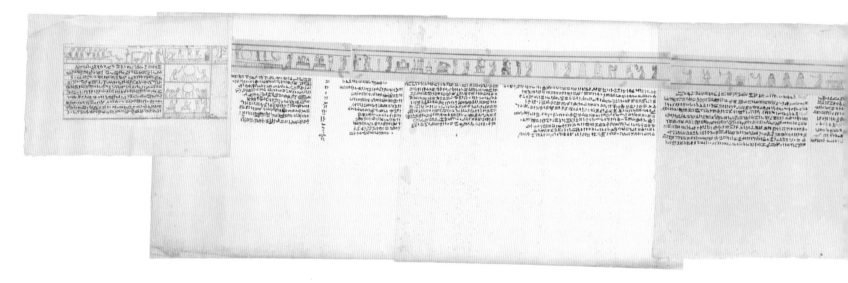

imperial Rome, others more recent) and works of Greek or Egyptian origin also featured frequently in early antiquities collections. Artefacts could not be placed in their social and historical context until Egyptian texts were properly translated, yet many were documented in drawings and published in the interest of sparking debate that might advance the understanding of ancient Egypt.

One of the most impressive efforts to document Egyptian religion, customs and architecture was made by Cassiano dal Pozzo (1588–1657), who assembled a vast array of drawings, casts, moulds and paper squeezes in Rome.[30] Scholars and aficionados from all over Europe visited the so-called Paper Museum whose contents, though largely unpublished,

20 (top)
Fragment of the mummy-wrapping of Aberuait inscribed with the Book of the Dead, which was previously misidentified as an Egyptian calendar
Saqqara, Ptolemaic Period, 332–30 BCE
Linen, H. 16.5 cm, W. 131 cm
Musée du Louvre, N 3059

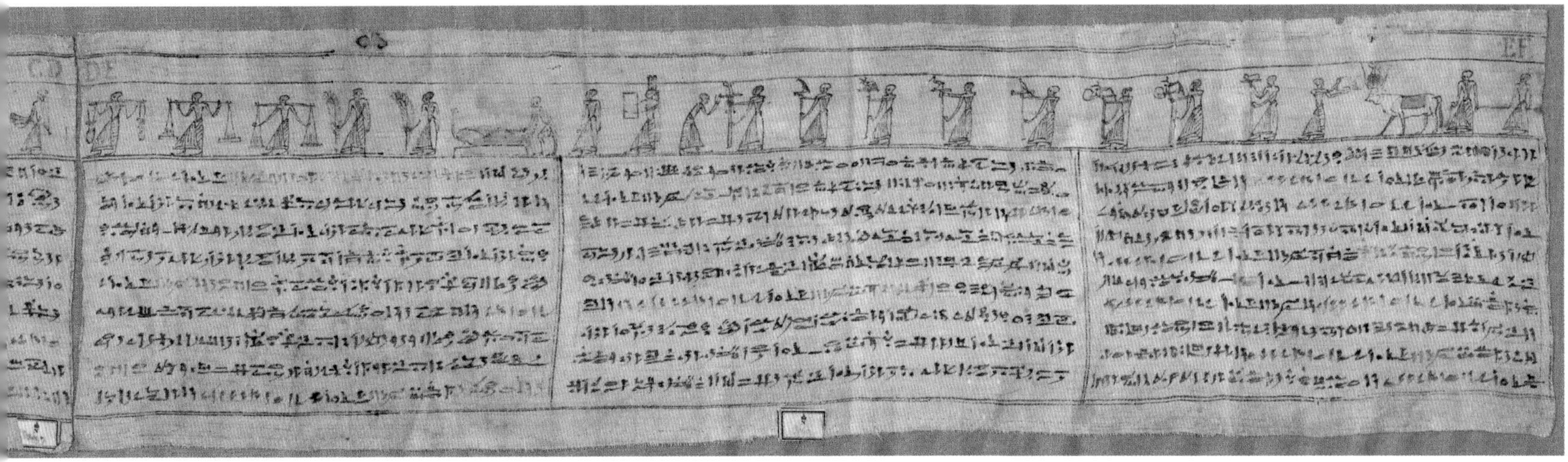

21 (bottom)
Modern facsimile of the mummy-wrapping of Aberuait, hand-drawn by Champollion
Paris, France, October 1811
Paper, H. 42 cm, W. 287.5 cm
Bibliothèque nationale de France, Département des Manuscrits, Egyptien 229

were the focus of intensive seventeenth-century study. Cassiano's collection was eventually dispersed, and in 1814 the British Museum acquired a set of drawings of the Egyptian objects of Charles Townley (1737–1805) (figs 22–23).

Likewise, the Kircherian Museum in Rome, assembled by German Jesuit polymath Athanasius Kircher (1602–1680), was one of many collections that began as a private cabinet of curiosities and was later incorporated into a national institution.[31]

In his effort to make sense of ancient Egyptian writing, Kircher used the Mensa Isiaca and Roman obelisks to develop a method for translating hieroglyphs.[32] Like other Catholic scholars, Kircher relied

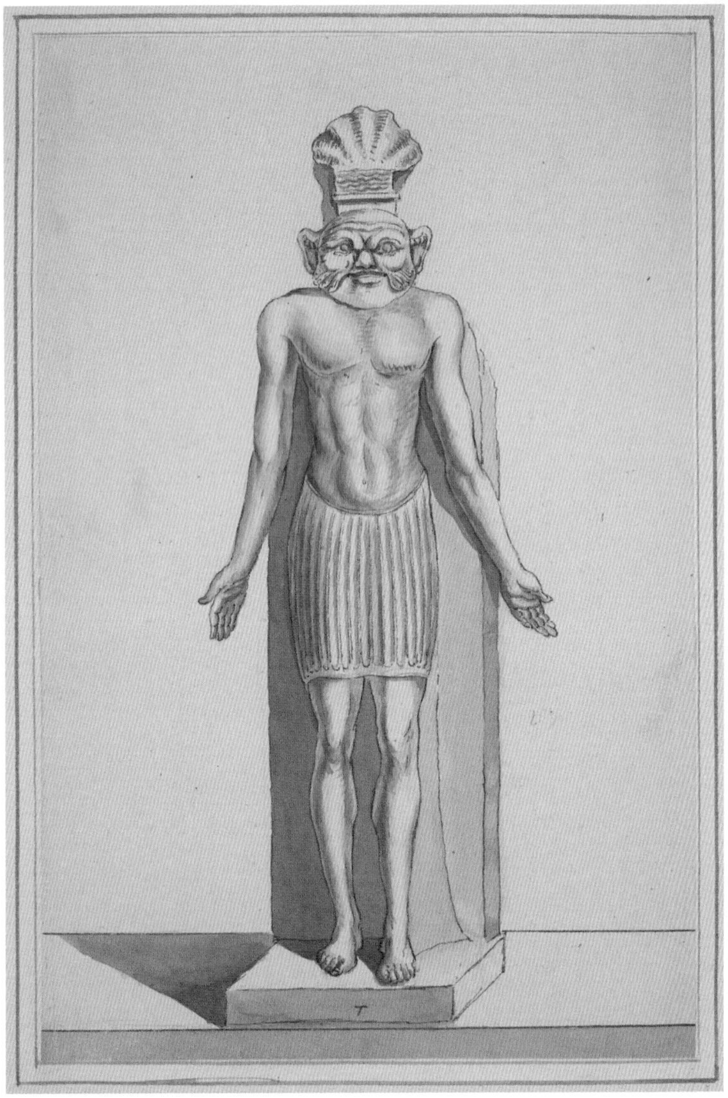

22 (facing page, left)
Drawing of a man wearing a Bes mask from the collection of Charles Townley
Italy (?), 1768–1805 CE
Paper, H. 22.8 cm, W. 15.1 cm
British Museum, 2010,5006.404

23 (facing page, right)
Figure of a man, perhaps a priest, wearing a Bes mask
Egypt, Roman Period, 1st century BCE–1st century CE
Schist, H. 63 cm, W. 16 cm
British Museum, EA47973

24 (above)
Sculptor's trial piece depicting an owl hieroglyph. The owl is one of the most common hieroglyphs and represents the sound 'm'.
Egypt, Ptolemaic Period, 332–30 BCE
Limestone, H. 16 cm, W. 13.5 cm, D. 2.3 cm
British Museum, EA38276

on the prophecies of the Egyptian Hermes as the basis for his attempt to restore and disseminate precious wisdom (see pp. 38–9). He believed that Hermes Trismegistus had invented hieroglyphs to encrypt the doctrines of the so-called *prisca theologia*, the single religion of remote antiquity from which all other monotheistic faiths arose. If the hieroglyphs, with their symbolic significance, could be read, the entire religious, philosophical and scientific system would be revealed.[33]

Arabic works on the history of ancient Egypt were now available in translation and Kircher was among the first Westerners to consult them, gaining access to previously unknown or forgotten traditions.[34] This led him to question the prevailing European view that hieroglyphs were symbols, relating them instead to the Coptic language. Convinced that Coptic was a corrupt form of the pristine ancient language that would ultimately enable scholars to understand hieroglyphs, Kircher identified several signs as alphabetic equivalents of Coptic letters and words.[35] He associated the 'rippling water' sign 𓈖 with the Coptic word for water, *mw*, thus correctly identifying the phonetic meaning of an Egyptian hieroglyph for the first time.[36] His suggestion that hieroglyphs represented sounds as well as ideas greatly influenced later European scholars.

Arriving in Rome in 1635, Kircher set out to translate the hieroglyphic inscriptions on obelisks. In 1650 he wrote the first of his great compendia of interpretations, the *Obeliscus Pamphilius*, in which he provided a sign-by-sign illustrated Latin translation, a dense web of esoteric and religion-tinged pronouncements. His work on the Pamphilian obelisk[37] on Bernini's Fountain of the Four River Gods in the Piazza Navona won him the nickname 'the father of the owls', perhaps because owls featured frequently in hieroglyphs, the so-called 'letters of the birds' (fig. 24). The obelisk was carved by Roman craftspeople, but the inscriptions are legible and demonstrate familiarity with hieroglyphic writing (fig. 25). They include the name of the emperor Domitian, using epithets borrowed from inscriptions of Ptolemy III Euergetes (256–221 BCE) and Ramesses II (1292–1225 BCE). The name of the latter king was incorrectly read by Kircher as a proclamation of the power of Osiris: 'Osiris is the source of all fecundity and vegetation; the holy Mophta draws his power of generation from the sky into his realm.'[38]

Kircher announced that the full decipherment of hieroglyphs was at hand and provided a sample using the human-headed scarab from the Mensa Isiaca (fig. 19).[39] He reconstructed six 'universally intelligible' signs: the scarab meant 'the world'; the head of Horus, 'the reason (sun) governing the world'; the concentric circles on the figure's shoulder symbolised the 'superior heavens'; the crescent on its head stood for 'the moon or Isis'; and

Latus.I. Orientale
Latus.II. Australe
Latus.III. Occidentale
Latus.IV. Septentrionale
INNOCENTIO·X·PONT·MAX·
ATHANASIUS KIRCHERIUS S.I.D.D.
PHILIUS
PAM
OBELISCUS
INNOCENTIUS·X
PONT·MAX·
EREXIT
ROMÆ

25 (facing page)
The Pamphilian obelisk, one of nineteen etchings from the catalogue of Rome's Palazzo del Collegio Romano collection, which was curated by Kircher.
Amsterdam, Netherlands, 1678
Paper, H. 71.3 cm, W. 51.5 cm, D. 2.5 cm
British Museum, M,33.6

26 (below)
Kircher's *Oedipus Aegyptiacus,* III.2
Italy, 1652–4
Paper, H. 37 cm, W. 42.5 cm (mounted)
British Library, G.2083, pp. 502–3

the cross within the crescent was read as 'flux and reflux, generation and corruption, the mixing of the elements, the disunited universe bound by love'. The supreme symbol was the winged sphere representing 'the union of the upper and lower world through *philo* (love)'. Since the Copts were Christians, Kircher assumed that the ancient Egyptians had experienced a similar revelation, so he associated the winged sphere with God; the beetle with Christ; and the *philo* with the Holy Spirit. The ambiguity of the hieroglyphic symbols was essential to Kircher's success, as it justified his abstract translations, even while rendering his readings doubtful.[40]

Kircher's spectacular multi-volume epic (over 2,000 pages in length), the *Egyptian Oedipus* (1652–4), put forward his claim to have solved the riddles of the Sphinx (fig. 26).[41] Throughout this and subsequent publications, he established a quasi-philosophical system of hieroglyphic interpretation that

27 (left)
Mould of a winged dung beetle from the Montecitorio obelisk's uppermost capstone
Rome, Italy, before 1789
Plaster, H. 39.5 cm, W. 45.7 cm, D. 3 cm
Thorvaldsens Museum, ThM L214

28 (below)
Relief or mould of part of the west side of the obelisk in the Piazza di Montecitorio
Rome, Italy, 1789
Plaster, H. 24.5 cm, W. 15.4 cm, D. 2.9 cm
Thorvaldsens Museum, ThM L206

29 (facing page)
Relief drawing of the east and south sides of the obelisk in the Piazza Monte Pincio by Andrea Roncalli, with comments by Zoëga
Rome, Italy, before 1797 CE
Pencil, pen and ink on paper, H. 82.9 cm, W. 28.4 cm
Thorvaldsens Museum, ThM D1161

captured the imagination of supportive colleagues who further promoted his methods. For example:

ḏd mdw in Wsir

Kircher translated the signs above as:

Cobra: life
Baton: control
Water wave: Typhon (a serpentine monster from Greek mythology)
Eye: vigilance
Flag: Anubis
Seat: altar

His translation of the phrase reads 'the life of things after defeating the Typhon, the humidity of nature through the vigilance of Anubis according to previous sacrifices'. The actual translation is 'speaking words by Osiris'.[42]

Not everyone agreed with Kircher's approach or his translations. According to the Englishman William Warburton (1698–1779), the belief that

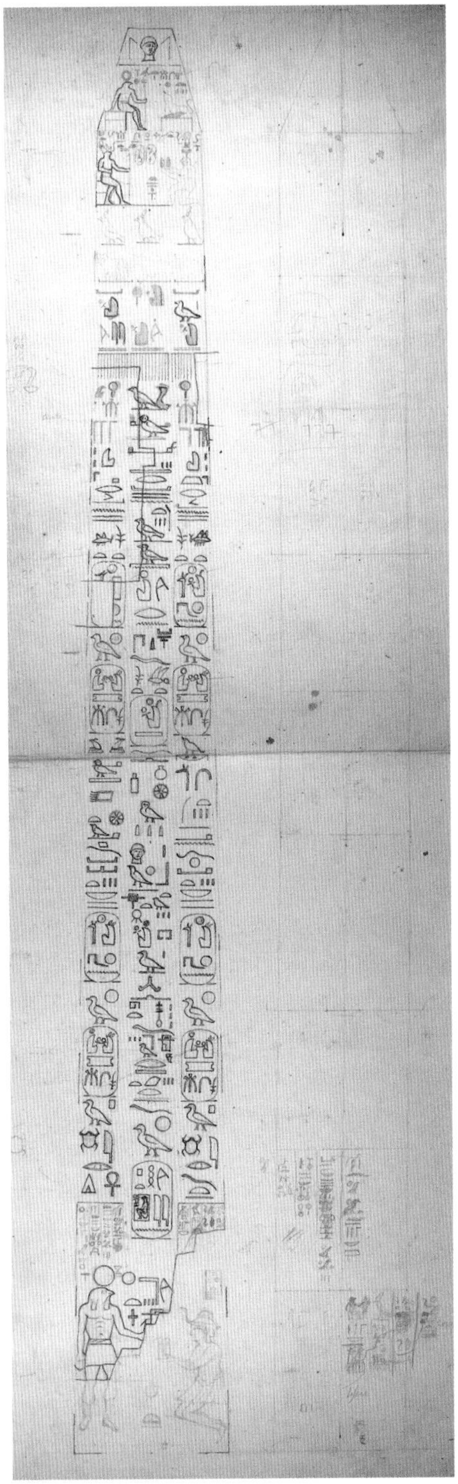

hieroglyphs were invented by Egyptian priests to hide privileged wisdom had caused a great misunderstanding.[43] He maintained instead that hieroglyphs represented an early and defective stage in the development of a language used to record banal affairs of state, laws, customs and moral decrees. An outspoken critic of Kircher, Warburton laid out a comprehensive, progressive scheme whereby all societies naturally developed a succession of increasingly perfect forms of spoken and written communication. He argued that Egyptian culture greatly pre-dated the Old Testament, and illustrated a progression of hieroglyphs from pictographic script to an alphabetic one.[44] He correctly affirmed that hieratic script derived from hieroglyphs. But as Jean-François Champollion later pointed out, Warburton had drawn a false distinction between hieroglyphs and other kinds of Egyptian writing.

In a letter dated 16 March 1825, Champollion wrote to his brother that he had visited the Rome atelier of the famous Danish sculptor Bertel Alberto Thorvaldsen (1770–1844), 'where Egyptian antiquities were abundant'.[45] The atelier, housing artefacts, casts, drawings and engravings of inscribed objects, was a must-see for anyone interested in ancient Egypt. The collection included some of the finest casts, pencil sketches and copper engravings of the obelisks of Rome. Many of the copies were probably created and/or gathered at the encouragement of Thorvaldsen's mentor, Georg Zoëga (1755–1809), who used them as sources for his work on hieroglyphs (see p. 61).[46] When Thorvaldsen returned to Denmark, the collection was gradually transported to Copenhagen (1835–45) and is now in the Thorvaldsens Museum.

Several casts in Thorvaldsen's collection were taken from an obelisk carved for Psamtek II (595–589 BCE) standing in Heliopolis (figs 27–28) that Emperor Octavian brought to Rome in 30 BCE to celebrate his conquest of Egypt. Unlike other Roman obelisks, it doubled as a gnomon, the part of a sundial that casts a shadow. Re-excavated in 1748, the obelisk was restored and re-erected by Pius VI in the Piazza di Montecitorio (1789–92) (see fig. 15).[47]

Another obelisk erected in the Piazza Monte Pincio offers a rare example of a hieroglyphic inscription probably composed in Rome and engraved by local craftsmen. Zoëga was the first to notice that many of the hieroglyphs were unlike those on other Egyptian monuments (fig. 29). This obelisk was dedicated to Emperor Hadrian's deceased lover, Antinous, to celebrate his deification. Rediscovered around 1630, it was moved to the palace grounds of Cardinal Francesco Barberini, who asked Kircher to translate its hieroglyphs in 1635. Following the obelisk's erection by Pius VII in the Piazza Monte Pincio in 1822, Champollion hastened to visit it; that same year he reproduced the names of Hadrian's consort Sabina from the obelisk, while complimenting the epigraphic quality of Zoëga's work in his seminal *Lettre à M. Dacier* (see p. 17).

FROM CABINETS OF CURIOSITIES TO PUBLIC MUSEUMS

Daniela Picchi

From the mid-sixteenth century onwards, anything that seemed to Europeans rare, curious, exotic or marvellous, including Egyptian antiquities, became a subject for learned collecting among individuals and small scholarly circles in aristocratic houses. These cabinets of curiosities, or *Wunderkammern*, were collections of objects, both natural and human-made, displayed in accordance with the tastes of their owners (fig. 30). The need to organise the contents of such cabinets soon turned what had been a simple interest in the 'wonderful' into a quest for systematic knowledge capable of making these collections into tools for education and scientific enquiry.

A good example of this is the *Theatrum sive Microcosmus Naturae*, a museum established by the Bologna scholar Ulisse Aldrovandi (1522–1605). Aldrovandi is considered the father of modern natural history for founding the first university professorship in the subject, and for establishing criteria used for the selection and cataloguing of the thousands of *naturalia* and *artificialia* in his collection. His intention was to simulate the natural world in a museum.[48] He left his collection in 1603 to the Bologna Senato, which exhibited it in the city's Palazzo Pubblico in accordance with Aldrovandi's own precise display and conservation instructions. University students, scholars and citizens were allowed to access the displays, so the collection's transfer from a private to a public building was the first step towards the creation of a modern public museum.[49]

Italy had more cabinets of curiosities than any other country and was, for this reason, a pioneer in the not always coherent or sequential journey that culminated in the concept of the modern museum. Between the years 1556 and 1560, artist and coin specialist Hubert Goltzius (1526–1583) stated that 380 of the 968 collections known to him belonged to Italy. The remainder were scattered across Holland, Germany, Austria, Switzerland and France.[50] Many of these included Egyptian antiquities, mainly small funerary objects and, sometimes, architectural elements or sculptures. Aldrovandi's universalist museum contained three shabtis (mummiform magical figures for the afterlife, see p. 190) and a scarab amulet, as well as two stone fragments with hieroglyphic inscriptions.[51] It is very difficult to establish the provenance of such objects. The collectors of the day relied on two possible acquisition methods, as well as frequently exchanging items with one another.

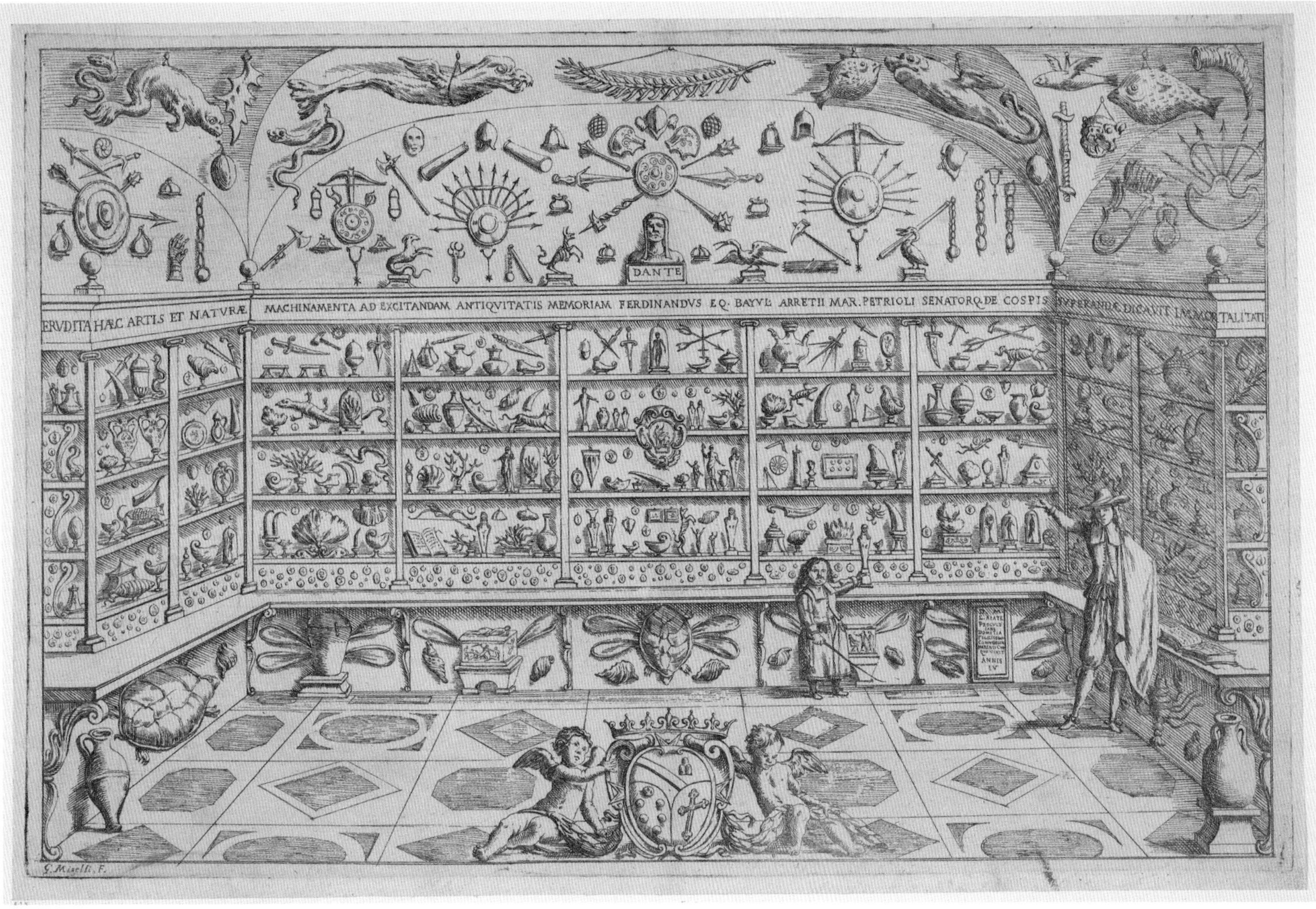

30
Engraving by Giuseppe Maria Mitelli of the curiosity cabinet of Ferdinando Cospi with shabtis (see p. 190) depicted in the centre
Bologna, Italy, 1677
Paper, H. 28.6 cm, W. 44.5 cm
British Museum, 1852,0612.471

First, extensive town planning work of the time in Rome and elsewhere brought to light antiquities that had been imported from Egypt in the Imperial Roman age, and these artefacts became available on the antiquities market.[52] One example is the unearthing in Rome in the early 1520s of the famous Mensa Isiaca, which, together with the obelisks erected by Pope Sixtus V, acted as the benchmark for all studies of Egyptian civilisation from the Renaissance to the early 1800s (fig. 19).

Secondly, in addition to its privileged relationship with the archaeological record, Italy's strategic position in the Mediterranean facilitated the sourcing of antiquities directly from Egypt. Those wanting to go to Alexandria and visit the Nile valley for religious, trading or exploration purposes could get there relatively easily. A well-known case is that of scholar and traveller Pietro della Valle (1586–1652).[53] His collection of antiquities, which reached Rome in 1623, included two famous mummies, two mummy masks made of cartonnage (layers of linen or papyrus covered with plaster), and a range of manuscripts that attracted the interest of the Jesuit father Athanasius Kircher.[54]

Even those who had no interest in travelling to Egypt personally, or were unable to do so, could buy antiquities and mummies of direct Egyptian provenance as the trade in these increased. Certain European merchants who were very active in Egypt played a key role, sourcing artefacts primarily from the Memphite area,[55] which they sold to travellers passing through Cairo or shipped from Alexandria to Europe. Many of the antiquities belonging to the Tuscan Grand Duke and Giovanni Nardi (1585–1654), his doctor and esteemed scholar, for example, came from the collection of Louis Bertier, a merchant from Lyon, France, operating in Egypt.[56] When Bertier moved from Cairo to Florence in 1642 he handed his collection over to Ferdinando II de' Medici (1610–1670) in exchange for an annuity.

Those without a direct relationship with this mercantile milieu could rely on middlemen such as Nardi, who played a key role in the acquisition of Egyptian antiquities for others in the Medici entourage. The Bologna marquis Ferdinando Cospi (1606–1686) was one of these. His famous *Wunderkammer* comprised objects similar to those owned by Nardi, such as shabtis and the so-called Ptah-Sokar-Osiris statuettes,[57] easily recognisable in the frontispiece of the Lorenzo Legati *Museo Cospiano* (1677) catalogue, which depicts the museum with its little custodian, a living marvel within a roomful of marvels (fig. 31).[58]

The language of ancient Egypt and Egyptian funerary rituals (the embalming of bodies in particular) were the most popular subjects of interest in the eighteenth century, as was the debate on the concept of the divine cutting across civilisations. A taste for the wondrous gave way to increasingly precise scientific investigation. More and more, interest in Egyptian civilisation involved the detailed reproduction of objects to scale, a preference for direct viewing of artefacts, and their classification and use as tools capable of furthering scholarship. A striking example is the Bologna marquis Luigi Ferdinando Marsili (1658–1730).[59] Marsili founded the Istituto delle Scienze in 1711 by donating his collections. He conceived its seven rooms as full-blown workshops capable of adding to scholarly knowledge through the fertile interaction between practice and theory. Its Stanza delle antichità (Room of antiquities) included about ten genuine Egyptian objects plus a fake worthy of attention, which bore a pseudo-hieroglyphic inscription freely inspired by the Nectanebo I (380–362 BCE) relief found near Chiesa di Santa Prisca on Monte Aventino in 1709

(figs 32–33). The Nectanebo relief, another of the few sources for the study of the Egyptian language available in the eighteenth century, was later donated to the Istituto delle Scienze by Benedict XIV (1675–1758, pope from 1740), together with two coffins and four mummies.

Although eighteenth-century collecting was powerfully conditioned by classical culture, driven by the excavation of important archaeological sites such as Pompeii and Herculaneum, Egyptian antiquities were increasingly collected and studied. The most resounding example is the collection of the Velletri cardinal Stefano Borgia (1731–1804), who collected 'treasures from the four corners of the world' and formed what came to be called the Museo Borgiano from 1782.[60] Borgia's modern scientific approach showed in the museum's structure, with its contents divided into ten classes, all of which were catalogued, restored, studied and published. The Egyptian antiquities

31 (facing page)
Mummiform figure from the previous Cospi collection, showing the creator god Ptah merged with the funerary gods Osiris and Sokar, in a so-called 'Ptah-Sokar-Osiris statue'. They support the rebirth of the deceased.
Egypt, 21st to 25th Dynasty, 747–30 BCE
Wood, H. 38 cm, W. 8 cm, D. 5.5 cm
Museo Civico Archeologico, Bologna, MCABo EG 341

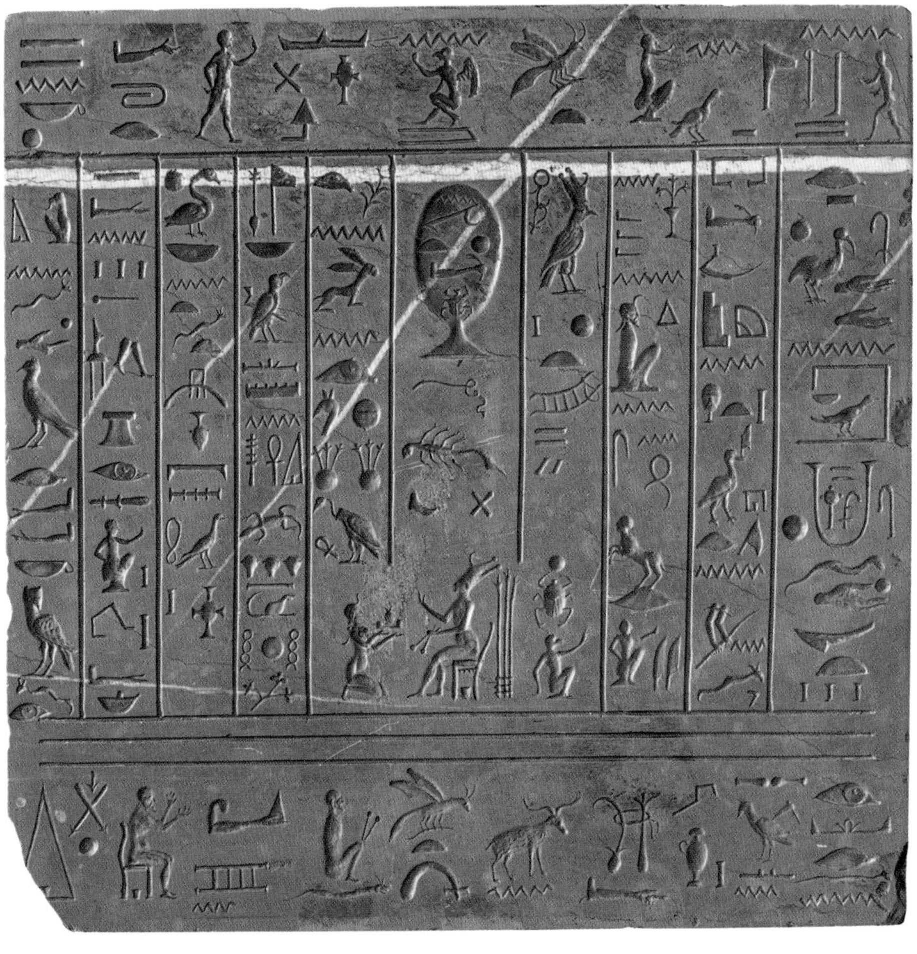

32 (right)
Fake with a pseudo-hieroglyphic inscription freely inspired by the Nectanebo I relief in Bologna (see fig. 33)
Italy, 1709–11
Marble, H. 23.5 cm, W. 24 cm, D. 5.5 cm
Museo Civico Archeologico, Bologna, MCABo EG 3707

33
Relief of Nectanebo I, who is depicted kneeling and offering jewellery and fabric to a number of demon-guardians. The hieroglyphs above the scene tell us that the pharaoh is thanking them for granting him power and victories in Egypt and abroad.
Heliopolis, 30th Dynasty, 380–362 BCE
Dolerite, H. 90 cm, W. 98 cm, D. 1.4 cm
Museo Civico Archeologico, Bologna, MCABo EG 1870

class was the most important, in both numerical and qualitative terms, with over 700 objects, among which were a statue of Pa-Maj, inscribed all over with magical texts, and an additional 1,800 Alexandrian coins and Coptic manuscript fragments (figs 34–35).

The collection was catalogued by Georg Zoëga,[61] who based his studies of the Egyptian language on Borgia's Egyptian objects, along with those in the other principal Italian collections (figs 36–37).

As a result of Napoleon's Italian campaign (1796–7) and the political events following his withdrawal, the eighteenth-century collecting world underwent profound upheavals. Collections changed hands or were broken up, primarily to the advantage of university museums and the various royal museums. In 1798, the Napoleonic Egyptian campaign and the consequent publication of the *Description de l'Égypte* (see p. 76) fuelled the rediscovery of ancient Egypt, which culminated in modern Egyptology and the creation of the principal European Egyptian collections. Italy, and the port of Livorno in particular, was the main collection hub for the thousands of objects leaving

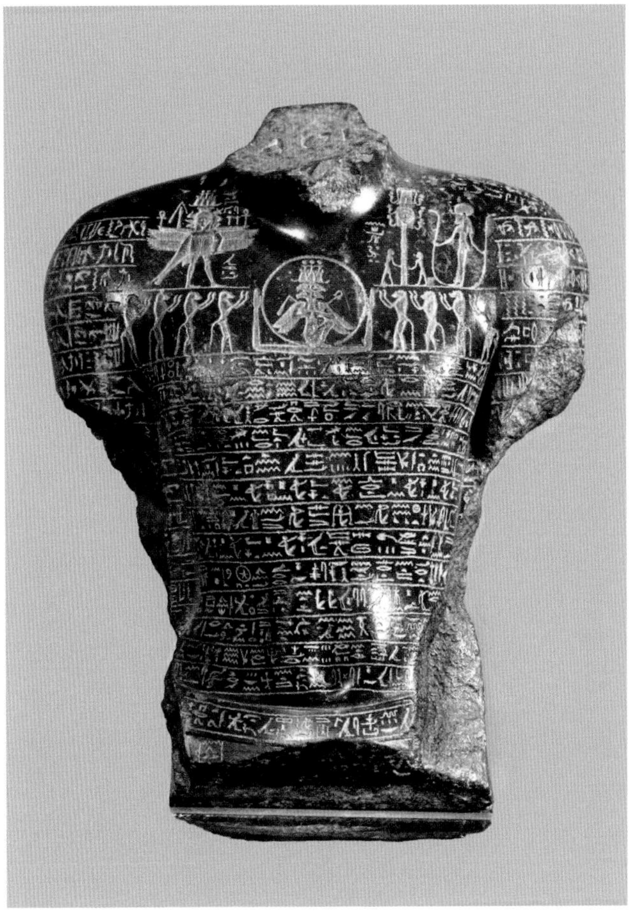

34 (right)
Magical statue of Pa-Maj, engraved with hieroglyphic texts and images of deities
Egypt, 30th Dynasty to early Ptolemaic Period, late 4th century BCE
Basalt, H. 26 cm, W. 20.5 cm, D. 19.5 cm
Museo Archeologico Nazionale di Napoli, inv. no. 1065

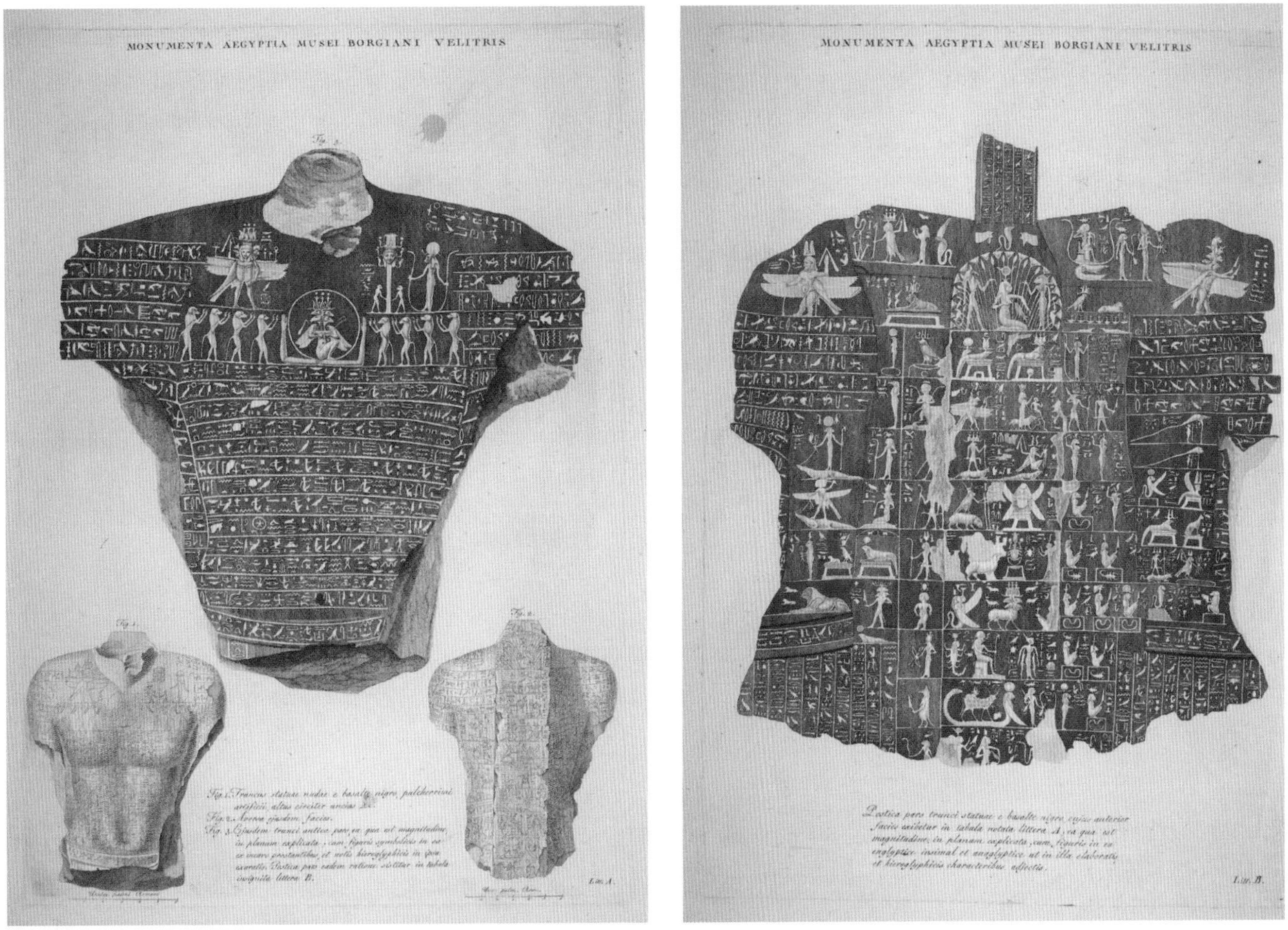

35 (below)
Engraving of front and back of the statue of Pa-Maj by an unknown artist
Probably Velletri, before 1850
Paper, H. 44.6 cm, W. 31.7 cm (left), H. 45.1 cm, W. 31.8 cm (right)
Thorvaldsens Museum, ThM E1416, E1418

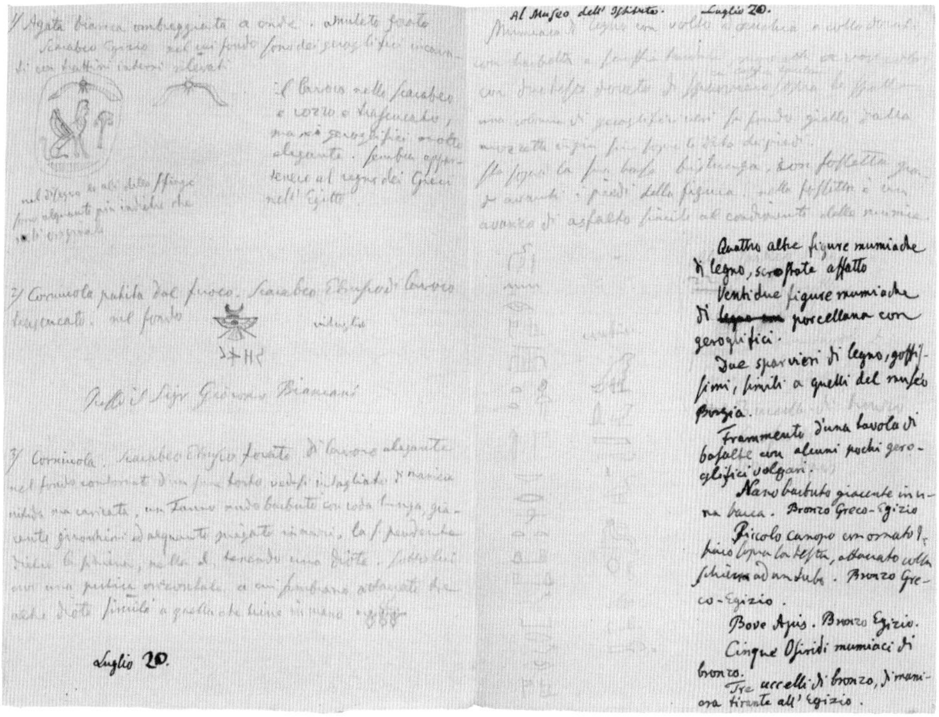
Al Museo dell' Istituto. Luglio 20.

Quattro altre figure mumiache di legno, scroftate affatto

Ventidue figure mumiache di ~~legno con~~ porcellana con geroglifici.

Due sparvieri di legno, goffissimi, simili a quelli del museo Borgia.

Frammenti d'una tavola di basalte con alcuni pochi geroglifici volgari.

Nano barbuto giacente in una barca. Bronzo Greco-Egizio

Piccolo canopo con ornato sopra la testa, adornato colla schiena ad un tubo. Bronzo Greco-Egizio.

Bove Apis. Bronzo Egizio.

Cinque Osiridi mumiaci di bronzo.

Tre uccelli di bronzo, di maniera tirante all' Egizio.

Luglio 20.

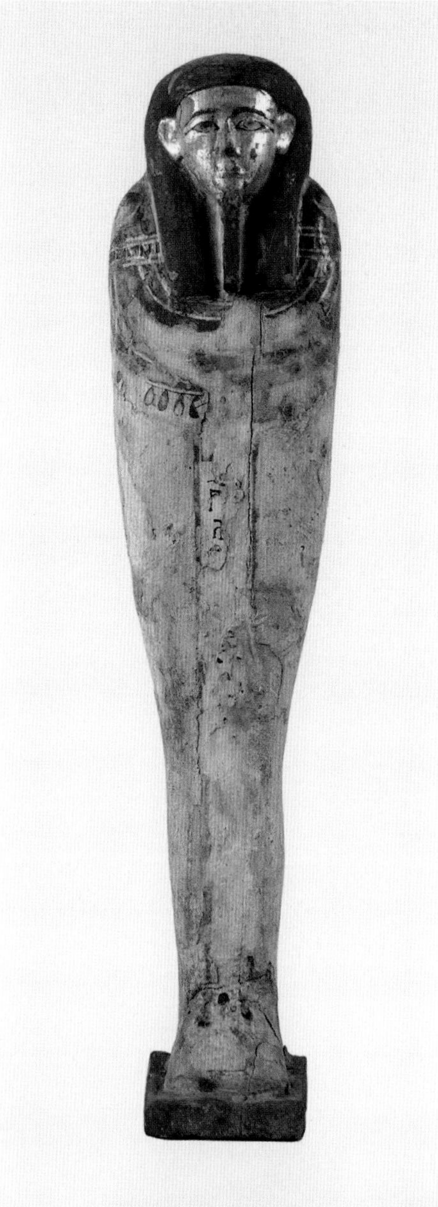

Alexandria for the European antiquarian market. Italy could, therefore, lay claim to two completely different but equally significant collecting histories.

First and foremost, there was the well-known acquisition in 1824 by Carlo Felice of Savoy (1765–1831) of around 8,000 antiquities collected in Egypt by the French consul, Bernardino Drovetti (1776–1852), with a view to setting up a museum in Turin which was to be Europe's first to focus entirely on Egyptian civilisation, the current Museo Egizio. A further striking example was the Egyptian collection of Bologna painter Pelagio Palagi (1775–1860), who, as the only private collector among many statesmen and monarchs, bought over 3,000 antiquities as well as Alexandrian and Ptolemaic coins between 1824–5 and 1845. His estate was ultimately bequeathed to the city of Bologna. The main nucleus of the collection was sold to him by the chancellor of the Austrian consulate in Egypt, Giuseppe Nizzoli, in 1831,[62] but this was supplemented by antiquities owned by the Belzoni family[63] and Venetian families such as Grimani and Nani, to cite just a few.

In the second half of the nineteenth century, the bulk of the older collections and those imported more recently either contributed to founding, or were simply funnelled into, mainly public museums. Italy still stands out in both the number and the distribution of such institutions.

36 (facing page, left)
Zoëga's drawing of and notes on the now-lost hieroglyphic inscription on the Ptah-Sokar-Osiris statue in Bologna (fig. 37)
Bologna, Italy, 20 July 1789
Paper, H. 20 cm, W. 28 cm
Royal Danish Library, NKS 357b fol., XIII, 3, 3, 6

37 (facing page, right)
Ptah-Sokar-Osiris statue from the previous Borgia collection
Egypt, Late Period to Ptolemaic Period, 747–30 BCE
Wood, H. 45.5 cm, W. 10.3 cm, D. 7.5 cm
Museo Civico Archeologico, Bologna, MCABo EG 335

ON THE THRESHOLD OF UNDERSTANDING

Ilona Regulski

The idea that hieroglyphs were symbols encoding sacred mysteries remained the dominant theory until the early eighteenth century, when scholars began focusing on aspects of Egyptian culture that could be measured, counted and otherwise precisely documented (figs 38–39). The engineering of Egyptian monuments replaced the meaning of hieroglyphs as the focus of fervid attention. The discipline of archaeology was taking shape, with interest in material remains overshadowing epigraphic matters, which were now mostly confined to general discussions of the probable nature and meaning of hieroglyphs.[64] Owing to this shift in priorities, few scholars after Kircher and prior to Champollion and Young made much progress in deciphering hieroglyphs. Some dismissed the medieval Islamic literature Kircher had drawn on as far-fetched, concluding that hieroglyphs could never be decoded at all.

While Rome remained the centre of research, travellers' descriptions of *in situ* Egyptian ruins became increasingly important sources of information. Following on from the eighteenth century's broadening and intensification of archaeological research, Danish antiquarian and coin specialist Georg Zoëga built on the work of previous scholars such as Bernard de Montfaucon, who saw Egyptian remains as art. Zoëga, the leading Egyptologist of the generation before Champollion, focused on obelisks within the comparative framework of ancient architectural practices.[65] He rejected the view that hieroglyphic inscriptions concerned occult sciences and religious and magical rites, embracing instead the classical scholars who understood obelisk inscriptions as praise of kings and gods.[66]

Zoëga's reputation as an expert in coins and classics came to the attention of the cleric (later cardinal) Stefano Borgia, who commissioned the Dane to catalogue his impressive collection of imperial coins from Egypt. Published in 1787, Zoëga's work was internationally acclaimed, making him the foremost authority on all things ancient Egyptian.[67] In 1788 Stefano Borgia recommended him to Pope Pius VI, who requested that Zoëga compose a history of the Egyptian obelisks that the Vatican was planning to re-erect in Rome. In 1797 Zoëga published *De origine et usu obeliscorum*, his crowning achievement.[68] This ponderous volume, celebrating the restoration of the magnificent obelisk raised in the Piazza Montecitorio,

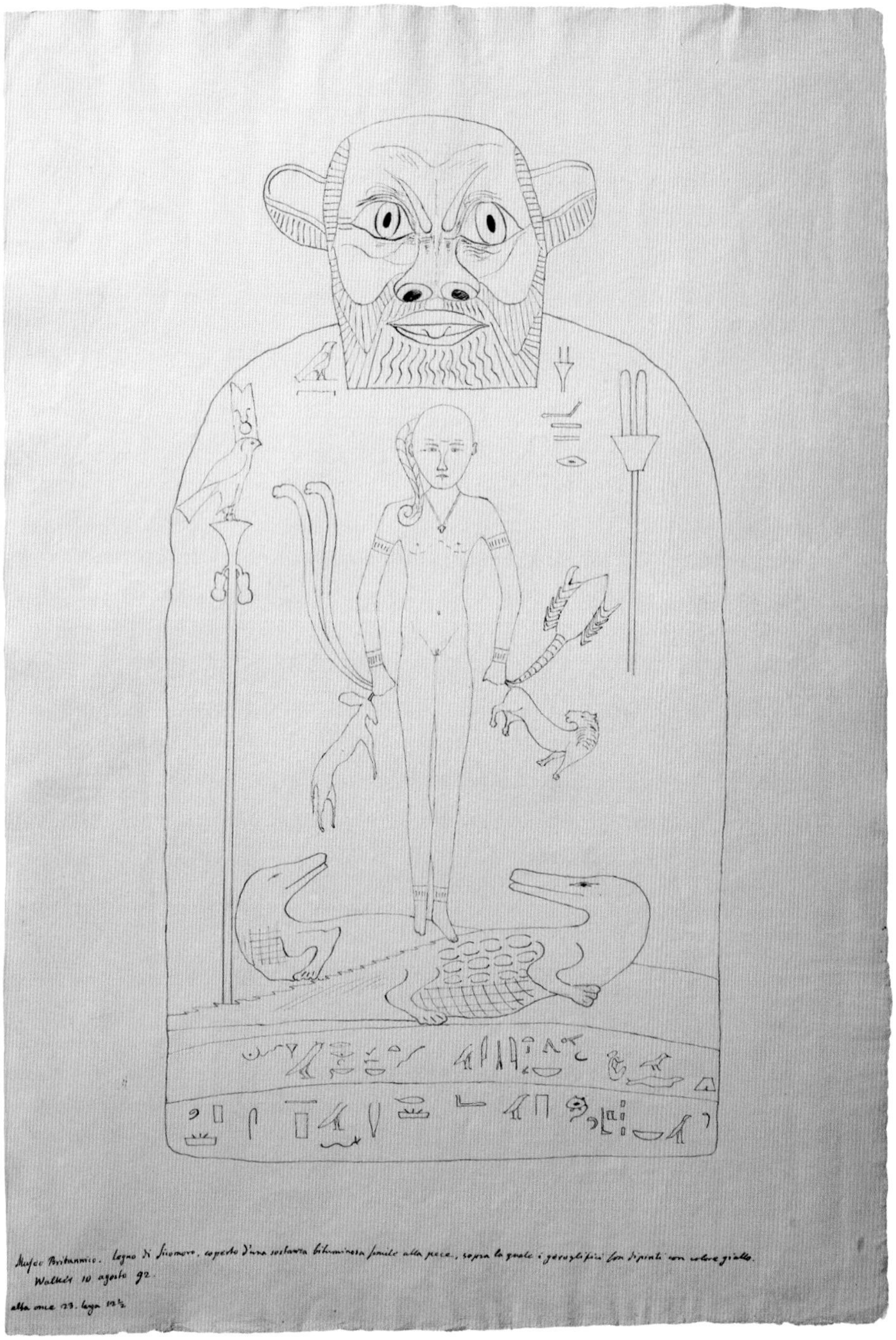

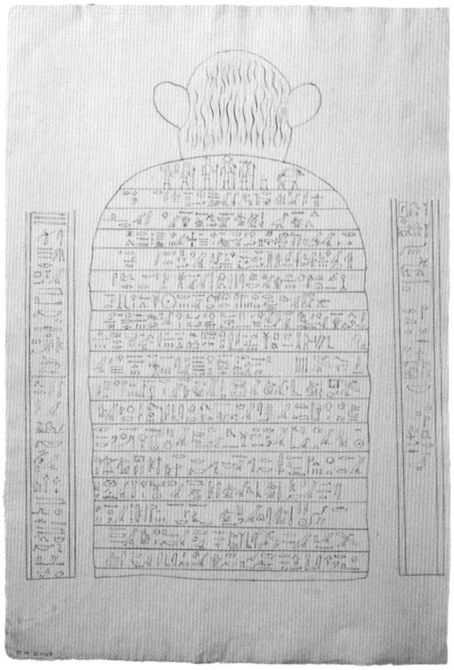

38
John Walker's drawing of a cippus representing Bes and Horus as a child (Harpocrates). Zoëga's inscription shows that he shared information with scholars in England: 'British Museum. Sycamore wood, covered with a bituminous substance like pitch, above which the hieroglyphs are painted in yellow. Walker 10 August [17]92.'
London, England, before 10 August 1792
Pencil, pen and ink on paper, H. 54.1 cm, W. 37.5 cm
Thorvaldsens Museum, ThM D1167r+v

39 (facing page)
Magical stela or cippus representing Bes protecting Harpocrates, with a hieroglyphic text on the back.
Egypt, Late Period, 747–332 BCE
Wood, H. 42.5 cm, W. 23.3 cm, D. 10.8 cm
British Museum, EA60958

summarised previous wisdom on the subject, variously criticised or fortified by the author's learned assessments.

Zoëga asked other scholars to gather inscriptions during their trips to Egypt (fig. 40). Thomas Ford Hill (1753–1795) copied some of the earliest inscribed Egyptian antiquities acquired by the British Museum,[69] and took rubbings to ensure their accuracy. Hill provided detailed descriptions and measurements followed by his hypotheses on the iconography, date and possible context of the pieces.

Zoëga was recognised as a leader in both Egyptian and Coptic language studies. Johan David Åkerblad (1763–1819) (see p. 94), who studied Coptic with Zoëga, described it as the 'language that served as a torch in all this research'.[70] Zoëga defined hieroglyphic characters as reproductions of ideas that were presented in a series, like letters in an alphabet or a sequence of thoughts. He believed the literate class had invented the system in the earliest times to use for inscriptions, and that the cursive script was a cruder form of hieroglyphs. An alphabet of twenty-five elements had developed from hieroglyphs, according to Zoëga, by a phonetic process in which sentences were broken into words, words into syllables, and syllables into letters. While unable to solve the riddle of decipherment, he intended his book as a guide to future scholars and was one of the first to offer accurate advice towards that end. Zoëga anticipated the importance that Coptic would hold for the scholars who later tackled the Rosetta Stone, discovered just two years after he published his masterpiece. His work made an immediate and powerful impression on Champollion.

Characteres Sacri sive Ιεροyραμμαlα των Αιγυπlιων.

in eorum Monumentis quæ in Britannia reperiuntur apparentes.

Tab. XXV.

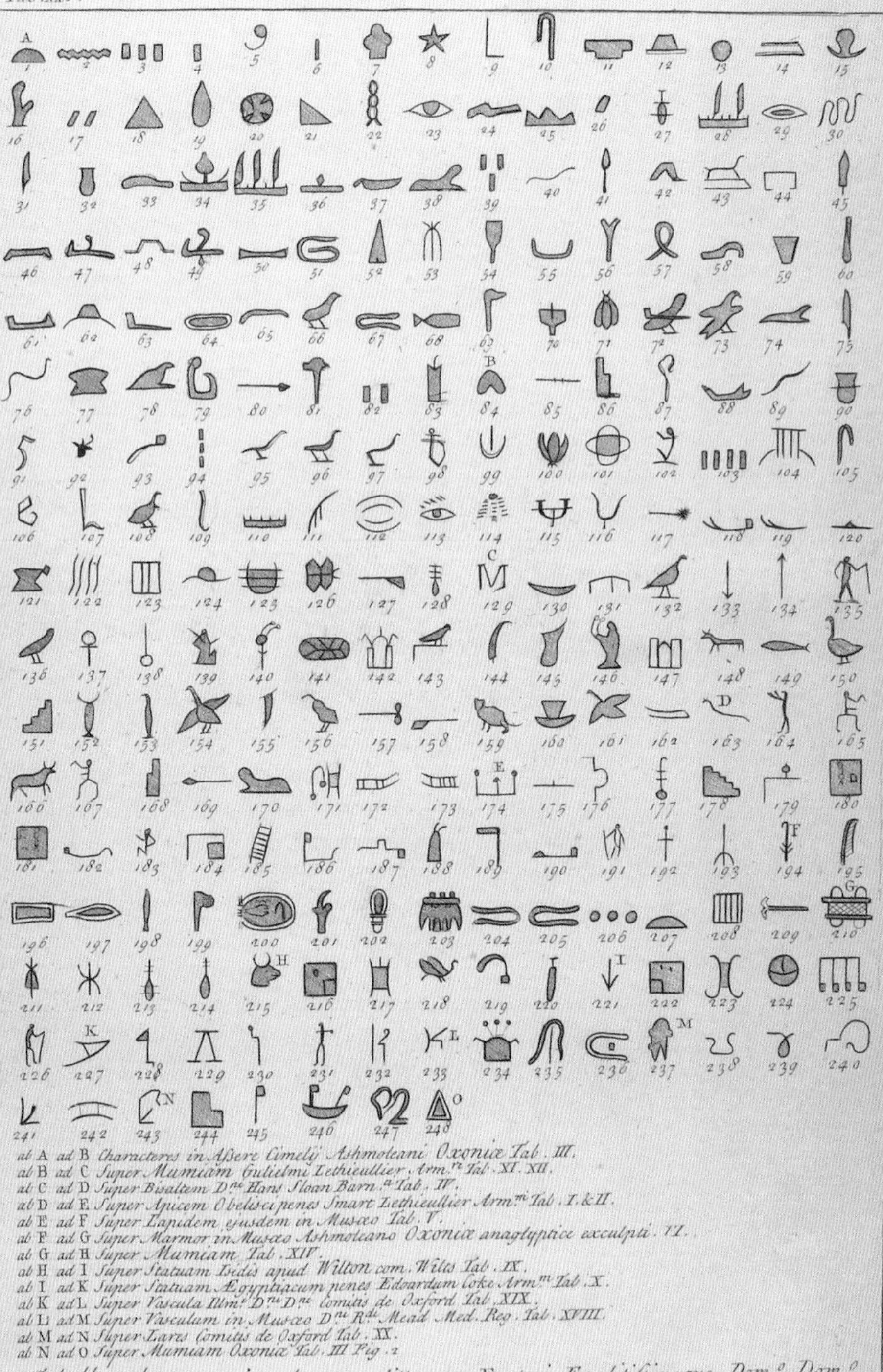

ab A ad B Characteres in Aßere Cimelij Ashmoleani Oxoniæ Tab. III.
ab B ad C Super Mumiam Gulielmi Lethieullier Arm.^{ri} Tab. XI. XII.
ab C ad D Super Bisaltem D.^{ni} Hans Sloan Barn.^{ti} Tab. IV.
ab D ad E Super Apicem Obelisci penes Smart Lethieullier Arm.^{ri} Tab. I. & II.
ab E ad F Super Lapidem ejusdem in Musæo Tab. V.
ab F ad G Super Marmor in Musæo Ashmoleano Oxoniæ anaglyptice exculpti. VI.
ab G ad H Super Mumiam Tab. XIV.
ab H ad I Super Statuam Isidis apud Wilton com. Wilts Tab. IX.
ab I ad K Super Statuam Ægyptiacum penes Edoardum Coke Arm.^{ri} Tab. X.
ab K ad L Super Vascula Illm.^{i} D.^{ni} D.^{ni} Comitis de Oxford Tab. XIX.
ab L ad M Super Vasculum in Musæo D.^{ni} R.^{di} Mead Med. Reg. Tab. XVIII.
ab M ad N Super Lares Comitis de Oxford Tab. XX.
ab N ad O Super Mumiam Oxoniæ Tab. III Fig. 2

Tabellam hanc, omnium bonarum litterarum Fautori Eruditißimoque Dom.^o Dom.^o
MARTINO FOLKES Arm.^{ro} ob Patrocinium suum Benevolentiamque humillimè

D.D.D. A. Gordon

THE DISCOVERY OF THE ROSETTA STONE

Patricia Usick

The understanding of hieroglyphs was lost as the culture of ancient Egypt was overcome by waves of conquest and occupation. The seventh-century Arab invasion brought Islam, and with it the Arabic language and a succession of rulers, culminating in the dominance of a quasi-independent military dynasty of former enslaved people, the Mamelukes. They ruled Egypt with repressive powers under the nominal authority of a governor ('pasha') in Cairo, installed by the sultan of the Ottoman Empire from the distant government of the Sublime Porte at Constantinople. The sultan's attempts to curtail the chaos caused by rival Mameluke factions under unruly provincial governors, the beys, led to an Ottoman army being sent to Egypt in 1786, but it was forced to withdraw the following year. General Napoleon Bonaparte was to encounter a ruling coalition of two beys: Murad and Ibrahim.

By the end of the eighteenth century, following the American and French revolutions, Europe was aware of the geographic and mercantile potential of Egypt and the weakness and corruption of the Ottoman Empire. The French count, Constantin Volney (1757–1820), travelling in Egypt from 1783 to 1786, published an influential account that revealed the political, social and economic decline of the country and posited his opinion on the benefits of a possible French invasion for both culture and trade. Warren Hastings (1732–1818), governor of Bengal for the British East India Company, had signed a commercial treaty with the Mameluke sheikh of Cairo in 1775, and the Company's troops were steadily establishing control in India. In December 1797, Tipu Sultan (1750–1799) of Mysore sought Napoleon's help against the increasing threat of British power in India and received an encouraging response indicating French support. In the margin of a book on Turkish warfare, Napoleon wrote: 'Through Egypt we shall invade India …'[71]

Fresh from his victories in Italy, but frustrated in his attempts to invade England, the charismatic Napoleon landed in Egypt on 1 July 1798, with a large force of 40,000 troops. Having taken the strategic island of Malta, he aimed to cut off the British from their lucrative overland trade with India, establish a French colony and then supplant British power in India itself. To this end he was accompanied by a Commission of Arts and Sciences, staffed by the most brilliant French minds of the day, who, in the spirit of scientific enquiry characteristic of the Enlightenment, would survey and

40 (facing page)
Engraving of hieroglyphs by John Smith. A number of these engravings were sent by Thomas Ford Hill to Zoëga as mentioned in a letter of 22 June 1792.
London, England, before 1737
Paper, H. 53 cm, W. 33 cm
Thorvaldsens Museum, ThM E1394

41
Drawing by Dominique Vivant Denon of the ruins at Apollonopolis Parva, Middle Egypt, study for Plate 80 of his 1802 book *Voyage dans la Basse et la Haute Egypte*
Egypt or France, 1799–1802
Paper, H. 13.1 cm, W. 28.8 cm
British Museum, 1836,0109.127

map Egypt, both ancient and modern.[72] The Commission comprised some 167 scholars, known as the *savants*: military engineers, astronomers, botanists, mathematicians, geographers and artists. Some were established figures, but others young students. In Cairo, they replicated the French Institute with an Institut d'Égypte, housed in a former palace, where they established a library and a printing press (requisitioned from the Vatican) with Arabic, Syriac and Greek fonts, held meetings and wrote papers, under the leadership of its permanent secretary, the mathematician Joseph Fourier. As General Desaix chased the Mameluke army south, he was accompanied by the antiquary and artist Baron Dominique Vivant Denon (1747–1825), who, at the age of fifty-two, was one of the most eminent *savants*. On his return to Paris with Napoleon, Denon would publish his travel journal and drawings of the great temple complexes of Upper Egypt to wide acclaim, and be appointed the first director of the Louvre Museum (fig. 41).[73]

In mid-July 1799, facing an impending attack from Ottoman naval forces wishing to avenge Napoleon's campaign in Syria, the French strengthened their shore defences. The castle fort at Rosetta (present-day Rashid) (fig. 42), a green and fertile Delta town on the western branch of the Nile, had been reconstructed by Sultan Qait Bey in the fifteenth century and was in a dilapidated state. Renaming it Fort Julien, after one of Napoleon's aides-de-camp who had been killed in an attack, the fort commander, d'Hautpoul, instructed young Lieutenant Pierre François Xavier Bouchard (1772–1822) to organise the demolition and reconstruction of the outer defences. A junior member of the Commission, Bouchard had taken his final engineering examinations at the Cairo Institut, having previously served in the new aeronautic squadron of Nicolas-Jacques Conté (the inventor of the pencil), which used hydrogen balloons for military observation. Bouchard and Conté

42
View in February 2022 of the fort in Rashid where the Rosetta Stone was discovered

each damaged an eye in an explosion during experiments with gas. Among the rubble of the foundations of the fort, the remains of an ancient stone appeared, seemingly of blackish granite, on which Bouchard recognised three fragmentary horizontal inscriptions: Egyptian hieroglyphs at the top, Greek at the bottom, and between them an unknown script, initially thought to be Syriac (see p. 90). On his tour of the Delta, Denon had noted the reuse of many such inscribed blocks in the fort,[74] and grasped that they probably came from the nearby ancient site of Sais. Realising its potential significance to the decipherment of hieroglyphs, Bouchard took the object (which would become known as the Rosetta Stone) to General Abdallah Jacques-François Menou (1750–1810), who had it cleaned and the Greek partially translated. Michel-Ange Lancret informed the *savants*, and Bouchard and the Stone sailed up the Nile to the Institut in Cairo, where its discovery and its arrival on 19 August 1799 were announced in the Commission's gazette, the *Courier de l'Egypte*, no. 37; this was the first mention of the Stone's potential to be 'the key' to the decipherment of hieroglyphs. The same issue announced the abrupt departure of Napoleon from Cairo for France. His military campaign, initially successful, had been disrupted by the Battle of the Nile on 1–3 August 1798. Admiral Nelson had destroyed the French fleet moored in Aboukir Bay, near Alexandria, and left the French army cut off in Egypt. Following an unsuccessful campaign in Syria and insurrection in Cairo, Napoleon had secretly arranged to return to Paris with Denon and some of his officers, leaving his army under the control of General Kléber.

At the news of the arrival of the Stone at Cairo's port in Būlāq, 'everyone ran to see the marvellous stone'[75] and spent weeks examining it in detail, hoping it would provide the key to the historic riches of ancient Egypt. The first and indispensable condition was to make exact copies. Two young orientalists, Louis Rémy Raige and Jean-Joseph Marcel, had recognised that the middle inscription was not Syriac but a cursive script of the Egyptian language, which they had seen before on papyrus and mummy bandages. To copy it by hand might take months and errors would be likely; therefore, they washed the Stone, leaving water in the indentations, then covered the surface with ink and printed it onto thin sheets of damp, coated paper, a technique that developed into lithography. By 24 January 1800, they had produced a white-on-black reverse copy which could be read with a mirror or against the light. Meanwhile Conté, independently, treated it like a copper engraving, producing a black-on-white image. Raige and Marcel began to translate the Greek, learning that it was a priestly decree in honour of a king Ptolemy (see p. 229), and included many Egyptian proper names. The text went on to direct that the decree was to be engraved on hard stone in sacred, vernacular and Greek characters and to be placed in every Egyptian temple. The script and the language of the vernacular section were unknown; the Frenchmen thought it perhaps related to Coptic, the modern vernacular, or some other ancient language. Using a pair of compasses, they searched mechanically for parallels of the proper names in the expected positions, starting with 'Ptolemy', and attempting to break down the sequence of signs. The engineer Adrien Raffeneau-Delile also took a sulphur cast, which avoided any printing errors. By that summer, General Dugua, the governor of Cairo, had returned to France with printed copies of the inscription.

In June 1800, General Kléber was assassinated by a student of the al-Azhar mosque, which the French had destroyed in the Cairo uprising of 1798, and General Menou, who had converted to Islam in Egypt and married an Egyptian woman, replaced him as commander-in-chief. On 8 March 1801 the British fleet landed at Aboukir Bay, near Alexandria, and Menou's army was defeated at the subsequent Battle of Canopus on

21 March, retreating to the walled city of Alexandria where the *savants* joined them. The British laid siege to the town. General Abercromby had been killed at Canopus, and General Sir John Hely-Hutchinson (1757–1832) now commanded the British army, while Hussein, Kapudan Pasha (the high admiral of the allied Turkish fleet) landed his troops at Aboukir. They marched on Cairo, where the French general Belliard surrendered. Menou surrendered Alexandria and signed the Capitulation on 31 August with the British and the Kapudan Pasha (fig. 43). Menou's first proposal for Article 16 was that the French should keep all their papers, plans, memoirs, collections of natural history and antiquities. Hutchinson refused, and passed the arrangements on to two scholarly Englishmen: one was travelling in Egypt purely by chance, and the other was there through diplomatic channels.

The antiquarian Reverend Edward Daniel Clarke (1769–1822) had been travelling through Europe and Asia with his wealthy young student, John Marten Cripps. In Cairo they met the like-minded William Richard Hamilton (1777–1859), diplomatic attaché and private secretary to Lord Elgin, the British Ambassador to Constantinople. Hamilton had been sent to Egypt to supervise the Capitulation. They visited the pyramids together and Clarke was shown some inscribed stones abandoned in the French Institut.[76] By September, Clarke and Hamilton reached Alexandria, where they informed Hutchinson that among the antiquities was a huge sarcophagus (stone coffin), taken from a mosque in Cairo and said to be the tomb of Alexander,[77] which was now hidden on a hospital ship awaiting departure.

Hamilton revised Article 16 so that, other than the *savants*' 'instruments of arts and science', all their collections, including 'Arabian manuscripts, statues and other collections which have been made for the French Republic' should be at the disposal of the generals of the British and Ottoman armies, thus reflecting the recent French confiscation of works of art from Italy and Europe. The *savants* protested to Menou that this gave away 'a property of science and art, the holiest of all'. Geoffroy Saint-Hilaire, Savigny and Delille insisted that the collections were not only private property, but would perish by changing hands, becoming (using the metaphor of ancient Egyptian) a dead language. They threatened to destroy everything; to throw it across the desert or into the sea. When Hamilton still refused, Geoffroy Saint-Hilaire exclaimed furiously that they would rather burn their treasures: 'For your fame, count on the remembrance of history; you too will have burned a Library at Alexandria!' This effected a sudden change in Hamilton, who agreed to plead their cause, and the *savants* eventually returned to France with the materials that would become their great and influential publication, the *Description de l'Égypte*.[78]

Art. 16.

Les Individus composant l'Institut d'Egypte & la Commission des arts emporteront avec Eux tous les papiers, plans, mémoires, collections d'histoire naturelle, et tous les monuments d'arts & d'antiquités recueillis par eux en Egypte.

16. Les Membres de l'Institut peuvent emporter avec Eux tous les Instruments des arts, & des Sciences qu'ils ont apporté de france, mais les manuscrits arabes, les Statues, & les autres Collections qui ont été faites pour la Republique francaise Seront considérés comm Proprieté publique, & seront à la Disposition des Généraux de l'armée combinée.

Monsieur le General Hope ayant déclaré sur quelques Observations du Général en Chef de l'armée francaise, qu'il ne pouvoit rien changer à cet article, il a été convenu, qu'il en seroit écrit à Monsieur le Général en Chef de l'armée anglaise.

Art 17.

Les Batiments qui seront employés au Transport de l'armée francaise & auxiliaire, ainsi que des Individus qui l'accompagneront, seront escortés par des batiments de Guerre des puissances alliées qui s'engagent formélement à ce qu'ils ne soient inquiétés d'aucune manière pendant leur Traversée.

17. Accordé avec une Semblable Réciprocité de la part du Général en Chef de l'armée francaise, qui s'engage à ce qu'aucun de ces batiments ne soient inquiétés pendant son séjour en france ni pour son retour. il s'engage également à ce qu'il leur soit fourni tout ce qui sera nécessaire,

Volumes of the *Description* would accompany Napoleon to his first exile in Elba, where he hung up illustrated plates and decorated his residence with painted Egyptianising motifs.[79] At Malmaison, the marital home established by his first wife Josephine, her many collections, reminiscent of the spirit of the age, included botanic and zoological specimens, neoclassical antiquities and a few Egyptian objects. The latter, once said to have been Napoleon's personal souvenirs (and thereby enhancing their prestige and financial value), can be shown to have been flattering gifts: two were from members of the *ancien régime*, anxious for their security in Napoleon's France.[80] There is no evidence that Napoleon himself collected antiquities in Egypt, but the display of Egyptian artefacts at Malmaison attests to his interest in them and their perceived cultural value alongside classical works.

Hutchinson instructed Clarke and Hamilton to recover all the antiquities and, in particular, to safeguard the Rosetta Stone and to copy the inscription in case it should be damaged (fig. 44). He gave them a copy 'made with red chalk upon paper by a member of the Institute' and instructed Colonel Tomkyns Hilgrove Turner of the Guards, a Fellow of the Society of Antiquaries, to oversee the recovery. Together, Clarke and Hamilton were shown the warehouses 'near the old port' by 'Monsieur Le Roy, Ordonnateur de la Marine', and were astounded by the number and quality of the antiquities, some of colossal size.[81] They scoured Alexandria for the other collections, finding 'Statues, Sarcophagi, Maps, MSS [manuscripts], Drawings, Plans, Charts, Botany, Stuffed birds, Animals, Dried Fishes, &c.'[82] Clarke and Cripps, then Hamilton, rowed out to discover the sarcophagus which had been hidden in the hold of the ship *La Cause* 'half-filled with filth and covered with rags of the sick people aboard'.[83] Hamilton wrote: 'This monument was resigned to us not without much regret, as it had long been considered one of the most valuable curiosities in Alexandria; but much greater reluctance was manifested by General Menou, when the claim was made for the Trilingular or Rosetta Stone, nor was it given up without frequent remonstrances on his part.'[84]

Menou claimed the Stone was as much his own property 'as the linen of his wardrobe or his embroidered saddles'[85] and Fourier listed each of the other antiquities as belonging to individual generals. Finally, on 12 September, Clarke, Cripps and Hamilton visited Menou's tent to collect the stone, having requested permission to make a copy. They were led to a small tent, divided by a curtain 'behind which Menou had his Charem'. The curtain was raised 'and Jacques Abd'allah made his appearance. A more grotesque figure can hardly be conceived'. Clarke thought him overweight and overdressed, and when the Stone was mentioned, Menou gave vent to his rage: 'You may tell your Commander-in-chief he has

43 (facing page)
Article 16 of the Capitulation for the Garrison of Alexandria, signed on behalf of Egypt, France and Britain
Alexandria, 1801
Paper, H. 33 cm, W. 21.5 cm, D. 6 cm (closed)
The National Archives, WO 1/345, pp. 450–1

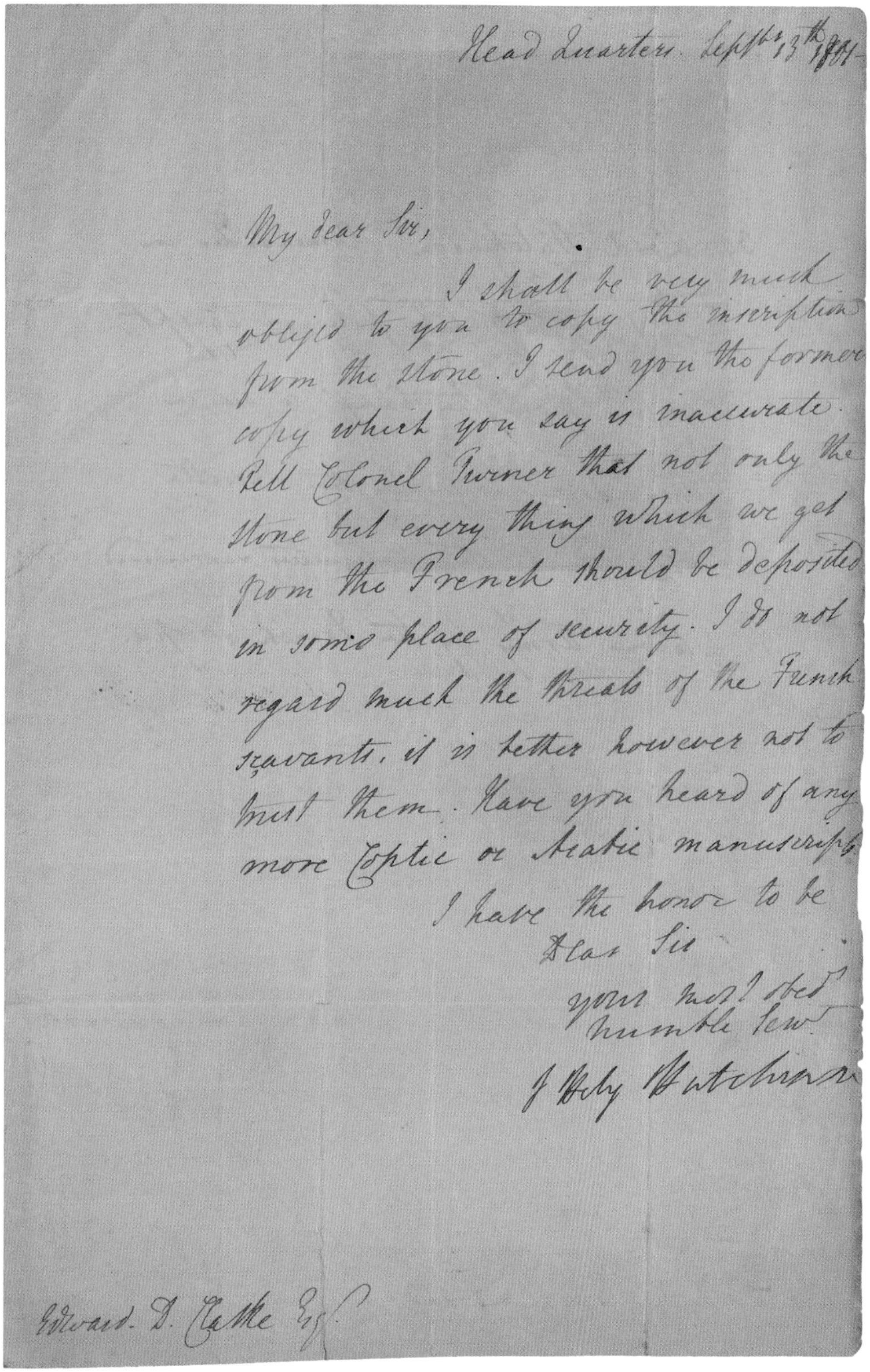

Head Quarters. Sept.r 13th 1801.

My dear Sir,

I shall be very much obliged to you to copy the inscription from the stone. I send you the former copy which you say is inaccurate. Tell Colonel Turner that not only the stone but every thing which we get from the French should be deposited in some place of security. I do not regard much the threats of the French sçavants, it is better however not to trust them. Have you heard of any more Coptic or Arabic manuscripts.

I have the honor to be
Dear Sir
your most obed.t
humble Serv.t
J Hely Hutchinson

Edward D. Clarke Esq.

as much right to make this demand as a highwayman has to ask for my purse!'[86] Hutchinson's response was to threaten a humiliating search of the officers' baggage. Clarke and Hamilton returned to Menou's tent, hearing him 'in strong terms of indignation remonstrating against the injustice of the demands made upon him: "Jamais on n'a pillé le monde!"' ('Never has the world been so pillaged!'), even threatening a duel with Hutchinson.[87] Clarke notes: 'However Colonel Turner soon brought this matter to a conclusion. The Rosetta tablet was taken from a warehouse, covered with mats, where it had been deposited with Menou's baggage; and it was surrendered to us, by a French Officer and Member of the Institute, in the streets of Alexandria'; pointedly adding, 'Mr Cripps, Mr Hamilton, and the author, being the only persons present, to take possession of it. The officer appointed to deliver it recommended its speedy conveyance to some place of safety, as he could not be answerable for the conduct of the French soldiers, if it were suffered to remain exposed to their indignation.'[88] They alerted Hutchinson, 'who gave orders for its immediate removal; and it was given in charge to General Turner, under whose direction all the monuments of Egyptian antiquity, resigned to us by the articles of the Capitulation, were afterwards conveyed to England' (fig. 45).[89] Despite this patriotic display, Clarke then visited the *savants* where a scholarly 'urbanity' prevailed, although they still refused to show him their map of Egypt.[90]

Clarke's report in his publications of 1805 and 1817 quite specifically contradicts the testimony of Turner, read to the Society of Antiquaries in 1810 and published in their journal, *Archaeologia*, in 1812. In the latter, Turner claimed that he alone collected the Stone. He states that the Stone, which he saw at Menou's house in Alexandria, was 'covered with soft cotton cloth, and a double matting', but when the French found it was to go to the British, 'the covering of the stone was torn off, and it was thrown upon its face, and the excellent wooden cases of the rest were broken off'. When he told Hutchinson of this treatment:

> he gave me a detachment of artillerymen, and an artillery-engine, called, from its powers, a devil-cart, with which that evening I went to General Menou's house, and carried off the stone, without any injury, but with some difficulty, from the narrow streets, to my house, amid the sarcasms of numbers of French officers and men; being ably assisted by an intelligent serjeant of artillery, who commanded the party ... During the time the Stone remained at my house, some gentlemen attached to the corps of sçavants [*savants*] requested to have a cast, which I readily granted, provided the Stone should receive no injury; which cast they took to Paris, leaving the stone well cleared from the printing ink, which it had been covered with to take off several copies to send to France when it was first discovered.[91]

44 (facing page)
Letter dated 13 September 1801, from General Hely-Hutchinson to Clarke
Alexandria, 1801
Paper, H. 31.4 cm, W. 20.5 cm
British Museum, EA76744

A Statue of white Marble of Roman Workmanship. 5„6. high - probably of Marcus Aurelius

... Workmanship preserved & 5„6 high without ... justly called Mark Septimius Severus.

... the head ... may easil... the head. ... Antony - ...

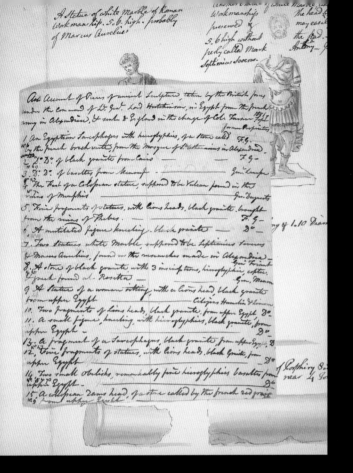

An Account of Pieces of ancient Sculpture, taken by the British forces under the Command of Lt. Genl. Lord Hutchinson, in Egypt from the french army in Alexandria, & sent to England in the charge of Col: Turner 1801 Sept

Former Proprietors

1 An Egyptian Sarcophagus with hieroglyphics, of a stone called by the french brechcritte, from the Mosque of St. Athanasius in Alexandria — F. G.

2. D°. D°. of black granite from Cairo — F. G.

3. D°. D°. of basaltes from Menouf — Genl. Lanusse

4. The Fist of a Colossean statue, supposed to be Vulcan found in the ruins of Memphis — Gen. Duguesty

5. Five fragments of statues, with Lions heads, black granite, brought from the ruins of Thebes. — F. G.

6. A mutilated figure kneeling - black granite — D°

7. Two Statues white Marble, supposed to be Septimius Severus & Marcus Aurelius, found in the researches made in Alexandria — Genl. Friant

8. A stone of black granite, with 3 inscriptions, hieroglyphic, coptic & greek found at Rosetta — Gen. Menou

9 A Statue of a woman sitting, with a Lions head, black granite from upper Egypt — Citizens Hamelin & Lironcourt

10. Two fragments of Lions heads, black granite, from upper Egypt D°

11. A small figure, kneeling, with hieroglyphics, black granite, from upper Egypt — D°

13. A fragment of a Sarcophagus, black granite, from upper Egypt D°

12. Five fragments of statues, with Lions heads, black Granite, from upper Egypt — D°

14 Two small obelisks, remarkably fine hieroglyphics basaltes from upper Egypt — D°

15. A collossean Rams head, of a stone called by the french red granite from upper Egypt —

...ny & 1.10 Diam...

...of Porphiry 8... near 4 Tons

16. A statue of a Woman sitting on the ground of black granite between the feet is a Model of a capital of a Column of the temple of Isis, at Dendera —

17. A fragment of a Statue with a lions head black granite, — Lord Hutchinson

18. A Stone with hieroglyphics, from the Camp of the 3d. Guards of the same unknown kind as the Memnon. — Col. Turner

A Chest of Oriental Manuscripts 62 Coptic, Arabic & Turkish, belonging to the library of the french institute at Cairo —

The whole of the above was on board H.M.S. Madras on her way home, except No. 8. & No. 16. and the Chest of Manuscripts, which are on board H.M.S. Egyptienne

T. H. Turner
Capt. 3d Guards

A large Sarcophagus, 10„ 2. long. 5„ 4. broad at the Circular end; and 4„3 at the square end. 3„10 high at the circular end, and 3„8½ at the opposite end — It consists of a curious kind of Breccia; is covered with hieroglyphics both within & without, & appears to have had a false bottom. It was converted by the Turks into a Bath or Cistern, there being a number of holes all around near the bottom. Its weight is about 9 Tons — Denon, in his "Voyage de la basse et haute Egypte" Vol mentions it, as one of the most curious Articles of Egyptian Antiquity he has ever seen, & strongly recommends that it may be made to decorate some Museum at Paris

It stood in the Mosque of St Athanasius at Alexandria.

[10]

Another Sarcophagus of black & white Granite, full of Hieroglyphics inside & out, with a figure of Isis carved at the bottom — This likewise appears to have been used by the Turks as a Bath or Cistern, there being one hole near the bottom at the rounded end. — Its length is 8„10. breadth 4:7 at one end, & 3„10 at the other end; and height 3„8½ Its weight about 8½ Tons.

[8]

A Colossal hand of red Granite 3„8 long. breadth across the Knuckles 2„7. breadth of the wrist 2„4. breadth of the Middle finger 9 inches weight near 2 Tons. The figure this hand belonged to must have been about 56 feet high.

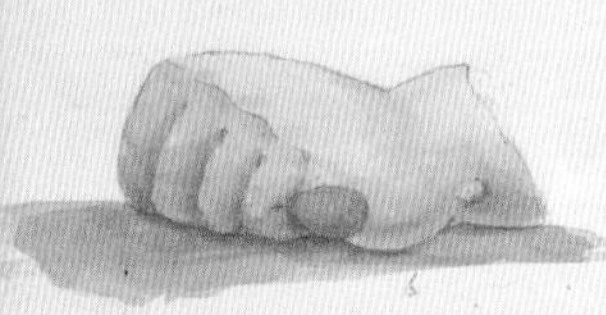

An Egyptian Deity, of black & red Granite 7 feet high, near 2 Tons in Weight NB This is in two pieces. and there are four more fragments which may be set up into two more similar figures. — There are also seven other fragments, of which it will be impossible to make out any whole figures. —

x 68
57 or 37

16 or 88

Two Obelisks of Basaltes, with hieroglyphics in pannels on each face. 8„6 long. 1„5 square at bottom & 1.2 at top. each weighing about 1¼ Tons.

[523] [524]

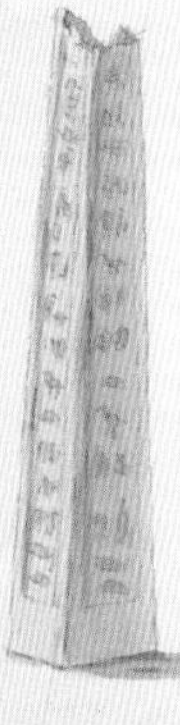

A part of a figure of black Granite; the upper part human, the lower of some quadruped — with hieroglyphics on the back 3„6. high

Another figure of the same kind. 1„6½ high with hieroglyphics both before & behind.

45 (facing page)
List of Egyptian monuments to be taken to England according to the terms of the Capitulation, drawn up by Colonel Tomkyns Hilgrove Turner
Alexandria, 1801
Paper, H. 39.8 cm, W. 54 cm, D. 0.4 cm (opened)
British Museum, AESAr.312

46 (right)
Printed engraving of the demotic text on the Rosetta Stone in the *Vetusta Monumenta*, a series of illustrated antiquarian papers on ancient buildings, documents and artefacts, published between 1747 and 1906 by the Society of Antiquaries of London
London, England, 1803
Paper, H. 57.2 cm, W. 45.5 cm, D. 9 cm (closed)
British Museum, Egypt and Sudan Library, RBC.2°.60

Having loaded the rest of the antiquities onto Admiral Bickerton's ship, *Madras*, Turner 'embarked with the Rosetta Stone, determining to share its fate', on board the *Egyptienne* frigate taken in the harbour of Alexandria, and arrived at Portsmouth, England, in February 1802. The Stone was sent to the Society of Antiquaries, where in July four plaster casts were taken and sent to the Universities of Oxford, Cambridge, Edinburgh and Dublin, and engravings of the Greek inscription were distributed internationally (fig. 46). King George III permanently deposited the Stone and the other antiquities in the British Museum. By August, being too heavy for the floors of Montagu House, they were temporarily housed under wooden sheds 'in the outer court' until a new gallery could be constructed.[92] Early in its museum history, the Rosetta Stone's incised signs were filled in with white chalk to make the shallow text more legible to the public,[93] and at some point the two sides of the Stone were painted with the words; 'CAPTURED IN EGYPT BY THE BRITISH ARMY 1801' and 'PRESENTED BY KING GEORGE III'. Despite much later searching, the missing fragments of the Stone, 'worth their weight in diamonds',[94] were never found.

EARLY EUROPEAN TRAVELLERS AND COLLECTORS IN EGYPT, 1815 TO 1835

John Taylor

The French Revolution and the Napoleonic Wars shattered the peace of Europe for a generation, but with the final defeat of Napoleon in 1815 order was restored. The first decades of the nineteenth century were also marked by growing stability in Egypt under the progressive (if often ruthless) rule of the Ottoman Viceroy Muhammed Ali (in office 1805–1848). Greater security created conditions more favourable for travel to, and in, Egypt, and in the following decades many Europeans flocked there. These included diplomats, military men, engineers, merchants, artists, botanists, geologists, mineralogists and an ever-growing number of casual visitors as Egypt became a popular tourist destination.

While the buildings of Islamic Egypt and the manners and customs of the inhabitants satisfied a thirst for the 'exotic', the main attraction for travellers was the monuments of pharaonic Egypt. The focus on antiquities was stimulated by publications such as Vivant Denon's account of the Napoleonic expedition to Egypt and Giovanni Belzoni's lively narrative of his explorations among the tombs and temples (see pp. 66, 133).[95] The French expedition's multi-volume *Description de l'Égypte* provided the reader with much weightier fare, but its influence was limited by its size, high cost and slow rate of publication (fig. 47).[96] Besides popular literature, enthusiasm was also fired by the arrival of Egyptian antiquities in growing numbers in European cities in the 1810s–30s. Some of these objects formed the nuclei of great museum collections, which were in the process of evolving from cabinets of curiosities, while others could be viewed at temporary exhibitions (see p. 54). The most famous of these shows was Belzoni's exhibition of statues, mummies and replicas of the newly discovered tomb of Sety I, staged in London in 1821 (see fig. 93). Although the huge sculptures and sarcophagi at first excited public astonishment and incomprehension, as monstrous 'curiosities', very 'alien' by comparison with the art of the classical world, with the decipherment of hieroglyphs they gradually became articulate witnesses to the lives, beliefs and habits of the ancient Egyptians, stimulating an increased hunger for accurate knowledge.

The consuls of the leading European nations, resident in Cairo and Alexandria for long periods, were among the first to respond to the new fashion for Egypt's past. They formed collections of antiquities, often

47 (facing page)
Map of the island of Elephantine and the town of Aswan in Egypt, plate 31 of the *Description de l'Égypte*
Paris, France, 1821
Paper, H. 72.1 cm, W. 55.7 cm, D. 4.7 cm (closed volume)
British Museum, Egypt and Sudan Library, RBC.2°1

A. Vol. I. ÎLE D'ÉLÉPHANTINE ET SYÈNE. Pl. 31.

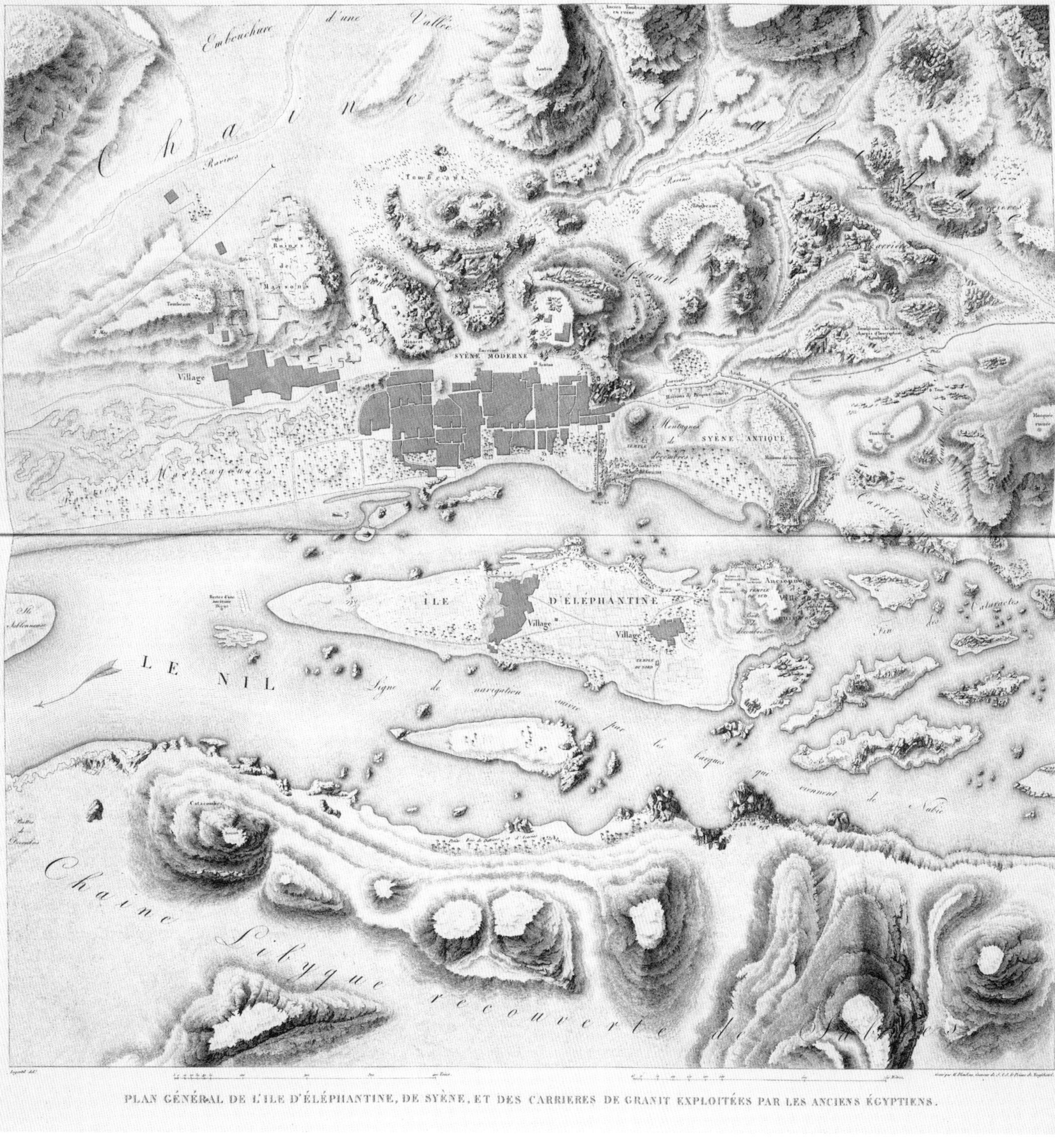

PLAN GÉNÉRAL DE L'ILE D'ÉLÉPHANTINE, DE SYÈNE, ET DES CARRIERES DE GRANIT EXPLOITÉES PAR LES ANCIENS ÉGYPTIENS.

numbering thousands of objects. The political climate of the 1810s–20s was favourable to this activity. Muhammed Ali recognised the Europeans' taste for antiquities, even if he did not share it himself, and, as he was anxious to have European support (particularly from France and England) in his efforts to pull Egypt into the modern world, he was willing to grant *firmans* (permissions) for the consuls to excavate, collect and remove pharaonic antiquities, which thus acquired something of the status of 'bargaining chips' in international diplomacy.[97] The consuls themselves usually provided the necessary funds, which they expected to recoup by selling their collections, if possible to one of the major European powers. They were motivated partly by commercial interests (and to provide for their retirement from the poorly paid post of consul) and partly by the desire to supply their native or adopted countries with significant Egyptian collections. They also persuaded themselves that by removing antiquities to Europe they were 'rescuing' them from an environment in which they were unappreciated.[98]

The Piedmontese-born consul of France, Bernardino Drovetti, a former army officer, was the first of the diplomats to begin collecting seriously.[99] He enjoyed the favour and confidence of Muhammed Ali and employed various European intermediaries in Egypt – mainly French and Italian – to buy antiquities from the inhabitants and to supervise excavations. The British consul Henry Salt (1780–1827), who arrived in Egypt in 1816, was an artist by training and had antiquarian interests, and he quickly became Drovetti's rival in collecting (fig. 48).[100] Sites with conspicuous standing monuments, such as Giza, Saqqara and Thebes (present-day Luxor), were targeted, as was Abydos, the ancient cult centre of Osiris. Imposing temples and tombs lay buried at these locations, many of their contents having survived untouched for centuries.

Both Salt and Drovetti were attracted to the same rich sites. With *firmans* as their authorisation they negotiated with local officials and villagers, who were employed to dig and were paid in proportion to the value of their finds. Salt, like Drovetti, used agents to collect for him, the first being Belzoni. The consuls behaved towards each other with formal politeness, as befitted their status as 'gentlemen', but these civilities masked a strong element of Anglo-French competition, and this rivalry was expressed more openly by their agents and the Egyptian working parties, who became (by virtue of their employment) partisans of the British and French. Frequent quarrels erupted over prized objects or promising spots to excavate, occasionally leading to violence. To try to mitigate this situation, Salt and Drovetti partitioned the ground at major sites such as Thebes and Abydos, thereby emphasising their near-monopoly on excavation and collection.[101] The traveller Frederick Henniker wrote: 'The whole of ancient Thebes is the private property of the

48 (facing page)
Drawing by Henry Salt of the dream stela of Thutmose IV, located between the paws of the Great Sphinx at Giza. In the story recounted on the stela, the Sphinx appears in a dream to Prince Thutmose, offering him the throne if he would only remove the sand covering the Sphinx's body.
Egypt, 1817
Paper, H. 63.5 cm, W. 50 cm, D. 2.5 cm (closed volume)
British Museum, AESAr.731

Granite Tablet in front of the Sphinx

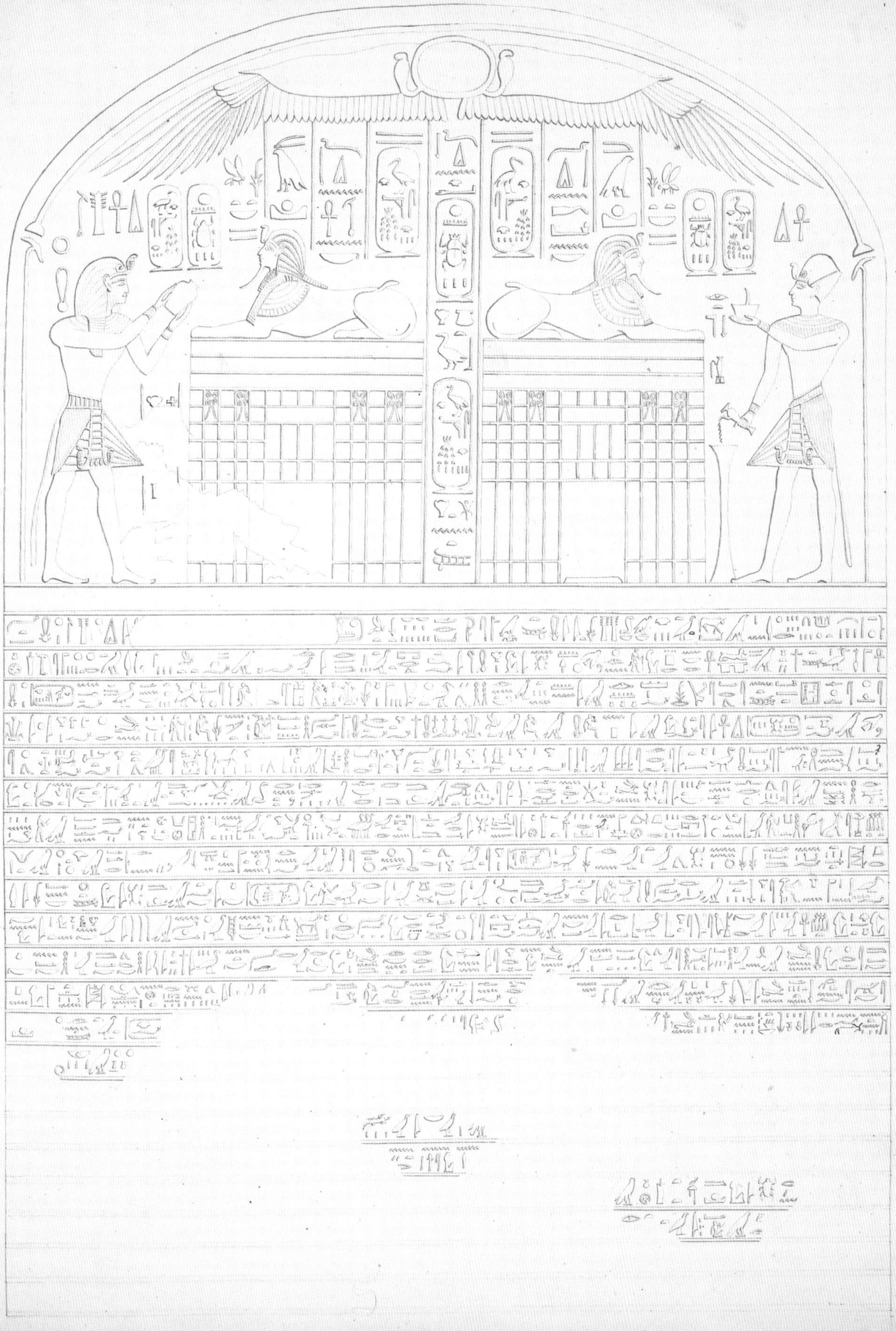

English and French consuls; a line of demarcation is drawn through every temple, and these buildings that have hitherto withstood the attacks of *Barbarians*, will not resist the speculation of civilised cupidity, virtuosi, and antiquaries.'[102]

Digging produced a wealth of objects that were considered desirable: statues in stone, metal and wood; sarcophagi, obelisks, stelae (inscribed commemoration slabs), mummies, coffins, papyri, shabti figures (see p. 190), scarabs, amulets and jewellery. Belzoni's transport of the colossal bust of Ramesses II from the Ramesseum in 1816 (afterwards presented to the British Museum) was only the beginning of four remarkable years of discoveries. He went on to excavate at Karnak, finding superb statues, and in the Valley of the Kings, where he found several tombs including that of Sety I. He also cleared Abu Simbel of sand and penetrated into the pyramid of Khafre at Giza. Not to be outdone, Drovetti's agents gathered equally impressive objects – notably Jean-Jacques Rifaud, who transported many statues from Karnak and Tanis.[103] Although Belzoni left Egypt in 1819 after quarrels with Salt and clashes with Drovetti's men, the English and French parties continued to build collections throughout the 1820s. A third key player in the 'war of the consuls' was Giovanni Anastasi (1780–1860), a Greek who acted as consul for Sweden and Norway.[104] Despite his diplomatic role, Anastasi was primarily a merchant, and through intermediaries he heavily exploited the sites of Saqqara, Abydos and Thebes. But although collections could be rapidly assembled, negotiations over their sale to the European nations were often complicated since museums hesitated over the cost of acquisition and the need to find suitable spaces to display the objects. Salt, having made a loss on the purchase of his first collection by the British Museum, sold his second to France, while Drovetti's first collection was rejected by the French and eventually found a home in Turin.[105]

The principal consular agents had the freedom to sell objects that did not find a place in their patrons' collections. Thus by 1824 the Greek Giovanni d'Athanasi (1798–1854), who succeeded Belzoni as Henry Salt's chief agent, was acting independently as one of the leading antiquities dealers in Egypt, as was the Italian Giuseppe Passalacqua.[106] D'Athanasi sold objects to many travellers who passed through Thebes, and he also had a base in Alexandria. These agent-dealers and the native Egyptians with whom they worked acquired deep knowledge of the structures, locations and contents of ancient tombs. In their activities they were motivated less by a quest for historical enlightenment than by a knowledge of what collectors wanted and how much they would pay. Objects were appreciated on an individual basis, for their perceived artistic merit or for their 'curiosity' value and, increasingly, for their inscriptions: the presence of cartouches (oval loops) containing royal names increased the desirability of stelae.

The significance of archaeological context and what would now be termed 'assemblages' for an understanding of the past was not generally appreciated. Objects found together were routinely dispersed and sold to different buyers, and the dealers were secretive about the findspots to protect their interests.[107] Pottery, so important to the modern archaeologist as a dating tool, was largely ignored in favour of more visually attractive items, and other classes of antiquity, regarded as having little worth, were routinely destroyed or damaged. One of the most frequently repeated observations in early nineteenth-century travel accounts is the burning of pieces of painted coffins as firewood.[108] When mummies were found they were quickly assessed for their saleability, 'inferior' specimens being roughly stripped to retrieve their amulets and jewellery, while those with more imposing trappings such as a mask or cartonnage coverings were placed in the vacant coffins to provide a more tempting 'package' for potential buyers.[109]

There were many short-term visitors who passed through Egypt en route to India or the 'Holy Land'. Most of them journeyed by boat along the Nile, calling at the main sites, and many bought antiquities, either directly from local villagers or from consular agents, though they complained about the monopolistic dominance of the consuls. Moyle Sherer, visiting Thebes in 1823, noted:

> Nothing is more difficult than to procure here any little antiques of value, to carry away with you as memorials of your visit: the Arabs, indeed, bring you little mummy ornaments … also scarabaei, rings of wood or pottery, scraps of papyrus, and a variety of trifles which I cannot name: but these are sure to be the mere refuse of the privileged collectors, and of the many sharp-witted non-descripts in their service.[110]

The great rise in tourism in the 1820s–30s pushed up the price of antiquities steeply, leading to ever more destructive ransacking of tombs. Travellers often expressed outrage at the rough treatment of human remains, though they themselves were willing to buy mummies, which were sometimes unwrapped on the spot and then discarded. Although many of these travellers published accounts of their visits, their knowledge of the country and its past was often only superficial. Many of them also defaced the monuments with graffiti. The French author Gustave Flaubert, who visited Egypt in 1850, commented on the Second Pyramid at Giza, 'One is irritated by the number of imbeciles' names written everywhere …'.[111]

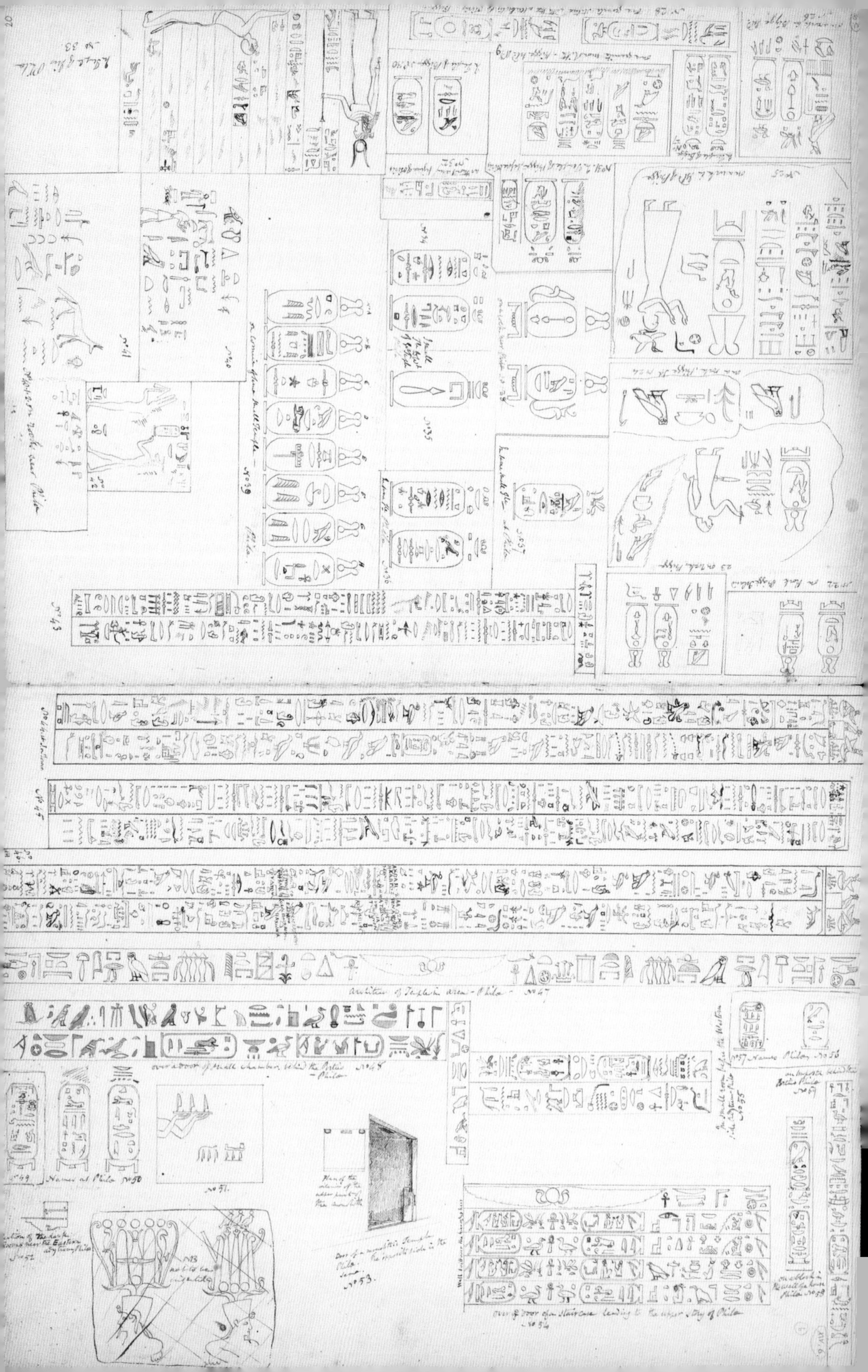

Architrave of Temple in area - Philae - No 47
over a door of small chamber behind the Portico No 48 - Philae
No 49 Names at Philae No 50
No 51
…tion of the dark rooms near the Eastern … Philae No 52
Plan of the interior of the upper part of the monolith
Door of a monolithic Temple in Philae. The … side is the same. No 53
Over ye Door of a Staircase leading to the upper story of Philae No 54
No 57 Names Philae No 56
No 55
on a block in the wall of a house Philae No 58

Alongside the committed collectors and casual visitors, there were others whose principal aim was to gather information and to record. Edward William Lane (1801–1876) spent many years in Egypt and wrote lengthy accounts of the topography and social life of the contemporary Egyptians.[112] John Gardner Wilkinson (1797–1875) and James Burton (1788–1862) also devoted long periods to the patient exploration of ancient sites and produced accurate copies of tomb paintings, inscriptions and other monuments.[113] Robert Hay (1799–1863) gathered a team of artists and architects for his lengthy expeditions of 1824–8 and 1829–34, making copious records of sites and monuments, as well as objects in the hands of dealers.[114] Hay, Wilkinson and their companions made accurate drawings, both by eye and using the camera lucida, an optical device employed as a drawing aid by artists and microscopists. They also took paper squeezes from walls, a process which, while reproducing the relief decoration faithfully, had the unintended effect of removing the ancient pigments when the damp paper was pressed into the relief. Generally these British copyists were acting on their own initiative, not representing national interests or receiving financial support from learned bodies. Other nations, however, were persuaded to provide state funding. The most grandly conceived scientific mission of the time was the Franco-Tuscan expedition, led by Jean-François Champollion and Ippolito Rosellini in 1828–9 (Chapter 3). Their teams spent almost a year and a half in Egypt, during which time the scholars journeyed up the Nile as far as the Second Cataract, copying monuments, carrying out excavations and buying antiquities. This was Champollion's only personal experience of Egypt; he boasted that he had gathered enough information to keep him busy for a lifetime, but in fact he had only three more years to live.

Although the work of the Franco-Tuscan expedition was published in the 1830s–40s, the immensely valuable copies and observations amassed by the independent artist-travellers, particularly those of Hay's team, remained largely inaccessible, owing in part to financial constraints, personal indecisiveness and the practical difficulties of publication.[115] Wilkinson's *Manners and Customs of the Ancient Egyptians*, a compilation based on his own observations and first published in 1837, quickly achieved the status of authority, but his extensive original copies of monuments remained inaccessible (fig. 49).

The papers of many copyists of this period – William John Bankes, Frédéric Cailliaud, Nestor L'Hôte, James Burton, Alessandro Ricci and others – have likewise slumbered in archives and only in recent years have begun to be systematically exploited (figs 50–53). Nevertheless, the sale of the great consular collections of antiquities in the 1820s–40s made London, Paris, Berlin, Turin and Leiden important focal points for the study of ancient Egypt. These growing museum collections were augmented by many objects brought back by private individuals. The arrival of these collections

49 (facing page)
Copies of the inscriptions at Philae, including royal names of Ptolemy and Cleopatra, by John Gardner Wilkinson
Philae, 1821–2
Paper, H. 48 cm, W. 73.5 cm
National Trust, on loan at the Bodleian Library, MS. Wilkinson dep. a. 14, plate 12/XIV.6

50
Stela of Nestjerenmaat, 'the lady of the house and chief chantress of Montu, lord of Thebes', standing in adoration of the god Ra-Horakhty. The text renders a funerary invocation in hieroglyphs.
Thebes, Third Intermediate Period, 1069–747 BCE
Wood and plaster, H. 27.5 cm, W. 25 cm, D. 3.7 cm
British Museum, EA8450

in European cities had a major impact on the development of Egyptology, by providing scholars with a body of material for study while simultaneously exciting curiosity and transforming public opinion. Egyptian artefacts began to be appreciated for their own artistic merits, and the inscriptions boosted the advance of knowledge. Following the initial decipherment of hieroglyphs, Champollion's study of the Drovetti collection in Turin and the Salt and Drovetti collections in the Louvre enabled him to make significant advances in understanding of the language and history of ancient Egypt.

Champollion's decipherment, occurring in the midst of this period, brought about changes. Although the ancient texts could not be fluently read until about the 1840s, there was an intensified drive to obtain specimens

51
Watercolour of the stela of Nestjerenmaat by Alessandro Ricci (1792–1834), an Italian artist who worked for Bankes and Salt
Egypt, 1818
Paper, H. 32.4 cm, W. 28.8 cm
British Museum, AESAr.1520

and copies of inscriptions, with the promise that the monuments could be appreciated on other than purely aesthetic grounds.[116] This marked the dawn of a more responsible attitude, with a reaction against the destruction and damaging of ancient monuments (both by government officials recycling ancient stonework for factories, and collectors heedlessly cutting sections of relief and painting from the walls of tombs and temples). At the conclusion of his visit to Egypt, Champollion urged Muhammed Ali to intervene against the destruction in order to protect the antiquities.[117] There was some immediate tightening of controls in 1829, when Ibrahim Pasha, the Viceroy's son, authorised a Turk to begin excavations, while 'Franks' (Europeans) were forbidden to do so. This first step was reinforced by an ordinance of

52 (facing page)
Cylinder seal inscribed with the name of king Pepy I and funerary cones stamped with the names of the deceased. Rows of such cones were set into the façades of tomb chapels, almost exclusively in the Theban Necropolis.

(cylinder seal)
Asyut, 6th Dynasty, 2321–2287 BCE
Glazed composition, L. 7.7 cm, diam. 2.9 cm
British Museum, EA47460

(cones)
Egypt, Late Period, 747–332 BCE
Pottery, L. 12 cm, diam. 8.6 cm (smallest), L. 14.8 cm, diam. 9.1 cm (largest)
British Museum, EA35672, EA35658, EA35651

53 (right)
Collection of Frédéric Cailliaud's drawings depicting funerary cones and a cylinder seal inscribed with four names of Pepy I. Champollion thought highly of Cailliaud's drawings, which arrived in France in November 1818.
France, *c.* 1818
Paper, H. 54.2 cm, W. 35.6 cm
Musée Dobrée

1835, by which antiquities were to be protected and their export from Egypt forbidden.[118] A fledgling museum was also established in Cairo under the supervision of Rifa'a Rafi' al-Tahtawi (1801–1873), but this was relatively short-lived.[119] The government's legislation did not stop all unregulated digging and antiquities trading, but did curtail it, at least temporarily, since harsh punishments could be meted out to Egyptians who broke this law. Travellers could still obtain antiquities, though less openly, but with the increased restrictions and with changes in diplomatic personnel, large-scale consular collecting began to decline. Salt had died in 1827 and Drovetti had left Egypt in 1829; their successors, John Barker and Jean-François Mimaut, formed smaller collections, which were disposed of by auction in 1833 and 1837 respectively.[120] Anastasi's third and last collection had been sent to Europe by 1841, but remained unsold until 1857, when it was finally auctioned in Paris. This did not mark the end of the antiquities trade, but when, exactly one year later, in June 1858, the Egyptian Antiquities Service was refounded, under the directorship of Auguste Mariette (1821–1881), a turning point had been reached in the treatment of Egypt's ancient past.

Al-Jabarti's account of Egypt under Napoleon

'On that day, General Bonaparte crossed to the Cairo side and settled in al-Azbakiyya in the house of Muhammad Bey al-Alfī, who had built and constructed it in al-Sākit district that same year. Moreover he had furnished it splendidly and has laid down fine carpets. The women left, abandoning all that it contained. The French entered it, stepping on the carpets with their shoes and sandals as was their custom, since they never take off their shoes with which they tread upon filth, not even when they sleep! Among their repulsive habits also is their practice of spitting and blowing their noses upon the furnishings. Their etiquette, however, is such that whenever one of them blows his nose or spits he rubs it with his shoes and so on.

Saturday, the eleventh of that month, was their appointed feast day. That morning, they fired several cannons and they placed upon every wooden pole one of their coloured *bandiera* [flags]. [After the festivities, a sumptuous dinner, and fireworks, the main flagpole remained] … the big pole underneath which a group of soldiers kept watch night and day because of its significance as an emblem, a symbol of the existence of their state, and a distinguished mark of their country – may God hasten its end.'[121]

Few Egyptian voices are recorded from the 1798 invasion of Egypt, except for that of the Egyptian scholar and historian al-Jabarti (1753–1825/1826), a remarkable witness to the first seven months of the French occupation of Cairo. His everyday accounts contrast with the many French proclamations claiming to support Islam and the freedom of Egypt from the depredations of the Mameluke rulers. Al-Jabarti instead presents the crushing reality of life under a despotic and violent military occupation for both the political elite and for ordinary Muslims, Christians, Copts and Jews. He writes scathingly of the turmoil, criticising what he saw as the injustice, lies and harassment of the military government under Napoleon, and its rapacious taxation through control of the local Diwan courts. French festivities, including fireworks and a novel red, white and blue hot-air balloon, were met with al-Jabarti's sarcasm. As a scholar, he was appalled by the poor grammar of the occupiers' Arabic translations of their proclamations and cynical of their content. However he was impressed by the *savants'* quarter of the city, with its library of books on science, geography, botany and zoology, which even contained a biography of the Prophet and a translation of the Qur'an. His appreciation of French military organisation contrasts with his view of the French as socially and morally depraved, especially in their reaction to the Cairo rebellion (21–22 October 1798), which he sees as a senseless riot by the lower classes. He chronicles their demands, the disturbances, and the violent French retribution and relentless destruction of the city's buildings, cemeteries and mosques in their attempts to fortify the city. – *Patricia Usick*

سنة ثلاث عشرة ومائتين

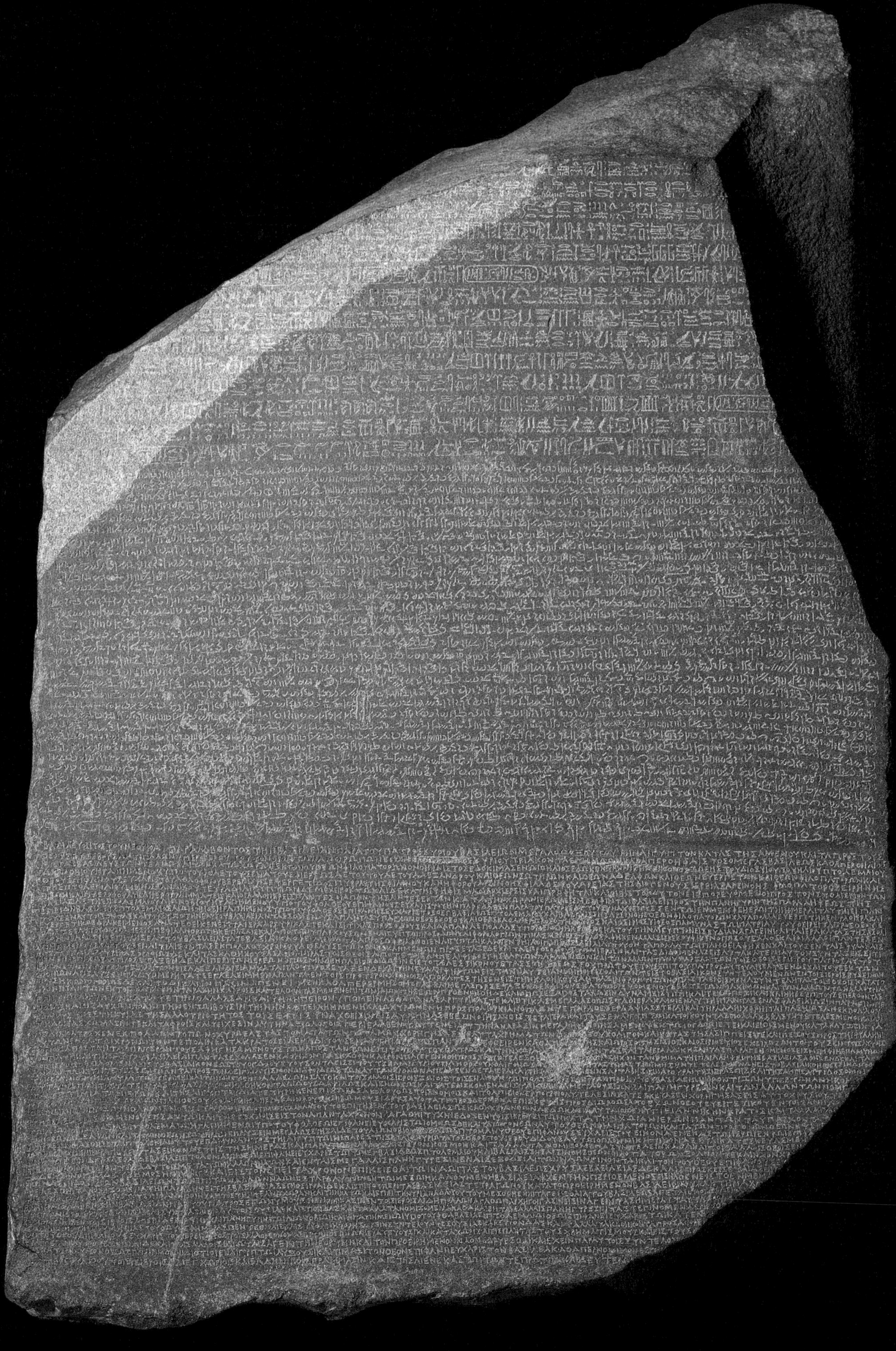

CHAPTER 2 The race to decipherment

THE RACE TO DECIPHERMENT

Ilona Regulski

Napoleon's expedition to Egypt (1798–9) and the subsequent publication of the *Description de l'Égypte* (1809–28), illustrating the monuments, people and cities of the storied country, fuelled public and scholarly interest in its ancient civilisation. Yet the evidence necessary to reconstruct Egyptian society and its writing system was still limited. European scholars had relatively few objects to work with, along with inaccurate copies of inscriptions created by predecessors and peers who could not read what they were copying. With the Rosetta Stone's discovery in 1799, hope soared that those ancient voices could be brought to life through the Greek version of its texts, especially in combination with the evidence available from Coptic, the last stage of the ancient Egyptian language. This proved harder than expected, and it would take another two decades.

The decipherment would hinge on two scholars, British polymath Thomas Young and precocious French philologist Jean-François Champollion. Although their work overlapped in significant ways, they differed in method and opinion, with each attracting supporters and detractors as their goal drew near. The breakthrough belonged to Champollion, a linguistic prodigy who mastered Coptic, ancient Greek, Latin, Hebrew, Syriac, Persian and Arabic. But the work of Young and others, though Champollion did not agree with all of it, helped solve the riddle of ancient Egyptian.

INFORMATION-SHARING IN THE EARLY NINETEENTH CENTURY

The Rosetta Stone was kept at first in Cairo, then London. To improve the chances of its decipherment, copies (prints and casts) were made and swiftly distributed to interested parties (see p. 68).[1] Within a year of the Stone's arrival in England in 1802, institutions in every western European country could boast a copy (fig. 54). Produced in haste, however, by artisans who were not all adept at copying such unfamiliar scripts, they contained mistakes. The situation improved in 1804, when translations of the Greek text and

54
Charcoal rubbing of the hieroglyphic section of the Rosetta Stone
England, 19th century
Paper, H. 52.5 cm, W. 35.9 cm, D. 6.4 cm (closed album)
British Museum, AESAr.574, no 46

annotated versions of the printed copies made by Jean-Joseph Marcel, a member of Napoleon's expedition, and artist and inventor Nicolas-Jacques Conté were published.[2] This marked a major shift in the publication of ancient Egyptian texts, away from incorporating the script into representations of figural art and towards proper text editions. Gradually the general content of the text on the Rosetta Stone grew clear, even though the dialect used by the Ptolemaic administration that created it was unfamiliar to scholars at the time.

DEMOTIC A-B-C'S

> The invention of the alphabet is commonly attributed to the Phoenicians, on the testimony of several authors; but the Egyptians can claim their right to the glory of such a beautiful discovery.
>
> *E.-F. Jomard, in* Description de l'Égypte[3]

Initially the Rosetta Stone's hieroglyphs were interpreted as a form of iconography, while the demotic script was understood as related to Coptic and essentially alphabetic. The first scholars to study the Stone had experience with alphabetic languages such as Phoenician (see fig. 185), which influenced their perception of Egyptian. Advances in Coptic studies led to laborious efforts to translate hieroglyphs through knowledge of the pharaohs' language in its later form.[4] Like many before them, French linguist Antoine Isaac, Baron Silvestre de Sacy (1758–1838) and Swedish diplomat Johan David Åkerblad considered Coptic a remnant of ancient Egyptian. Silvestre de Sacy, Champollion's teacher, frequently met with Åkerblad, who had worked on Coptic manuscripts with Georg Zoëga in Rome.[5] Among the first to focus on the demotic portion of the Rosetta Stone, de Sacy and Åkerblad shared the fundamental assumption that it was an ancestral (alphabetic) form of Coptic.

They began by seeking the similarities in proper names, looking for repetitions of sign sequences in the demotic that might correspond to a repeated word in the Greek. Using spatial comparison, de Sacy identified five names, including 'Alexander', using the Greek inscription, but he did not explain how he arrived at these readings, and realised that the letters of a demotic word were not necessarily laid out spatially as in Greek or Coptic writing. Åkerblad adjusted de Sacy's reading of 'Alexander', and identified words such as 'Greek', 'temple' and 'Egyptian'. By comparing all the places where temples were mentioned in the Greek inscription with similar locations in the demotic, he reasoned, the corresponding group of signs in demotic must signify temples. Åkerblad then searched for the Coptic word for 'temple' and tried to locate demotic signs corresponding to letters in the Coptic script.[6]

Having obtained a set of letters in this fashion, Åkerblad identified other demotic words using his Coptic-based 'alphabet'. Although many of his twenty-nine sign equivalents remained valid over the years, Åkerblad's alphabet was incomplete and he was unable to translate more words. His work appeared only in French, but nonetheless received considerable attention in England, as did de Sacy's, bolstering expectations that decipherment was within reach. Young, however, was unconvinced. He wrote to Åkerblad:

> I must confess that all the learning and ingenuity, which you have displayed, only serves still more to convince me of the extreme hopelessness of the attempt to read [translate] the Inscription of Rosetta, by means of any imaginable alphabet, into tolerable Coptic, and of the necessity of adhering strictly, in the first instance, to the plan, which I have adopted, of comparing the inscription with itself and with the Greek only.[7]

Young agreed overall with Åkerblad's translation but did not see how Coptic helped.

55
Print portraying Thomas Young
London, England, 1830
Paper, H. 27.3 cm, W. 18.5 cm
British Museum, 1866,1013.655

THOMAS YOUNG'S LAST OBSESSION

Described as 'The Last Man Who Knew Everything',[8] Thomas Young made landmark contributions to the fields of physics, optics, mechanics, physiology, linguistics and musical harmony before directing his attention to Egyptology (figs 55–56). His efforts to decipher the Rosetta Stone facilitated Champollion's ultimate success, but his richest gift to Egyptology was his decoding of demotic script. He made the first major advances in this area, correctly understanding that demotic was composed of both ideographic (symbolic, pictorial) and phonetic (sound) signs.

In July 1814 the forty-one-year-old Young joined the ranks of researchers poring over the Rosetta Stone, as 'the amusement of a few of my leisure hours'.[9] Like Åkerblad, Young maintained that the intermediate, demotic section of the Rosetta Stone was the key to understanding hieroglyphs, but he did not believe it consistently conveyed complicated grammatical or even syntactic information. Instead, Young thought the sign sequences should be treated as meaningful logograms – as words – regardless of what the corresponding sounds in Egyptian speech might have been. He initially referred to the middle script on the Stone as 'Egyptian', but he later called it 'enchorial' (meaning 'used by the people'), basing the name on the last line of the Greek text on the Rosetta Stone, which refers to signs 'of the country'. The Egyptian translation of the Greek instead refers to 'demotica', which became Champollion's preferred term.

Young's *Memorandums* (1814) represented the first serious attempts to work on all the inscriptions of the Rosetta Stone (hieroglyphs, demotic and Greek) with Latin and English translations. He hoped to retrieve the meaning of the Egyptian text by breaking the Greek into sections and trying to match them with the demotic. Since the demotic had thirty-two lines, he divided the fifty-four lines of Greek into thirty-two parts, breaking at places that made sense. Young noted that the termination of the lines on the right were more regular than those on the left, suggesting that the demotic writing proceeded from right to left. Young then looked for demotic characters that occurred repeatedly, pairing them with Greek words that appeared an equal number of times. He identified a sequence of signs that might correspond to the Greek word *basileios* ('king') because that word, with its several derivatives, appears in the Greek text some forty times. A difficulty typical of ancient Egypt's writing system arose: none of the groups occurred with the same frequency in demotic, and the sequences were not all written in an identical way.[10] Young nonetheless considered this method of spatial correspondence reliable enough and rapidly isolated more sequences. He found a total of eighty-six sign groups, almost all of which had several variants in their orthography (how they were written or spelled).

Young used a similar method to compare hieroglyphs with the demotic script (fig. 57). He noticed a resemblance between some demotic signs and the corresponding hieroglyphs, suggesting that demotic might relate to the hieroglyphic script much as modern handwriting does to its printed equivalent.[11] But the hieroglyphic inscription contained at least a hundred different characters, too large a number to accommodate any alphabet.[12] Some hieroglyphic sequences might correspond directly to words, he realised, but not all did. A sign resembling an object might, in one case, refer to that object, while in another, it might represent an aspect of a person associated with the object. For example, a sceptre might signify an actual sceptre or, alternatively, the power of a sovereign. In that case, the relation of a sign to other signs in one sequence might differ from its relation to signs in another, making interpretation strongly dependent on context. Such a complex and unstable system reinforced Young's conviction that hieroglyphic scripts were inferior to alphabetic systems.

Young's work betrayed increasing scepticism regarding the Coptic language, as he reassessed the special relationship with ancient Egyptian

56
Medal of Thomas Young
London, England, mid-20th century
Copper alloy, D. 0.3 cm, diam. 5.1 cm
British Museum, 1964,0405.3
Donated by Melville, P.C.

57
Young's work on deciphering the Rosetta Stone, showing his attempts to match sequences of signs between demotic line 22 and hieroglyphic line 6
London, England, 1814
Paper, H. 23 cm, W. 19 cm
British Library, Add 27281, f. 92

ascribed to it since the Middle Ages. He accepted the idea that Coptic was a descendant of the ancient Egyptian language, but doubted whether even an early form of Coptic was similar enough to be a reliable guide in decoding the ancient scripts. He suggested that phonology (the organisation of sounds to form speech) was used only for Greek and Roman proper names, which revealed the infiltration of foreign elements into a purely logographic Egyptian script. He surmised that the cartouche (oval loop) around names signalled that the enclosed characters had been rendered phonetically. Young relied upon a rebus-like connection to extract sounds from a limited set of signs, though he also redeployed Åkerblad's alphabet, with modifications, for Greco-Roman names.[13] He shared his 'conjectural translation' of the Rosetta Stone, a word list and a thirteen-sign addendum to Åkerblad's Coptic-Egyptian alphabet with de Sacy, leading to extended correspondence between the two (1814–16).[14] Shortly afterwards, Young received a letter from de Sacy's student, Jean-François Champollion, about his work.

Young deepened his studies by comparing the Rosetta Stone's demotic with the script found on mummy wrappings and papyri (figs 58–59).[15] In early 1816 he obtained volume 2 of the *Description de l'Égypte*, which contained engravings of three lengthy papyri, one written in hieroglyphs and two in the cursive hand (hieratic). The publication was a boon to both Young and Champollion, providing them with many hieroglyphic and cursive signs. Young made careful sign-by-sign copies of the papyri, placing hieroglyphs directly beneath what he deduced were the corresponding cursive signs. He identified the title *epiphanes* (meaning 'God Manifest' or 'the Glorious/Illustrious'), which he also found six times in the Rosetta Stone.[16] Matching spatially similar sign sequences, Young identified the corresponding word in both the demotic and the hieroglyphic. Elaborating on the link between the scripts, he concluded that the cursive hieratic script of the papyri was related to hieroglyphs, and that the demotic was a degraded form of the hieratic, and consequently closely linked to hieroglyphs as well. Agreeing

58
Fragment of mummy-wrapping with funerary text in demotic; 'Long live his soul for eternity before Osiris, ruler of the West.'
Egypt, Late Period to Ptolemaic Period, 747–30 BCE
Linen, H. 7.5 cm, W. 30.1 cm, D. 0.5 cm
British Museum, EA73747

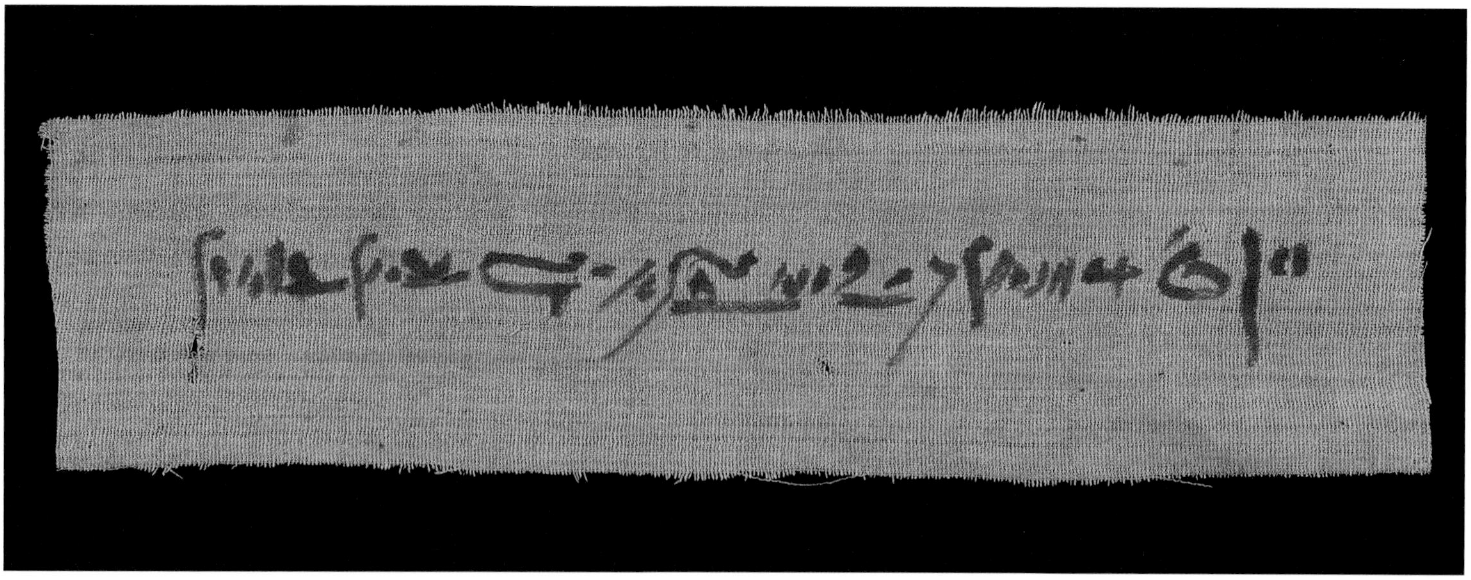

59
Book of the Dead of Padihorpara in cursive hieroglyphs, published by Thomas Young in 1823 and later used by Champollion to show the frequency of homophones (different signs indicating the same sound) in the hieroglyphic writing system
Egypt, Ptolemaic Period, 332–30 BCE
Papyrus, H. 20.9 cm, W. 57 cm, D. 0.2 cm
British Museum, EA9907,4

with his French correspondents that hieroglyphs involved meaning without sound, Young declared that aside from royal names, the cursive and demotic scripts were neither alphabetic (composed exclusively of one-letter signs) nor phonetic (sound-based).

In his seminal article 'Egypt' for the *Encyclopædia Britannica* (1819), Young discussed how phonetics might work in the hieroglyphic and demotic signs for 'Ptolemy' (fig. 60). Elaborating on Åkerblad's determinations, Young read the cartouche of Ptolemy as follows:

> The square block and the semicircle at the beginning of the name are the *p* and *t* identified by Åkerblad;
> the next character is a kind of knot, often omitted in hieroglyphs and always absent in the demotic;
> the lion corresponds to the *lo* of Åkerblad, perhaps to be read *olt* or *ole*;
> the next character was known to have some reference to 'space' and, equivalent to the Coptic *ma*, read either *ma* or simply the *m* of Åkerblad's alphabet;
> the two 'feathers' answer to the three parallel lines of the demotic text, and seem to have been read *i* or *e*;
> the 'bent line' was read *osh* or *os*, for the Coptic *shei*, and seems to have corresponded to the Greek letter sigma.

Putting these elements together, he read *P-t-lo/olt/ole-m(a)-i/e-osh/is*. He did not consider the final seven signs phonetic, but rather adjectives: the

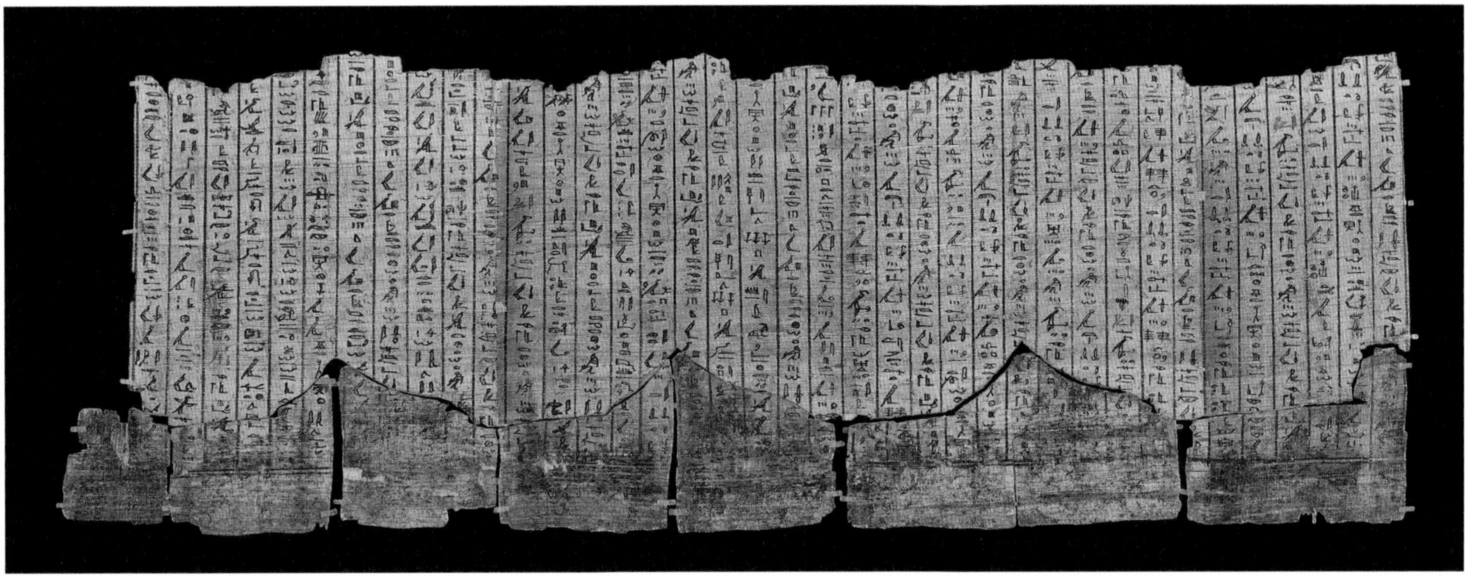

LAGIDAE

PTOLEMAEUS

Col. 51 At Philae

There seem to be capricious variations of the name of a Ptolemy – perhaps one of the latest, "beloved by Vulcan and Isis". The name occurs in other parts of the temple nearly in its usual form – The globe bearing serpent with

Col. 52 the oval alas it seems to mean uniting offspring, as is more demonstrable at Ombos – The epithet perhaps giver of laws – It seems as if Ptolemy Epiphanes had been called after his death simply "Vulcanian", for the epithet epiphanes and eucharistus have not been observed, though the name is found at Ombos. At Karnak however Philo sole seems to be called by the same name.

The two epithets, … or … occur at Ombos, with the same preceding title as here

The inscription copied by Mr. Hamilton, shows that the Ptolemy concerned in the temple at Ombos must have been Philometor, the dedication being in his name and that of Cleopatra, to Aroeris Apollo and the other gods of the temple from the infantry and cavalry in the nome. … ΘΕΟΙΣ ΚΑΙ … ΤΩΝ ΣΥΝΝΑΩΝ.

Hence we are enabled to draw many conclusions from the names in Col. 74, which would however have been more satisfactory if they had been more completely copied –

1. The characteristic of this sovereign and royal pair seems to be … a double battle axe, …, or …, or … ; or rather besides the dual of god, and before the epithet … loving or rivers loving or … perhaps for …

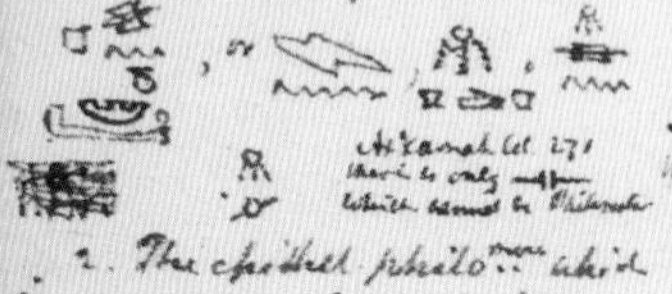

At Karnak Col. 271 there is only … which seems to be Philometor

2. The epithet philo… which is never wanting, is followed by

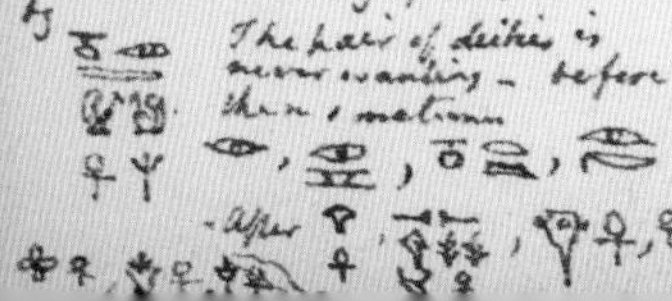

The pair of deities is never wanting – before them, sometimes

– After …

BERENICE ?

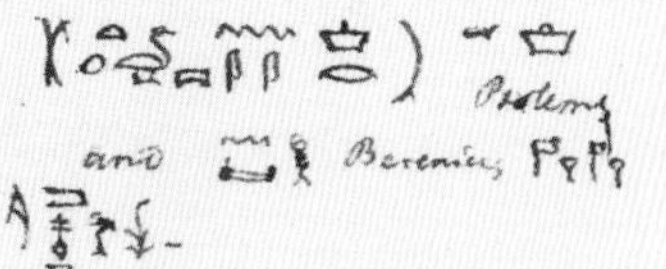

Ptolemy and Berenice

Col. 224 – "Corbeille en panier à anse"

Now a basket is … Bsp, … EN to offer? … always … the good KEN, the KENEKWOC of Kircher – CCWOC signifying simply gregarious – and the original word being XNY, gain, profit, … it from XNYAHWN … glorious!!! The enchorial texts makes it Bazos for the child which is a simpler contrivance, and comes about as near. It was probably engraved by a Scotchman, who thought … much better than … – "combien il y a peu loin du sublime au ridicule" –

The father's name can scarcely be any thing but Ptolemy – This therefore settles the date of Berenice – … this name Arsinoe? 200 next leaf

3 We may besides remark the distinction of god and goddess, sometimes present and sometimes absent …, and the mode of expressing the dual by … – which occurs in many other cases – in the name of Thoth it seems to express ὁ μέγας καὶ μέγας of the R. Inscr. It is here preceded by …

The supposed Nilometer cannot mean "mother" since it would occur in many other inscriptions in this sense.

The Philometores occur also in a prominent situation in the great temple at Edfou – The same epithet precedes the name of the father, as if it were paramount to Epiphanes … Eucharistus

Col. 89 The double name is over a single figure sacrificing a gazelle, at Edfou, in the great temple – The characteristic is here …, with …, which seems to be some sort of pair

In a grotto at El Kab over one of the female guests at a banquet, we …

In the Memnonium not entirely distinguishable Col. 182, to 184 Different – yet able to form

is in question Col. 260

In both places followed by the case But both seem for the Memnonium

CLEOPATRA ??

At Ombos, between Ptolemy and Aeroditi we have which might be Cleopatra – and it may not

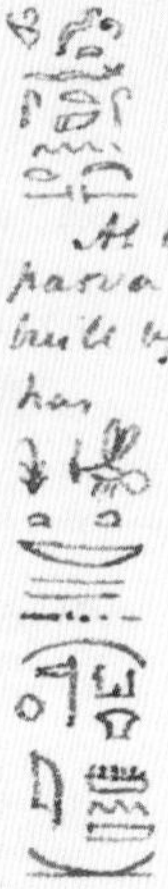

At Qous, Apollinopolis parva, where the temple was built by the Philometores, we have

But in a banner preceding it there is a child – and there is no feminine termination – The name however is clearly the same with that of the statue of Montfaucon – the real coleman, called by him Isis – We are therefore quite certain that it is either the wife or a child of Ptolemy Philometor – and the resemblance of the … to the … makes it not improbable that it may be Cleopatra Perhaps too … The preceding … makes this alternative also the more probable.

… is like nothing but a fishmonger's knife at El Kab

… occurs also at Medinet Abu Col. 154 – followed by … and the corresponding name … followed by … – They seem to be man and wife – though we have a … in the inscription, as if … were … – The temple seems to have been dedicated to Ammon Thoth & Phthah, and perhaps Hieracion, Col. 153 –

Col. 237 – at Karnak … may perhaps be Philadelphus Ptolemaei et Berenices – The Philometores seem to have been represented by a name similarly composed. It is true that … may be inaccurate but it is as good a basket as the other; and in Col. 255 the name … looks very much like Philadelphus – and it is not the same as … – In short it must be either the saviour gods or the philadelphi – and it is most like the latter. But there there must be an error in copying, for it seems to be "and Berenices", which is not coherent … or either supposition.

Another variety Col. 240

Perhaps ΚΛΕΟΒΡΑΤ The Θεοι however is certainly that of a young man instead of a woman

Col. 260, 261 at Karnak

… Clearly the same, and Cleopatra's name included.

Col. 277, 278 At Kar.

The Θεοὶ ἀδελφοὶ are certainly with Ptolemies – not Philadelphi – and the σύνθρονοι θεοὶ also Philae Serapis cynocephalus standing on a crocodile. The king's head is seen as a … the queen as … or Isis –

PHILOMETORES

Heliotheus PTOLEMAEI Col 29, 30

The essential part of the name appears to be the two figures flags with the intervening branched disc: the latter are beloved by the Nile, or Philopotamius, and perhaps respecting the god, or some particular god – Whether the two circles preceding the name of Ptolemy have the same meaning as the disk and the circle, is not quite certain, but it seems most probable that they have – Ptolemy is called … as usual. The Description of the plates observes that the name [Heliotheus] is the most common in all the temples at Philae, and is also found at Ombos

The same name occurs in the … in the small … at Karnak – though not fully

Montfaucon has a statue with a name somewhat similar, which is also made the son of a Ptolemy – but here Vulcan is substituted for the disc with branches or rays, which seems to belong to the sun. … The two deities seem synonymous with … as the 3 in Cleophon's father –

At Karnak Col. 271

snake and ankh meant 'immortal' or 'ever-living', while the twisted rope meant 'loving' or 'beloved'.

Young did not accept that phonetic writing was used before Alexander's conquest of Egypt in 332 BCE, when Greek began to infiltrate the Egyptian writing system. He was willing to admit that some phonetics had been used for the names of native pharaohs, but through syllables, not alphabetic letters. His 'Egypt' article discussed the name of Ramesses on the obelisk of Heliopolis. Using Coptic phonetic values, he read: 'for we have RE, the "sun", MES, "a birth", and SHESH, "a pair"'.[17] This was the only instance where Young thought that Coptic might be used to render the sounds of pharaonic names. Champollion, who probably read Young's article, may have taken this as a hint that phonetics could have been used throughout the pharaonic period, a possibility that Young entertained but eventually dismissed.

MORE PIECES FOR THE PUZZLE

> All the inscriptions on temples, and the generality of the manuscripts found with the mummies, appear to relate to their ridiculous rites and ceremonies: I see nothing that looks like history.
>
> *William John Bankes, letter to Hudson Gurney, early 1816*

Keen to strengthen his case, Young enlisted the assistance of his close friend, British explorer William John Bankes (1786–1855), in gathering bilingual data. Bankes visited Egypt in 1815 and studied an obelisk inscribed with the names of Ptolemy VIII Euergetes II (*r.* 170–116 BCE) and his second consort, Cleopatra III.[18] Located on the island of Philae (near Aswan), the obelisk's lower pedestal had three Greek inscriptions recording communications between Euergetes and the priests of Isis at Philae. When compared with the Greek, the hieroglyphic inscriptions on the obelisk appeared to be royal protocol and the epithets of Osiris, Amun and Isis, to whom the monument was dedicated. Bankes copied the Greek inscription, as did mineralogist Frédéric Cailliaud (1787–1869),[19] whose drawings arrived in France in November 1818 (see p. 83).

During his second trip to Egypt in 1818, Bankes searched for the hieroglyphs Young had described as being of special interest (figs 61–62). These represented 'the names of the kings, whom they commemorate, and those of the deities to whom they are dedicated'. The deities were 'generally distinguished by a hatchet or a sitting figure which follows them', while the kings' names were enclosed 'by an oval' also known as a cartouche. Young

60 (facing page)
Thomas Young's reading and explanation of Ptolemaic king names
London, England, 1814
Paper, H. 25 cm, W. 18.5 cm
British Library, MS Add 27282, f. 77

1

Welbeck Street Tuesday 10 Feb. 1818 3

Dear Sir

I send you a few memorandums, which I shall be much obliged by your forwarding to your son, for the chance of his receiving them before his return to Egypt, as I doubt not that so enlightened and enterprising a traveller will be as willing as he is able to assist in promoting the investigation of the hieroglyphical antiquities of that singular country: and I trust that a few hints of what has already been done will enable him to effect this purpose, with considerably less labour than might otherwise have been bestowed on it.

1. The great desideratum of all is the recovery of the lost fragments of the Rosetta Stone, which to an Egyptian antiquary would be worth their weight in diamonds. The part found by the French contains little more than one third of the inscription in the "sacred characters"; and this portion, imperfect as it is, has afforded an explanation of above fifty hieroglyphics; a number which would be more than doubled by the discovery of the remainder. Mr. Salt was empowered by the British government to expend a liberal sum in digging in the neighbourhood of Fort St. Julien, or otherwise, in pursuit of this object; but there is reason to fear that it has wholly escaped his memory.

2. A duplicate of this stone is described by Dr. Clarke as having been seen by him in the house occupied by the Institute at Cairo, but in imperfect preservation. It would be of the utmost importance to have this duplicate brought to England, since the slightest traces might possibly be rendered intelligible by a careful comparison: and it is indeed hoped that Mr. Salt has already taken measures for this purpose.

3. The inedited inscriptions on the ruins of buildings still existing in Egypt, and even on unwrought blocks and rocks are far too numerous to be copied by any single traveller: it becomes therefore of importance to be directed to the most important parts of them: which are commonly the names of the kings whom they commemorate, and those of the deities to whom they are dedicated. The names of the deities are generally distinguished by a hatchet or a sitting figure which follows them; those of the kings universally by an oval ring which surrounds them, preceded by a reed and a bee: and frequently followed by a goose and a circle, and then a second name, which is that of the father.

4. The inscriptions almost universally relate to the figures over or before which they are placed; and they are always read from the front to the rear of the figures; but they are arranged from right to left, or from left to right, almost indifferently.

Specimens

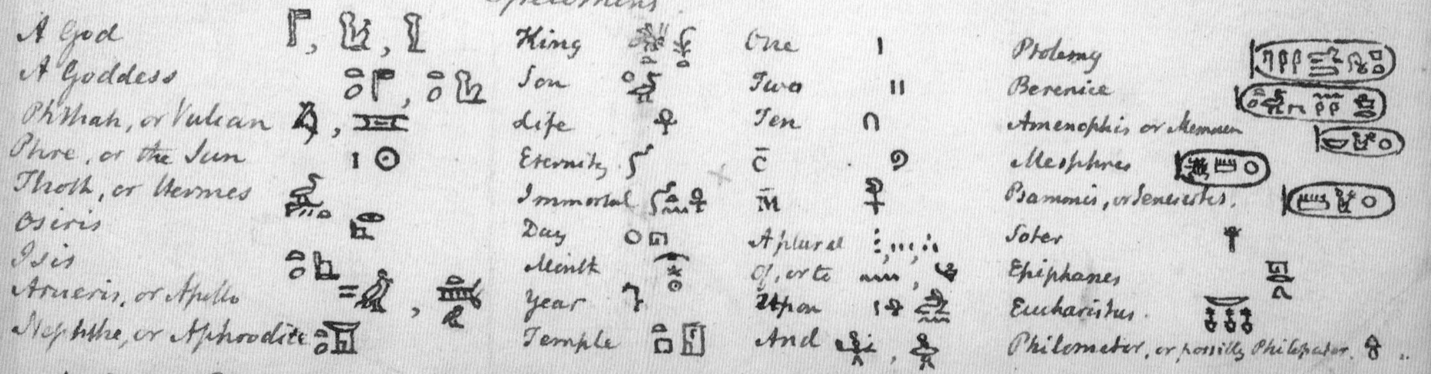
A God
A Goddess
Phthah, or Vulcan
Phre, or the Sun
Thoth, or Hermes
Osiris
Isis
Arueris, or Apollo
Nephthe, or Aphrodite
King
Son
Life
Eternity
Immortal
Day
Month
Year
Temple
One
Two
Ten
C
M
A plural
Of, or to
Upon
And
Ptolemy
Berenice
Amenophis or Memnon
Mesphres
Psammis, or Senesertes
Soter
Epiphanes
Eucharistus
Philometor, or possibly Philopator

H. Bankes Esq

I am, dear Sir, your faithful and obedient servant Thomas Young

61 (facing page)
Letter by Young to Bankes's father containing instructions for copying and checking inscriptions. The letter outlines what Young himself had already achieved. On his return to England, Bankes presented his copies of Greek and hieroglyphic inscriptions to Young.
London, England, 1818
Paper, H. 22.7 cm, W. 18.4 cm
British Museum, AESAr.387, vol. II, p. 3

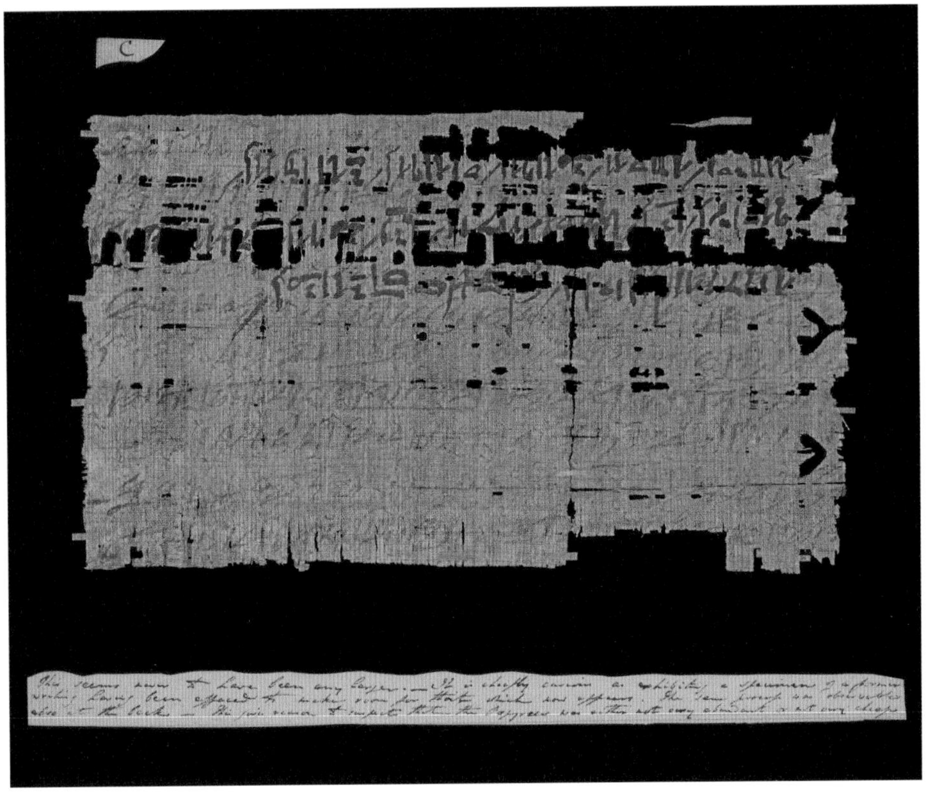

62 (right)
Late Ramesside letter reused (palimpsest) to write a short charm against ill health or similar. Bankes is known to have collected papyri at Thebes on his second journey to Upper Egypt in 1818. This papyrus is still mounted on early 19th-century grease-paper, with a notation by Bankes himself marking it as document 'C'.
Thebes, 20th Dynasty, 1186–1069 BCE
Papyrus, H. 12.7 cm, W. 22.3 cm, D. 0.2 cm
British Museum, EA75025

provided hand-drawn examples, including the cartouches of names he had identified as Ptolemy and the Ptolemaic queen Berenice.

Young also encouraged Bankes and his party to look for fragments of the Rosetta Stone and to visit a bilingual stone kept 'in the house of the institute in Cairo'. In response to Young's request to see the latter, the editor of the *Description*, Edme-François Jomard (1777–1862), described a 'trilingual monument' he had seen at Menouf in the Nile Delta. Unfortunately, both stones were badly preserved, but Young still hoped to obtain copies of these 'other known fragments of trilingual stones'. Henry Salt (1780–1827), then consul-general in Egypt (see p. 78),[20] also promised to help Young.

Bankes stopped north of Luxor to visit the ruins of two temples at Hu, known under the Ptolemies as Diospolis Parva. The porch or gatehouse (propylaeum) of one temple bore a Greek inscription with the name Cleopatra followed by Ptolemy, reversing the usual sequence. Among the temple's hieroglyphs, Bankes recognised Young's hieroglyphic signs for Ptolemy near a male figure. A parallel scene displayed another cartouche near a female figure that, based on the Greek, Bankes figured was Cleopatra. Turning to the obelisk at Philae, Bankes at once established Young's

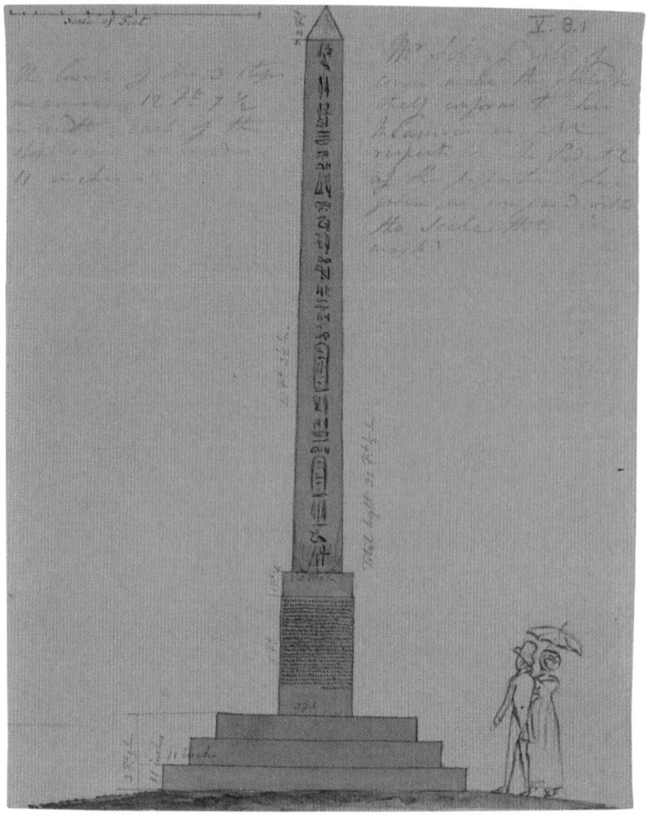

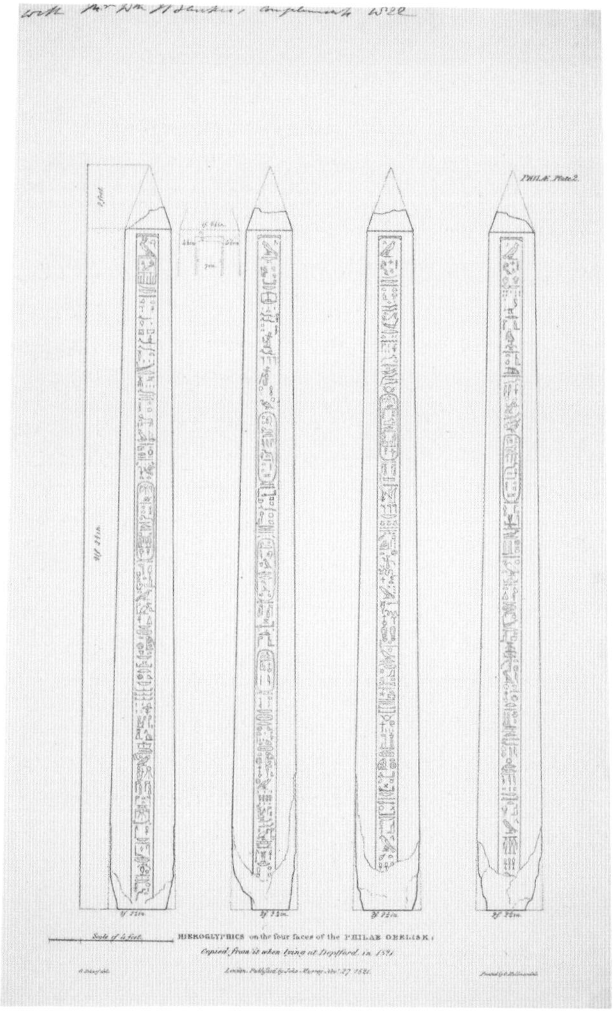

63 (above left)
Bankes's drawing of the Philae obelisk erected at Kingston Lacy
England, *c.* 1821
Paper, H. 18.3 cm, W. 22.6 cm
National Trust, on loan at the Dorset History Centre, D-BKL/H/J/6/5/B/1

64 (above right)
A model of the Philae obelisk
England, mid-19th century
Stone, H. 34 cm, W. 12.5 cm, D. 12.5 cm
British Museum, EA55204
Donated by Selina Theresa Mangles

65 (left)
Annotated print of Bankes's copy of the hieroglyphs on the Philae obelisk. This is the print that would have been distributed to colleagues in Europe.
London, England, 1821
Paper, H. 44.4 cm, W. 28 cm
British Museum, AESAr.26, p. 61

sequence for Ptolemy. Then, beneath one inscription, he saw signs identical to those on the Diospolis Parva temple that he had just linked to Cleopatra.[21]

Bankes had the obelisk removed from Philae and transported to London by museum agent Giovanni Belzoni in 1818. It arrived in September 1821 without its base block, which had been stranded in a cataract of the Nile. The obelisk was reunited with its base and erected in 1830 at Kingston Lacy, Bankes's country home in Dorset, where it still stands.[22] Bankes had its inscriptions copied and sent to interested individuals and institutions (figs 63–65). He published the obelisk's text in 1821, with only the hieroglyphic name Ptolemy tentatively identified. It was hoped that the hieroglyphs were a translation of the Greek text on the obelisk base, a theory first contested by Jean-Antoine Letronne (1787–1848)[23] and eventually by Champollion.[24]

CHAMPOLLION'S TRIALS, ERRORS AND TRIUMPHS

66
Etching of Champollion by the artist Eugène-André Champollion (1848–1901)
France, 19th century
Ink on paper, H. 29.7 cm, W. 21 cm
Musée Champollion, inv. 03.03.1

Champollion (fig. 66) was seventeen years old when he took his first serious shot at translating the text of the Rosetta Stone. Encouraged by his older brother and fellow scholar, Jacques Joseph (1778–1867), Champollion concentrated on the demotic script where others had already made progress. Most early work had focused on the relationship between the Stone's three scripts, and whether or not they were alphabetic. Champollion had read the 1802 analyses of Åkerblad and de Sacy, who identified some proper names and a few words in the demotic section and claimed (but did not prove) the existence of an alphabet in the demotic script. Champollion agreed with them in trying to produce meanings for specific words through links with their Coptic equivalents.[25] Yet, he could make no sense of the demotic inscription.

In August 1808 Champollion studied the papyri published by Baron Dominique Vivant Denon, a member of Napoleon's expedition (see p. 66), with the premise that they were written in a cursive script similar to the one on the Rosetta Stone. One of the papyrus documents, the *Book of Breathings Made by Isis,* was written for Nespautitawi (Spotous), an important Theban official during the reign of Cleopatra VII (51–30 BCE) (fig. 67).[26] 'At the first sight of this manuscript,' Champollion wrote to his brother, 'I thought it was impossible to decipher it.'[27] But he soon noticed repeated clusters of signs and tried to apply his own version of Åkerblad's demotic alphabet to them.

Although he successfully identified sixteen 'letters', he could not understand their meaning. The papyrus was written in hieratic, not demotic, which explains his failure.

Discouraged, Champollion abandoned further analysis of the hieroglyphs on the Rosetta Stone and turned to the study of Coptic. To understand the distant past, he needed the cultural information preserved through language and writing, and in Coptic he found the perfect time machine: the liturgical language of Egyptian Christianity, long believed to contain the remains of ancient Egyptian.[28] Because of its fixed structure, Champollion considered Coptic 'the most perfect and the most rational language known'.[29]

In Grenoble, in 1805, Champollion met a Coptic monk named Rafaël de Monachis who became his tutor, and he began attending masses with members of Paris's Coptic community.[30] Most had served with the auxiliary units of Napoleon's Armée d'Orient, often as translators. Champollion's ties

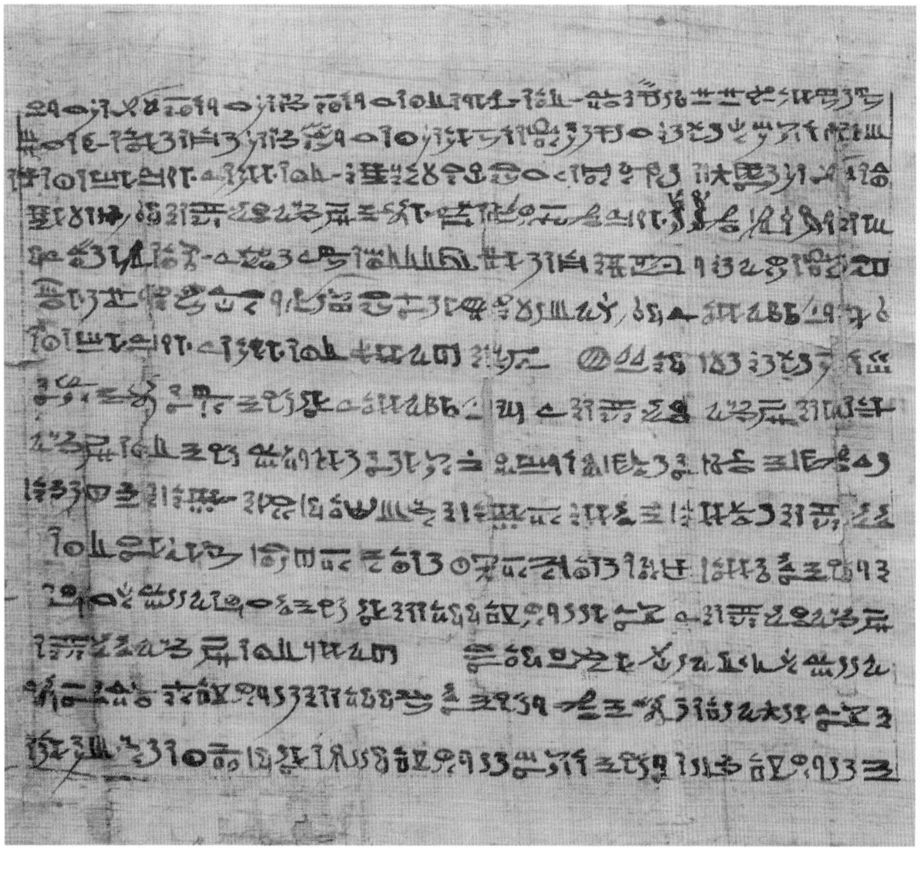

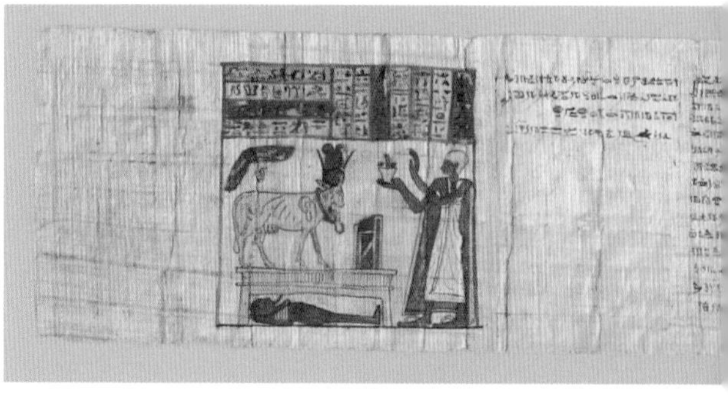

to the community fired his commitment to the language, history and culture of ancient Egypt. He became fluent in Coptic, translating, annotating and cross-referencing materials in the libraries of Paris and Grenoble. 'I am so Coptic,' he wrote, 'that for fun I translate everything that comes to my mind into Coptic; I speak Coptic to myself.'[31] Styling himself as *saghir* ('little one' in Arabic), he grew a beard like his mentors' and cultivated a refined Arabic speaking style. His knowledge of Arabic enabled him to digest the contents of Coptic grammars and dictionaries compiled by medieval Arab scholars (fig. 68), which he found superior to those written by Europeans such as Kircher. He studied the development of the Coptic dialects, Bohairic, Sahidic and Fayyumic (see p. 22), since it was believed that the oldest dialect would retain the clearest and most reliable links to the pharaohs. The great age of Sahidic, Champollion concluded, made it of vital importance to anyone investigating ancient Egypt (fig. 69).[32]

In assembling his Coptic materials, Champollion paid special attention to the names of ordinary things such as plants and animals, and words that seemed to share common roots, the smallest unit in language that carries meaning. He sorted roots thematically with variations and derivatives to track their persistence throughout the language's history.[33]

Champollion tried matching Coptic roots with demotic characters in the Rosetta Stone and focused on the six extra Coptic letters believed to have phonetic equivalents in the demotic (fig. 70). He wanted to see if he could translate some of the Greek sentences into Coptic, then pair the Coptic equivalents with the demotic sentences.[34] This could only work if the structure of Coptic was similar to demotic and demotic words were spelled alphabetically, like Coptic words.[35]

Remnants of early Coptic had survived over millennia, as evidenced in the names of cities, towns and prominent geographical features such as the Nile.[36] For practical reasons the phonetic representation of

67
(below) The *Book of Breathings Made by Isis* for Nespautitawi, written in hieratic, and (left) detail. This is one of four papyri that were owned by Vivant Denon and studied by Champollion.
Thebes West, Ptolemaic Period to Roman Period, *c.* 99 BCE–99 CE
Papyrus, H. 20 cm, W. 218 cm
Huis van het boek, inv. 42/88

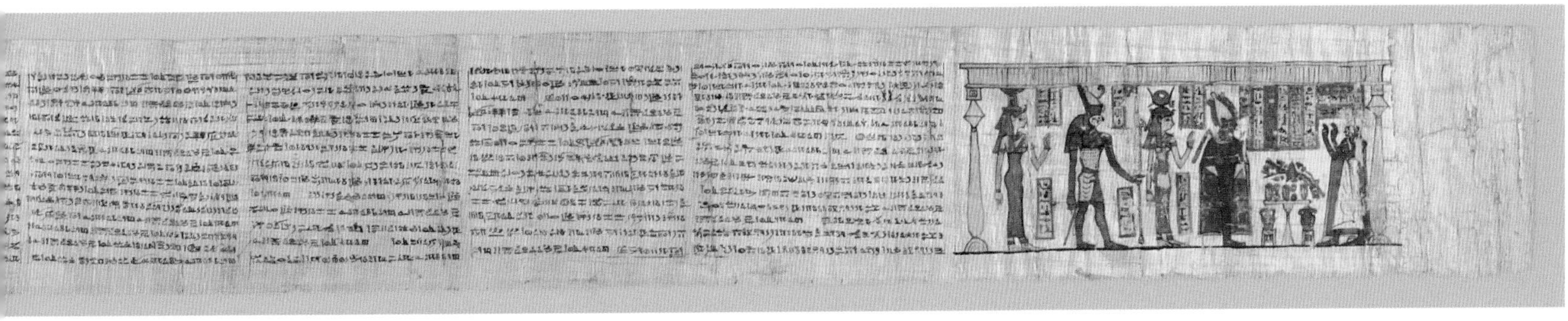

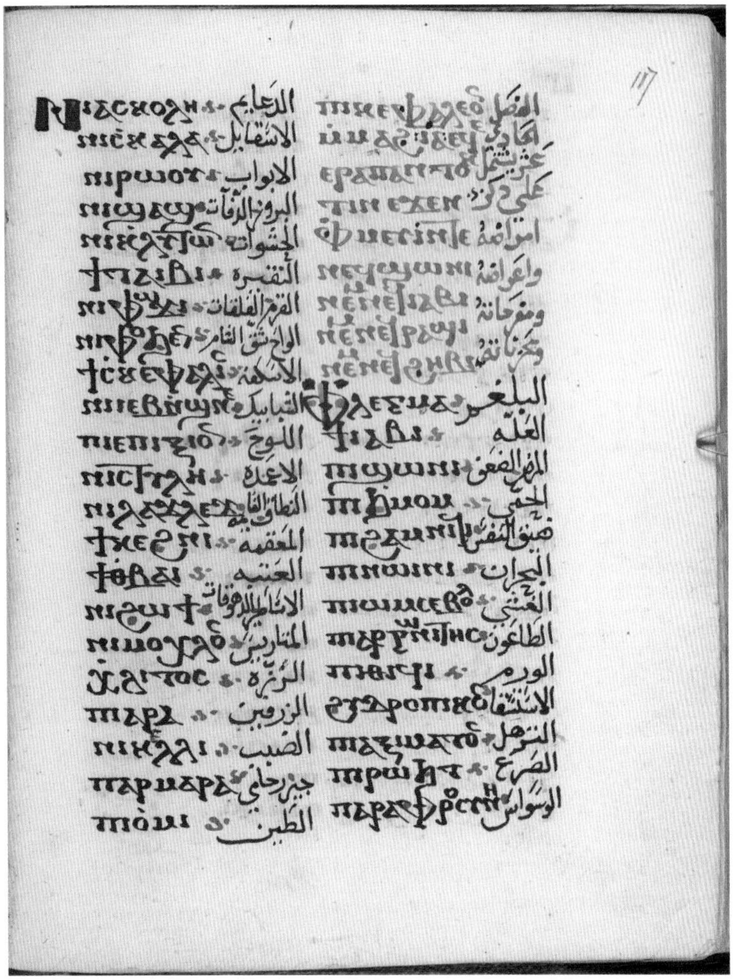

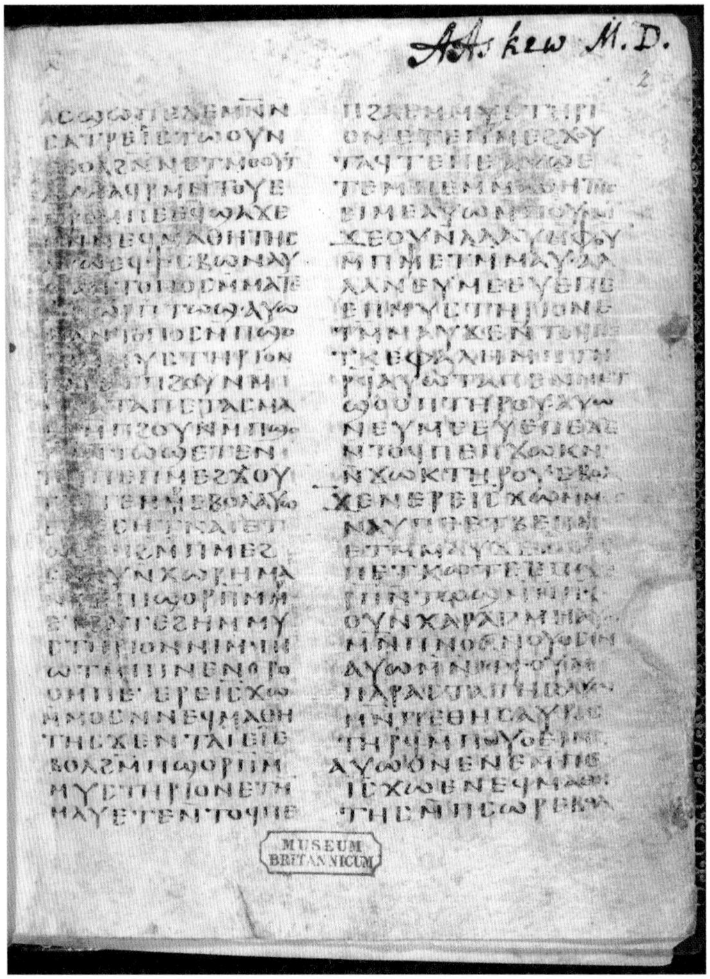

toponyms (place names) tends to be conserved even when they are written in different languages with different scripts. Using Coptic lists of the towns and villages of Egypt and the maps published in the *Description de l'Égypte*, Champollion tried to connect ancient toponyms with their modern equivalents (fig. 71). He believed that these names were derived from ordinary words describing nature and physical objects, linked to ancient Egyptian culture and religion.

For example, the Greek toponym Syène (modern Aswan) is derived from a combination of the ancient particle *ca* (sa), attributing the ability or power to do something, and the Coptic root *oyhn* (ouèn)/*oyen* (ouan). The reading 'to (cause to) open' stresses Aswan's strategic location as the southern gateway to Egypt. Champollion also showed that a toponym could reveal which deity was consecrated to the place; for example,

68 (left)
Treatise on Coptic grammar, including a name list, by the Egyptian/Coptic scholar Abu al-Barakat, who was also known as Ibn 'Kepir' in some parts of Europe. This *Scala Magna* is one of the many Arabic manuscripts that were brought to Europe by Pietro della Valle (1586–1652).
Egypt, 13th century CE
Paper, H. 22.5 cm, W. 18 cm, D. 5 cm
British Library, MS Or 1325, f. 117a

69 (facing page, right)
The Askew Codex with Sahidic Coptic translations of the Gnostic *Pistis Sophia*, spiritual teachings of the resurrected Jesus to his disciples. Until the discovery of the Nag Hammadi library in 1945, the Askew Codex was one of three surviving codices containing full copies of all the Gnostic writings that have survived until recent times.
Egypt (?), *c.* 3rd–4th centuries CE
Parchment, H. 23 cm, W. 19 cm, D. 4 cm (closed)
British Library, MS 5114, f. 002r

70 (top right)
Champollion's notes using the Coptic language to assign sound (phonetisation) to demotic script
Paris, France, 1814–22
Paper, H. 47 cm, W. 27.1 cm, D. 2.6 cm (closed)
Bibliothèque nationale de France, Département des Manuscrits, NAF 20352, p. 12

71 (bottom right)
Writing board with a list of words (known as an onomasticon) in hieratic, recording types of people on one side ('young boy', 'lad', 'ship builder', 'head carpenter') and Upper Egyptian towns on the other. The classifier ⊗ indicates that the preceding word is the name of a town, as Champollion discovered.
Egypt, 21st or 22nd Dynasty, 1069–715 BCE
Wood, H. 13.3 cm, W. 28.5 cm, D. 2.7 cm
British Museum, EA21635
Donated by Sir Ernest A T Wallis Budge

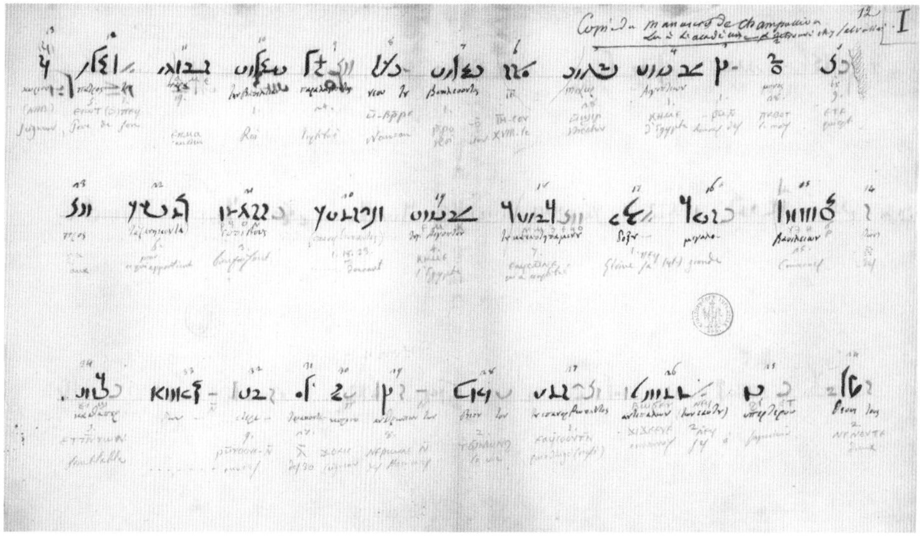

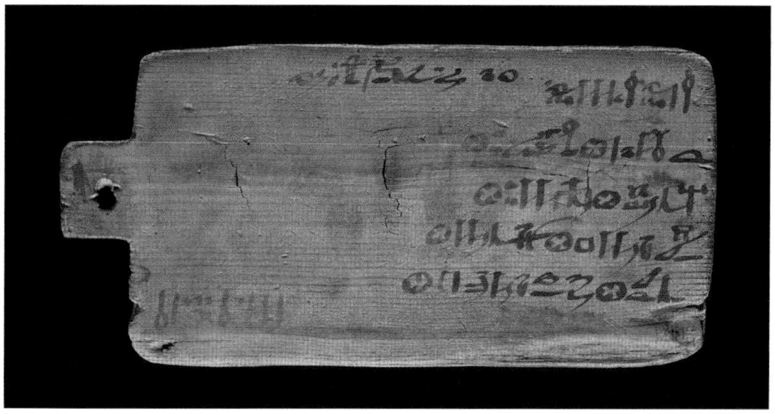

Hermopolis was the city of the god Hermes. In 1811 he published a substantial introduction to what would become his two-volume study of ancient Egyptian geography.[37]

From Coptic, Champollion gained both an idea of the structure of the ancient Egyptian language and a vocabulary pivotal to his understanding of hieroglyphs. Yet Coptic also misled him just as it had his predecessors. Ancient words could not be easily transcribed into later forms of Coptic, since many possible meanings for a word or phrase coexisted, and the boundaries between these semantic units proved hard to draw.

BREAKING THE CODE

In 1810 Champollion proposed that if the hieroglyphic section of the Rosetta Stone represented the names of Ptolemy, Berenice, Arsinoe and Alexander that were present in the Greek section, then hieroglyphs must have had the power to be spoken. However, he initially ascribed an alphabetic element only to the hieroglyphic rendering of non-Egyptian names, not the rest of the script.[38] He studied the five cartouches in the Rosetta Stone's hieroglyphic inscription containing Ptolemy's name and titles. By October 1813 he was convinced that hieroglyphs did not exclusively represent ideas or even words, but that at least some of the images of familiar natural objects were alphabetic. He further determined that the cursive script that he studied on papyri was also phonetic.

Champollion had two copies of the Rosetta Stone inscription, the *Vetusta* engraving (see fig. 46) and the reproduction intended for publication in the *Description de l'Égypte*, but he distrusted the quality of both. On 10 November 1814 Champollion wrote to the Royal Society of London requesting 'a plaster cast [of the Rosetta Stone] from a mould made on the original'. He also asked for confirmation of the accuracy of several passages in the demotic inscription of the Rosetta Stone that only someone with direct access could provide (fig. 72). His requests were passed to Young, the Royal Society's foreign secretary, who had been working on the Rosetta Stone for several months.

On 19 April 1818 Champollion wrote to his older brother of his findings regarding hieroglyphs. He said that he had identified the articles (words such as 'the', 'an' and 'a' in English), the formation of plurals and some conjunctions (linguistic elements that link two or more words or phrases). It was progress, yet not enough: 'The results of my work have already overturned all the ideas I had about hieroglyphics until now,' he wrote. 'But I cannot end it without the engraving of the Commission. My tracing of the English engraving is poor in some parts as well as the English original.'[39] By June 1818 Champollion had two new copies of the Rosetta Stone inscriptions, both based on the *Description*. With these at hand, his understanding leapt ahead.

Champollion observed that there were more correspondences between demotic and hieroglyphic sequences than there were between demotic and Coptic equivalents. But there were far more hieroglyphs than demotic signs. If demotic was alphabetic, it could not be closely connected to (ideographic) hieroglyphs, yet both belonged to the same writing system. Gradually, like Young, Champollion rejected the idea that demotic was purely alphabetic. The large number of different hieroglyphs also suggested that they were not

72 (facing page)
Champollion's letter to the Royal Society, written 10 November 1814 in Grenoble. As the society's secretary, Young responded to the letter, drafting his reply at the bottom of the page.
Grenoble, France and London, England, 1814
Paper, H. 33 cm, W. 22 cm
British Library, Add 21026, f. 16

apparences bien diverses, je ne vais que pas à pas & avec une extrême défiance. On ne doit pas même douter que cette partie essentielle de l'antiquité Egyptienne ne fut aujourd'hui plus avancée, si une copie moulée, comme je le dis, du beau monument de Rosette était déposée dans chacune des principales bibliothèques de l'Europe et envoyée à ses Académies les plus célèbres; ce nouveau Présent fait aux amis des bonnes lettres serait digne du Zèle & du Désintéressement qui animent la Société Royale.

J'ose recommander mon ouvrage à son Indulgence, et c'est avec beaucoup d'empressement que je saisis cette occasion de lui payer mon tribut d'admiration & de reconnaissance pour ses grands & utiles travaux; Je n'en ai pas moins à vous offrir, Monsieur le Président, l'hommage de mon dévouement

Grenoble le 10 Novembre 1814. J. F. Champollion le jeune

Monsieur Le Président de la Société Royale a reçu l'exemplaire de votre ouvrage sur l'Egypte que vous avez bien voulu adresser à la Société, mais il ne l'a pas encore presenté a la Société, puisqu'a en juger par votre lettre il parait douteux si vous avez eu l'intention de l'envoyer à la Société Royale ou a la Société d'Antiquités qui a seule le mérite de l'avoir fait graver ~~publié~~ ~~une~~ la ~~copie de~~ l'Inscription de Rosette : et il l'a cru de son devoir de vous demander ~~Monsieur~~ de nouvelles instructions sur la présentation de votre ouvrage a l'une ou a l'autre Société.

J'ai eu beaucoup de plaisir et d'interet Monsieur, a faire les comparaisons que vous souhaitez entre les deux copies de l'inscription — En général, celle de la Société Antiquaire me parait ~~la plus exacte, et même~~ presque parfaite (quelquefois pourtant la copie françoise est la plus exacte): mais dans la plupart des endroits que vous avez cités il y a quelque obscurité dans les traits originaux qui sont un peu confus ou usés, et ce n'est qu'en comparant les diverses parties de la pierre qu'on peut s'assurer de la véritable leçon ~~Par exemple~~ Autant que j'ai pu distinguer les traits dans un jour qui n'étoit pas très favorable, on doit lire ainsi

L. 2. ~~dans le mot [illegible] pourroit etre ou [illegible] ou [illegible] : le nom de Vulcain est~~ comme l. 4 et 6

~~[illegible] Encore [illegible] - Le [illegible] est un peu confus~~

N.° 1 L. 2 [illegible]

N.° 2. [illegible]

N.° 3 L. 5 [illegible]

N.° 4 L. 5 [illegible] , non pas [illegible]

N.° 5 L. 6 [illegible]

N.° 6 L. 6 [illegible]

entirely ideographic.[40] Counting 1,419 hieroglyphic signs on the Rosetta Stone,[41] Champollion reasoned that this many ideas could not possibly be conveyed in the 486 words of the Greek text. If hieroglyphs were not alphabetic, and not exclusively ideographic, then they must represent a hybrid system.

Investigating the demotic sequence corresponding to 'Alexandria', Champollion suggested that the word was constituted from a phonetic component – the name itself – plus an ideographic sign indicating the way in which the phonetic component should be understood, in this case as a place name. Champollion had discovered the determinative, a unique set of qualifying signs that indicate the nature of either a single sign or a group (see p. 25). For example, an angle sign  at the end of the name of queen Arsinoe transformed the meaning of 'king' into 'queen'. Champollion noted that angles also terminated the hieroglyphic names of goddesses. This proved that sign sequences could comprise both phonetic and non-phonetic elements.

With this novel conclusion, Champollion turned to older cursive scripts, which he now understood were written in hieratic, with texts from papyri and mummy wrappings providing ample study material. Since demotic borrowed its signs from hieratic, the latter could not be alphabetic either. Like demotic, he concluded, hieratic was a simple modification of the hieroglyphic system and differed only in the shape of its signs, not their meaning.[42] Because it was written on papyrus and not carved into monuments, hieratic had lost any 'figurative' resemblance to physical objects.[43] He asserted that hieratic and demotic scripts were graphically equivalent, differing principally in the material ease with which each could be inscribed. For example, he pinpointed the hieratic version of the semicircle-plus-oval  as a female signifier and linked it to the angle sign in demotic. Demotic was used in daily life and needed to convey practical affairs efficiently: hence the sign system was shortened. Champollion concluded that none of the three scripts was purely alphabetic, but included signs that represented words or concepts, and that most characters were 'signs of things and not of sounds'.[44]

READING ROYAL NAMES

Lecturing in August 1821, Champollion reiterated his belief that signs (hieroglyphic and demotic) could only be used as alphabetic letters when writing non-Egyptian names. Yet, a letter sign could apparently be separated from the sign's basic semantic value and used phonetically. For example,  (*r*) means 'mouth' but could also simply designate an '*r*' sound, unrelated to that meaning. Now on the verge of a breakthrough,

73
The stela of Pasherenptah III (right) containing cartouches of Cleopatra III (above) and Ptolemy XII. Pasherenptah's autobiography recounts that immediately after his appointment as high priest of Ptah in 76 BCE at the age of fourteen, he performed the coronation of Cleopatra's father, Ptolemy XII Auletes.
Saqqara, Ptolemaic Period, 41 BCE
Limestone, H. 72.5 cm, W. 61 cm, D. 14 cm
British Museum, EA886

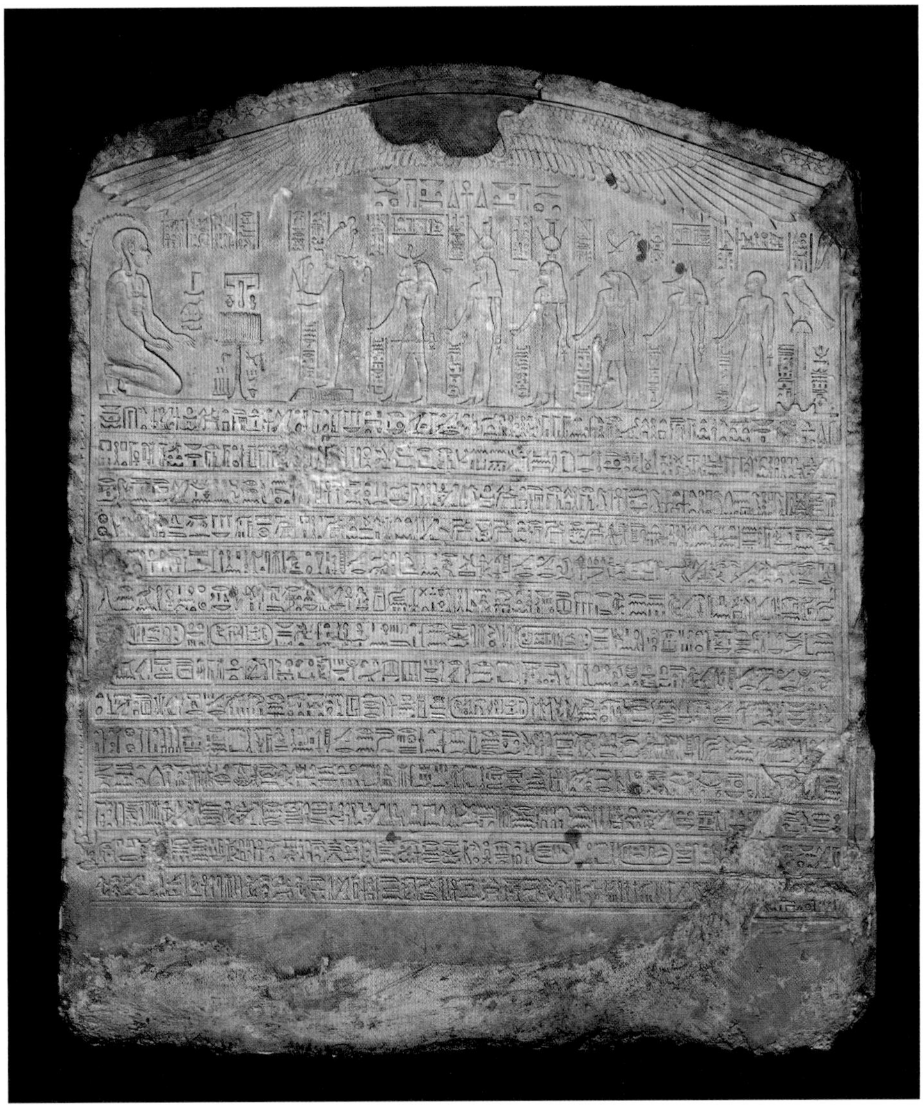

Champollion refined previous readings of the cartouche of Ptolemy to *P t o l m y s* and tested other cartouches of Ptolemaic royals (fig. 73).

In 1821 Champollion identified the demotic spelling of Cleopatra in a bilingual papyrus lately purchased in Egypt by Casati, an Italian collector (fig. 74).[45] The eighteen lines of demotic text, dated to year 36 of the reign of Ptolemy VI Philometor (146 BCE), are followed by a six-line Greek inscription and a list of witnesses in demotic. Champollion noticed that Cleopatra had four letters in common with Ptolemy: *l o p t*.[46] The third lion-like sign in Ptolemy's cartouche was the same as the second sign in Cleopatra's name, which should be identified, therefore, as an alphabetic *l*. Young's syllabic

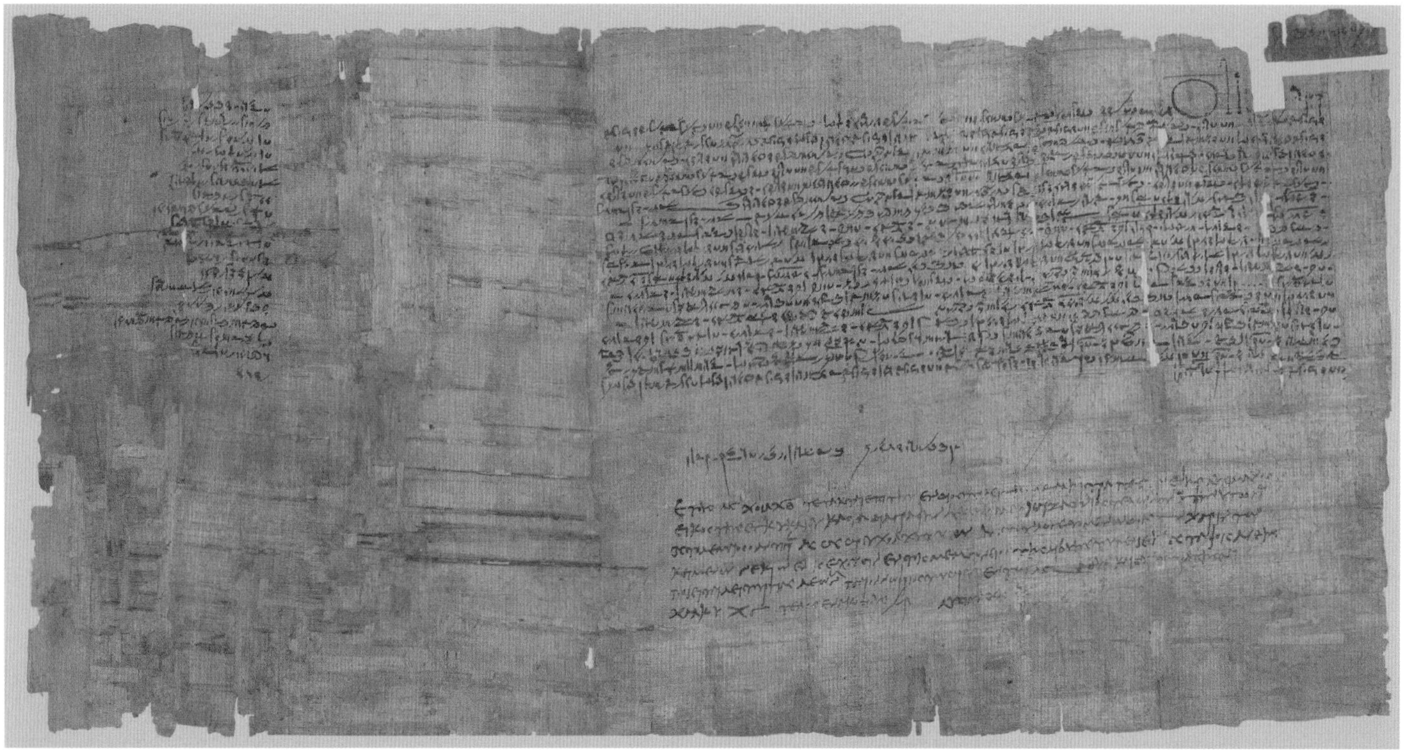

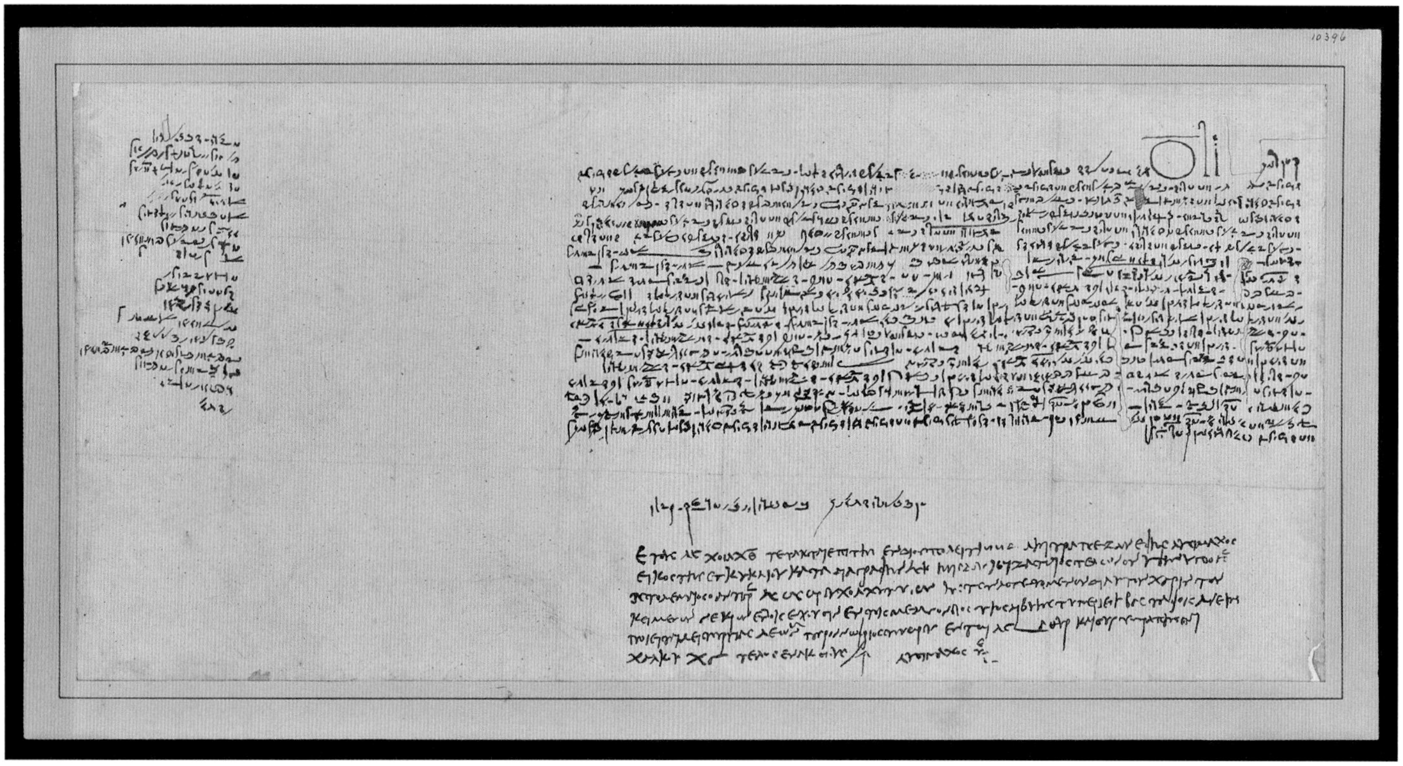

74 (facing page, top)
The Casati papyrus, dated year 36 of Ptolemy VI Philometor
Thebes, Ptolemaic Period, 146 BCE
Papyrus, H. 32.5 cm, W. 63 cm
Bibliothèque nationale de France, Département des Manuscrits, Egyptien 218

75 (facing page, bottom)
Facsimile of the Casati papyrus presented by Thomas Young to the British Museum
Paris, early 19th century CE
Cardboard, H. 27.3 cm, W. 59 cm
British Museum, EA10396
Donated by Thomas Young

reading of *ole* or *olt* for this sign (see p. 101) was consequently incorrect. Champollion also recognised that the final *t* indicated the feminine, as in Semitic languages that he knew well. Champollion now had fourteen alphabetic values: three for vowels and eleven for consonants. He tried them on other Greco-Roman cartouches and names known from classical literature: Alexander, Caesar, Domitian and Trajan. In discussions with Young, Champollion maintained that the Greek inscription on the Casati papyrus was not an accurate translation of the demotic, but he did not share his copy of the Greek with Young, who was consequently unable to check Champollion's readings (fig. 75).

In 1822 Young received a papyrus from George Francis Grey, an Oxford clergyman and antiquarian, that coincidentally was a Greek translation of the demotic text on the Casati papyrus, confirming the latter as a receipt for the sale of a share of income from tombs at Thebes (present-day Luxor) (fig. 76). To Young, the Greek text confirmed his suspicion that Champollion had read some of the Roman names incorrectly.[47] He identified Antimachos and Antigenis, but Champollion read them as Antiochus and Antigonus.[48] To explain the discrepancy, Young wrote on 23 November 1822 that the Grey papyrus offered evidence 'in favour of the extensive employment of an alphabetic mode of writing during the Greco-Roman period more so than the Rosetta Stone inscription'. Champollion was unconvinced (fig. 77).

The texts on the Philae obelisk (see p. 101) provided Champollion with another missing link. In January 1822 he saw Bankes's copy of the inscriptions but was dismayed by its quality: 'this English engraving, of very small proportion, executed by artists poorly accustomed to the style of Egyptian monuments' was 'inferior in all respects to the beautiful drawings of the obelisks given by the Egypt commission'.[49] Champollion nonetheless noted that one of the cartouches contained the proper name of a woman, a Ptolemaic queen, as indicated by the unvoiced sign for the feminine.

During his 1818 voyage to Egypt, Bankes had correctly identified the hieroglyphic cartouches of Ptolemy and Cleopatra in the temples of Diospolis Parva and Philae (see p. 103). Bankes also found Cleopatra on the base of the Philae obelisk and made a note of her name in the margins of at least one of the lithographs he distributed in France.[50] Young had, meanwhile, published a phonetic reading from the demotic of Cleopatra in his 1819 *Britannica* article, two years before Champollion did the same. But neither Bankes nor Young explained their readings or backed them up with a methodology applicable to other scripts. Champollion claimed to have obtained his reading of the demotic Cleopatra from the Casati papyrus, independently of Young or Bankes. In choosing not to acknowledge their

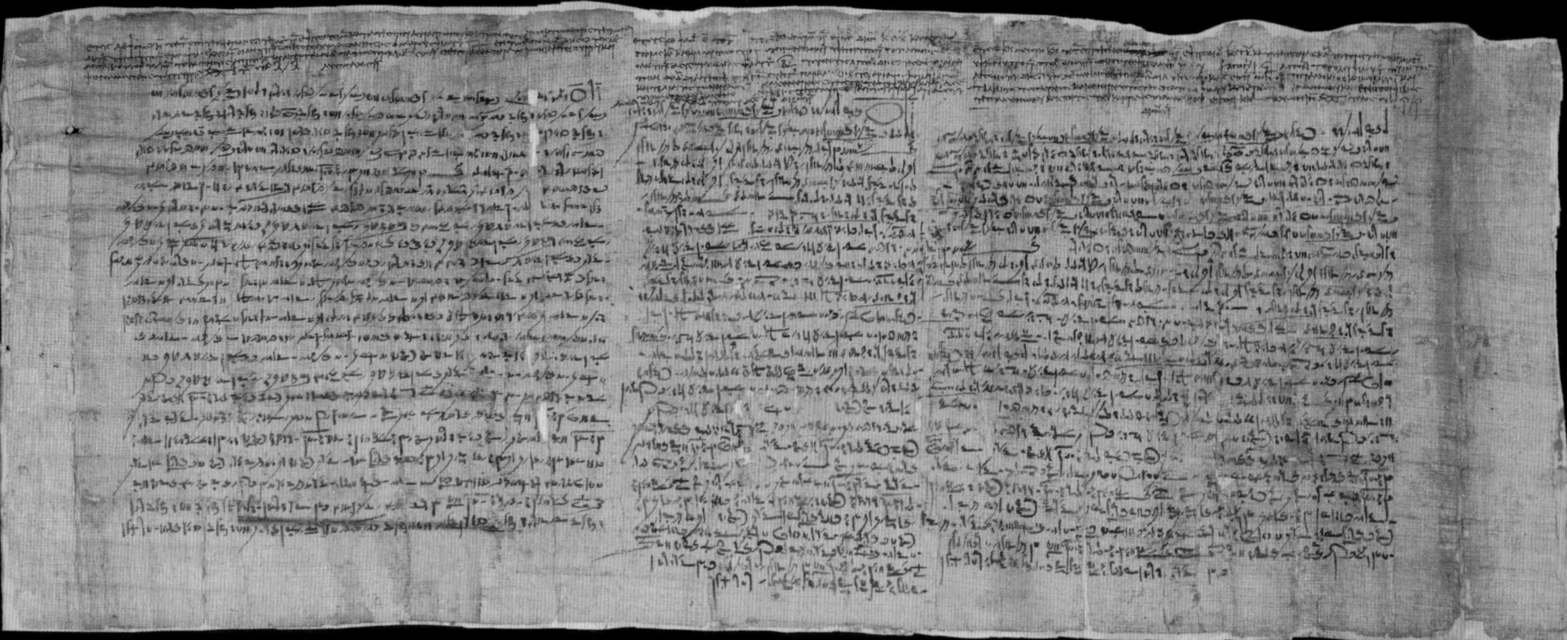

contributions to decipherment, Champollion raised scholarly hackles. According to Salt, Bankes later alleged that Champollion had translated the cartouche of Cleopatra thanks to his marginal notes.

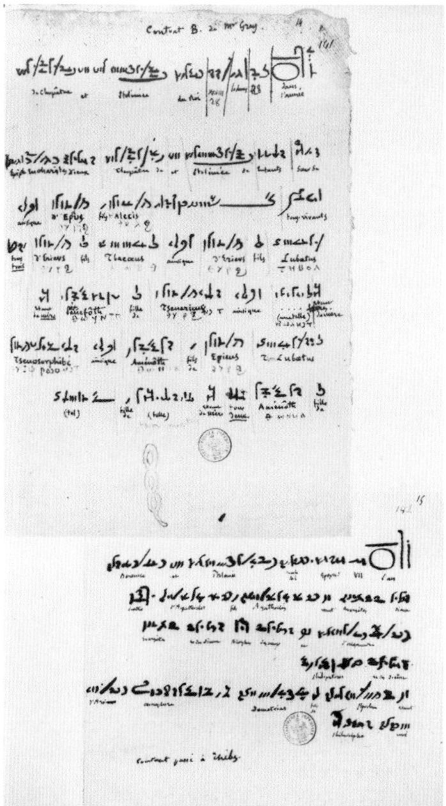

EUREKA!

Champollion had been guided by both the advances and the shortcomings of his peers and predecessors, but he was certainly the first to grasp the structural logic of the ancient Egyptian language in its varied forms. The story goes that on 14 September 1822 he visited his brother, thrusting notes into his hands and gasping, 'look, I've got it!' (*je tiens mon affaire, vois!*), before collapsing in a dead faint. His notes formed the basis of a historic letter to M. Dacier, secretary of the Académie des inscriptions et belles-lettres (27 September 1822), in which Champollion outlined his findings and the reasoning behind them (fig. 78).[51] His work was published in meticulous detail in 1824, and with these tools in hand scholars could finally translate the texts and records of a civilisation that had persevered for thousands of years. Champollion's 1822 revelatory letter to Dacier marked the birth of Egyptology.

In the letter, Champollion stated that all Egyptian scripts represented things or ideas, not sounds, but he made one crucial exception. Hieroglyphs could represent sounds when used phonetically to write non-Egyptian proper

76 (facing page, top)
Papyrus Grey, named after its former owner, George Francis Grey
Hermonthis, Ptolemaic Period, 153 BCE
Papyrus, H. 32.5 cm, W. 81 cm, D. 1 cm
Bodleian Libraries, MS. Egypt a.4(P)

77 (facing page, bottom)
Champollion's notes on the papyrus Grey
Paris, France, *c.* 1822
Paper, H. 48.5 cm, W. 61.5 cm (closed)
Bibliothèque nationale de France, Département des Manuscrits, NAF 20314, fol. 141

names, such as Ptolemy and Berenice.[52] Given the relationship between the scripts, he was able to use the demotic to make phonetic interpretations of hieroglyphic signs for foreign words. He proposed phonetic transliterations (approximate renderings of the sounds, using the Western alphabet) for the cartouches of many Greek and Roman rulers of Egypt, and a hieroglyphic and demotic 'alphabet' supposedly used only for writing foreign names. From the names of Ptolemy and Cleopatra alone, Champollion generated consonants and vowels corresponding to letters a, ai, e, k, l, m, o, p, r, s and t.

Since the three scripts on the Stone were variants of one another, at least some hieroglyphs must have been expressed in speech. Champollion now detected a fuller phonetic structure than previously imagined.[53] Moreover, the conservative character of Egyptian culture, he argued, would not have tolerated a massive revision of the writing system, so if spelling based on pronunciation was present at any time, it must have been there from the start.[54] Champollion's eureka moment regarding the phonetic aspect of Egyptian language literally knocked him off his feet.

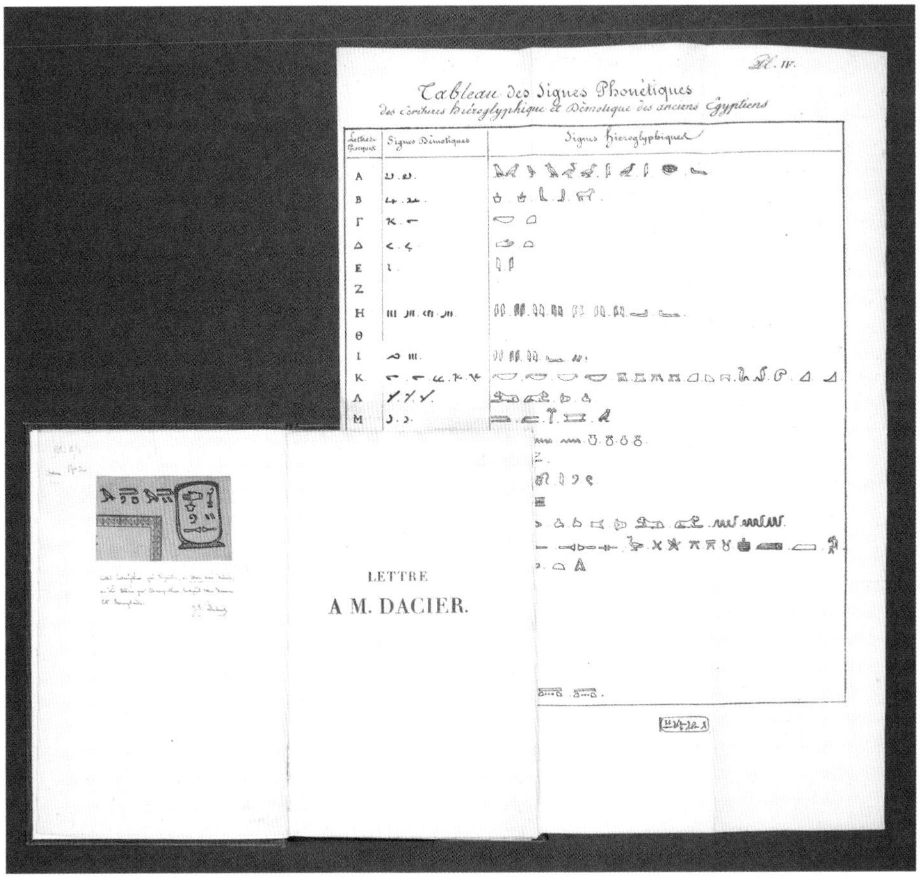

78
Copy of Champollion's *Lettre à M. Dacier*
Paris, France, 1822
Paper, H. 44.5 cm, W. 49 cm (opened, including insert)
British Museum, Egypt and Sudan Library, RBC.CHA

Champollion discovered phonetic elements in the cartouches of two pharaohs of the New Kingdom (1520 to 1075 BCE): Ramesses and Thutmose. The name in the first cartouche combined a sun disc with a sign depicting three fox skins tied together, followed by two identical horizontal signs representing a doorbolt 𓇳 𓄟 𓊃𓊃 (figs 79–80).[55] He knew the last two signs as *s* from the cartouche of Ptolemy, and the sun disc as *ra* was known from Coptic. Despite the unknown middle hieroglyph, Champollion linked *Ra – ? – ss* with the famous pharaoh Ramesses, who is mentioned in the Bible, attributing the value *m* to the middle sign.

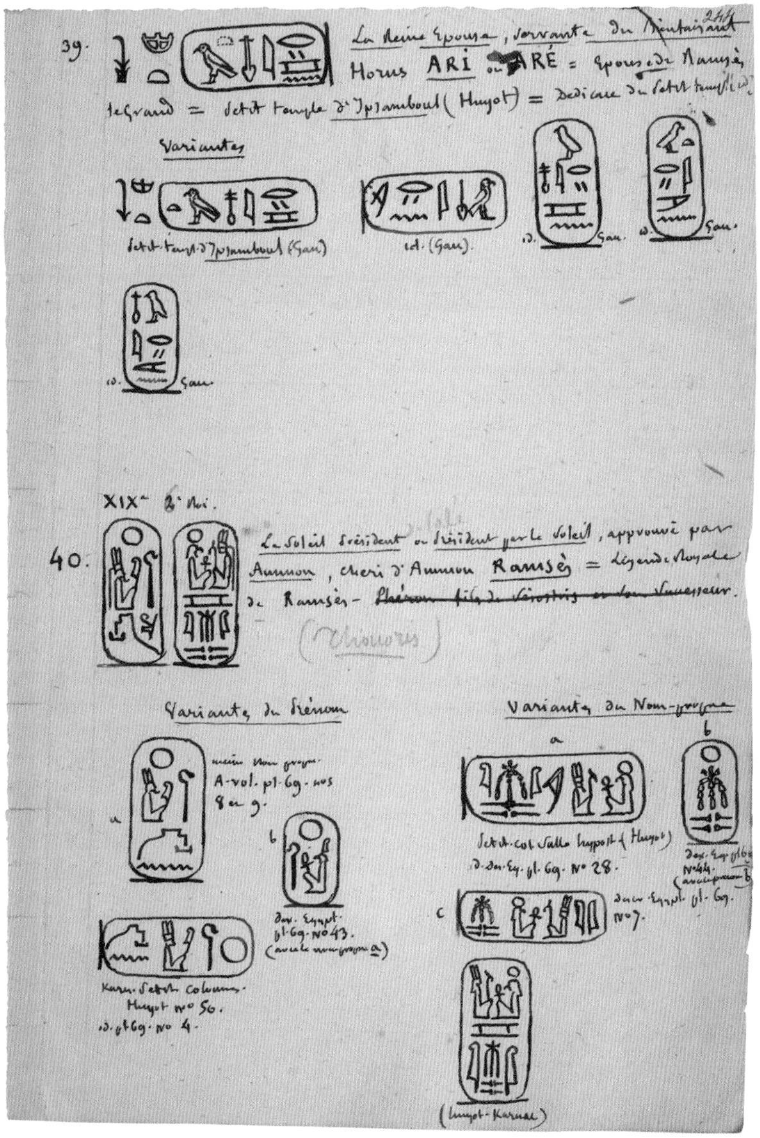

79 (left)
Champollion's copy of the cartouche of Ramesses, based on a now-lost drawing by Jean-Nicolas Huyot (1780–1840), the French architect of the Arc de Triomphe in Paris, who travelled in Egypt with Bankes. The spelling suggested by Huyot's drawing is in fact quite rare.
Paris, France, *c.* 1824
Paper, H. 47 cm, W. 27.6 cm, D. 5.8 cm (closed)
Bibliothèque nationale de France, Département des Manuscrits, NAF 20337, p. 244

80 (facing page, top)
Lintel showing names of Ramesses III, written with the seated god Ra instead of the sun disc, and a vertical s-sign 𓋴 (a piece of folded cloth) instead of the door bolts 𓊃
Egypt, 20th Dynasty, 1184–1153 BCE
Limestone, H. 64.5 cm, W. 141 cm, D. 12.5 cm
British Museum, EA 1344

81 (facing page, bottom)
Fragment of a relief with cartouches of Thutmose I
Deir el-Bahari, New Kingdom, 1504–1492 BCE
Limestone, H. 31.5 cm, W. 18.5 cm, D. 16 cm
British Museum, EA 1456
Donated by the Egypt Exploration Fund

The second king's cartouche showed an ibis followed by the same middle sign as in Ramesses' cartouche, and a horizontal doorbolt for *s* (fig. 81). Champollion knew the ibis was the sacred animal of Thoth and figured this must be *Thot–m–s*, the great Thutmose of whom the classical authors spoke. The middle sign seemed to be confirmed, once again, as *m*.

The fortuitous comparison of these two names gave Champollion the key to the entire hieroglyphic writing system, apart from one small mistake. The middle sign was, in fact, the two-letter sign *ms*, while the horizontal sign *s* only complemented the pronunciation of the previous sign.[56] Nonetheless, Champollion had illuminated the combinational nature of Egyptian writing: in the same cartouche, which itself he recognised as a determinative, purely phonetic signs were used alongside signs representing an entire word (Ra and Thoth).

In his letter to M. Dacier, Champollion did not include his readings of the pharaohs' names, as he was still feverishly testing his system. Consequently, some reviewers called his phonetic rendering of Greco-Roman names a mere addendum, useful mainly for determining the chronology of Ptolemaic rulers. But Champollion's letter was the product of a long, upward trek towards decipherment, and with his next publication, *Précis du système hiéroglyphique des anciens Égyptiens* (1824), he planted his flag on the summit.

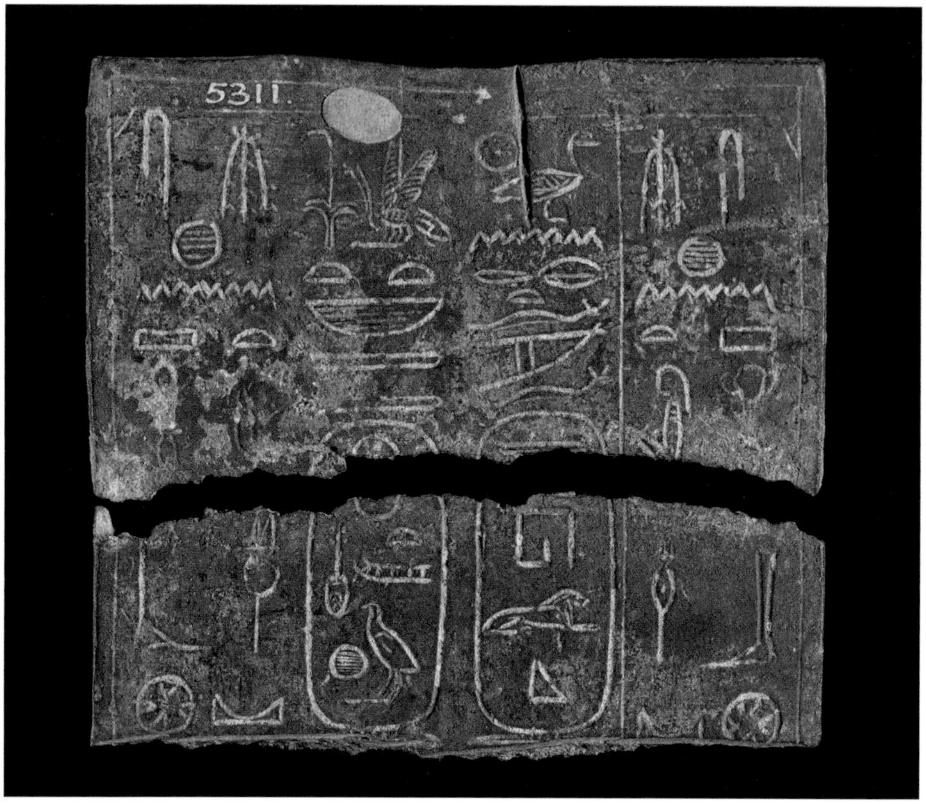

UNTANGLING A HYBRID SYSTEM

Champollion was now certain that, throughout Egyptian history, hieroglyphic script had had a major phonetic component.[57] He tested his idea by reading pre-Alexandrian names already known in Greek inscriptions, such as Xerxes, the Persian king who occupied Egypt between 485 and 465 BCE and Taharqa (figs 82–84, see p. 155).[58] The discoveries multiplied.

Recognising the flexible, economical ways in which ancient Egyptians used their written characters was Champollion's most astute observation: one sign could have different functions, and more than one sign could represent the same sound (homophones). The letter *t* is an example: it could be written with a small bread sign 𓏏 or with a hand 𓂧. Collating the characters in sequences, Champollion enlarged his earlier phonetic 'alphabet' with homophone signs.[59] This enabled him to read the names of deities known from classical literature, and also the names of people that incorporated names of gods. He discovered that *ms.n*, meaning 'born of',

82 (above left)
Alabaster jar inscribed with the name of Xerxes in Egyptian hieroglyphs and in cuneiform script representing the Persian, Median and Assyrian languages
Halicarnassus, Turkey, Achaemenid period (or Egyptian 27th Dynasty), 485–465 BCE
Calcite, H. 28.2 cm, diam. 17.5 cm
British Museum, 132114

83 (facing page, right)
Plaque inscribed with the names and epithets of Taharqa in hieroglyphs. On 14 August 1824, Champollion wrote to his brother that he saw a cartouche of *thr-ḳ3* and speculated that this would be the 25th Dynasty king Taharqa (Taraka or Téarko) whom he already knew from inscriptions at Naga and Gebel Barkal in Sudan.
Egypt, 25th Dynasty, 690–664 BCE
Bronze, H. 8.3 cm, W. 9 cm, D. 1 cm
British Museum, EA5311

84 (right)
Letter by Champollion to his brother in which he tested his newly cracked system on pre-Alexandrian royal names such as Taharqa. He recognised d (hand) + h (meander) + r/l (lion) + q (half mountain) in 'thr-q', a combination of letters he had encountered on monuments in Nubia.
Turin, Italy, 14 August 1824
Paper
Archives départementales de l'Isère, 185 J 18, fol. 23

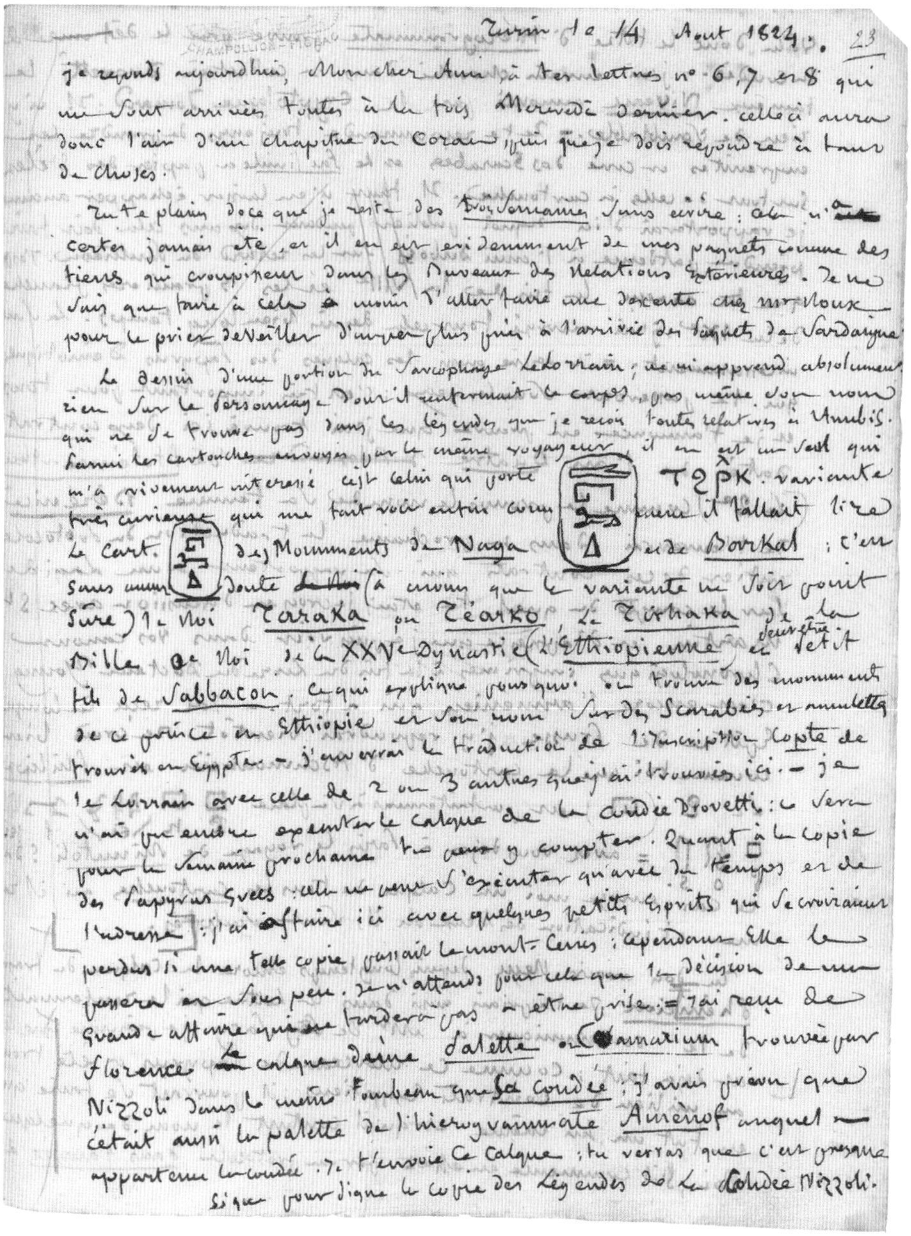
Turin le 14 Août 1824. 23
je réponds aujourd'hui, Mon cher Ami, à tes lettres nº 6, 7 et 8 qui me sont arrivées toutes à la fois Mercredi dernier. celle-ci aura donc l'air d'un chapitre du Coran, puisque je dois répondre à tant de choses.

indicated family members, and correctly identified the goose sign *z3* on funerary stelae and papyri as meaning 'son of'.

Champollion expected a determinative to appear near common names indicating they should be read phonetically, just as for royal names, and duly identified the seated man determinative (fig. 85), gaining insight into its varied use. He noted that name indicators referred to the individual in question, but did not guarantee that all signs in the name should be read alphabetically as well as phonetically. He realised that hieroglyphic writing employed two kinds of signs: some expressing sounds one-to-one, others representing larger semantic units.

Champollion's revolutionary *Précis du système hiéroglyphique des anciens Égyptiens* (published April 1824, with 400 pages and 24 sample texts and tables) presented the essence of decipherment as he wished it to be understood (fig. 86).[60] He demonstrated how Egyptian scripts had always been fundamentally both phonetic and ideographic, and how phonetic hieroglyphs provided the key to a system used to write the spoken language through time. He explained how to decode the hieroglyphic names and titles of gods, kings and private individuals. He described 450 signs or sign sequences but claimed to have identified 864 distinct characters. The alphabetic signs comprised but a fraction of this number, the vast majority being two-, three- and four-letter signs, or those belonging to the figurative and symbolic categories.

After the *Précis*, Champollion continued to elaborate, confirm and add translations for sign sequences gleaned from new materials (figs 87–88). In 1828 he made the long-dreamt-of journey to Egypt (see Chapter 3), collecting inscriptions but also impressions of the place, people and monuments that had occupied his thoughts for so long. His decipherment granted the world entry into a distant, prodigiously creative past. Champollion spent his last few years exploring it, translating inscriptions until his death, aged forty-one, in 1832. The vista of discovery he opened was staggering.

RIVALRY AND LEGACY

The political turmoil that rocked France during Champollion's life continuously threatened to disrupt his research; his allegiance to the exiled Napoleon made him suspect in the eyes of the subsequent Royalist regime. His relations with prominent scientific figures, such as Joseph Fourier and Silvestre de Sacy, both helped and hindered him.

85 (above)
Fragment of a stela of the priest Horiraa with hieroglyphic and demotic inscriptions attesting his role in the Memphite cults of Ptah and Bastet. The seated man determinative appears near the end of line 2, after Horiraa's name. The first sign in line 3 is the feminine equivalent, classifying the (now-lost) name of his mother.
Memphis, 30th Dynasty to early Ptolemaic Period, 380–30 BCE
Limestone, H. 19.8 cm, W. 21.8 cm, D. 5 cm
British Museum, EA20945

86 (facing page, top)
Champollion's *Précis du système hiéroglyphique des anciens Égyptiens*
Paris, France, 1824
Paper, H. 23.4 cm, W. 15.6 cm
Bibliothèque nationale de France, Département des Manuscrits, BnF RES-X-2617, pl. XII

87 (facing page, bottom)
Preparations for Champollion's Egyptian grammar, indicating pronouns and verb conjugations
Paris, France, after 1822
Paper, H. 40.6 cm, W. 27.3 cm (closed)
Bibliothèque nationale de France, Département des Manuscrits, NAF 20345, pp. 98–9

Page 213

Pl. XII.

Futur TAPE

Subjonctif

Impératif 99

Affixes du Présent

		Copte	Passé	
1re	masc.	ϣ · ϯ		NAI
1re	fem.	ϣ · ϯ		NAI
2e	masc.	K · Ϫ		NAK
2e	fem.	TE		NE
2e				NAY
3e	masc.	ϥ		NAϤ
3e	fem.	C		NAC
1re	plur. com.	N		NAN
2e	plur. com.	TEN		NATEN
3e	pluriel com.	CEΝΑ		NAY.

marqué comme en copte par … ua. avant le radical.

ANTI NAI OYWN …

EI ЧA

Viens (ЧA EI) ouvre moi ô Anubis!

Rituel papyr. Cailliaud. Vetmenoph.

… nom d'action verbal.

pat

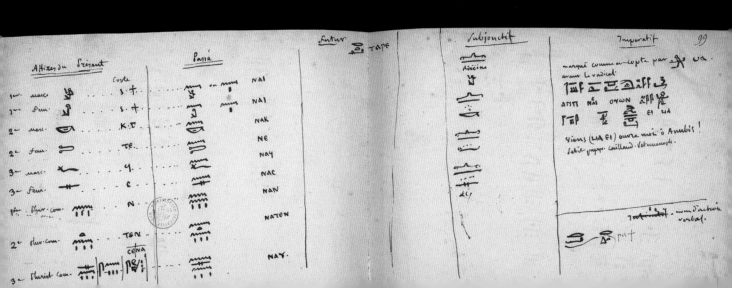

Champollion's peers were obliged to recognise his accomplishments, but scholarly competition aroused tensions in the course of the work. Young felt that Champollion had overlooked his role in deciphering Greco-Roman names. Champollion's mentor, de Sacy, had reportedly warned Young to be wary in his correspondence with Champollion, lest he co-opt Young's discoveries.[61] Perhaps as a result of the Frenchman's criticism of the quality of his engravings of the Philae obelisk, Bankes was outright 'hostile to Champollion', calling him 'a dirty scoundrel'.[62] The day after Champollion read his letter to M. Dacier, Young confided to a friend: 'You could say that he [Champollion] found in England [*chez* Young] the key to unlock the door, and you often find that it is the first step that counts. But if he borrowed an adjustable key, the lock was so horribly rusted that no normal arm would have had enough strength to turn it.'[63] In other words, Champollion's system left much to be desired and was still a heavy lift.

In 1823 Young published *An Account of the Recent Discoveries in Hieroglyphic Literature and Egyptian Antiquities*, aiming to establish his work as the basis for Champollion's achievement. Young conceded that Champollion had extended the phonetic list for foreign names but maintained that Åkerblad had laid the groundwork in this regard. In his 1824 *Précis*, Champollion acknowledged Young as the first to correctly identify several sound signs for foreign names, in particular those for Ptolemy and Berenice. But Young's failure to accept the phonetic aspect of hieroglyphic script beyond the spelling of foreign names had stalled his progress.

Despite these frictions, the two devoted readers of ancient Egyptian scripts corresponded amicably in later life. When Champollion became curator of the Louvre's Egyptian collection (1826), he offered Young access to materials related to the demotic, which was Young's main concern and the decipherment of which was his greatest contribution to Egyptology. In his final months, Young completed the *Rudiments of an Egyptian Dictionary in the Ancient Enchorial Character*, published posthumously in 1829.

Young and Champollion took different approaches to Egyptian writing because of their attitudes towards antiquity. As was common at the time, Young considered Egyptian culture vastly inferior to the Greek, and incapable of producing a sophisticated writing system. His rejection of any concerted reliance on Coptic reflected a certain disdain for ancient Egypt. Champollion was biased in the opposite direction; he felt that ancient Egypt was the source of much that was revered in ancient Greece and that Egyptian art and architecture were in some ways superior.[64] To read the ancient scripts was to enter an enticing world he dearly wished to understand.

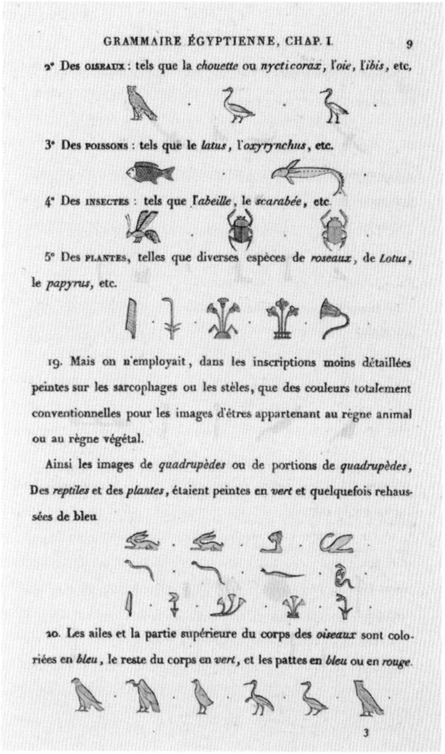

GRAMMAIRE ÉGYPTIENNE, CHAP. I. 9

2° Des OISEAUX : tels que la *chouette* ou *nycticorax*, l'*oie*, l'*ibis*, etc.

3° Des POISSONS : tels que le *latus*, l'*oxyrynchus*, etc.

4° Des INSECTES : tels que l'*abeille*, le *scarabée*, etc.

5° Des PLANTES, telles que diverses espèces de *roseaux*, de *Lotus*, le *papyrus*, etc.

19. Mais on n'employait, dans les inscriptions moins détaillées peintes sur les sarcophages ou les stèles, que des couleurs totalement conventionnelles pour les images d'êtres appartenant au règne animal ou au règne végétal.

Ainsi les images de *quadrupèdes* ou de portions de *quadrupèdes*, Des *reptiles* et des *plantes*, étaient peintes en *vert* et quelquefois rehaussées de bleu

20. Les ailes et la partie supérieure du corps des *oiseaux* sont coloriées en *bleu*, le reste du corps en *vert*, et les pattes en *bleu* ou en *rouge*.

3

88

Printed version of Champollion's Egyptian grammar, with hieroglyphs coloured in by hand
Paris, France, 1836
Paper, H. 34.3 cm, W. 23.5 cm, D. 4.1 cm (closed volume)
British Museum, Egypt and Sudan Library, RBC.4°.CHA

Thomas Young to the Archduke John of Austria, 2 August 1816

'With respect to the utility of the knowledge to be acquired from an interpretation of all the existing inscriptions, a few historical details are the utmost that we could reasonably expect to obtain: the great mass of Egyptian monuments of all kinds relates exclusively to the religious and superstitious rites observed towards the ridiculous deities and the idolised heroes of the country. I have sufficiently ascertained the characters implying units, tens, hundreds, and thousands; but in the inscriptions connected with astronomical representations, scarcely any of these numbers are observable: so that we can entertain but slight hopes of finding any very accurate records of astronomical phenomena, among the monuments of so foolish and so frivolous a nation.

After all, however, notwithstanding our contempt for their absurdities, it must not be denied, that a knowledge of the literature of that country, which is confessedly the parent of the earliest civilisation on record, does present to the imagination an objects of the highest possible curiosity; and if a single individual should fail in completing the whole discovery, it may be presumed, that his labours will hereafter be continued by others with renewed ardour, and perhaps under more favourable circumstances. They must, however, remember, when they undertake such a task, that it is not by the gigantic exertions of fancied talents, but the stubborn perseverance of indefatigable industry, that we can ever hope to obtain, for ourselves and our successors, an admission into the hidden treasures of nature and art.'[65]

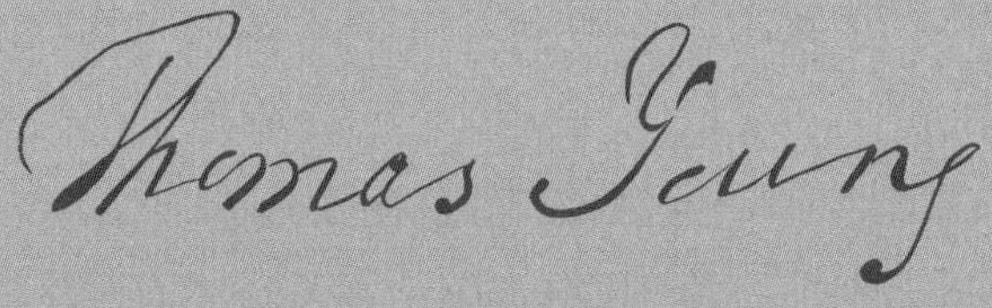

CHAPTER 3 The impact of decipherment

THE IMPACT OF DECIPHERMENT

Ilona Regulski

As newly arrived collections in Europe started to be unpacked and Champollion improved his understanding of hieroglyphs, the impact of decipherment became more obvious. Every inscription could now potentially be read and reveal how ancient Egyptians had lived and experienced the world.

By 1824 Champollion had exhausted the Egyptian research materials available in Paris. He needed fresh resources. The illiberal but influential Duke of Blacas d'Aulps (1771–1839) brought Champollion to the attention of King Louis XVIII and emphasised how greatly French glory would be enhanced if the young scholar continued to outshine his English counterpart in the matter of reading the ancient scripts. Financial support soon followed, which allowed Champollion to inspect new inscriptions in Italy, before moving on to Egypt four years later.

BEYOND CRACKING THE CODE

Ilona Regulski

READING HISTORY

Between 1824 and 1825 Champollion spent many months in Turin, where Drovetti's collection was being unpacked (see p. 60). There were 5,268 objects, including statues, papyri, stelae, sarcophagi, mummies, bronzes, amulets and items from daily life. Champollion was the first person since the Roman period who could accurately identify the statues from their inscriptions and establish centuries of royal succession.[1] Among the thousands of pieces, he discovered a papyrus that is now known as the 'Royal Canon' (Museo Egizio, Cat. 1874),[2] an extensive list showing the names of pharaohs in cartouches, in chronological order of their reigns. He compared this with another list he had learned about through Alessandro Ricci's collection of drawings in Florence.[3] This was the king list from Abydos, comprising thirty-four royal names (figs 89–90).

89
King list from the temple of Ramesses II at Abydos
Abydos, 19th Dynasty, *c.* 1250 BCE
Limestone, H. 140 cm, W. 376 cm, D. 25 cm
British Museum, EA 117

> The Turin collection is in short the most beautiful possible commentary on the Table of Abydos: it has monuments of 14 successive kings of the 18th Dynasty. These contemporary monuments will undoubtedly suffice to stop the more robust scepticism and will push back the domain of positive history which, from what I see here, will never go back, as I had already seen by studying the drawings of Huyot and the commission, well beyond this same 18th Dynasty, where the details of the chronicle also begin.
>
> Champollion to his brother, 23 July 1824, Turin[4]

The Abydos king list was originally part of the temple of Ramesses II, which is located just west of the prominent, and now more famous, temple of his father Sety I. These memorial temples of two of the most powerful kings of the Nineteenth Dynasty (1292–1189 BCE) belonged to a sacred

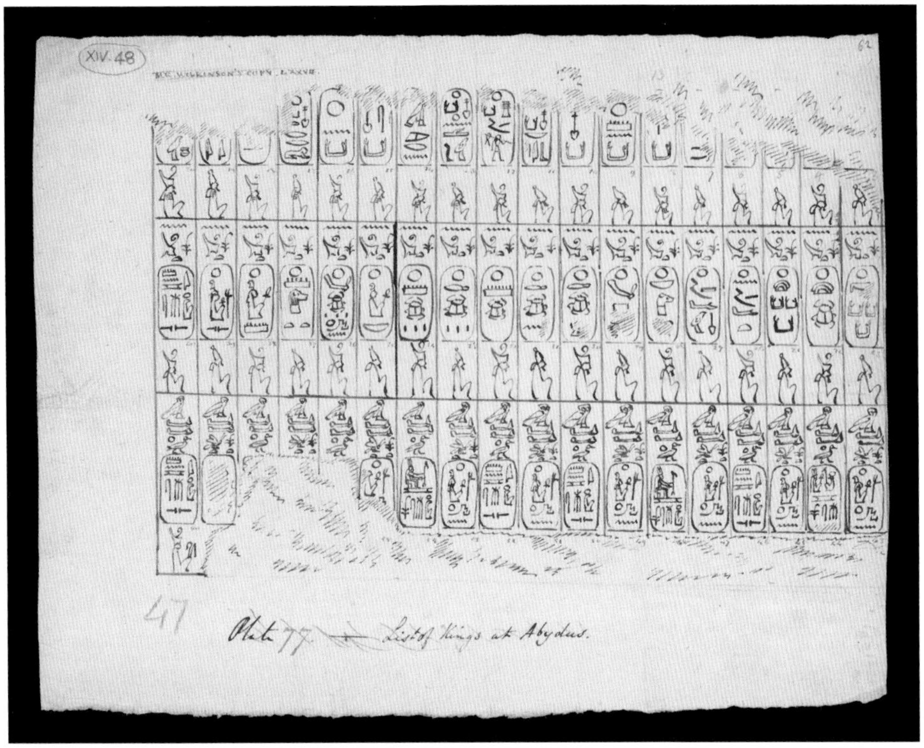

90
Copy of the Abydos king list by John Gardner Wilkinson
Abydos, 1821–2
Paper, H. 21 cm, W. 27.3 cm
National Trust, on loan at the Bodleian Library, MS. Wilkinson dep. a. 14, fol. 62/XIV.48/plate 77

landscape that had shaped the important site of Abydos since the beginning of Egyptian history.[5] By showing themselves worshipping their predecessors, Sety and Ramesses stressed their legitimacy in an ancient lineage of powerful kings.

The fragments of Ramesses' list were discovered, excavated and copied by William John Bankes during his second voyage through Egypt in 1818 (see p. 101). Bankes did not remove the Abydos king list, partly owing to his ambivalent attitude towards breaking up intact monuments for the sake of collecting.[6] Made up of half a dozen separate pieces, the list was cut out by the French consul-general Jean-François Mimaut (1774–1837) and taken to France in 1837. His collection, including the king list, was acquired by the British Museum in the same year.

The list's surviving part contains sections of three rows of cartouches.[7] The upper row lists the relatively short-lived kings of the Seventh and Eighth Dynasties. The middle row names kings from Senwosret II (Twelfth Dynasty) to Ramesses II (Nineteenth Dynasty), but it omits Sobekneferu, the last ruler of the Twelfth Dynasty (a woman), all the kings of the Second Intermediate Period when Egypt was not a unified kingdom, the female pharaoh Hatshepsut, and the Eighteenth Dynasty monarchs between Amenhotep III and Horemheb (the Amarna Period, see p. 158). By omitting the kings of the Intermediate Period, female rulers and the 'heretic' Amarna royalty, Ramesses provides us with his own view of history and who he considered to be legitimate kings. The bottom row gives the two alternating names of Ramesses II.

The king list was of such importance that Champollion requested an 'exact' copy of the inscriptions. Bankes refused, for he was furious that Champollion had not admitted seeing Bankes's written insertion of the name Cleopatra on a copy of the Philae obelisk (see p. 115). A few years later, but before its final removal, Champollion was able to inspect the king list himself during his journey to Egypt.

PUSHING BACK HISTORY

It had not been widely understood in Europe that Egypt's civilisation was much older than that of classical Greece or Rome. Referring to the work on chronology by the Egyptian historian Manetho (third century BCE), Champollion used the Turin Royal Canon and the Abydos king list to push back Egyptian history by thousands of years.[8] His early dates for Egyptian civilisation contributed to a nineteenth-century secular movement that portrayed claims about resurrection, miracles and the historical reliability of the Bible as hostile to science and progress. This put him at odds with those who insisted on making Egypt a mere player in Christianity's grand narrative.[9] The Church was incensed by arguments that used 'pagan' carvings to contradict the truth of the Scriptures. The reactionary king of France Charles X introduced notorious legislation against sacrilege in 1825, which encouraged an atmosphere of Catholic intolerance that would affect work on Egyptian chronology.

The ceiling of the temple of Dendera, north of Thebes, was decorated with one such controversial inscription, known as the Zodiac of Dendera, which had been discovered and drawn by Napoleon's *savants* (fig. 91). Some scholars had attributed its inscriptions to pre-classical antiquity. But Champollion, studying drawings of the ceiling, used his readings of the Greek epithet *autokrator* ('the absolute ruler'), and the names of Tiberius Claudius and Nero to establish that the reliefs of the temple were sculpted during the Roman period. Ironically, these readings initially improved Champollion's standing among monarchists and the clergy as they implied that the temple, and thus also the Zodiac, dated from Greco-Roman times, eliminating its challenge to religious orthodoxy.

When Champollion entered the buried temple at Dendera from its roof on 16 November 1828, and gazed at the ruined ceiling, he discovered that

91
Marble copy of the Zodiac of Dendera. Vivant Denon and other *savants* drew the zodiac with as much care as the darkness, heat and discomfort allowed. A wax model was created one-third of the original's size, from which an engraving was made and published in 1804. This reproduction was completed later and exhibited at the 1819 Paris Salon, shortly before the arrival of the original in Paris.
Paris, France, 1819
Marble, H. 112.5 cm, W. 112.5 cm, D. 5.5 cm
Fitzwilliam Museum, E.1.1862

92 (facing page, top)
Box of Ptahmes with hieroglyphic texts and images of funerary servants and the four sons of Horus. The object was acquired by Champollion on his trip to Egypt and still bears his identification marks.
Egypt, 18th Dynasty, 1550–1295 BCE
Wood, H. 39.5 cm, W. 24 cm, D. 21 cm
Musée du Louvre, N 2692

the cartouches that the *savants'* drawing had shown with the epithet *autokrator* were, in fact, empty. The members of the Commission had added the word later, thinking they had overlooked it when in the field. Nonetheless, Champollion concluded that the decadent style of carving was typical of the Greco-Roman period. His reputation as the saviour of Christian belief deeply troubled Champollion. As he later announced to his friends, 'they would soon change their minds' once he started applying his alphabet to 'monuments whose antiquity will frighten them'.

IN EGYPT AT LAST

Champollion had become friends with the Pisan professor Ippolito Rosellini (1800–1843) in whose company he visited the Italian peninsula to look at

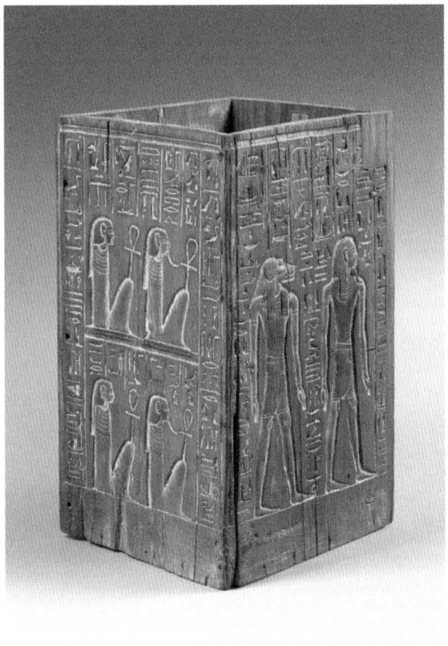

Egyptian monuments. The two men planned a joint expedition to Egypt with the aim of accurately recording reliefs and inscriptions and collecting objects through excavation.[10] These excavations were to be carried out by Champollion and Rosellini, each on behalf of his own government, 'on land chosen by draw'. Champollion arrived in Alexandria on 18 August 1828 and remained in Egypt for a year and a half. He returned to France on 6 December 1829, with a hundred pieces acquired for the national museum that was to become the Louvre (fig. 92).[11] These still bear the marks he added for identification.

The Franco-Tuscan expedition visited many monuments Champollion knew from drawings and descriptions, such as the temple of Dendera and the tomb of king Sety I (fig. 93). When Sety's tomb was discovered by

93 (below and right)
Inscribed fragment from a pillar of the tomb of Sety I. A later ink graffito reads 'the one who protects Maat', which perhaps identifies the depicted goddess.
Valley of the Kings, 19th Dynasty, 1294–1279 BCE
Limestone, H. 50 cm, W. 39 cm, D. 21 cm
British Museum, EA884
Donated by Colonel T P Thompson

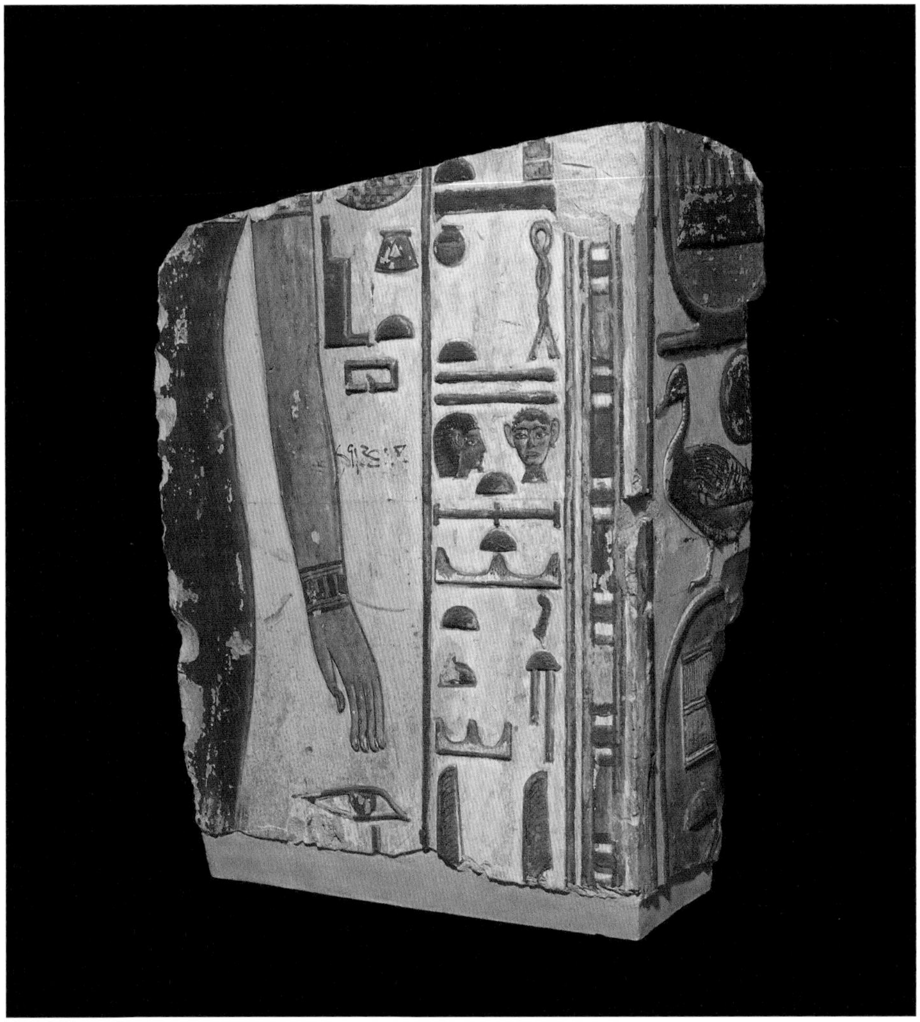

Giovanni Battista Belzoni (1778–1823) on 17 October 1817, it was believed to be the tomb of Psamtek I, but Champollion correctly attributed it to Ramesses' father, pharaoh Sety I.[12] Its beautifully coloured reliefs had been recorded by Salt's party years earlier (see p. 126).[13] Eight drawings are annotated by Salt as work done by Alessandro Ricci, who travelled with Bankes and Salt and would join the Franco-Tuscan expedition. As Belzoni stated, Ricci practised hieroglyphs for some time before starting to copy the reliefs in the tomb of Sety I.

The decipherment of hieroglyphs made the fundamental difference between what had been discovered previously and what the Franco-Tuscan expedition could and did achieve. Previous scholars had reproduced inscriptions with the maximum possible fidelity, but Champollion and Rosellini held the keys to interpretation (fig. 94). Champollion, therefore, considered his 1828–9 expedition to Egypt a follow-up to Napoleon's own expedition, the drawings from which he often criticised as inaccurate.[14]

The members of the expedition shared all their results, according to the official agreement which stated that the two directors should obtain 'two identical sets of drawings and notes'. Stored at Pisa, several of these

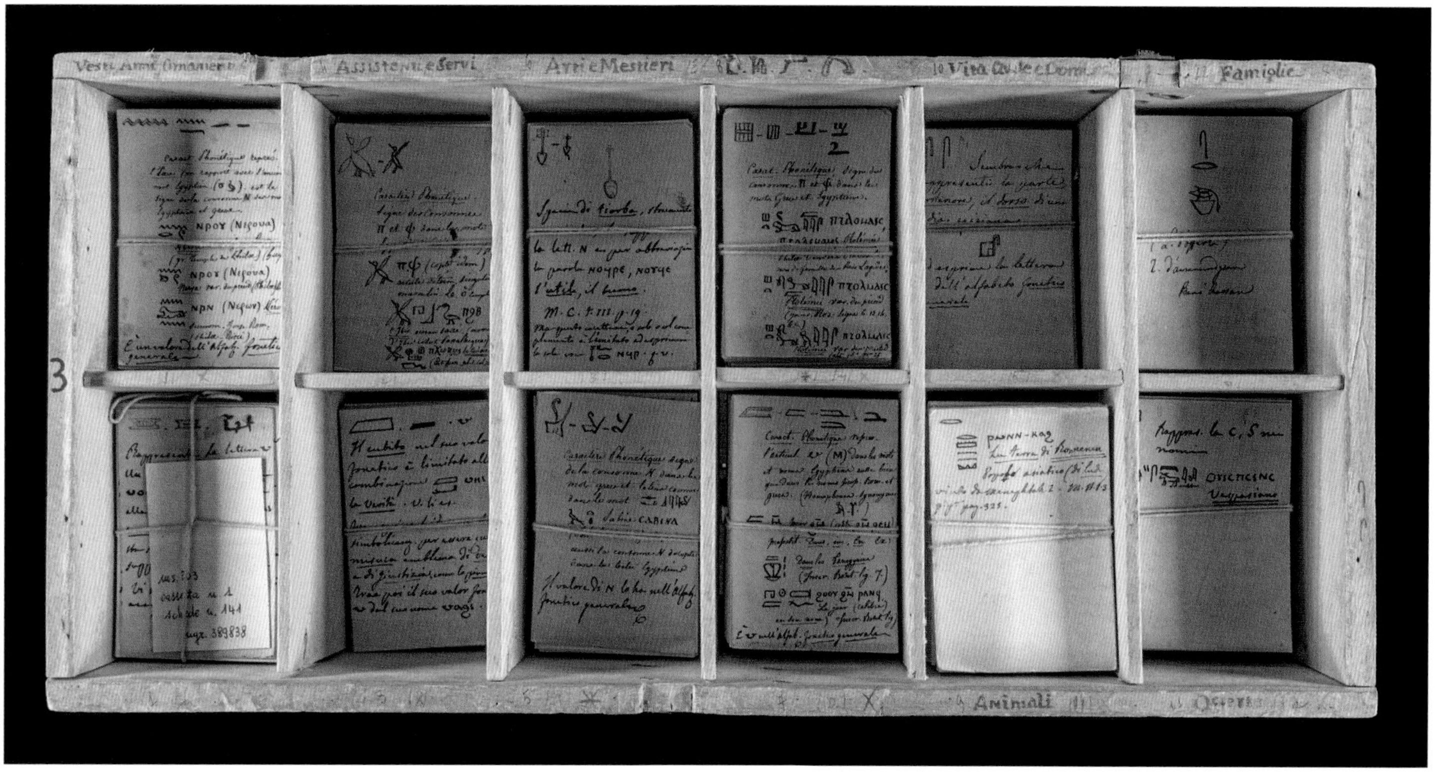

94 (facing page)
Box with filing cards recording Ippolito Rosellini's work on his dictionary
Pisa, Italy, after 1828
Wood and paper, H. 11 cm, W. 55.7 cm, D. 25.2 cm
Pisa University Library, Box 3

95 (right)
Drawings of birds, identified by their hieroglyphic names; by Giuseppe Angelelli (1803–1844), 'copied from M. Bertin'
Egypt, 1828–9
Paper, H. 30.1 cm, W. 22.7 cm
Pisa University Library, Ms.272-c133

drawings are inscribed with the signature of their Tuscan author followed by the words 'copied from' and the name of the French artist (fig. 95).[15] These copies expanded Champollion's collections of signs and provided him with further evidence from which to draft his grammar and dictionary, both of which were edited by his brother and published posthumously (see figs 87–88). On 1 January 1829 Champollion wrote to M. Dacier that there was nothing to add to his alphabet as it could be applied successfully to all the monuments of Egypt.

APPROACHING ANCIENT EGYPTIAN POETRY

Richard Bruce Parkinson

> Champollion discovered the ancient language of Egypt, but his successors were able to reconstruct its grammar and syntax and to translate the many masterpieces uncovered from its literature. It is up to the younger generation of Egyptologists to establish its poetics.
>
> *Baron Textor de Ravisi*[16]

On 22–3 July 1828, en route to Egypt, Jean-François Champollion saw the collection of the provincial official and collector François Sallier (1764–1831) in Aix-en-Provence, France. He realised that it contained 'non-funerary' manuscripts, including 'two rolls containing types of odes or litanies in praise of a pharaoh'.[17] One text was a poetic account of the Battle of Qadesh (see p. 146), but the other was *The Teaching of King Amenemhat*, a work composed in Middle Egyptian which is much more fictional and dramatic (fig. 96). In this, the dead king Amenemhat I appears to his son, Hamlet-like, and describes in despair how he was murdered. The fact that a king's name featured on the papyrus was presumably why it caught Champollion's attention, but beyond this chronological interest, it opened up wider views to Egyptologists, including poetry.

Classical accounts had implied that Egyptian writings were either historical, or hermetic 'sacred writings' (see p. 38), and so the first 'hierologists' were not expecting to find anything resembling 'literature', which everyone in Europe assumed to have begun with the Greeks. The French Egyptologist Emmanuel de Rougé (1811–1872) first spoke of the possibility of literature in 1852, when he described a roll with the scribe Inene's copy of the Late Egyptian *Tale of the Two Brothers* as 'the first sample of Egyptian genius in a purely literary genre', and 'a work of pure imagination' (see fig. 191).[18] His phrase 'pure imagination' reflects contemporaneous ideas of literature as something autonomous and unrelated to other mundane aspects of culture.

Other comparisons were also influential: the wine merchant and Egyptologist François Chabas (1817–1882) was struck by one text's similarity with the biblical story of Potiphar,[19] and Gaston Maspero (1846–1916) noted similarities with the Arabic *Thousand and One Nights*.[20] In 1857 the British Museum curator Samuel Birch summarised attitudes to Egyptian writings, which he described as 'peculiarly monumental', but he admitted that 'even

96

The Teaching of King Amenemhat. In this fictional work, the dead king dramatically describes how he was murdered by his bodyguard and instructs his son to trust no one. Although the poem provides a vivid picture of kingship during the Middle Kingdom, it may have been composed later.
Egypt, 19th Dynasty, 1295–1186 BCE
Papyrus, H. 23.4 cm, W. 30 cm, D. 0.2 cm
British Museum, EA10182,1

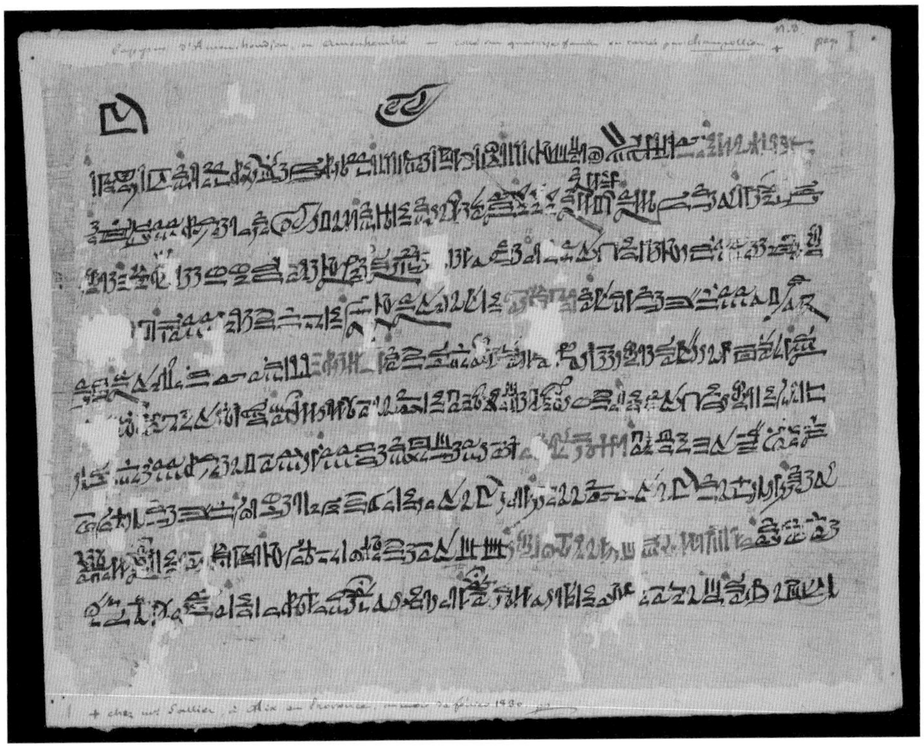

works of imagination were extant in Pharaonic time'.[21] As late as 1872, Maspero could comment that any association of 'these two words *Egypt* and *literature*' was still unexpected.[22] Nevertheless, there was a growing awareness that some texts were written in verse and could be lyric poetry.[23]

In 1865–6, the judge Charles Wycliffe Goodwin (1817–1878) produced a study of what is widely regarded as the masterpiece of Egyptian poetry, *The Tale of Sinuhe*, describing it as 'an Egyptian tale of four thousand years ago' (fig. 97, see p. 143). He considered it to be 'short and simple' with 'little claim upon the attention of the modern reader, plied with sensation novels, except its antiquity', even though the poem is now regarded as one of the most stylistically and psychologically complex works to survive from the ancient world. He recognised that the owner must have 'delighted' to read such works; another claim was that even the prophet Abraham might 'have heard Saneha [Sinuhe] talked of'.[24] His rather dismissive judgements were echoed by some reviewers, although one commented enthusiastically that it was 'curious to be brought face to face with the real life and actual thoughts of a man living in so remote an age'.[25]

These first readers of Egyptian literary texts saw them as almost 'pre-historic', and their approaches betray a lack of engagement with the

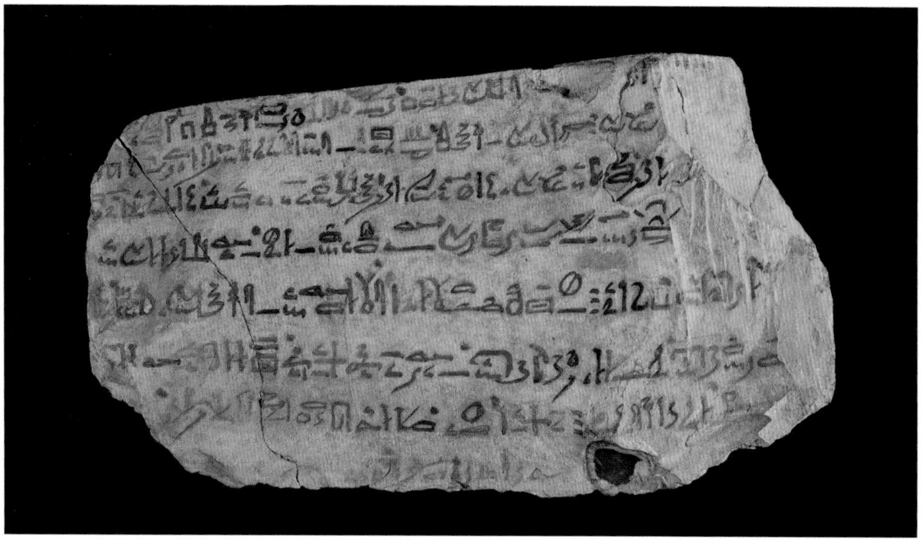

97
Ostracon with the final stanza of *The Tale of Sinuhe*. While on an expedition to Libya, Sinuhe learns of the king's sudden death (1908 BCE) and flees. He travels eastwards, leaving Egypt, and eventually reaches Palestine. As he builds a seemingly successful life abroad, he in fact remains restless as he longs for home.
Thebes, 19th Dynasty, 1295–1186 BCE
Limestone, H. 17 cm, W. 29 cm, D. 5 cm
British Museum, EA5629

cultural otherness of these texts, as was common for most non-Western writings: in 1835 the politician Thomas Macaulay had written that 'I have never found one [orientalist] who could deny that a single shelf of a good European library was worth the whole native literature of India and Arabia'.[26] Discussions of ancient texts were inevitably part of the dynamics of colonisation, and Enlightenment Europe often denied cultural difference by regarding non-Western ancient cultures as primitive ancestors, focusing on narratives of progress and the triumph of science. There was also a sense that such texts must be rescued from their original cultures, and that they required acquisition, transformation and representation by modern (European) scholars before they could be properly appreciated. The French decipherment of the hieroglyphic script ensured that the core location of Egyptian philology was not Egypt but Europe, and the poems were judged – unsympathetically – in assimilative terms of European expectations. Thus, the Oxford professor of Egyptology Francis Llewellyn Griffith (1862–1934) remarked that 'the educated Egyptian had no more subtlety than a modern boy of fifteen, or an intelligent English rustic of a century ago',[27] and in Adolf Erman's (1854–1937) contemporaneous *Life in Ancient Egypt*, literary style was linked to the 'unimaginative' character of the ancient and modern Egyptians, which was in turn ascribed to their 'monotonous' surroundings; Egyptian writings were often characterised as 'childish', 'deficient' or 'Oriental'.[28]

Such early colonialist approaches left little space for empathetic engagement, despite the rapid progress of philology. Although critics acknowledged that literary texts were distinctive, they often treated them exactly like other types of historical document. Even at the beginning of the

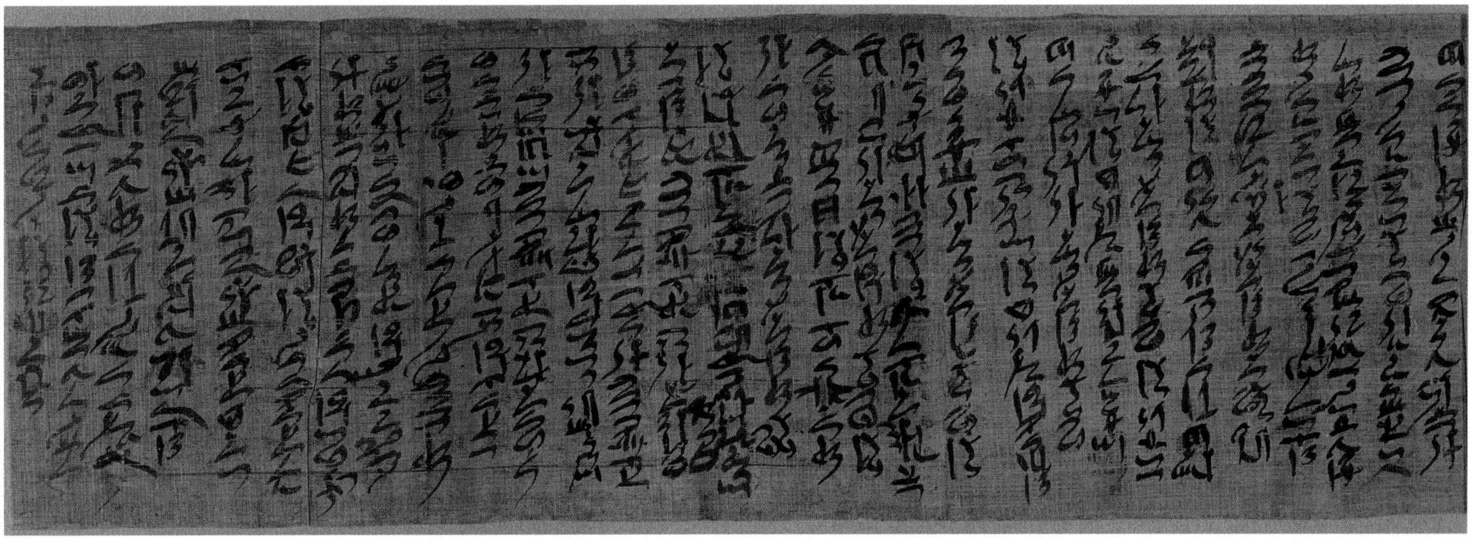

98
Papyrus with the final sections of *The Dialogue of a Man and his Ba*
Egypt, 12th Dynasty, 1985–1795 BCE
Papyrus, H. 16.4 cm, W. 350.5 cm
Ägyptisches Museum und Papyrussammlung, Staatliche Museen zu Berlin, P. Berlin 3024

twentieth century, literature in general was still often considered in relation to factual causes, such as the historical context – and thus literature itself required little explicit definition. In this general context, Erman produced a comprehensive and groundbreaking anthology of Egyptian literature in 1923, including lyrics and commemorative and religious texts as well as fictional narratives. His masterly survey of the known genres revealed a rich range of forms, but the unfamiliar styles of writing remained problematic. He claimed a threefold significance for these works, in a notable order: first, their age; second, their 'insight into an active intellectual life'; and third, an insight into ancient Egyptian 'poetry'.[29] Around the same time, the British Egyptologist T. Eric Peet (1882–1934) commented in a comparative study that 'there is more poetry in each line of [Keats's *Ode to a Nightingale*] than in the whole of the Egyptian lyric' of *The Dialogue of a Man and his Ba* (fig. 98).[30] Yet the *Dialogue* is one of the most emotionally transparent and lyrical works to survive; a man in despair at the suffering of life speaks:

Death is to me today
  like a sick man's recovery,
  like going out after confinement.
Death is to me today
  like the smell of myrrh,
  like sitting under a sail on a windy day.
Death is to me today
  like the smell of flowers,
  like sitting on the shore of Drunkenness.

Death is to me today
like a well trodden path,
like a man coming home from an expedition.
Death is to me today
like the sky clearing,
like a man grasping what he did not know before.
Death is to me today
like a man longing to see home,
having spent many years taken in captivity.

Despite their reservations about literary quality, these pioneering scholars were aware that they saw the works only in part, and Peet also perceptively remarked that 'as long as our ignorance is so great, our attitude towards the criticism of these ancient literatures must be one of extreme humility'.[31] We know little about the sound of the words (apart from the consonants), and all the visceral effects of poetry are inaccessible. Literature in any culture is a complex phenomenon that is hard to define, and poetry is often, as the poet Robert Frost (1874–1963) famously remarked, what gets lost in translation.

Modern Romantic expectations that poetry is the spontaneous utterances of an individual author have also influenced analyses. *The Words of Khakheperreseneb* is a densely meditative monologue from the late Middle Kingdom, in which the author remarks:

If only I had unknown utterances
and extraordinary verses,
in a new language that does not pass away,
free from repetition,
without a verse of worn-out speech
spoken by the ancestors!

This has often been read as a spontaneous outpouring of personal despondency or an individual's distinctive ideas about literary conventions, because only one manuscript was preserved on an Eighteenth Dynasty writing board from Thebes (fig. 99). However, another copy was soon identified on an ostracon in the Cairo Museum, showing that this poem had been an established part of the literary canon, and as such was used as a set text in scribal education; further copies on other writing boards have recently been identified.[32] The poem cannot be understood intuitively from a modern viewpoint or in the framework of modern European genres. With the identification of new manuscripts and texts, and with new discoveries being made in excavations and museum collections, the range of Egyptian

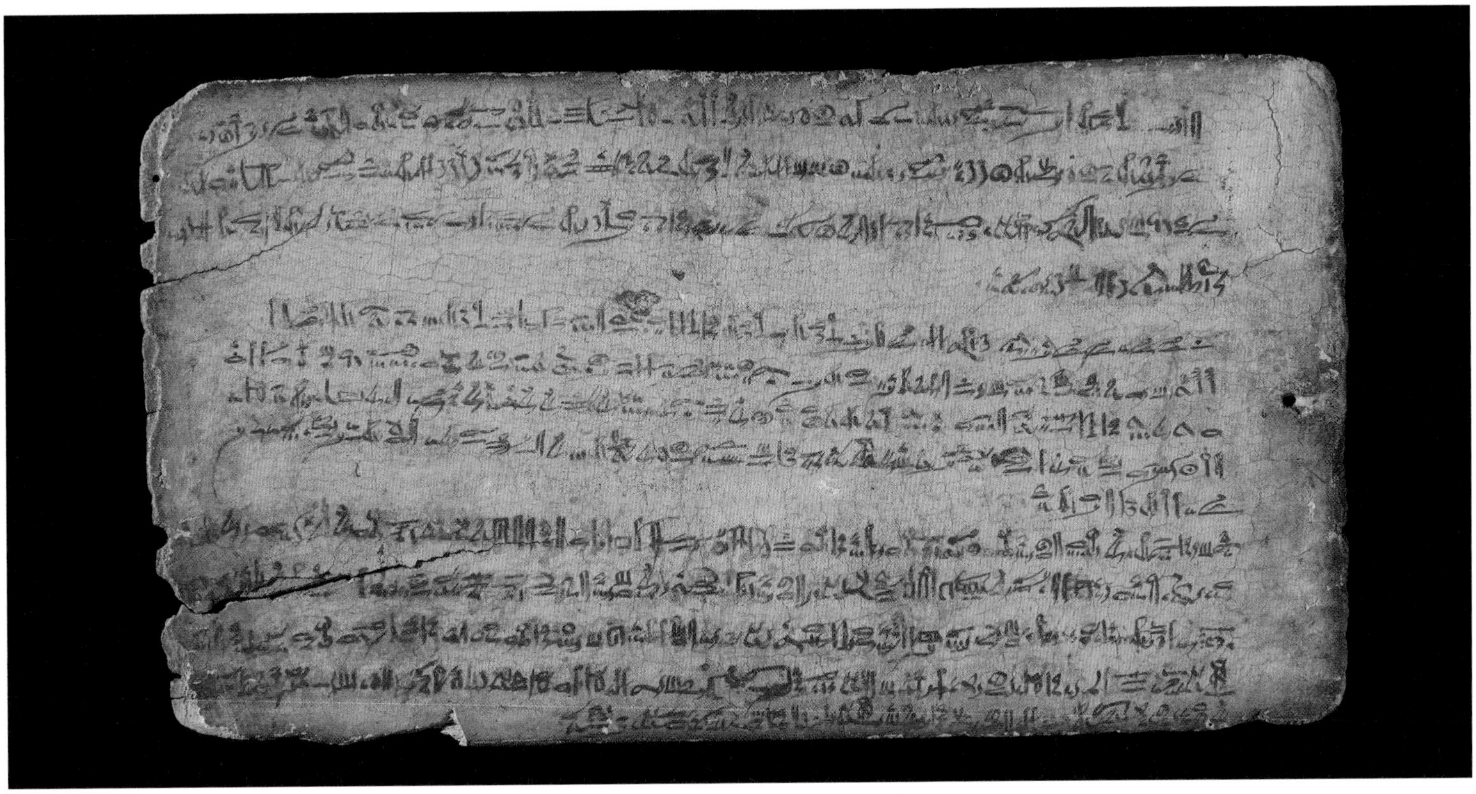

99
Writing-board inscribed with
The Words of Khakheperreseneb
Egypt, early to mid-18th Dynasty,
1550–1350 BCE
Wood and plaster, H. 30.2 cm, W. 55.6 cm,
D. 0.9 cm
British Museum, EA5645

literature is emerging as broader and more diverse than Champollion imagined – a self-reflexive, intertextually complex corpus of works including, for example, love songs and works of entertainment and humour, as well as dramatic compositions (but no plays), and poems of mixed emotional tonality (but without the genres of comedy and tragedy).

The differences in form and style from European writings have often encouraged Egyptologists to regard these texts primarily as sources of grammar, lexicography, or cultural and political history. Academics rarely engaged with the texts' aesthetic or emotional qualities, possibly in part because they were, in the words of the great Marxist critic Raymond Williams, 'trained to detachment … consistently abstracting and generalizing'.[33] They have often seemed unresponsive to forces such as the Arabic word '*tarab* (delight)', which were arguably integral to the poems' creation and their original impact. For example, with the lyric quoted above, published discussions of the verse 'like sitting under a sail on a windy day' concentrate on the lexicography of the single word 'sail', overlooking the visceral impact of this simple, sublime and highly evocative line. However, scholars such as the Swiss Egyptologist Antonio Loprieno (b. 1955) have championed the use of modern literary and cultural theory to deepen our engagement

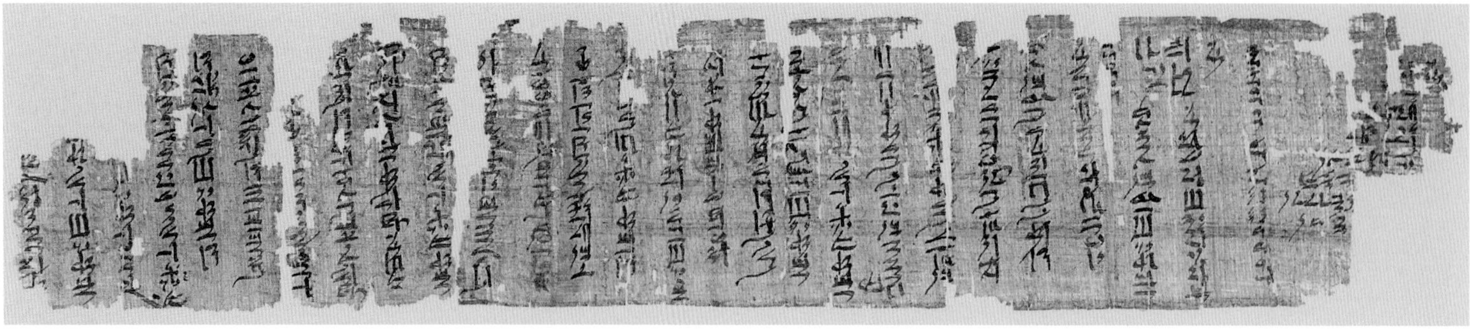

with these texts, although even these approaches were developed primarily for European literature and so their usage can risk being Eurocentric. A renewed study of the manuscripts has increased awareness of the poems as material artefacts, shaped by various cultural forces, which continually changed their form and meaning through time. Performances of translations have also provided a way of reimagining and communicating the emotional and dramatic aspects that these works had for their intended audiences.[34]

The poems are still usually read within a specialist Egyptological context, and Americo-European reactions to these poems outside the academic community have often been profoundly superficial and trivialising. The 1954 film *The Egyptian* was a dull Hollywood travesty of *The Tale of Sinuhe*, despite its lavish staging and archaeologically informed design. A radically different reception can be seen in the works of modern Egyptian writers and artists: Naguib Mahfouz (1911–2006) produced a romantically evocative rewriting of *Sinuhe* as a short story in 1942, and in 1970, the Egyptian director Shadi `Abd al-Salam (1930–1986) created a mesmerically poetic film of *The Tale of the Eloquent Peasant* (although significantly he had to use European translations to write the script) (fig. 100).[35] These modern versions reveal the works' potential to be part of a living tradition of high art.

The ancient writers hoped that their words would endure better than 'pyramids of bronze, / with stelae of iron', and would 'speak to the future' (see fig. 142).[36] The words of the poets often mediated between the ideals of their society and individual experiential reality in a manner that can still, in the words of the literary critic Wolfgang Iser, 'confront people with themselves'.[37] Egyptian literature is now regularly included in such canonical series as the Oxford World's Classics, and in anthologies of world literature: our dialogue with these texts is expanding.[38] In 1878 Baron Textor de Ravisi had imagined Egyptian poetry in a predictably orientalistic manner as 'this beautiful mummy'; however, perhaps now his 'Sleeping Beauty'[39] is finally starting to wake and be heard by new audiences across the world.

100
Papyrus with *The Tale of the Eloquent Peasant,* a story of a peasant who is robbed and receives justice through his elegant speeches
Thebes, 12th Dynasty, 1985–1795 BCE
Papyrus, H. 14.3 cm, W. 72.5 cm, D. 0.2 cm
British Museum, EA10274

The Tale of Sinuhe

'For now God has acted so as to be gracious to one
with whom He was offended,
whom He led astray to another country.
Today, he is satisfied.
A fugitive takes flight because of his surroundings;
but my reputation is in the Residence.
A creeping man creeps off because of hunger;
but I give bread to my neighbour.
A man leaves his land because of nakedness;
but I have bright linen, white linen.
A man runs off because of the lack of someone to send;
but I am plentiful of serfs.
Good is my house, spacious my dwelling place;
and memory of me is in the palace.
Whatever god fated this flight
– be gracious, and bring me home!
Surely You will let me see the place where my
heart still stays!
What matters more than my being buried in the land
where I was born?
This is my prayer for help, that the good event befall,
that God give me grace!
May He act in this way, to make well the end of someone
whom He made helpless,
His heart sore for someone He compelled
to live in a foreign country!
Does this mean that He is so gracious today as to hear
the prayer of someone far off
who shall then turn from where he has roamed the earth
to the place from which he was carried away?
May the king of Egypt be gracious to me,
that I may live on his grace!
May I greet the Mistress of the Land who is in his palace,
and hear her children's messages!
So shall my limbs grow young again, for now old age
has fallen:
weakness has overtaken me,
my eyes are heavy, and my arms weak;
my legs have ceased to follow, and my heart is weary;
I am near to dying.
May they lead me to the cities of eternity!
May I follow the Lady of All,
and then she shall tell me that all is well with her children!
May she pass eternity above me!

Now the Majesty of the Dual King Kheperkare was told
about the state of affairs in which I was.
And his Majesty sent to me,
with bounty of royal giving,
to gladden the heart of this humble servant
like any ruler of a country
and the royal children who were in his palace let me hear
their messages.'

The official Sinuhe fled to Canaan (present-day Palestine) after hearing about the sudden death of king Amenemhat I. Leaving Egypt behind around 1875 BCE, Sinuhe became an important local chief successfully fighting many enemies, but here, as an old man, he prays for a return to his homeland.[40]

CHAPTER 4

Rediscovering ancient Egypt

PHARAOH AND EMPIRE

Ilona Regulski

As the decipherment of hieroglyphs became a political and imperial undertaking, stories of an ancient society with colonial ambitions of its own began to emerge. In 1828, on his way to Egypt, Champollion discovered a papyrus with the poem of Pentaour recounting the Battle of Qadesh in the collection of François Sallier (1764–1831) in Aix-en-Provence (fig. 101, see p. 157). He failed to recognise the literary character of the text; for him the importance lay in its historical information. In one of the ancient world's largest chariot battles, fought beside the Orontes River in 1275 BCE, Ramesses II sought to seize Syria from the Hittites and recapture the city of Qadesh.[1] With neither side achieving an outright victory, the battle led to the world's first recorded peace treaty, and the only one from the Near East for which both sides have survived (fig. 102).

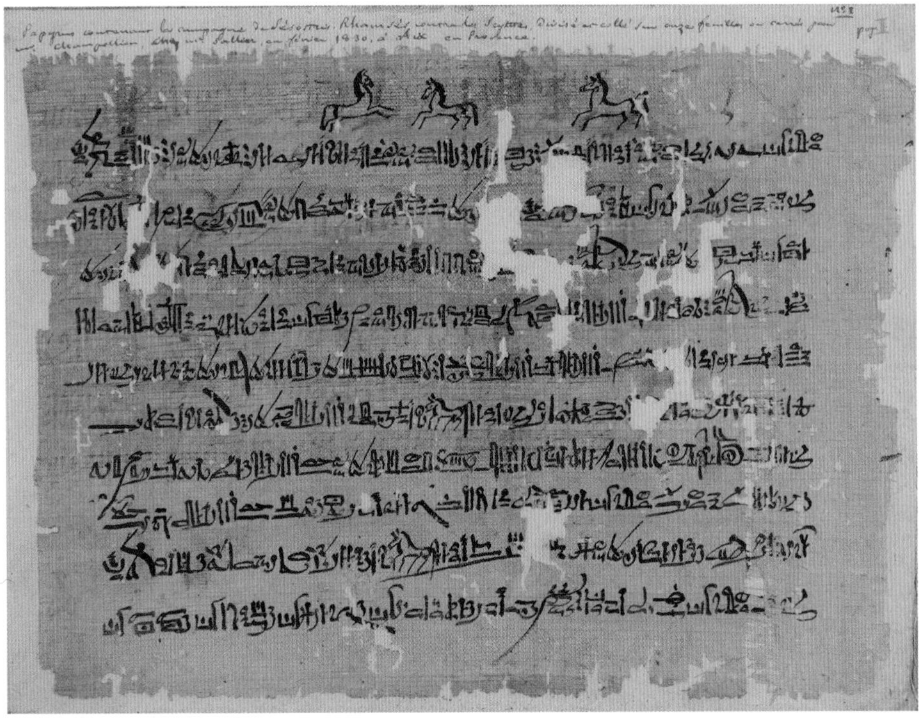

101 (below left)
Papyrus Sallier III featuring the poem of the Battle of Qadesh. After the death of François Sallier in 1831, his collection of papyri was sold to the British Museum; a note states that they were 'stuck onto fourteen squared sheets by Champollion at M. Sallier's in the month of February 1830'.
Egypt, 19th Dynasty, 1274–1186 BCE
Papyrus, H. 21 cm, W. 29.8 cm, D. 0.2 cm
British Museum, EA10181,1

102 (facing page, top)
Cuneiform tablet with peace treaty between Ramesses II and Hattusili III, following the Battle of Qadesh
Bogazkale, 19th Dynasty, *c.* 1275 BCE
Clay, H. 3.9 cm (smallest piece), H. 6.9 cm (largest piece)
Staatliche Museen zu Berlin – Vorderasiatisches Museum, inv. nos VAT 06207, VAT 06207bis, VAT 13572

103 (facing page, bottom)
Watercolour of Ramesses II receiving suppliants after the Battle of Qadesh, from the Great Hall of the Temple at Abu Simbel. The painting is by Salvatore Cherubini (1797–1869), one of the five illustrators of the Franco-Tuscan expedition.
Egypt, 1828–9
Paper, H. 65 cm, W. 140 cm
Pisa University Library, Ms_300_2_c130-132

Champollion read the names of fifteen foreign nations, including Ionians, Lycians, Ethiopians and Arabs, and uncovered information about the chiefs who had been taken hostage and the tribute required from the defeated nations (fig. 103). This enabled him to identify a pair of hieroglyphic signs used to specify the names of foreign countries and individuals given in a foreign language.

SECURING BORDERS

The ancient Egyptians perceived the Asiatics in the east and the Nubians in the south as the two opposite poles of a hostile world outside the Nile valley. In the Egyptian worldview, they represented chaos and disorder, and their subjugation became a popular topic as soon as social status was expressed in writing and iconography (fig. 104).

To patrol the deserts to the east, Egyptians recruited a semi-nomadic people whose homeland ranged from Egypt to the Red Sea. Their duties encompassed the security of desert roads and wealthy institutions such as

temples and cemeteries, which were often located at the desert edge, and they were referred to as the 'Medjau'. The term became a general designation for desert police, and such groups later included Egyptians (fig. 105).

To the south, the ancient Egyptians ruled Lower Nubia (ancient Wawat) as a conquered province. Kings from the Twelfth Dynasty (1985–1795 BCE) protected their own access to highly valued African resources such as gold, valuable stones and minerals, as well as sub-Saharan trade goods, by erecting a series of massive fortresses in Nubia. Each of these was at first staffed by rotating garrisons.[2] Functionaries from all branches of the administration were part of the occupation of Nubia, but best represented were the departments that secured order, such as the police and army. Intef-Dedu was a commander in the army of Senwosret I and recorded the subjection of Lower Nubia on a pair of stelae set up in the temple at Buhen on the west bank of the Second Cataract of the Nile.

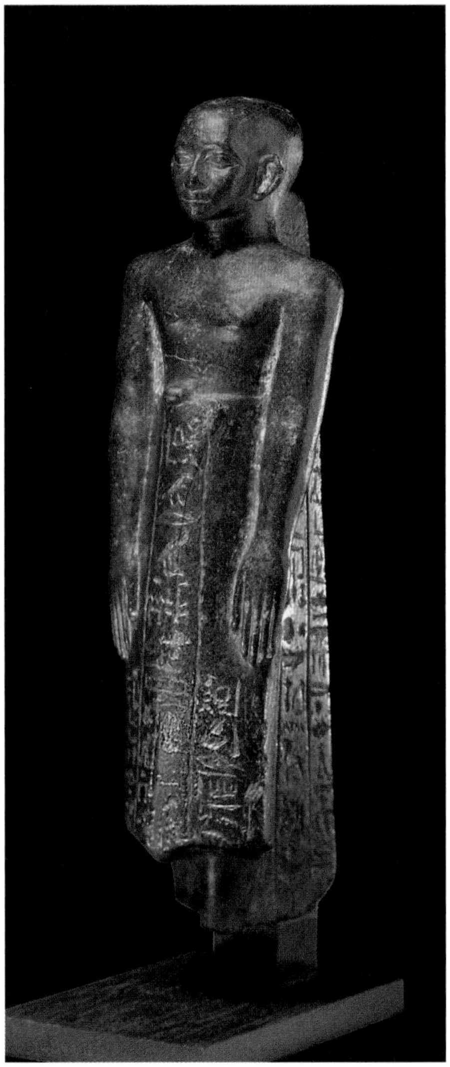

Investigating one of the stelae *in situ* in 1828, Champollion noted that it was damaged and some of the hieroglyphs copied by his predecessors in 1819 had already gone (fig. 106).[3] The stela had been assigned to the French but was loaded onto Rosellini's boat by mistake and ended up in the Museo Egizio in Florence (E2540).[4] The second stela was donated to the British Museum by Sir Henry George Lyons in 1894 (EA1177).

As time passed and Egypt's rule expanded southwards, soldiers began to settle more permanently in the Nubian fortresses and engaged with the local communities (figs 107–109).[5] The fortress of Buhen was abandoned after the New Kingdom but isolated communities continued to reside there until the waters of Lake Nasser submerged the site in 1964.

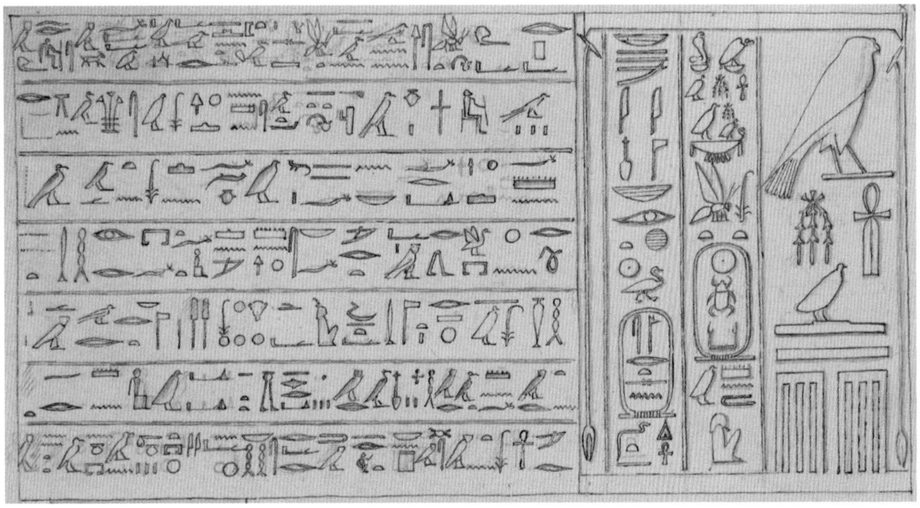

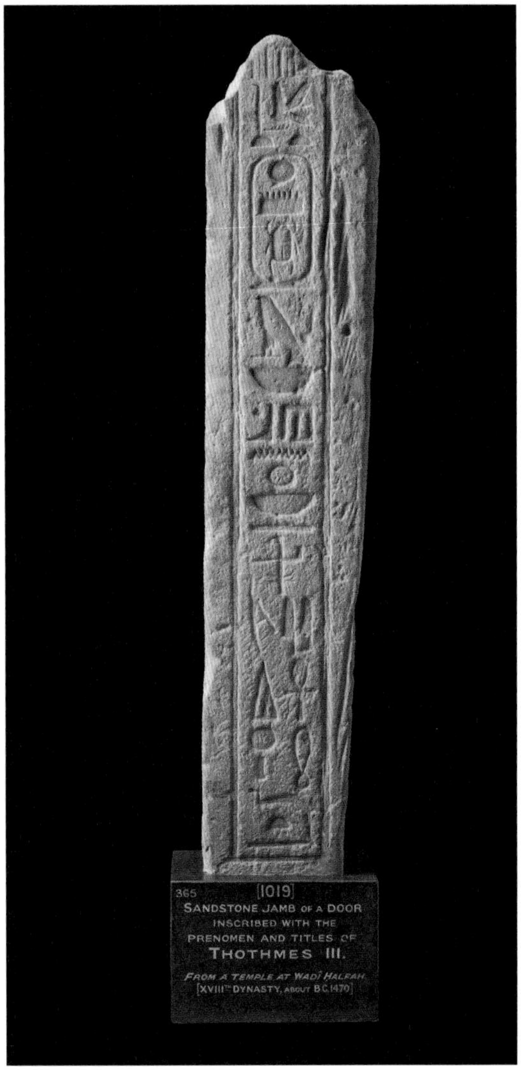

104 (facing page, top right)
Label showing king Den during the 'First occasion of smiting the East'. Such labels could be attached to goods or boxes containing linen.
Abydos, 1st Dynasty, *c.* 2985 BCE
Ivory, H. 4.5 cm, W. 5.3 cm, D. 0.3 cm
British Museum, EA55586

105 (facing page, bottom right)
Statue of Nebhepetra, senior lector priest and guard at the temple of Amun-Ra in Karnak. Autobiographical information on the back pillar of the statue reveals that Nebhepetra was also a 'Medjau'.
Thebes, 12th Dynasty, *c.* 1900–1800 BCE
Serpentine, H. 19.5 cm, W. 6.4 cm, D. 5.9 cm
British Museum, EA83921

106 (facing page, bottom left)
Drawing of one of the two inscribed stelae of the official Intef-Dedu from the north temple at Buhen. It is attributed to Henry William Beechey but Alessandro Ricci could also be the creator.
Buhen, 1819
Paper, H. 18.3 cm, W. 22.3 cm
National Trust, on loan at the Dorset History Centre, D-BKL/H/J/6/12/C/5

107 (above left)
Redware pottery bowl
Buhen, 12th Dynasty, 1985–1795 BCE
Ceramic, H. 9.2 cm, diam. 13.6 cm
British Museum, EA65695
Donated by the Egypt Exploration Society

108 (above right)
Drabware pottery bowl
Buhen, Middle Kingdom to early Second Intermediate Period, 2055–1600 BCE
Ceramic, H. 4.7 cm, diam. 10.8 cm
British Museum, EA65701
Donated by the Egypt Exploration Society

109 (right)
Doorjamb bearing an incised hieroglyphic text including the name of Thutmose III
Buhen, 18th Dynasty, 1479–1425 BCE
Sandstone, H. 149 cm, W. 33.5 cm, D. 25 cm
British Museum, EA1019

REWRITING CONQUEST

Egypt's traditional enemies would eventually live up to their reputation and cause the destabilisation and fragmentation of the Egyptian state. By 1700 BCE west-Semitic rulers referred to as 'Hyksos' conquered Lower (northern) Egypt and extended their influence up the Nile from their capital at Avaris in the eastern Delta.[6] The term Hyksos is derived, via the Greek Ὑκσώς, from the ancient Egyptian expression *ḥḳꜣ-ḫꜣś.wt* (pronounced 'heqau khasut'), meaning 'rulers from foreign lands'. They were referred to by Champollion as 'Shepherd Kings', based on a later change in pronunciation of 'khasut' to 'Shasu', which was then understood to mean 'lord of shepherds'.[7] Champollion also spoke of them as 'Arabs', 'Bedouins' or 'Bedouin Arabs', emphasising that the Egyptians perceived them as foreign. Trying to reconstruct their place in history, Champollion understood that they had coexisted with indigenous rulers in the south and theorised extensively on the legitimacy of their rule (fig. 110).[8] It is now commonly accepted that the term Hyksos refers to individual foreign rulers of the Second Intermediate Period (1650–1550 BCE), rather than to a people (figs 111–113).

A period of warfare culminated in the defeat of the Hyksos in around 1650 BCE by Ahmose I, who reunited Egypt (fig. 114). In a letter to his brother dated 25 August 1824, Champollion remarked that Ahmose's cartouche is also present on the Abydos king list and that he should thus be added to the beginning of the Eighteenth Dynasty. One month later, Champollion changed his mind and moved Ahmose to the end of the Seventeenth Dynasty. We know now that it was in fact Ahmose's predecessor Kamose, last king of the Theban Seventeenth Dynasty, who fought decisive battles against the Hyksos and that Ahmose then made the final conquest and founded the Eighteenth Dynasty.[9] New evidence discovered in 2000 by a British Museum team at the site of Elkab provides evidence for an even more nuanced view of this period. The new inscription narrates how the most profound military threat in this southern region of Egypt came from the Kingdom of Kush, in present-day Sudan, and its allies, rather than from the Hyksos in the north.[10]

The epic scale of events during the Second Intermediate Period explains Egypt's aggressive invasions during the subsequent New Kingdom. Egypt's self-confidence was boosted, and violent interactions with traditional enemies became a literary topic. Poetry as well as monumental display celebrated how the great military leaders of Egypt expanded its territory through a series of successful battles.[11]

The numerous invasions of Libyan tribes between 1300 and 1200 BCE were equally traumatic as they brought invaders from an unexpected part of the ancient world. The distressing experience of war once again led to

FACING PAGE

110 (left)
Letter from Champollion to his brother
Turin, Italy, 4 September 1824
Paper
Archives départementales
de l'Isère, 185 J 18, fol. 30

111 (top right)
Fragment of a vase with the name of the Hyksos ruler Apepi
Tell el-Yahudiya, 15th Dynasty, *c.* 1555 BCE
Chert, H. 7.1 cm, W. 5.1 cm, D. 1.1 cm
British Museum, EA32069

112 (centre right)
Scarab inscribed with the name of the minor Hyksos ruler Yakubher
Egypt, 15th Dynasty, 1650–1550 BCE
Glazed steatite, H. 1 cm, W. 1.6 cm, D. 2.2 cm
British Museum, EA40741

113 (bottom right)
Scarab with name of the Hyksos king Kayan
Saqqara, 15th Dynasty, *c.* 1600 BCE
Glazed steatite, H. 1 cm, W. 1.4 cm, D. 2 cm
British Museum, EA30500

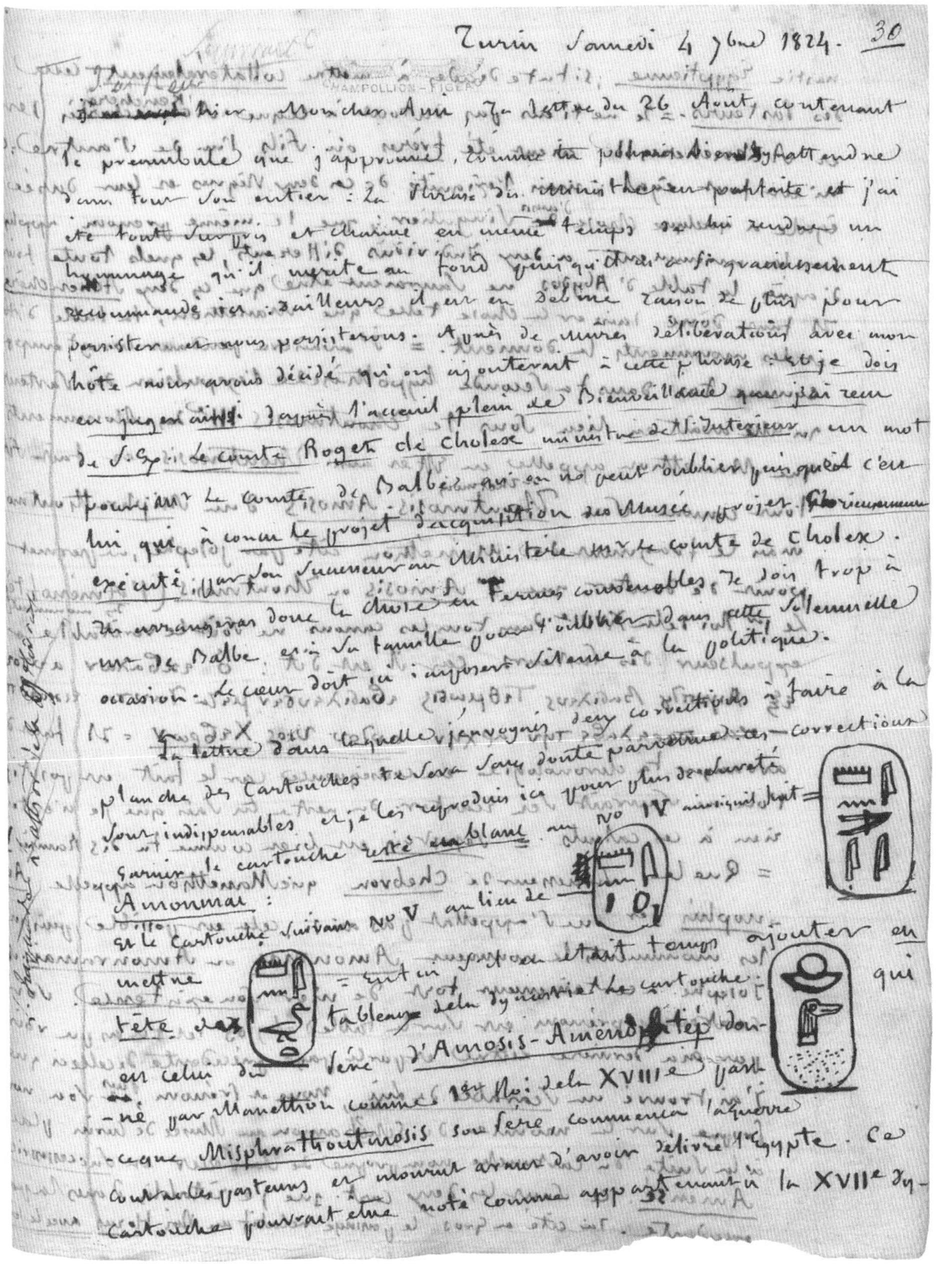
Turin Samedi 4 7bre 1824. 30

narrative representations of the conflicts being copied on temple walls and other monuments for centuries (fig. 115). It was during this time that Egypt's reigning monarch came to be identified by his palace, the 'Great House', or *pr-ꜥꜣ* (pronounced as 'Per-aa'), which evolved into the modern term 'pharaoh' (fig. 116).

As Egypt once again became riddled with conflict during the Third Intermediate Period (1069–747 BCE), its enemies either seized lands

114 (above)
Shabti of Ahmose; a rare representation of the warrior king and founder of the 18th Dynasty
Thebes, 18th Dynasty, *c.* 1550 BCE
Limestone, H. 28.8 cm, W. 8.2 cm, D. 6.5 cm
British Museum, EA32191

115 (left)
Casts of part of the northern exterior wall of the hypostyle hall in the temple of Karnak, recording king Sety I slaughtering the Libyan chief and trampling his people
Karnak, 1830–40s
Plaster, H. 95.5 cm, W. 70 cm (smallest piece), H. 90.4 cm, W. 139 cm (largest piece)
British Museum, EA91038,a, h, i

adjacent to its borders or weakened the bonds between the Egyptian king and his vassal rulers. From the eighth century BCE onwards, the country was frequently ruled by foreign empires, including those of Kush, Assyria and Persia. Piankhy's Victory Stela (fig. 117) elaborately recounts how the Kushites from the south reunified Lower Egypt and Upper Egypt during the Twenty-fifth Dynasty (747–656 BCE) and merged it with the Nubian state, creating a major power whose only rival in the Near East was Assyria.[12] The

116
Statue of Sety II holding a ram's head representing the god Amun. This is the only seated statue of Sety II and a rare example of a king seated with an emblem on his knees.
Thebes, 19th Dynasty, 1200–1194 BCE
Quartzite, H. 164 cm, W. 49 cm, D. 85 cm
British Museum, EA26

Kushites assimilated into society by reaffirming ancient Egypt's religious traditions and using its writing system. They also introduced a marked renaissance in pharaonic art.

The turbulent administrative, political and military developments in Egypt during the last thousand years BCE were bound up with changes in language. As the central government collapsed in the Third Intermediate Period (1069–747 BCE), hieratic developed in separate ways in different parts of the country. A cursive form of the administrative script developed into

117 (left)
Cast of Piankhy's Victory Stela from Gebel Barkal (Sudan), announcing Piankhy (747–716 BCE) as pharaoh of all Egypt. The stela highlights his divine kingship by naming him 'Son of Ra' (Ruler of Lower Egypt) and 'Beloved of Amun' (Ruler of Upper Egypt). The original is in the Egyptian Museum in Cairo.
Cairo, 1891
Plaster, H. 177 cm, W. 145.8 cm, D. 47.5 cm
British Museum, EA1121
Donated by the Government of the British Protectorate of Egypt

118 (facing page)
Papyrus with administrative text in late cursive hieratic. The sheets were purchased by Alexandre Louis Henry de Vaucelles (1798–1851) during his 1826 journey through Egypt.
Thebes, 25th Dynasty, 690–664 BCE
Papyrus, H. 35 cm, W. 70 cm (top), H. 35 cm, W. 152 cm (bottom)
British Museum, EA87512,1–2

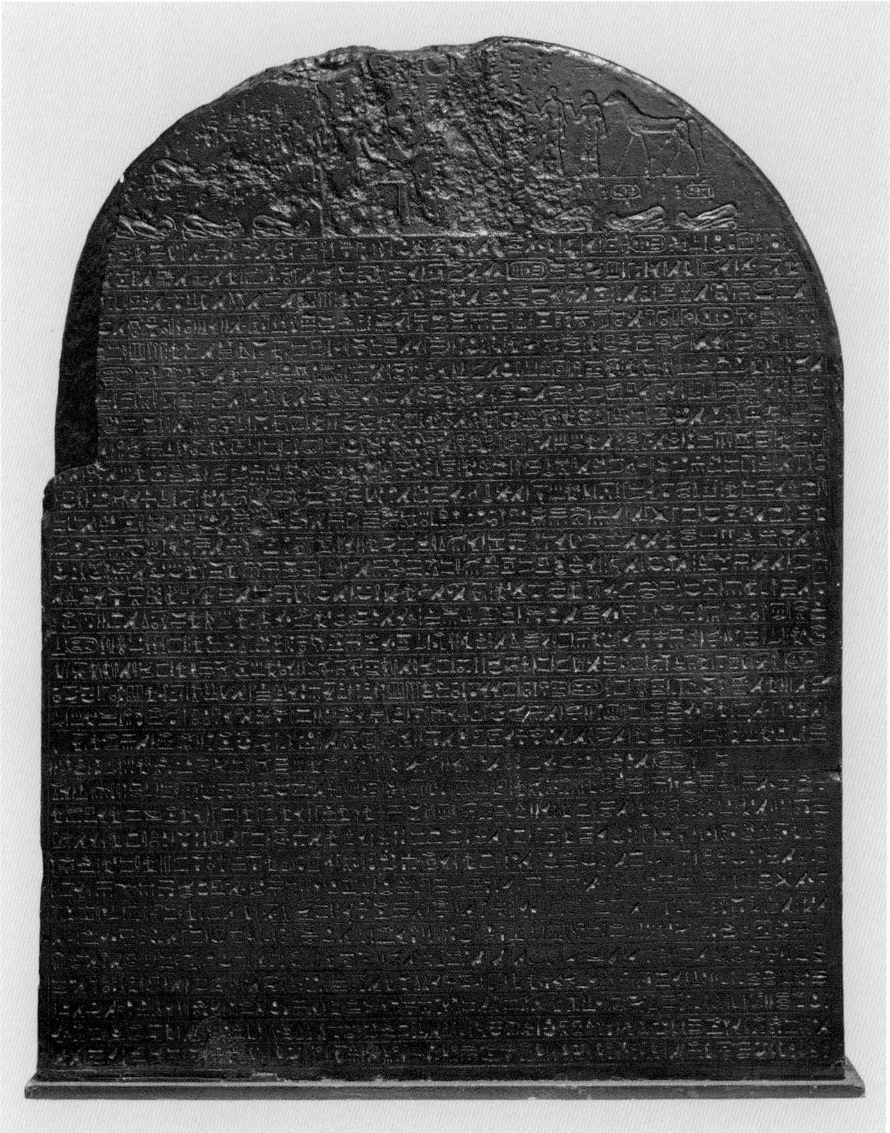

the highly abbreviated 'abnormal hieratic'[13] in the south of Egypt.[14] The evidence is sparse. In 2016 the British Museum was able to acquire a unique account of silver payments in 'abnormal hieratic' dating from the reign of the Kushite king Taharqa (690–664 BCE) (figs 118–119). Champollion correctly attributed Taharqa, who was known from the Bible, to the Twenty-fifth Dynasty (747–656 BCE) and labelled him the 'Ethiopian' (see fig. 84).[15] Most of what was known of Taharqa up to then had been based on literary sources from the heartland of Kush, near the Fourth Cataract in present-day Sudan.

The late cursive hieratic used in the north developed into demotic during the eighth and seventh centuries BCE. In 644 BCE, Psamtek I subdued the local potentates in the Delta and reconquered the south of the country, with the help of foreign (mainly Greek and Carian) mercenaries. As part of his administrative reforms, early demotic was introduced to the south of Egypt and employed across the whole country.[16] As these reforms were concluded, abnormal hieratic was phased out.

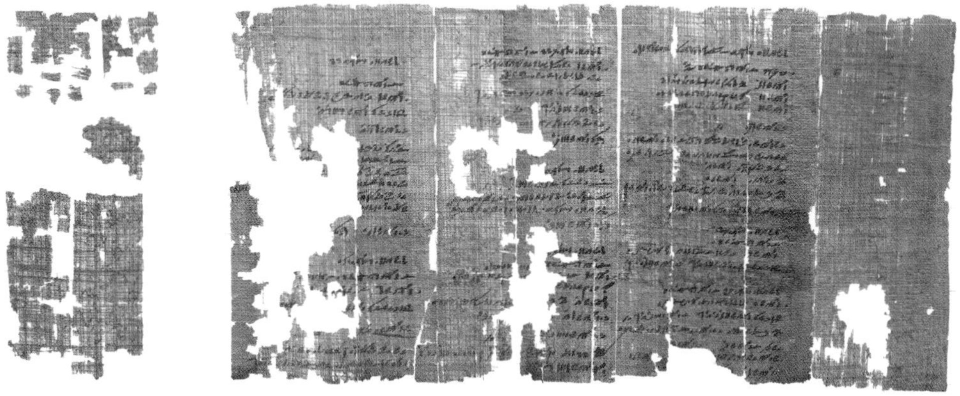

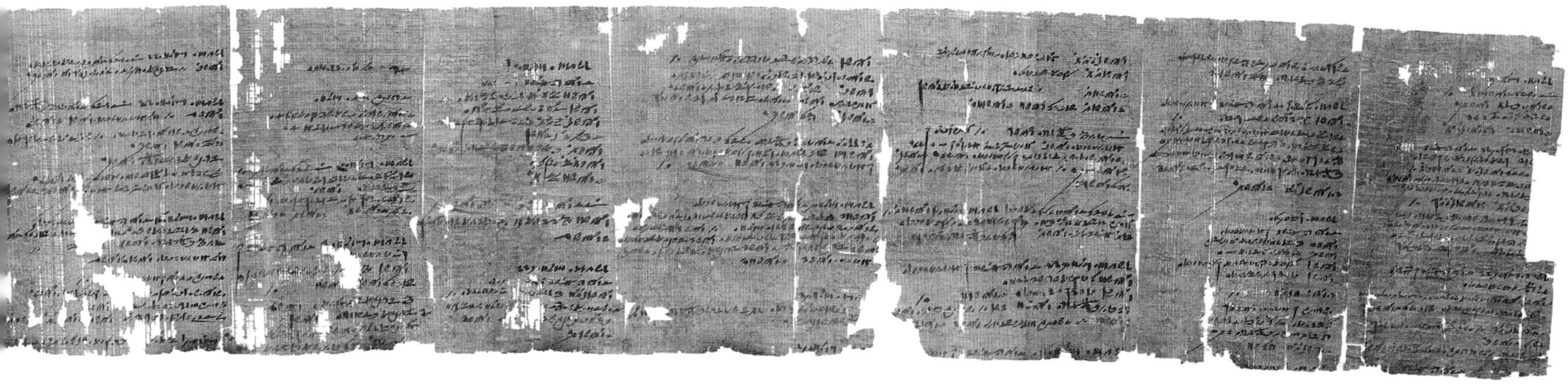

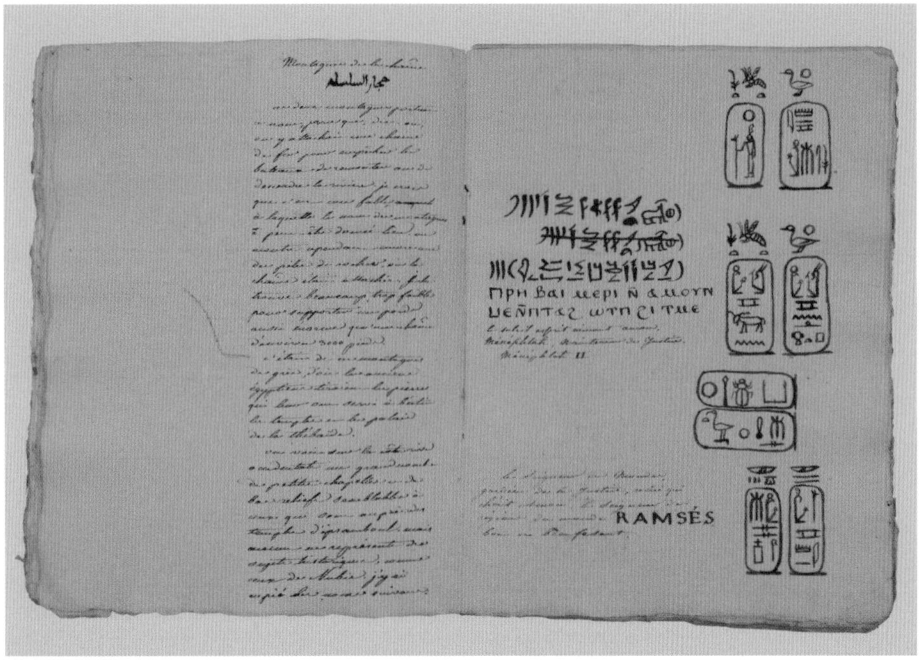

The final centuries of pharaonic rule were a period of great unrest and anarchy, with rival factions competing for power. Following the first Persian occupation of Egypt (525–404 BCE), it was up to obscure rulers, sometimes of foreign origin themselves, to fight for Egypt's fading independence. King Hakor, the penultimate ruler of the Twenty-ninth Dynasty, was possibly not a native Egyptian but came from a North Arabian nomadic tribe living in Palestine (fig. 120). This explains the occasional demotic writing of his name with a 'foreigner' determinative ϯ.[17]

119 (left)
Notebook of Alexandre Louis Henry de Vaucelles, which was kept with the papyrus sheets (fig. 118) but sold separately in Paris on 17 December 2015. The young traveller studied hieroglyphs in the school of Champollion and was among the first European explorers to go beyond the Second Cataract of the Nile into the land of Nubia.
Egypt, 1826
Paper, H. 23.5 cm, W. 37 cm
Antiquariat Inlibris, Vienna

120 (right)
View of the inscription on the back pillar of the Statue of Hakor
Tell Basta, 29th Dynasty, 393–380 BCE
Limestone, H. 31 cm, W. 12 cm, D. 19 cm
British Museum, EA1825
Donated by the Egypt Exploration Fund

King Ramesses II speaking at the Battle of Qadesh, 1274 BCE

'More than a hundred thousand charioteers,
More than ten thousand brothers and sons
Who are united as one heart.
The labours of many people are nothing,
Amun is more helpful than they;
I came here by the command of your mouth,
O Amun, I have not transgressed your command!
Now though I prayed in the distant land,
My voice resounded in Southern On.
I found Amun came when I called to him,
He gave me his hand and I rejoiced.
He called from behind as if near by:
"Forward, I am with you.
I, your father, my hand is with you.
I prevail over a hundred thousand men,
I am lord of victory, lover of valour!"
I found my heart stout, my breast in joy,
All I did succeeded, I was like Mont.
I shot on my right, grasped with my left.
I was before them like Seth in his moment.
I found the mass of chariots in whose midst I was,
Scattering before my horses;
Not one of them found his hand to fight,
Their hearts failed in their bodies through fear of me.
Their arms all slackened, they could not shoot,
They had no heart to grasp their spears;
I made them plunge into the water as crocodiles plunge,
They fell on their faces one on the other.
I slaughtered among them at my will,
Not one looked behind him,
Not one turned around,
Whoever fell down did not rise.'[18]

FOREIGN VOICES IN EGYPT

Travellers and traders from places ranging from the Mediterranean to the Indian subcontinent came to Egypt and brought their languages with them (fig. 121). Some left a profound impression on the structure and usage of the Egyptian writing system.

The first foreign writing system with which the Egyptians came into contact was cuneiform (a modern term, meaning 'wedge-shaped'), originating from Mesopotamia (present-day Iraq). There is evidence for cuneiform texts in Egypt from about 1500 BCE onwards, but the most substantial group was found at the site of Amarna, the short-lived capital of Egypt during the reign of king Akhenaten (1352–1336 BCE).[19] Most of them are letters written in the Akkadian language from rulers of the lands north of Egypt who were keen to ensure that the Egyptian king did not develop close alliances with any of their rivals. There are also tablets inscribed with myths, epics, syllabaries, lexical texts and other lists – the kinds of texts that were used to learn cuneiform writing. A small number of the letters (labelled with dates in hieratic script) were sent from Burnaburiash of Babylon and Tushratta of Mitanni to Amenhotep III and Akhenaten (fig. 122). The rulers addressed one another as 'brother' and sent messages such as congratulations on accession to the throne, an announcement of their own accession or complaints concerning delay in receiving, or poor quality of, royal gifts.

Achaemenid Persian rule over Egypt (526–404 BCE) introduced Old Persian cuneiform to Egypt (fig. 123). The language and writing system used for the imperial Achaemenid administration in Egypt was Aramaic, however, a Semitic language rendered in a simple alphabet of twenty-two signs, mostly consonants, with only limited possibilities for indicating vowels (fig. 124). Particularly interesting is the documentation from the military settlement in Elephantine, near present-day Aswan, which housed Judean mercenaries at the Egyptian southern border of the Persian Empire.[20] Aramaic was the lingua franca of the entire Near East, but it did not have an enduring impact on Egyptian writing. Only very few Aramaic loan-words in later Egyptian can confidently be attributed to the period of Persian domination.[21]

During the Late Period (747–332 BCE), Egypt encountered another Semitic writing system: Ancient South-Arabian (fig. 125).[22] Although actual attestations of this writing system are rare in Egypt, it has long been thought that the exotic South Arabian script made a significant impact on Egyptian writing by introducing an alphabetic sequence for arranging Egyptian word lists.[23] In earlier periods of Egyptian history, word lists would have been organised following the logical order of semantic categories, such as

121 (above)
Hieratic writing board with personal names of people from the island of Crete. The text starts 'Making the names of the Keftiw' followed by phonetically spelled names. Such attempts to accurately render the pronunciation of foreign names provide a glimpse of the Cretan language.
Egypt, New Kingdom, 1550–1069 BCE
Wood, H. 14 cm, W. 25.6 cm, D. 0.5 cm
British Museum, EA5647

122 (below)
Cuneiform tablet bearing a letter from Tushratta of Mitanni to Amenhotep III of Egypt negotiating a royal marriage
Amarna, 18th Dynasty, *c.* 1350 BCE
Clay, H. 8.7 cm, W. 7 cm, D. 2.5 cm
British Museum, E29793

123 (right)
Cylinder seal and impression with a cuneiform inscription mentioning king Darius in the Old Persian, Elamite and Babylonian languages
Thebes, Achaemenid,
6th–5th centuries BCE
Chalcedony or prase, H. 3.7 cm, diam. 2 cm
British Museum, 89132

124 (below)
The Aramaic funerary poem on this stela was erroneously identified as Phoenician when it was discovered in 1704. The stela depicts the deceased woman Taba on her deathbed surrounded by four deities, a scene that is typical of ancient Egyptian iconography.
Memphis, 5th–4th century BCE
Limestone, H. 50.5 cm, W. 33.7 cm, D. 5.2 cm
Bibliothèque Inguimbertine, Carpentras, inv. no. 2007.0.16

geographical for place names (fig. 126, see p. 109). From the fourth century BCE onwards, there is solid evidence that words in such lists could be arranged according to their first letter, especially in the sequencing of proper names where a 'logical' order was more difficult. This implied the notion of an alphabet. To help writers memorise the alphabet, each Egyptian letter was given a name; birds whose name began with the consonant in question were chosen, for example, the letter 'd' is *djandja*, from the bird name *ḏnḏn,* possibly a swan. The South Arabian alphabet, with its large inventory of twenty-nine consonants, would have been able to express most of the sounds of the Egyptian language.

Alphabetic canons may have been present in Egypt long before the Greco-Roman period, however, and it has recently been suggested that they were borrowed from a Northwest Semitic tradition sometime during the fourteenth to twelfth centuries BCE.[24] Other scholars have even argued for an Egyptian origin of the canon between 2000 and 1500 BCE.[25] Recent discoveries have revealed the existence of the so-called *halaḥam* order (*h-l-ḥ-m*) in Egypt some 1,000 years earlier than previously assumed.[26] This order may be the earliest known alphabetically organised text in world history. The *halaḥam* order is one of the two alphabetic canons used in the Middle East from the late fourteenth to early twelfth centuries BCE onwards.[27] The other sequence, *a-b-g* (aleph-beth-gimel), was the precursor of the Greek α-β-γ and Latin a-b-c.[28] Such alphabetic consciousness may have had a long tradition and was possibly the most important contribution of pharaonic Egypt to the development of the alphabet.

The most profound encounter with a foreign language and script began with the arrival in Egypt of Greek-speaking immigrants, mostly mercenaries,

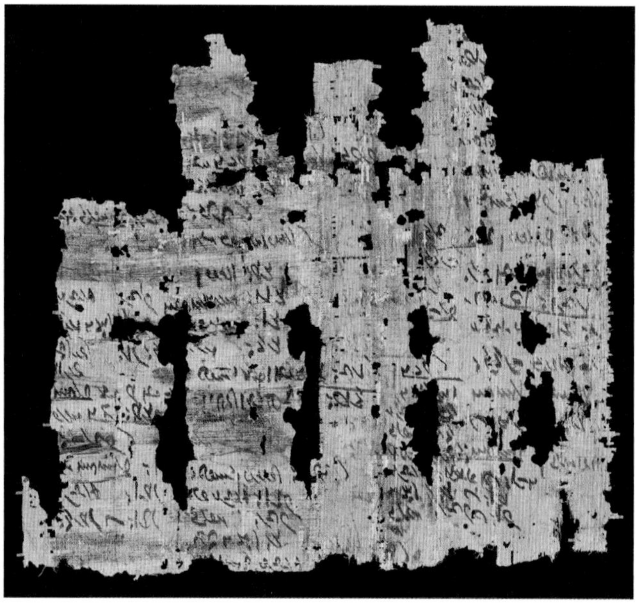

and their families from the seventh century BCE onwards. They were given incentives, such as grants of land, and settled mainly in the northwestern Delta region of Egypt, where the rulers of the Twenty-sixth Dynasty had established a capital city at Sais and an international port and trade node at Naukratis on the Canopic branch of the Nile.[29] Simultaneously, the Carian language and writing was introduced into Egypt by Carian mercenaries serving in the Egyptian army, but it did not have lasting impact (fig. 127).

At Naukratis, temples devoted to Egyptian gods operated next to Greek sanctuaries, and numerous Greek inscriptions dedicated to the local gods reflect different traditions merging in ritual practice (figs 128–130, see p. 165).

A group of cat statues found at Naukratis illustrate how its Greek inhabitants supported local cults as an expression of loyalty towards the Ptolemaic Dynasty, which had manipulated these cults for political advantage. The long-established Egyptian belief in the protective power and sacredness of cats is well documented and fed into the visual arts and elaborate animal cults of the Late Period and Ptolemaic era. The cat votive sculptures are a Ptolemaic, Hellenised expression of the Egyptian goddess Bastet, called Boubastis for a Greek audience.

The domestic cat in limestone was carved in Egyptian style, seated with its tail positioned like that of a sphinx, using materials and techniques uncommon in Greek workshops (fig. 131). The fragmentary demotic inscription on the front of the base dates the piece to between 8 April

125 (left)
Sphinx with hieroglyphs and Proto-Sinaitic hieroglyphs, an early form of alphabetic writing and the ancestor of the ancient South Arabian script. It was probably used by local people working in Sinai alongside the Egyptians as local guides or traders.
Serabit el-Khadim, Middle Kingdom, *c.* 1800 BCE
Sandstone, H. 15.4 cm, W. 23 cm, D. 10 cm
British Museum, EA41748
Donated by the Egypt Exploration Fund

126 (right)
Alphabetical list of demotic personal names followed by the name of a god, for example 'Ptah is content'. Combined with the pieces in Copenhagen and Cairo, the order is: *h – [...] – n – [...] – p – i – a – g – x – t.*
Egypt, Late Period to Ptolemaic Period, 4th–early 3rd century BCE
Papyrus, H. 26.3 cm, W. 29.2 cm, D. 0.2 cm
British Museum, EA10852

127 (left)
Funerary stela of Piabrm with Carian inscription. Carian was an alphabetic script used in southwestern Anatolia (modern Turkey) until the 3rd century BCE. It is still being deciphered but we can understand that Piabrm's father erected the stela for her and that her family came from Milas.
Saqqara, Late Period, *c.* 6th century BCE
Limestone, H. 63.5 cm, W. 31.3 cm, D. 10 cm
British Museum, EA67235
Donated by the Egypt Exploration Society

128 (top right)
Stamp seal in a shape of a cartouche with an Aramaic inscription
Naukratis, Late Period, *c.* 5th century BCE
Copper alloy, H. 7.3 cm, W. 3.6 cm, D. 1.8 cm
British Museum, 1886,0401.1706
Donated by the Egypt Exploration Fund

129 (centre right)
Chian pottery rim with dedication inscription by a woman called Aigyptis, perhaps one of the famous sex workers of Naukratis
Naukratis, 26th Dynasty, *c.* 575–550 BCE
Ceramic, H. 3.4 cm, W. 6.9 cm, D. 0.2 cm
British Museum, 1924,1201.755

130 (bottom right)
Stamped amphora handle made in Brindisi, Italy and found in Naukratis, Egypt
Naukratis, Ptolemaic Period, *c.* 130–50 BCE
Ceramic, H. 7.7 cm, W. 3.6 cm, D. 3.3 cm
British Museum, 1955,0920.89
Donated by the Egypt Exploration Fund

266 BCE and 22/28 (?) August 227 BCE. The male cat creeping forward in Parian marble is of Greek workmanship (fig. 132). Parian marble was imported from the island of Paros in the Aegean Sea. The Greeks hardly represented cats before the fourth century BCE, raising the question whether cats were present in Greece at all.[30] The limestone base for this cat is inscribed with a dedication, Γαλατεία Θευδότου Βουβάστι, 'Galateia daughter of Theodotos to Bubastis', placing the group within a Bubasteion, a temple of Bastet at Naukratis (fig. 133).

After Alexander the Great's conquest in 332 BCE, and continuing into the Ptolemaic and Roman periods, the Greek language became increasingly dominant in the country's administration, but also in literary texts and day-to-day exchanges. It had already become necessary to render Egyptian names and other words in Greek spelling; for example, the Egyptian name *Pꜣ-ḏi-zmꜣ-tꜣ.wj* became Potasimto.[31] Such usages of 'Greco-Egyptian' simply employ the nearest approximation in the Greek alphabet, for example

FACING PAGE
131 (left)
Egyptian-style cat with demotic inscription
Naukratis, Ptolemaic Period,
c. 332–200 BCE
Limestone, H. 50 cm, W. 17 cm, D. 36 cm
British Museum, 1905,0612.3
Donated by the Egypt Exploration Fund

132 (top right)
Cat in Greek style
Naukratis, Ptolemaic Period,
c. 325–227 BCE
Parian marble, H. 31 cm, W. 61 cm,
D. 18 cm
British Museum, 1905,0612.7

133 (bottom right)
Base for Greek-style cat
Naukratis, Ptolemaic Period,
c. 325–250 BCE
Limestone, H. 11 cm, W. 50 cm, D. 18 cm
British Museum, 1905,0612.20

ф for *f*, and should not be confused with Coptic.[32] Greco-Egyptian was used by both Greeks and Egyptians, which may be surprising. While Greeks may have felt little pressure to try to accurately write down unfamiliar sounds that most of them would not have been able to pronounce anyway, Egyptians would have hesitated to insert strange demotic signs when writing for a Greek supervisor. Perhaps they were only trained in writing Greek and were thus incapable of using signs from older scripts to represent their spoken language.

The addition of demotic signs to express those sounds of the Egyptian language that did not exist in Greek – the definition of Coptic (see p. 21) – is not attested until 100 CE (fig. 134). Even when Coptic was introduced, Greco-Egyptian remained in use, especially in the magical sphere, perhaps because such texts were copied from earlier examples.

BILINGUAL EGYPT

Cary J. Martin

'Discovering that you are learning Egyptian letters, I was delighted for you and for myself.' So begins a letter written in Greek in the second century BCE by a woman to her husband. And she continues: 'Because now, when you return to the city, you will teach the slave boys in the establishment of Phaloubes the enema doctor, and you will have a means of support for old age.'[33] The letter does not state that the addressee was being taught to speak Egyptian – he was most likely a bilingual Egyptian – but rather that he was learning to read and write the language. As the letter shows, he was already literate in Greek. The relevant medical 'textbooks' he would use in his work would be in Egyptian rather than Greek and these 'Egyptian letters' would have been the cursive demotic script of day-to-day affairs – not the sacred hieroglyphs.[34]

When this letter was written, Greeks had been settled in Egypt for many centuries and more than 150 years had passed since Alexander the Great's invasion.[35] The two principal languages spoken in the countryside were Greek and Egyptian.[36] But should we consider these to be on an equal footing? To what extent was the population bilingual? Greek was the language of the Macedonian ruling family, of the majority of the professional soldiers who had served under the Ptolemies and who had been given land grants and settled in the countryside,[37] and of the merchants and traders who had seen the commercial opportunities opened up by the Ptolemies and had flocked to Egypt in the third century BCE. It was the language of business and of administration at the higher levels.[38] Did

134 (facing page)
Papyrus with magical invocations using the Old Coptic script to write an older language that is a mixture of Middle and Late Egyptian and demotic. Graphically, it makes use of demotic-derived signs covering sounds which cannot be written with Greek signs. Some of these have not survived in 'standard' Coptic writing.
Oxyrhynchus, Roman Period,
c. 2nd century CE
Papyrus, H. 29.10 cm, W. 16.8 cm, D. 0.2 cm
British Museum, EA10808
Donated by the Egypt Exploration Society

these Greek speakers also learn Egyptian? And what about the Egyptian population? Did they see the new regime as remote and inaccessible or as an opportunity for self-advancement – did they learn Greek?

The Ptolemies did not seek to impose a 'one-size fits all' system on Egypt. The indigenous temples remained powerful and benefited from considerable royal patronage, while in the Greek cities of Alexandria, Naukratis and the new foundation of Ptolemais, in the south,[39] Greek temples were built for the worship of Greek gods. The royal court, the higher levels of the administration and the military appear to be entirely Greek-Macedonian, but the world of the temples looks unmistakably Egyptian. Appearances, however, can be deceptive. This was not an either/or binary situation. The same individual could belong to both worlds and adopt the appropriate identity in each one. This would often mean having a double name – one Egyptian and one Greek. This became very common in society, but it is usually hard to recognise in our sources because, in most situations, only one name was employed.[40] In administrative or military matters, the individual's Greek name would be used; in the cultural or religious environment, the Egyptian. For example, in Akoris in Middle Egypt between 150 and 100 BCE lived an Egyptian called Dionysios son of Kephalas. He was a professional soldier and a priest of Thoth. His archives are bilingual and he wrote excellent Greek and demotic. In the Greek papyri he is referred to by his Greek name, Dionysios; in the demotic he is called Plenis.[41] In only one text is his double name used.[42]

For members of the military who were settled on the land, there would have been gradually increasing familiarity with Egyptian customs and Egyptian religion.[43] We can see this in the extensive bilingual archive – more than fifty texts – of the cavalryman Dryton son of Pamphilos and his family. Dryton was of Cretan descent, his father having immigrated to Egypt probably in the latter part of the third century BCE (see fig. 121).[44] He married twice and his second wife was a local Egyptian woman, who had a double Greek/Egyptian name, Apollonia-Senmonthis.[45] Their daughters also had double names and married men with Egyptian names, at least two of whom were members of the military. The documents that they had drawn up following these marriages were in demotic and they gave their children only Egyptian names.[46] In her business dealings Apollonia used her Greek name and called herself a Greek, but in documents that concerned affairs of her family it was her Egyptian name that she preferred.[47]

A statue now in the Nelson-Atkins Museum in Kansas belonged to a certain Harcheb, an Egyptian name which literally means 'Horus of Chemmis', who also had the Greek name Archibios, the latter being an almost phonetic rendering of the former.[48] The statue probably dates to the second half of the second century BCE, but may be earlier, and originally stood in a temple in Mendes in the eastern Delta. Harcheb's titles include that of *dioiketes*, finance minister, as well as royal scribe and overseer of royal fields, and he also had responsibility for the collection of taxes. It is highly likely that this is the same individual who is attested in some Greek texts from Tebtynis. On his statue belt, his double name was used – Harcheb who is also called Archibios son of Pamnevis and Senobastis. In the inscription on the back, where he is portrayed making an offering to the divine triad of Mendes, only his Egyptian name is given. We have here an example of a Hellenised Egyptian who held a senior position within the Ptolemaic court.

Another Egyptian who had risen to become an important member of the Ptolemaic administration is Dioskourides, who lived in the first half of the second century BCE. His name is Greek, but on his Egyptian-style sarcophagus, now in the Louvre, it is written alphabetically in Egyptian hieroglyphs (see p. 117). He appears in a number of Greek documents, where he carries the important titles of *archisomatophylaks*, 'chief bodyguard', and also, like Harcheb above, *dioiketes* (finance minister). On his sarcophagus there is a long Egyptian autobiography which begins: 'Honoured before Thoth, the twice great, lord of Hermopolis, prince and governor, unique friend'.[49]

When we find Greek and Egyptian scripts together it is usually on non-monumental texts, as for example in the many hundreds of bilingual mummy-labels, which date predominantly to the Roman period (fig. 135). The combination of Egyptian and Greek texts that we find on the Rosetta Stone and the other decrees is in fact quite uncommon.[50] It was usual practice for monuments to keep to one style and one language.[51] A good example of this can be found in a group of hieroglyphic stelae and Greek tombstones that belonged to a leading family whose members were both high-ranking soldiers and Egyptian priests.[52] These come from the vicinity of Edfu, probably from the same tomb, and date to the latter part of the second century BCE. The hieroglyphic stelae are classically Egyptian, with a winged sun disc above an offering scene, and the names inscribed on them are Egyptian. The tombstones, on the other hand, are in Greek style, the names are Greek and the Greek inscriptions are written in perfect elegiac couplets, a Greek poetic form. The same people are honoured in both. The Aphrodisia of the Greek texts is the Hathority of the Egyptian – Egyptian Hathor was equated with Greek Aphrodite. The name of her father Euagoras was rendered as *ỉwwrs*.[53]

In the administration of justice, the Ptolemies early on in their rule established – or consolidated – a dual legal structure in which cases were heard according to the nationality of the parties: Egyptian courts applying

135
Mummy-label of Senpsais the Elder, daughter of Peteube(s)tis (?), inscribed in demotic and Greek. She was fifteen years old when she died (the demotic and the Greek indicate the age slightly differently: according to the demotic, she died when she was within sixteen years; according to the Greek, she lived fifteen years).
Akhmim, Roman Period,
2nd–3rd century CE
Wood, H. 6.2 cm, W. 11.9 cm, D. 0.7 cm
British Museum, EA23215

Egyptian laws and Greek courts using Greek laws. From the first part of the second century BCE survives a very detailed account of a trial, written in demotic, held in an Egyptian court. Over time, however, this system began to break down. If a family has been living in the Egyptian countryside for 200 years, how do you differentiate a Greek from an Egyptian? In 118 BCE a royal decree was issued that stipulated that it was the language in which a document was written, not the ethnicity of the parties, which would determine in which court a case would be heard.[54] The complexity of the situation can be seen through a series of documents written in both Greek and demotic from the extensive bilingual family archive of the Theban mortuary priests. These concern a legal dispute that ran from 125 to 117 BCE over the ownership of a house located near the temple of Karnak at Thebes.[55] The defendants were Egyptian mortuary priests; the plaintiff was a Greek soldier. Written on one of these texts, Papyrus Grey, are copies of three demotic legal documents of sale, recording purchases by three mortuary priests of parts of a building site in Thebes, with a statement written in Greek at the top of each text that the sales tax had been paid (see fig. 76). The original documents date to 153, 153–152 and 146 BCE and the copies were made as part of the evidence that was put together by the defendants.[56] But as the proceedings were held before a Greek court, these documents had to be translated into Greek. The hearing was held in 117 BCE in Greek and the verdict of the court – the Egyptians were successful – also recorded in Greek. The Egyptians had a Greek lawyer. We do not know whether they were able to follow the proceedings without a translator, but just four years later, one of the defendants, Horos, drew up a sale and division of his property for his children.[57] Unlike the earlier legal documents from the archive, this was written in Greek. When he died some eighteen months later, a memorandum was prepared that detailed the expenses of his embalming and burial. This was written in demotic.[58]

In these family archives, containing a mixture of demotic and Greek papyri, it is the texts recording transactions between family members that are written in demotic Egyptian. The Greek texts typically relate to dealings with the authorities, where the documentation would of necessity have to be in the language of the rulers. However, the Greek-speaking authorities gradually extended control over more aspects of the administration and it became a requirement during the second century that, even when an agreement was drawn up in demotic, it had to be registered in the Greek record office to be valid.[59] Where tax had to be paid on a transaction, a receipt was issued, also in Greek. These were regularly written on the demotic papyrus directly below the main text (see fig. 181).[60]

Over time there was a gradual encroachment of the Greek-speaking administration into many aspects of day-to-day business. Indeed, the requirement for documentation to be in Greek resulted in demotic, outside the world of the temple, being increasingly marginalised.[61] Egyptians would have learned to speak Greek and, for the literate minority, also to write it. But for the Greeks in the countryside, marriage to Egyptian women would have also brought the Egyptian language, culture and religion into the family home. What about the children and grandchildren of these Greek-speaking fathers and Egyptian-speaking mothers? They would have been bilingual. Would they have considered themselves to be Greek or Egyptian?

THE CONCEPT OF TIME

Ilona Regulski

For many historians, the main attraction of the Egyptian script is not its pictorial character or presumed structure, but its antiquity. Champollion did not just decipher a writing system; he uncovered one of the oldest written languages in human history.

Writing was 'invented' around 3250 BCE, firstly in order to organise the distribution and storage of goods. Since only a happy few were able to read and write, it – indirectly – also served as a means for cultural and elite display. The oldest Egyptian text at the British Museum dates to around 3100 BCE and mentions 'accounts from Upper Egypt' in addition to the name of Sekhen/Ka, who ruled over Upper Egypt just before the first unification of Egypt's regions into one state (fig. 136).

The decipherment of hieroglyphs has not only affected our understanding of Egyptian chronology, but also revealed detailed information on how the ancient Egyptians measured time, organised the year, and commemorated ancestors (or expunged them from history). Among the ancient Near Eastern peoples, the Egyptians were often praised for their painstaking chronicles by classical writers. The Greek historian Herodotus

136
Jar with an administrative notation in ink. This is the oldest legible Egyptian inscription in the British Museum collection.
Abydos, late Predynastic, *c.* 3100 BCE
Pottery, H. 27.2 cm, diam. 12.4 cm
British Museum, EA35508
Donated by the Egypt Exploration Society

(484–425 BCE) more than once expressed his admiration: 'The Egyptians, by their practice of keeping records of the past, have made themselves much the best historians of any nation of which I have had experience'.[62] Egyptian consciousness of the longevity of their state was displayed to Herodotus by the priests of the temple of Ptah at Memphis, who read a long king list from a papyrus which listed pharaohs from the first human king Menes onwards. In addition to official records, a wealth of informal written sources confirm the Egyptians' deep awareness of the passing of time.[63]

REPURPOSING THE PAST

King lists and historical narratives were one way in which the Egyptians drew upon their past. Others included archaism (a conscious imitation of a previous style); restoration or usurpation of earlier works of art; reuse of building materials; and either ancestor cults or the erasing of a predecessor's memory (known as condemnation of memory, *damnatio memoriae*).[64] Texts, architecture and works of art often referred to elements of the remote past.[65] Revival of the past and the commemoration of ancestors was a trend set by kings.[66] In particular, periods of civil strife, when the central administration was disrupted, necessitated the collection of precedents and models in order to emphasise the legitimacy of rulers. The same tendency towards revival was employed in the non-royal (but still elite) sphere.

The block statue was one of the most common and longest-surviving types of non-royal sculpture in ancient Egypt, so it provided artists with a link to bygone times.[67] Such statues, depicting a person in a squatting posture with knees drawn up to the chest (figs 137–141), were copied throughout Egyptian history.[68] The cloak worn by the individual envelops the entire body except for the feet and hands. The type was invented during the early Twelfth Dynasty (around 1900 BCE), but subtypes emerged over time that depicted the squatting person with, for example, a stela, a little shrine known as a naos, or a small statue in front of the legs (fig. 139). Inscriptions allow us to identify the individuals and date the objects more precisely.

The ancient Egyptians had a strong sense of their own past and were keen to align themselves with the achievements of their ancestors. Authorship was rarely attributed in pre-classical antiquity, though achieving long-lasting fame was a hallmark of greatness. One of the texts from a private library at Deir el-Medina commemorates eight 'great' authors of the past (fig. 142, see p. 180). These learned scribes foretold the future and their sublime writings caused them to be remembered:

FACING PAGE
137 (top left)
Block statue of the treasurer Sahathor, originally placed inside a stela that functioned as a shrine (EA569). The funerary inscription on the stela mirrors the text on the statue, addressing deities such as Osiris and Anubis.
Abydos, 12th Dynasty, *c.* 1900 BCE
Limestone, H. 42.5 cm, W. 20 cm, D. 26 cm
British Museum, EA570

138 (top right)
Block statue of Kamose with a writing palette on his left thigh
Egypt, 18th Dynasty, *c.* 1400 BCE
Granodiorite, H. 59 cm, W. 26.8 cm, D. 37 cm
British Museum, EA1210

139 (bottom left)
Block statue of Parenu with a relief representation of Osiris flanked by Isis and Horus at the front of the legs
Egypt, 19th to 20th Dynasty, 1295–1069 BCE
Limestone, H. 35 cm, W. 21.5 cm, D. 29 cm
British Museum, EA1085

140 (bottom centre)
Block statue of the prince Ouaibre, chief of Upper Egypt, controller of the domains of Neith (patron goddess of Sais) and director of the gate of foreign territories. The statue has been in the Louvre since 1816 and was studied by Champollion.
Sais, 26th Dynasty, *c.* 595–525 BCE
Granodiorite, H. 102 cm, W. 45 cm, D. 66 cm
Musée du Louvre, A 91

141 (bottom right)
Block statue of Padiamennebnesuttawy
Karnak, Ptolemaic Period, 332–30 BCE
Black granite, H. 24.8 cm, W. 12 cm, D. 17.3 cm
British Museum, EA48035

48035

> Is there any here like Hordedef? Is there another like Imhotep? There is none among our people like Neferti, or Khety their chief. I shall make you know the name of Ptahemdjehuty and Khakheperresonbe. Is there another like Ptahhotep, or likewise, Kaires?[69]

Some of the scribes mentioned are well known from other sources, especially from so-called Teachings or Instructions. These are didactic works, mostly ascribed to famous sages, and they discuss general matters of life and moral principles in the form of short sayings and warnings. They are sometimes addressed by a wise man to his children as advice on 'the way of living correctly' in keeping with the moral norms and expectations of Egyptian society. The learned scribes in Qenherkhepshef's papyrus, quoted above, are paired according to the themes of their work. Neferti and Khety did not work or live at the same time, but they both address the topic of royal succession as it relates to the historical king Amenemhat I. (As the founder of a new dynasty (the Twelfth) he had to justify his right to rule.) Ptahhotep and Kaires are authors of Instructions which, from the civil servant's point of view, deal with Egyptian hierarchy and the interdependencies of the individual social classes.

142
Papyrus Chester Beatty IV, from the library of Qenherkhepshef, with monotheistic hymns on the recto and a student's miscellaneous texts on the verso. The so-called 'Miscellanies' have been identified by scholars as a distinct genre in ancient Egyptian literature.
Deir el-Medina, 19th Dynasty, 1295–1186 BCE
Papyrus, H. 21.5 cm, W. 61.2 cm, D. 0.2 cm
British Museum, EA10684,5
Donated by Sir Alfred Chester Beatty and Lady Edith Chester Beatty

143
Ostracon with a version of the Loyalist Teaching of Kaires on the recto and a copy of the *Tale of Sinuhe* on the verso
Deir el-Medina, 19th to 20th Dynasty, 1295–1069 BCE
Limestone, H. 15 cm, W. 21.6 cm, D. 4.1 cm
British Museum, EA5632

> If you are a wise man, establish a home and love your wife. Fill her belly, clothe her back. Ointment is a good remedy for her limbs. Make her happy as long as you live. She is a good field to her master.
>
> Instructions of Ptahhotep, ll. 323–30

The Teachings vary in their tone and didactic emphasis, one of the most exhortatory being the Loyalist Instruction of Kaires (fig. 143).[70] His Teaching stresses the dependence of the elite on their servants and subordinates: field-labourers should not be overworked lest they run away; a harsh master ultimately undermines his own prosperity. Its authorship had long been contested as the name of the teacher did not survive in any of the known copies.[71] This changed in 2005 when a new copy of the text was discovered in a tomb at Asyut in Middle Egypt.[72] It had been jotted down as an exercise on the wall of the tomb of the local governor Iti-Ibi-Iqer and, fortunately, the beginning of the text with the author's name was preserved. The Teaching of Kaires can now be given its place among those of other respected scribes of the Old Kingdom (2686–2181 BCE). Although these scribes are named as authors, the Teachings were probably conceived slightly later; the Asyut copy dates to the Eleventh Dynasty (2055–1985 BCE) in the Middle Kingdom.

Some notable figures of the past became real heroes, even gods, such as Imhotep, the architect of Egypt's first pyramid. Deification (worshipping people as gods) became widespread in later Egyptian history, especially during the Ptolemaic period. Amenhotep son of Hapu, a high official during the reign of the Eighteenth Dynasty king Amenhotep III (1390–1352 BCE), was greatly revered during his lifetime and by following generations and was worshipped as a god a thousand years later. To this effect, a decree instructing the endowment of his mortuary temple was composed and inscribed on a stela during the Twenty-first Dynasty (1069–945 BCE) (fig. 144). According to the text, this was based upon an earlier decree issued in year 31 of king Amenhotep III.

Other individuals, by contrast, were forgotten or deliberately erased from memory. Usurpation was the practice of replacing the names of predecessors with one's own on monuments and royal statuary. Most famously, Ramesses II usurped dozens of monuments, not to defame his predecessors but to promote his own kingship. Usurpation could also, however, be linked to the *damnatio memoriae* (fig. 145).[73] An individual's name or image might be violently obliterated or hacked out, most famously by the pharaoh Akhenaten, who attempted to replace the state god Amun with a new deity. Subsequently, Akhenaten's own monuments were destroyed and his capital city of Amarna abandoned by his successors, who returned to traditional religion. The name of his father, king Amenhotep III, was also regularly effaced or usurped, perhaps because of his relationship to the heretic ruler (fig. 146).[74] In other cases, names were altered or erased simply because they were no longer of interest.[75]

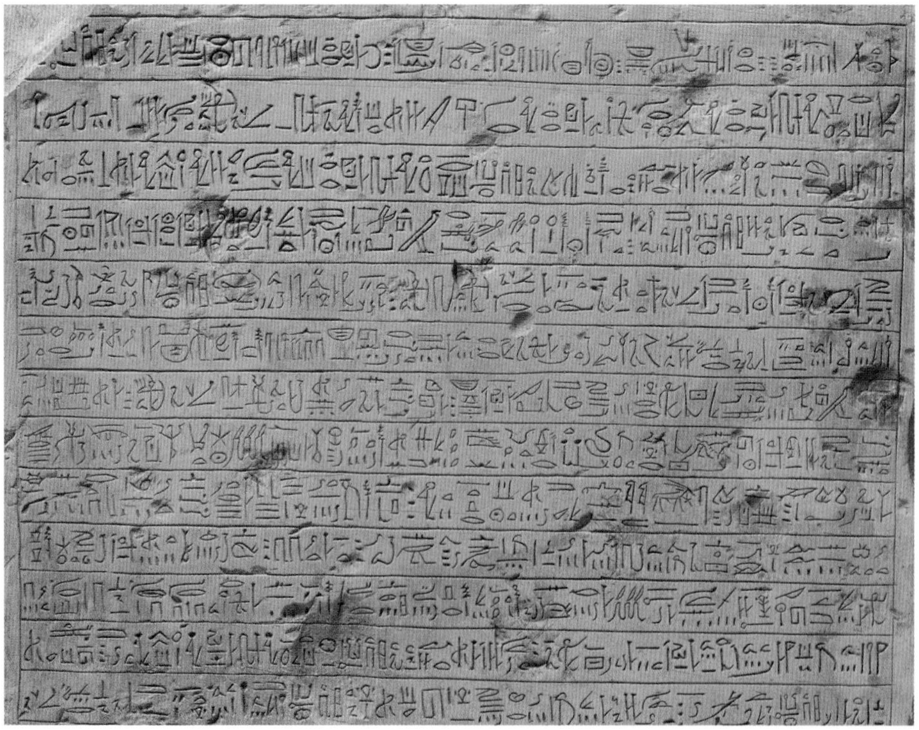

144 (left)
Detail of a decree 'dated' to year 31 of Amenhotep III, protecting the people and property of the funerary foundation of Amenhotep son of Hapu. This is one of the earliest known stelae inscribed in hieratic, a script usually reserved for writing with brush and ink.
Egypt, 21st Dynasty, 1069–945 BCE
Limestone with inlaid pigment, H. 81.5 cm, W. 63 cm, D. 10 cm
British Museum, EA138

145 (facing page, left)
Kneeling figure holding a stela with a hymn to the sun god. The name of the dedicator has been erased.
Egypt, 18th Dynasty, 1390–1352 BCE
Limestone, H. 26 cm, W. 11.5 cm, D. 18 cm
British Museum, EA24430

146 (facing page, right)
Fragment of a box-cover with erased royal names
Egypt, 18th Dynasty, 1390–1352 BCE
Ebony, H. 50.6 cm, W. 3 cm, D. 0.2 cm
British Museum, EA38271
Donated by Spencer Joshua Alwyne Compton, 2nd Marquess of Northampton

24430

MEASURING TIME AND THE ORGANISATION OF THE YEAR

From the beginning of Egyptian history, the year was named after the most important event that took place. In a label of Den, sixth king of the First Dynasty, a year is named after the ritual run of the king during the Sed festival, a ceremony celebrating his continued rule. The label, which may have been attached to goods or a box, depicts the king seated on a throne in a booth and also running around ritual boundary markers (fig. 147). The four text registers are bordered on the right side by a large year-hieroglyph.

The people of Egypt depended upon the Nile River, with its reliable seasonal flooding that fertilised the land. Thus, the Egyptian year was organised according to seasonal cycles and their associated festivals. In Turin, Champollion discovered that the ancient Egyptian year was divided into twelve months and three seasons. In a letter to his brother (23 November 1824), he explained how the fourth month of the flooding season (Akhet; June–September) is followed by the first month of the growing season (Peret; October–February) and the fourth month of Peret is followed by the first month of the harvest season (Shemu; March–May). In hieroglyphs, each season is followed by one, two, three or four half-moons (the sign for month) or one half-moon followed by one, two, three or four strokes, to indicate the month. As each regular month was formed of exactly thirty days, five extra days were added – we know now – to bring the calendar in line with a 365-day year. These additional, so-called 'epagomenal' days at the end of the year were used to celebrate the gods' birthdays. The division of the year into seasons and months is as follows:

Season	**Month**	**Egyptian (New Kingdom)**	**Greek**
I Akhet	1st Month of Flood	*ḏḥw.tj*	Thoth
II Akhet	2nd Month of Flood	*pꜣ-n-ỉp.t*	Phaophi
III Akhet	3rd Month of Flood	*ḥw.t-ḥr.w*	Athur
IV Akhet	4th Month of Flood	*kꜣ-ḥr-kꜣ*	Khoiak
I Peret	1st Month of Growth	*tꜣ-ꜥ(ꜣ)b.t*	Tybi
II Peret	2nd Month of Growth	*mḫr*	Mekhír
III Peret	3rd Month of Growth	*pꜣ n-ỉmn-ḥtp.w*	Phamenṓth
IV Peret	4th Month of Growth	*pꜣ n-rnn.t*	Pharmouthí
I Shemu	1st Month of Low Water	*pꜣ n-ḫnw.w*	Pakhṓn
II Shemu	2nd Month of Low Water	*pꜣ n-ỉn.t*	Paüní
III Shemu	3rd Month of Low Water	*ỉp-ỉp*	Epiphí
IV Shemu	4th Month of Low Water	*msw.t Rꜥ*	Mesorḗ
Epagomenal days	Those upon the year	*ḥrj.w rnp.t*	epagómenai

147 (above)
Year label from the reign of Den. In addition to the Sed festival, the label refers to the destruction of a stronghold and the taking of captives, the delivery of precious Lebanese oil and the name of the high official Hemaka who oversaw the events.
Abydos, 1st Dynasty, 3100–2890 BCE
Ebony, H. 8 cm, W. 5.5 cm, D. 0.7 cm
British Museum, EA32650
Donated by the Egypt Exploration Fund

148 (facing page, top)
Feast list on the back pillar of a statue group of the parents of Iymhotep. Important feasts such as the Opening of the Year, New Year's Day, the Wag festival, the Thoth feast and the festival of Sokar are mentioned.
Egypt, Late Period, 747–332 BCE
Wood, H. 27.2 cm, W. 14.5 cm, D. 8.3 cm
British Museum, EA41516

149 (facing page, bottom)
New Year's flask. The edge band is inscribed on both sides with invocations to the deities Ptah and his wife Neith.
Thebes, 26th Dynasty, 664–525 BCE
Glazed composition, H. 14.1 cm, W. 10.9 cm, D. 7.2 cm
British Museum, EA4770

The Egyptians did not fully align their civil calendar with the solar year, as we do by adding a leap day every four years, until the reign of Emperor Augustus (30 BCE–14 CE). This means that their calendar was a 'wandering' one. The seasons were originally named after events: the Nile flood (Akhet), the cultivation (Peret) and the harvest (Shemu). As the calendar wandered, these seasons no longer aligned with the actual events. There is evidence that a civil calendar coexisted with a lunar one.[76] An average lunar month is 29.53 days. The original lunar calendar (354 days) was thus out of sync with the solar year of 364/5 days and had to be replaced as soon as a mature farming civilisation developed. Lunar-based religious events such as the Wag festival, honouring the memory and souls of the dead, had to be assigned a fixed date or incorporated into other feasts (fig. 148).[77] However, the lunar-based festivals were not immediately abandoned. Two Wag festivals were recorded for some time: one on day 18 of the first civil month (Akhet), and another movable event celebrated at the traditional lunar date. The joy of these festivals was expressed through drunkenness and the giving of libations (fig. 149).

For the ancient Egyptians, every day of the year had significance and calendars were drawn up in which each day was specified as lucky or unlucky, good or bad. Superstitious beliefs, such as the thirteenth being the unluckiest day of the month and Friday the unluckiest day of the week, are very ancient and have a wide geographical distribution. In Egypt, many days in the year were the anniversaries of events in the mythological history of the gods and thus acquired a happy or unhappy reputation. The papyrus Sallier IV, named after its previous owner, is one of the most extensive calendars to survive from ancient Egypt (fig. 150). To designate a day as good or bad, the author of the papyrus labels each day with the sign for 'good' 𓄤 in black ink or 'bad' 𓊢 in red ink (underlined in the example below). A day may be entirely good, entirely bad, or partly good and partly bad. In the Sallier papyrus, each day is considered as consisting of three equal parts, and a wholly good day is accordingly labelled 𓄤𓄤𓄤 and a wholly bad day 𓊢𓊢𓊢. A day of which the first two-thirds were good and the evening bad was marked 𓄤𓄤𓊢 and so on.

> 2nd month of the inundation, day four: bad, good, bad. You shall not come forth from your house in any way on th[is da]y. Everyone, who is born on this day, will die of an epidemic on this day![78]

The ancient Egyptians were one of the first civilisations to divide days into equal parts using timekeeping devices such as sundials, shadow clocks and water clocks. Obelisks were used as sundials by reading their shadows as they moved with the (apparent) progress of the sun across the sky during the day.

Monitoring the passage of time in detail was necessary to understand and predict natural phenomena such as day and night, and the annual Nile flood, but also to regulate civic and religious duties related to the temple cult. The Egyptian time system divided day and night into twelve hours.

Water clocks (*clepsydra*) were shaped like flower-pots, with sloping sides, and had a small outlet near the bottom that allowed water to drip out at a steady rate until the vessel was emptied (fig. 151). The marks on the inside served to measure each hour as the water level decreased. The outflow water clock was possibly invented during the Eighteenth Dynasty (1550–1295 BCE) and had the potential to be accurate to within about fifteen minutes. Ptolemaic and later water clocks were increasingly used in Lower Egypt and their measurements were modified to time the hours of the night more accurately. Their iconography, often showing the king making offerings to deities, suggests that these devices were used by priests to determine the hours for the performance of nocturnal temple rituals.

While water clocks may have been used for timing civil night, star-clocks were used to indicate astronomical night (i.e. the hours between sunset and sunrise, excluding twilight). Star-clocks first appeared on coffin lids from the Asyut region during the Ninth or Tenth Dynasty (c. 2100 BCE), presented as grids representing the motions of selected stars that appear consecutively on the horizon throughout one rotation of the Earth (fig. 152). Because a new star group reappeared in the eastern sky at dawn every ten days, after a period of being obscured by the sun's light (heliacal rising), the ancient Greeks called these groups *dekanoi* (δεκανοί) or 'tenths'. The ancient Egyptians referred to them as *b3k.tjw*, '[those] connected with work'. They are arranged in 36 intervals of 10 days, for a total of 360 days, and 12 stars per interval, one for each hour of the night.[79] The rising of each star marked the beginning of a new hour of the night. Champollion coined the term 'determinative' (see pp. 25, 112) partly based on the word *wnw.t* 'hour': 'The star [sign] is the determinative of all divisions of time', he noted, meaning that this sign indicates which words belonged to the category of time units.[80]

150 (facing page, top)
Papyrus Sallier IV with a calendar of lucky and unlucky days. The text contains many errors, which led to it being interpreted as a schooling exercise.
Thebes, 19th Dynasty, 1295–1186 BCE
Papyrus, H. 17.8 cm, W. 59 cm, D. 0.2 cm
British Museum, EA10184,6

151 (facing page, bottom)
Clepsydra (water clock) showing Philip Arrhidaeus (323–317 BCE) making offerings to several deities. Champollion used Philip's cartouche to identify the letter h.
Tell el-Yahudiya, Ptolemaic Period, *c.* 320 BCE
Basalt, H. 34 cm, W. 30, D. 7 cm
British Museum, EA938

152 (right)
Lid of the anthropoid inner coffin of Hornedjitef with a star-clock on the inside. Hornedjitef held many priestly offices.
Thebes, Ptolemaic Period, *c.* 240 BCE
Wood and pigment, H. 194.5 cm, W. 60.8 cm, D. 37.5 cm
British Museum, EA6678

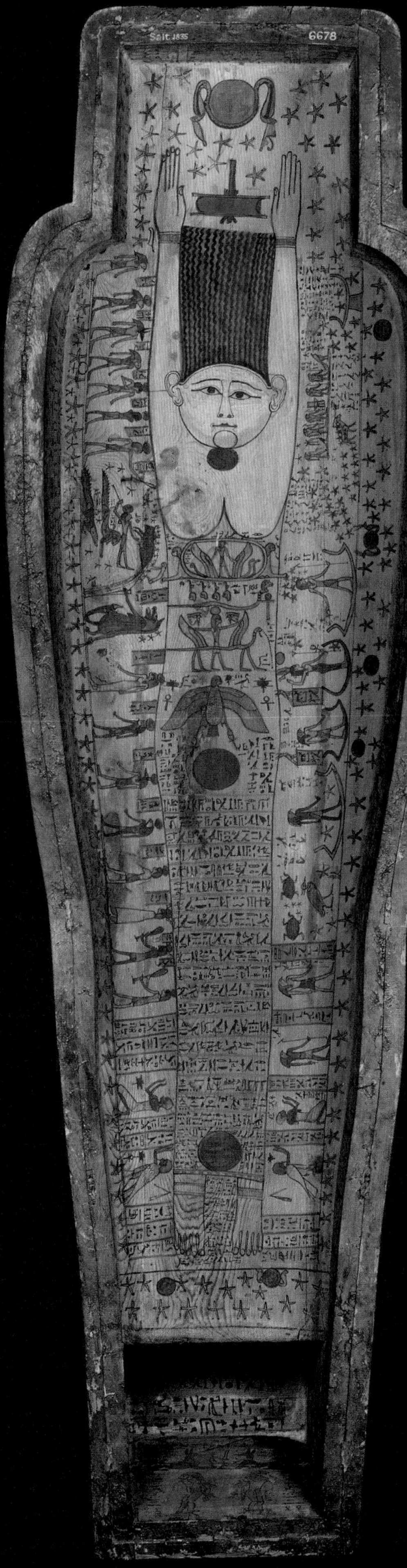

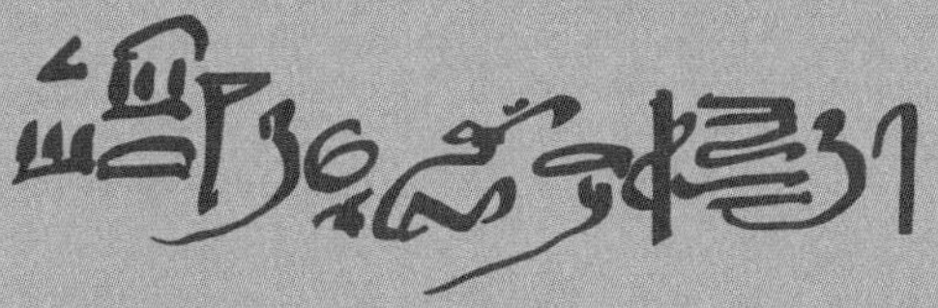

Scribes remembered in Chester Beatty IV papyrus, 1295–1186 BCE

'But, should you do these things, you are wise in writings.
As for those scribes and sages from the time which came after the gods
– those who would foresee what was to come, which happened –
their names endure for eternity,
although they are gone, although they completed their lifetimes and all their people are forgotten.

They did not make pyramids of bronze, with stelae of iron.
They recognised not how heirs last as children, with [offspring] pronouncing their names;
they made for themselves heirs as writings and the Teachings they made.
They appointed [for themselves] the book as the lector-priest,
the writing board as Beloved-Son,
the Teachings as their Pyramids,
the pen as their baby,
the stone-surface as wife.
From the great to the small are given to be his children:
the scribe, he is their head.

Doors and mansions were made: they have fallen,
their funerary priests leaving,
while their stelae are covered with earth,
their chambers forgotten.
(Yet) their names are (still) pronounced over their rolls
which they made, from when they were.
How good is the memory of them and what they made –
for the bounds of eternity!

Be a scribe! Put it in your heart,
that your name shall exist like theirs!
The roll is more excellent than the carved stela,
than the enclosure which is established.
These act as chapels and pyramids
in the heart of him who pronounces their names.
Surely a name in mankind's mouth
is efficacious in the necropolis!

A man has perished: his corpse is dust,
and his people have passed from the land;
it is a book which makes him remembered
in the mouth of a speaker.
More excellent is a roll than a built house,
than a chapel in the west.
It is better than an established villa,
than a stela in a temple.

Is there any here like Hordedef?
Is there another like Imhotep?
There is none among our people like Neferti,
or Khety their chief.
I shall make you know the name of
Ptahemdjehuty and Khakheperresonbe.
Is there another like Ptahhotep,
or likewise, Kaires?

These sages, who foretold what comes –
what came from their mouths happened –
one benefits from the lines written in their books.
To them the offspring of others are given,
to be heirs as if their own children.
They hid from the masses their magic,
which is read from their Teachings.
Departing life has made their names forgotten;
it is writings which make them remembered.'[81]

THE AFTERLIFE

Ilona Regulski

> He has taken away the breath from my nose, (although) my days had not yet come. He has brought me to this place, although my food was on earth.
>
> *Ancient Egyptian Coffin Texts, spell 89*

153
Ba-statue expressing the mobility of the soul after death. The reunification of the deceased body with the soul after their temporary separation is an essential part of the burial ritual, as it facilitates rebirth.
Egypt, Late Period to Ptolemaic Period, 747–30 BCE
Wood, H. 11.3 cm, W. 4.1 cm, D. 7.2 cm
British Museum, EA61884

Like people in many other cultures, the ancient Egyptians rendered death acceptable by redefining it as an individual's progression into another state of being (fig. 153). Preparation for death, one of the most powerful forces driving ancient Egyptian culture, generated a wide variety of evidence related to funerary rituals, including architecture, images, artefacts and texts. Yet our understanding of what happened during burials and funerary ceremonies was long hampered by a lack of understanding of the textual accounts and a focus on disturbed and dispersed archaeological contexts.

SCATTERED ACCOUNTS OF MUMMIFICATION

Among the most popular objects to appear in early cabinets of curiosities were what we now call canopic jars, a set of four sealed containers that preserved the organs of their deceased owner. The link with human remains was forgotten by the early eighteenth century, so the canopic jars were misunderstood as simple representations of either Egyptian gods or holy elements of Egyptian life. Champollion interpreted them correctly as ritual objects used during the embalming process. Intrigued by these jars, he submerged one in a pot of boiling water on 12 November 1812, in an attempt to loosen the thick, hard substance inside. He explained the figures on the lids as 'emblems of the four great qualities of God: the woman expresses the goodness with which the soul is received by his court; the hawk the god who gives life; the jackal the god who bestows death and the baboon the god of divine justice'.[82]

In fact, the lids are sculpted to represent the four sons of the god Horus. A protective inscription on each jar specifies the name of the donor and the respective guardian deity: the human-headed god Imset preserved the liver and was protected by the goddess Isis; the jackal-headed Duamutef preserved the stomach and was protected by the goddess Neith; the baboon-headed Hapy preserved the lungs and was protected by the goddess

Nephthys; and the falcon-headed Qebehsenuef preserved the intestines and was protected by the goddess Serqet.

As the cabinets started to be dispersed, sets of canopic jars were split up and individual pieces moved from one collection to another. In 1719 the Benedictine monk Dom Bernard de Montfaucon (1655–1741) made drawings of three alabaster canopic jars in the possession of François Xavier Bon de Saint-Hilaire (1678–1761) and in the cabinet of Vivant Denon.[83] His copies were so good – at a time before decipherment – that it was later possible to read the names in the inscriptions as that of Ahmose, son of Pediptah and Tentnefertem. Two jars were purchased by Lord Leverhulme and ended up in the Lady Lever Art Gallery, Liverpool, England (figs 154–155).[84] The third and fourth jars are now in the Musée Calvet in Avignon, France, and the Louvre in Paris (figs 156–157).[85] The set probably came from Memphis, dating to around the Twenty-sixth Dynasty.

The ancient Egyptian treatment of the human body after death never ceased to intrigue. When the cartonnage and coffin of Baketenhor arrived in

154 (left)
Canopic jar of Ahmose, representing Duamutef (jackal)
Egypt, Late Period, 747–332 BCE
Calcite, H. 33 cm, diam. 16.1 cm
Lady Lever Art Gallery, LL 5136, LL 5137

155 (right)
Canopic jar of Ahmose, representing Qebehsenuef (falcon)
Egypt, Late Period, 747–332 BCE
Calcite, H. 38 cm, diam. 16.4 cm
Lady Lever Art Gallery, LL 5134a, LL 5135

156 (left)
Canopic jar of Ahmose, representing Hapy (baboon)
Egypt, Late Period, 747–332 BCE
Calcite, H. 31.5 cm, diam. 17 cm
Musée du Louvre, E 13137

157 (right)
Canopic jar of Iahmes, representing Imset (human)
Egypt, Late Period, 747–332 BCE
Calcite, H. 30 cm, diam. 11 cm
Musée Calvet, no. 115

Newcastle, England, in 1821, local individuals petitioned the Literary and Philosophical Society of Newcastle to allow an unwrapping, for 'there is a scientific purpose to be served' (fig. 158).[86] At a certain point, the mummy was carefully removed from and then returned to her painted cartonnage, but she was never actually unwrapped. Thomas Young was consulted about the inscription on Baketenhor's cartonnage in 1822, just months before Champollion's breakthrough.[87] He concluded that the religious iconography was typically meant to invoke or conciliate the goodwill of divinities, 'somewhat in the nature of letters of credit to the next world'. A year later, Champollion identified the inscription as a prayer addressed to several deities for the soul of the deceased.[88] Speculations about the association of the deceased with Osiris demonstrate a reasonable knowledge of ancient Egypt.

The correspondence with colleagues in Newcastle highlights Champollion's confident grasp of the language (fig. 159). He identified various gods and titles, but struggled with phonetic values of the signs,

158
Cartonnage and mummy of Baketenhor
Egypt, 22nd Dynasty, 945–715 BCE
Human remains and organics, H. 30 cm, W. 175 cm, D. 40 cm
Great North Museum: Hancock, AREGYPT605

reading the sign *pr* 𓉐 as *p* and the sign *ḥr* 𓁷 simply as *h*. In 1823 Champollion was on the verge of discovering that certain characters in private pharaonic names could represent two (biliteral) or three (triliteral) letters rather than being just single alphabetic signs. Champollion recognised how groups of signs were used but did not always understand their full meaning. For example, he concluded that the term *mꜣʿ-ḫrw* 'always follows the proper names of the deceased of both sexes and is a sign of the species' but only translated the term correctly in his grammar as 'true of voice', indicating the deceased as having been judged morally righteous.[89] Champollion's reading was impressively accurate, especially considering he had only made his major breakthrough in decipherment the previous year. In a second letter (1827), Champollion was able to offer a full breakdown of the offering formula.[90] In 1992 the inscription was correctly read as follows:

> An offering which the king gives to Re-Harakhty, chief of the gods [to] Atum, lord of the two lands, [and to] Osiris, Foremost of the Westerners, so that he may give offerings and provisions to the Osiris, the Lady of the House, Baketenhor-nakht, daughter of the gods' father Nakhtefmut, true of voice.[91]

The decision not to unwrap Baketenhor ensured the preservation of the mummy and has enabled more recent non-invasive, non-destructive examination using modern technology. In 1964 a radiographic survey of Baketenhor revealed that she was an adult female measuring 1.57 metres in height.[92] Objects were identified between the wrappings, including several amulets, a winged pectoral (brooch) and an embalming plaque. A full computerised CT scan in 1993 determined that she had a full set of teeth, no signs of arthritis or bone disease and was estimated to have been between twenty-one and thirty-five years of age when she died.[93] The brain had been removed through the nose, while implants, possibly stones, had been placed behind the eyelids, as well as packing material in the mouth and throat.

159 (facing page)
Champollion's response on 31 October 1823 to an enquiry by Joseph Lamb (1781–1859) about the inscription on the cartonnage of Baketenhor, in a later transcript translated into English. Their warm correspondence testifies to a collegial relationship and offers a different perspective to the popular narrative of rivalry between the British and the French.
Paris, France and Newcastle, England, 1823 and 1827 (originals)
Paper, H. 32.7 cm, W. 20 cm
Great North Museum: Hancock, NEWHM : 2022.H62

Copied from NEWCASTLE MAGAZINE, 1824, Vol. III. p.92.

Paris, Oct. 31, 1823.

Sir,

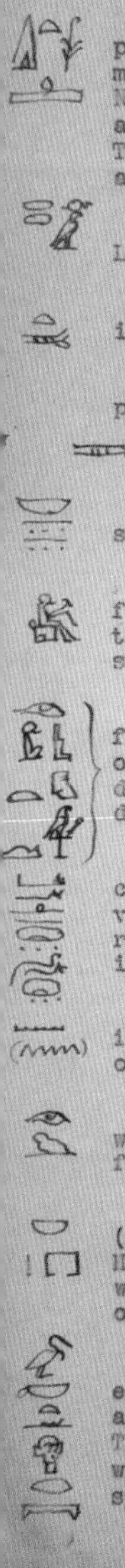

I desire to return you my sincere thanks for your kindness in presenting me with an exact copy of the inscription on the Egyptian mummy presented to the Literary and Philosophical Society of Newcastle. This inscription contains the usual formula - a prayer addressed to several divinities for the soul of the deceased. The Gods, to whom supplications are made on the mummy in question, are three;

1st. The Sun, in the Egyptian language Phre, with the title, Lord of the Gods.

2. The Egyptian God Mars, whose entire hieroglyphic name is written, in short, on your mummy.

This name (the figures which stand first under No 2) is phonetic and answers to the letters T.M.

1. The significance of this sign is still unknown to me. ? a sledge for stones etc

2. This divine name is accompanied with the title which signifies Master of the Worlds.

3. The character which terminates the name of the God is figurative; it represents the God himself. It is thus that in the first name, the sun is indicated by a hawk, having the head surmounted by a discus, the ordinary emblem of Phre.

3. The third divinity named in the legend is Osiris, followed by the title, which answers to the idea of Supreme Ruler of Amenti, or the Egyptian Hades, where the souls were judged and dispersed among the various celestial regions, according to their degrees of merit acquired on the earth.

4. These hieroglyphics, which are found more or less complete on all mummies, are a usual formula, which begins by the verb to give, and by which they supplicate the Gods to grant repose or their favour to the soul of the deceased, whose name immediately follows.

5. This hieroglyphic (N) is the preposition to, which indicates the following groups, as being the indirect complements of the verb to give, which is of the third person.

6. This group is one of the names of Osiris, which, as well as the preceding name of the same God, (see above) is always found before the proper name of the deceased of both sexes.

7. This group is composed of the character, Master, (NHB, Neb in the Egyptian language) and of the character, House, HV, in the Egyptian language, which forms the complete word Nebei, which signifies a Master or Mistress of the House, and answers to our honarary titles, Sir or Madam.

8. These signs contain the name which the individual embalmed bore. I am persuaded that the first two characters are a mystic title signifying daughter. The five others, TSHRPE, Teshorpe, or Tashorpe, are the name of the deceased, who was a woman, as is proved by the figurative character or sign of the species (9), a woman holding a flower of the Lotus.

10. These signs are also determinative, but their ~~significance~~

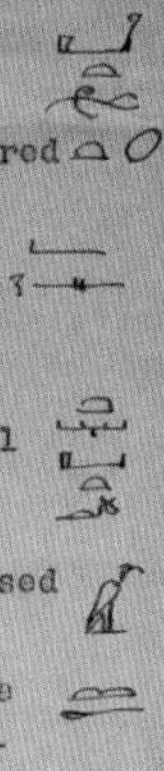

signification is unknown to me. - In a note in the original letter, it is stated by Mr Lamb, that M.C. has since discovered this to mean "only daughter".

11. This group, which is read CTN, Setan, signifies daughter of.

12. This is a title.

13. The name of the mother of the deceased. Several signs being yet undecided or unknown, I cannot give the pronunciation. ?

14. This group signifies, Mother, and here is only used to determine the proper name preceding.

15. This group always follows the proper names of the deceased of both sexes, and is a sign of the species.

The entire legend answers pretty nearly to the following phrases.

May she be approved by Phre, the Lord of the Celestial Gods, and by T-M. (Egyptian Mars), Lord of the Worlds. May Osiris, the Supreme Ruler of Amenti (Hades), grant repose to the Osirian Lady, her daughter Tashorpe x x daughter of x x (mother) deceased.

This, Sir, is all that it is possible to advance with certainty upon the legend which you had the goodness to send me. I hope that these ideas, collected in haste, will satisfy you. I seize this occasion to renew the expression of the distinguished sentiments with which I have the honor to be, Sir,

Your very humble and obedt servant,

J. B. CHAMPOLLION.

A Monsieur
Monsieur Lamb,
Rue Lepelletier, No 6,
Pecs le nouvel Opera, Paris.

READING ANCIENT RITUAL

Champollion tried to understand and reconstruct the 'Grand Funerary Ritual', a prototype text that contained prescriptions and prayers for funerary ceremonies. Using two printed versions of the 'Papyrus Cadet' as published in the *Description de l'Égypte*,[94] Champollion contemplated the organisation of the text and tried to fill some of the gaps (figs 160–161).

In 1827 Champollion studied the papyrus of Djedmutiusesankh, discovered or purchased in Egypt by Giuseppe Passalacqua between 1821 and 1825 (fig. 162).[95] Champollion added his signature beneath the papyrus after he elaborated on Passalacqua's note (his insertions are underlined below):

> Papyrus from the Passalacqua collection, in hieratic or priestly script, containing prayers for the happy wandering of the soul of a woman named Thetmouthis, daughter of a guardian of the temple of the goddess Mouthis (Isis). (Father's name is deleted)

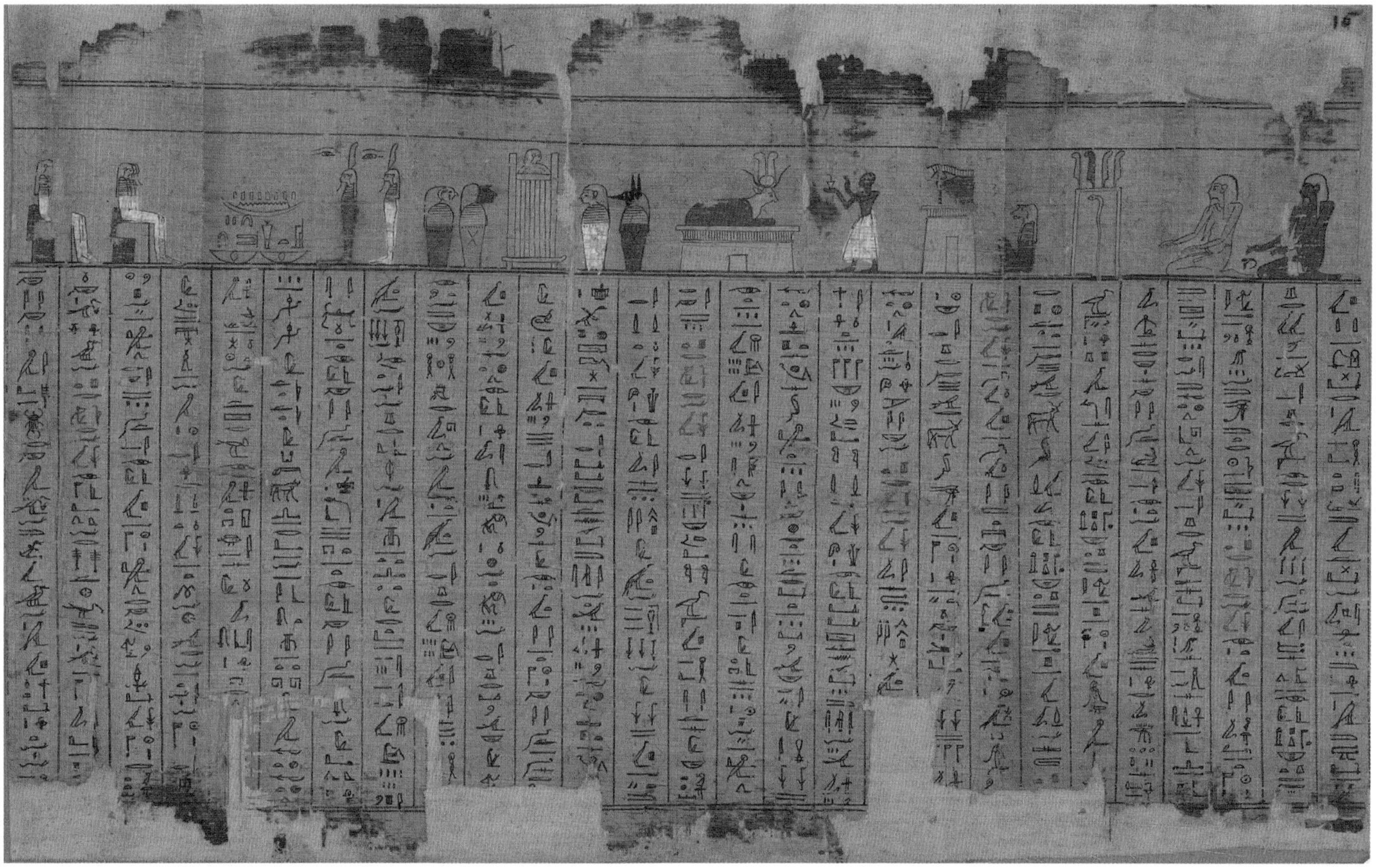

160 (facing page)
Book of the Dead of Padiamennebnesuttawy or the Papyrus Cadet after its previous owner, Jean-Marcel Cadet (1751–1835). This frame shows the beginning of Chapter 17 with a vignette in the upper banner. The papyrus is written in cursive hieroglyphs, which were used for religious documents.
Thebes, Ptolemaic Period, 332–30 BCE
Papyrus, H. 26 cm, W. 43.5 cm
Bibliothèque nationale de France, Département des Manuscrits, Egyptien 4

161 (right)
Champollion's proposed reconstructions of the Papyrus Cadet
Paris, France, 1814–22
Paper, H. 47.6 cm, W. 31.3 cm (closed)
Bibliothèque nationale de France, Département des Manuscrits, NAF 20310

162 (below)
Book of the Dead of Djedmutiusesankh, with Champollion's signature
Thebes, 21st to 22nd Dynasty, 1069–715 BCE
Papyrus, H. 13.2 cm, W. 52.8 cm
Private collection of David and Molly Lowell Borthwick

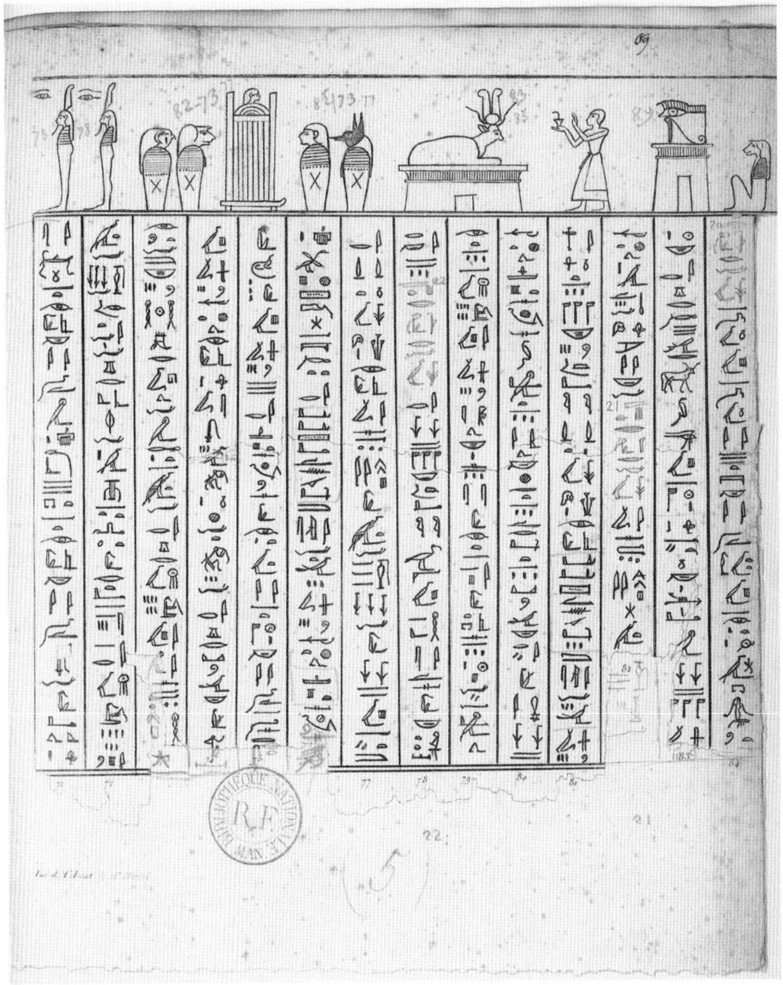

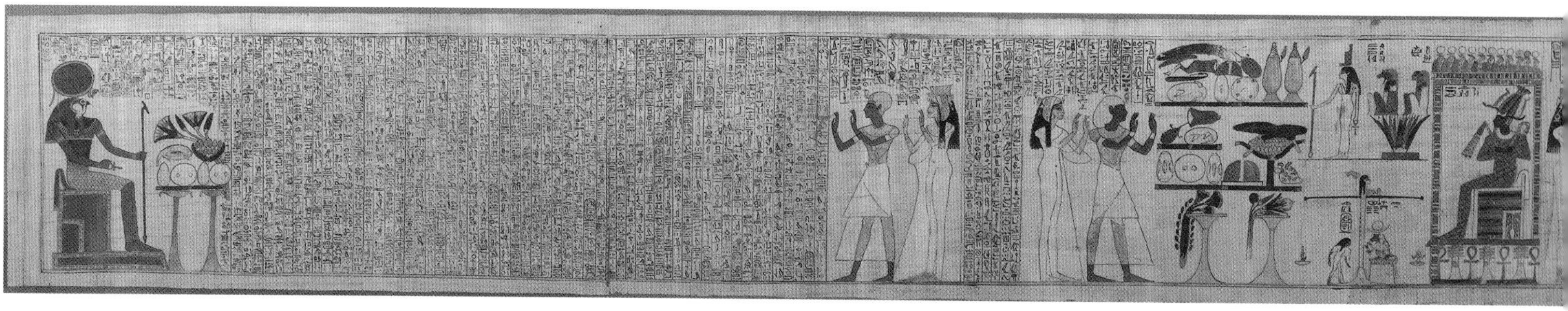

Its modest size recalls the abbreviated Book of the Dead papyri that are known from Thebes during the Third Intermediate Period (*c.* 1069–747 BCE), but such adaptations of the genre were unknown to Champollion at the time. Twenty years after Champollion's 1822 breakthrough, the father of German Egyptology, Karl Richard Lepsius (1810–1884), published a Ptolemaic guide for the soul in the afterlife under the title *Das Todtenbuch der Ägypter*.[96] Lepsius's designation, 'Book of the Dead', has remained in use ever since. This corpus of mortuary spells is now better understood as a development from the Coffin Texts of the Middle Kingdom, which in turn evolved from the Old Kingdom Pyramid Texts.

Such traditional terminology is misleading, and gives the impression that the texts on tomb walls and coffin boards were solely composed for the deceased. But the Egyptians' investment in preparations for the afterlife contained a wealth of information regarding the world of the living. Most of the surviving mortuary texts are funerary adaptations of manuscripts that were originally composed to accompany ritual performances. There was no single or canonical Book of the Dead; people seem to have commissioned their own personal selection of religious and magical spells.

Nedjmet is one of very few owners of a Book of the Dead about whose life we know any details; she was married to king Herihor (1070 BCE), shown prominently in the vignettes, and was also the mother of a king (fig. 163).[97] Surviving letters on papyrus written by the powerful army commander Piankh show that she was involved in the political murder of two policemen who had made rebellious speeches: 'Have these two Medjay [policemen] brought to my house and get to the bottom of their words in short order, and have [them] killed and have them thrown [into] the water by night.'[98] Such an act, if revealed on judgement day, would have led to her damnation. On her Book of the Dead papyrus, which was over 14 metres long, she is shown standing by the scales in anticipation of her heart being weighed against the feather of Maat, goddess of truth and justice (figs 164–165).

163 (top)
Fragment of the Book of the Dead of Nedjmet, wife of king Herihor. The section to the right of this papyrus is in the Louvre (E 6258) and the central section was formerly in Munich but is now lost.
Egypt, 21st Dynasty, *c.* 1069 BCE
Papyrus, H. 34 cm, W. 416 cm, D. 0.2 cm
British Museum, EA10541
Donated by King Edward VII

164 (facing page)
Squatting figure of Maat upon a pedestal. The goddess of truth and justice can be represented as a feather or as a female figure with a feather on her head.
Egypt, Late Period, 747–332 BCE
Copper alloy, H. 11.5 cm, W. 3.1 cm, D. 3.4 cm
British Museum, EA60383

165 (above)
Heart amulets were often wrapped inside the mummy bandages. The jasper amulet is inscribed with hieroglyphs from Chapter 30B of the Book of the Dead.

(from left to right)
Egypt, date unknown. Breccia, H. 4.9 cm, W. 3.8 cm, D. 2.4 cm. British Museum, EA24393

Egypt, date unknown. Red jasper, H. 2.7 cm, W. 1.6 cm, D. 0.6 cm. British Museum, EA8090

Egypt, 18th to 19th Dynasty, 1350–1250 BCE. Jasper, H. 5.3 cm, W. 3.5 cm, D. 1.8 cm. British Museum, EA15619

LIFE AFTER LIFE

Possible destinations in the afterlife were presented as idealised versions of Egypt, where people could continue many earthly activities, preferably only the pleasant ones. To avoid having to work, the deceased would be equipped with small magical figures who could take their owner's place when labour was required (fig. 166).[99] They are called shabtis, from the ancient Egyptian *wšb.tj* (*weshebti*), 'answerer'. According to the magic spell often written on the figures, they were supposed to answer on behalf of the dead person if they were called to the tasks of 'making the fields arable', 'flooding the banks' or 'conveying sand from east to west'.

In keeping with the ancient Egyptian worldview that the afterlife was a continuation of life, Egyptians sought to communicate with deceased relatives. Letters to the Dead were not meant simply to convey greetings, but were often prompted by unfortunate events in the writers' lives.[100] In those cases, the deceased, or some other person in the beyond, is charged with being the cause of these misfortunes. The recipient of such a letter is either requested to stop exerting malign influences, or to institute legal proceedings in the afterlife against a fellow spirit suspected of creating the problems. It was thought that hostile spirits could harm their living descendants: not just by causing physical injury, but also in terms of inheritance issues or confiscation of property. The latter is the subject of a letter written on a bowl from Qaw el-Qebir (fig. 167, see p. 195). In this letter, a person called Shepsi informs his late parents about problems with his inheritance, possibly triggered by his brother, who is causing trouble from the netherworld. Shepsi argues that he has acted in his parents' best interests, both in life and in death: in order to remain immortal in the afterlife, the dead need the living to carry out their mortuary rituals and keep their tombs in good order. The letters were recited and deposited in tombs, where the dead person would be sure to read them. This took place as part of a larger ritual performance, which included an invocation offering and execration rites such as the 'breaking of the red pots', which were intended to ward off danger.[101]

The idea of preserving the memory of the deceased and their position in society on earth is expressed by ancestor busts (fig. 168). These busts were plain and often without inscriptions, perhaps because they were generic images of unspecified ancestors or because the person to be remembered was well known to the family.[102] They could be set into household shrines, though several were found near tombs. The bust of Muteminet, sistrum player of Amun, Mut and Khonsu, could have belonged to the tomb chapel of her son Amenmose at Thebes, as a bust of her husband was also discovered there.[103]

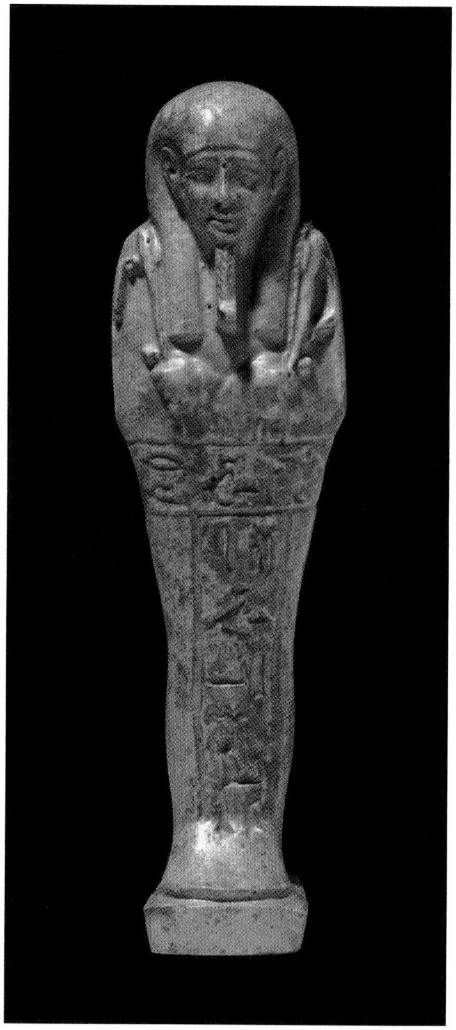

166
Shabti of Tarudj
Saqqara, 26th Dynasty, 664–525 BCE
Glazed composition, H. 15.6 cm, W. 4.4 cm, D. 3.2 cm
British Museum, EA9180

167 (above)
Letter to the Dead written on a bowl. On the inside of the bowl, Shepsi wrote to his deceased father; on the outside, he wrote to his deceased mother (see p. 195).
Qaw el-Qebir, 7th to 8th Dynasty, 2181–2125 BCE
Clay, diam. 19.5 cm
Petrie Museum, UC16163

168 (right)
Ancestor bust of Muteminet, who is identified by the inscription as the sistrum player of Amun, Mut and Khonsu, the divine family of Thebes
Thebes, 19th Dynasty, 1295–1186 BCE
Limestone, H. 51 cm, W. 26 cm, D. 29 cm
British Museum, EA1198

169
Stela of Userwer with offering formula and Appeal to the Living. Userwer is depicted with his wives and other family members. The stela was never finished; the grid and preliminary drawings are still visible.
Egypt, 12th Dynasty, 1985–1795 BCE
Limestone, H. 52 cm, W. 48 cm, D. 6.5 cm
British Museum, EA579

To mitigate the risk that the memory of an individual would fade into oblivion after death, the deceased called upon the living to read their names and recite the list of offerings out loud, so that the gifts would become real (fig. 169). Inscribed on stelae or tomb walls, these Appeals to the Living characteristically start with 'O you who live upon earth ... '. They often address a specific audience, such as priests, necropolis workers, scribes and royal dignitaries, who had regular access to temples and tombs.[104]

THE BUSTLING BUSINESS OF DEATH

The job of the necropolis workers did not end with the burial (fig. 170); patrons were also charged fees for maintaining the mortuary cult and protecting the tomb. We know from demotic texts that the rights to mummies and tombs and the income accrued from them were carefully defined among the necropolis workers, who may have been organised in guilds. Detailed registers were drawn up to record who was responsible for each mummy and who received the payment.[105]

On 14 July 157 BCE the scribe Harekusis, son of Imouthes, wrote an agreement between two groups of mortuary priests concerning duties that were to be carried out whenever the parties were professionally approached about the funeral of a citizen of Asyut (fig. 171).[106] Party A were to give various provisions to party B, including quantities of cloth on different days during the mummification process and possibly ceremonial clothing for specific individuals involved (fig. 172). Certain clauses stipulate items that were not to be provided, or appointments that they were not to make, presumably because other parties were responsible for these tasks. There were strict demarcation lines between the different groups of

170 (above)
Mummy-label of Tatetriphis with an extract from the 'Book of walking through eternity' in hieratic. Only the second half of line 3 and the beginning of line 4 on side A are written in demotic. Since mummified bodies were sometimes temporarily stored awaiting their turn to be buried, inscribed wooden labels were attached to the corpses for identification.
Akhmim, Roman Period, 2nd century CE
Wood, H. 5.6 cm, W. 10.6 cm, D. 0.6 cm
British Museum, EA23198

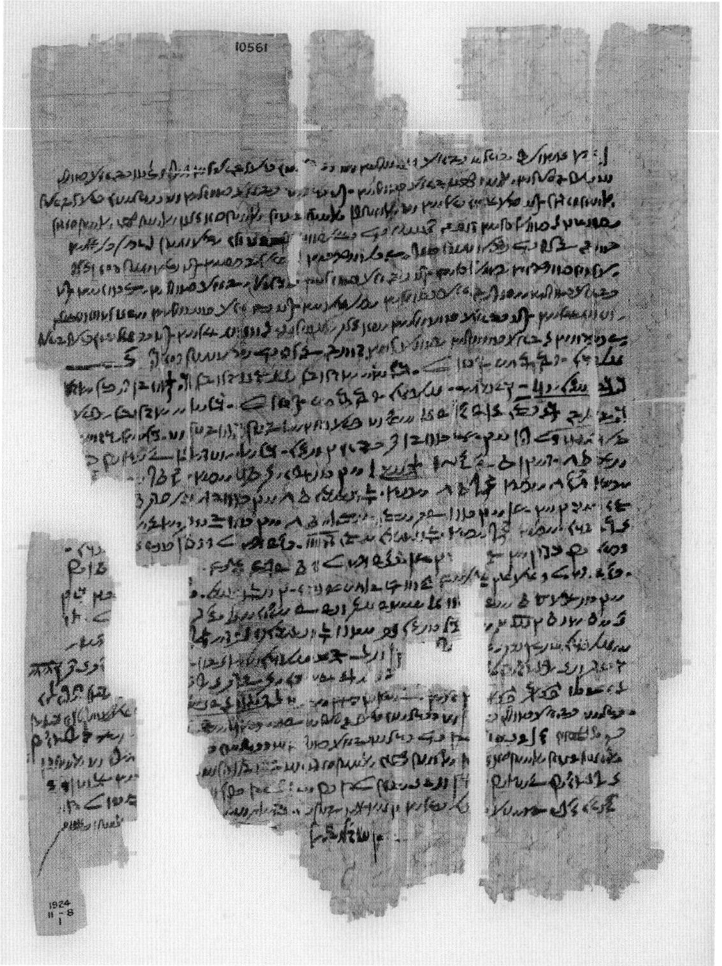

171 (right)
Agreement between lector priests, who accompany the embalming with recitations, and other men outlining their duties. The documents show that the business stayed in the family and responsibilities were passed on from father to son. The site of Asyut yielded one of the most extensive surviving archives.
Asyut, Ptolemaic Period, 157 BCE
Papyrus, H. 31 cm, W. 23.3 cm, D. 0.2 cm
British Museum, EA10561

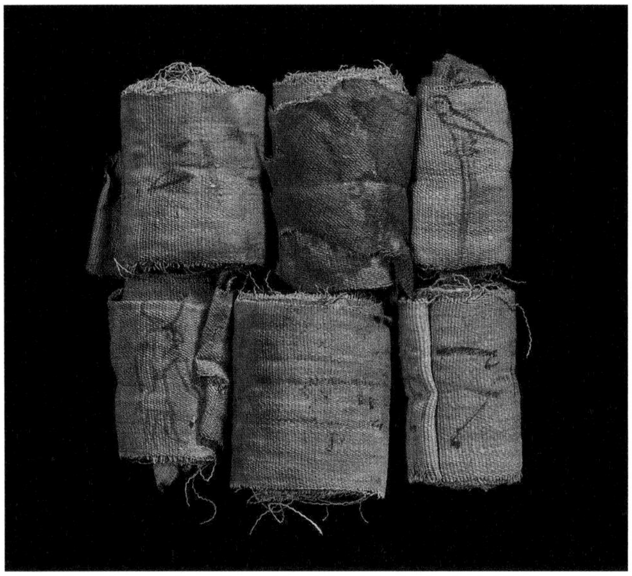

mortuary priests, both in terms of responsibilities and territorial jurisdictions. The 35th day was of particular ritual significance and the text states that no one else was allowed to 'carry out the ceremonies' of this day. The document ends with a penalty clause and royal oath.

As death became a lucrative industry, so such arrangements often led to disputes. The writer and recipient of a text on an ostracon (stone flake or pottery sherd) from Ptolemaic Thebes each thought they had purchased or inherited the rights to a certain burial (fig. 173).[107] The dispute became so hostile that one of the parties went so far as sealing up the tomb, thereby preventing any further mummies from being interred or removed. The case had been referred to the appropriate authorities to be resolved. The writer of the text had lost the dispute and accordingly signed a written oath stating that his claim had been invalid and issuing instructions for the tomb to be reopened, therefore allowing the other person to carry out his duties. The text on the interior of the ostracon is a summary of that on the exterior, suggesting that this is simply a draft for a more comprehensive record.

172 (left)
Inscribed pieces of linen with vignettes from the Book of the Dead and other funerary texts
Egypt, Ptolemaic Period to Roman Period, *c.* 100 BCE–200 CE
Linen and resin, H. 2.9–4.8 cm, W. 3.5–6.6 cm, D. 6.5–8 cm (rolled)
British Museum, EA15039

173 (right)
Ostracon with a dispute over the rights to a tomb
Egypt, Ptolemaic Period to Roman Period, 332 BCE–395 CE
Pottery, H. 9 cm, W. 10.5 cm, D. 1 cm
British Museum, EA5679

Shepsi's Letter to the Dead, 2181–2125 BCE

'It is Shepsi who addresses his father, Inekhenmut:

This is a reminder of your going to the prison, to the place where Sen's son Hetepu is, when you brought the foreleg of an ox, when I, your son, came with Enwaf, and when you said, "Welcome to me, both of you. Sit down and eat meat." Is it in your presence that I am being injured by my brother even though there is nothing that I, your son, did or said? Although three khar-measures of Upper Egyptian barley were charged against him as a loan (from me): a bolt of cloth, a mace(?), six hekat-measures of Upper Egyptian barley, a bundle(?) of flax, and a cup, and although he had done what ought not to have been done, I prepared him for burial, brought him back from the city of […], and interred him among his necropolis companions. Since you had said regarding me, your son, "It is in my son Shepsi that all my property shall be vested," he has done this against me, your son, very wrongfully.

Now my fields have been taken possession of by Sher's son Henu. Now that he (my brother) is with you in the same city (of the dead), you must institute litigation with him since you have witnesses at hand in the same city. Can the man who wields the javelin be joyful while his rulers are repressed?

It is Shepsi who addresses his mother, Iy:

This is a reminder of the fact that you said to me, your son, "You shall bring me some quails that I may eat them" and I, your son, then brought you seven quails and you ate them. Is it in your presence that I am being injured so that my children are disgruntled and I, your son, am ill? Who, then, will pour out water for you?

If only you might decide between me and Sobekhotep, whom I brought back from another city to be interred in his own city among his necropolis companions after tomb clothing had been given to him. Why is he injuring me, your son, so wrongfully, when there is nothing that I said or did? Wrongdoing is disgusting to the gods!'[108]

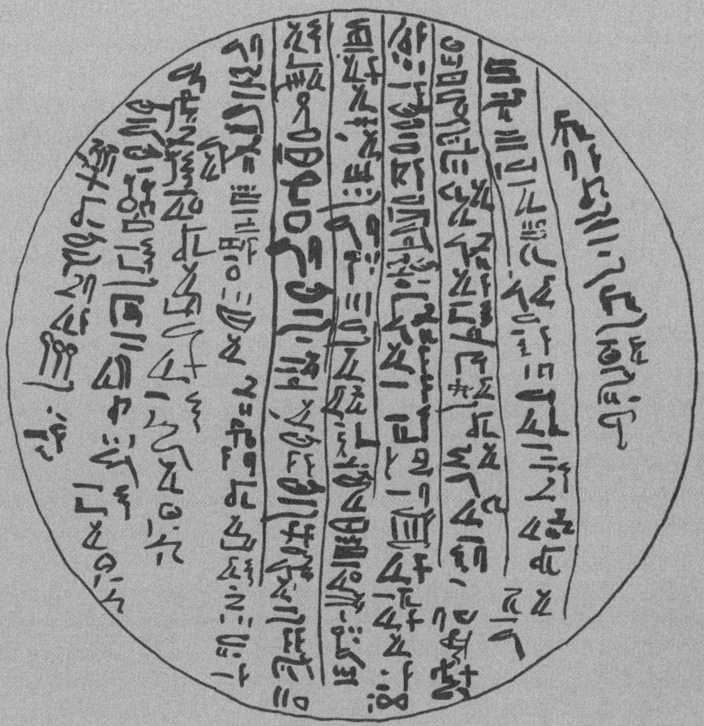

PERSONAL STORIES

Ilona Regulski

Champollion paved the way for other scholars to refine our knowledge of the Egyptian writing system. Thanks to the decipherment of hieroglyphs we know that, just like us, ancient Egyptians made jokes, sent letters, enjoyed literature, married and divorced, and negotiated business deals. Access to the vast scope of written culture preserved from ancient Egypt allows us to reconnect with these ancient people in a way that was not possible before the ingenious act of decipherment. The secular nature of much ancient Egyptian writing may be surprising to some, as expressions of passion, politics and personal beliefs have often been overshadowed by religious prayers and monumental propaganda both in scholarly studies and in more general assumptions about ancient Egypt.

ACCOUNTING, MATHEMATICS AND CONSTRUCTION

Susanne Beck

The ancient Egyptians used numbers based on a decimal system for counting and to solve mathematical problems. The numbers 1, 10, 100, 1,000, 10,000 and 100,000 were written with individual hieroglyphic signs (fig. 174). Egyptian numbers do not have a place value (or values based on a digit's position within a number; for example, the position of 4 in 743 tells us that it is worth 40). Instead, multiples of 1, 10, 100 and so on were written by repeating the relevant sign. Therefore, the number 743 would have been written with the sign for 100 repeated seven times, the sign for ten repeated four times, and the sign for one repeated three times: 𓍢𓍢𓍢𓍢𓍢𓍢𓍢𓎆𓎆𓎆𓎆𓏤𓏤𓏤. There was no sign for zero, but it was expressed by words that mean 'none' or 'there is not'.

The Egyptians did not express fractions as we do, with a single round numerator (the top figure) and a single round denominator (the bottom figure below the line). We would write, for example, $\frac{5}{8}$. The Egyptians used the smallest denominator possible, adding a second fraction to express the extra value: so $\frac{5}{8}$ was written $\frac{1}{2}$ $\frac{1}{8}$ (a half – that is, four-eighths – and one-eighth). This has the advantage that direct comparison of fractions is easier: comparing $\frac{5}{8}$ and $\frac{4}{7}$ with each other, we can only tell that both are a bit more than $\frac{1}{2}$. The Egyptian notation as $\frac{1}{2}$ $\frac{1}{8}$ and $\frac{1}{2}$ $\frac{1}{14}$ (a half and

174
Table with the Egyptian numbers in hieroglyphs. The numbers 1 to 9 are represented by an equivalent number of strokes.

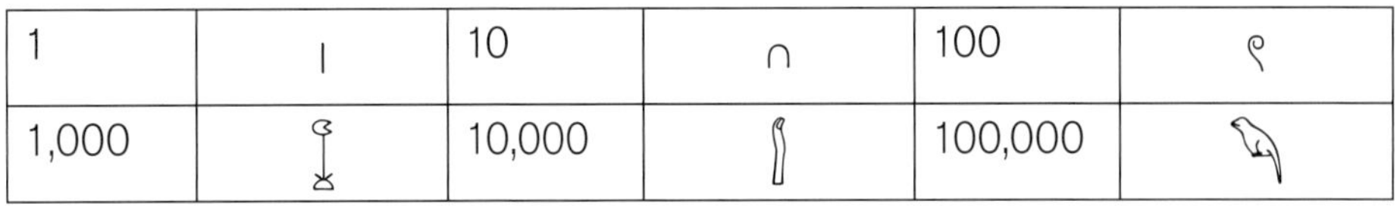

1	2	3	4	5	6	7	8	9
I	II	III	IIII	III II	III III	IIII III	IIII IIII	III III III

one-eighth, and a half and one-fourteenth) clearly shows that the former has a greater value.

The most famous document illustrating the advanced mathematical knowledge of the ancient Egyptians is the Rhind Mathematical Papyrus, discovered near the mortuary temple of Ramesses II in Thebes (modern-day Luxor) (fig. 175). The manuscript is named after the Scottish antiquarian and archaeologist Alexander Henry Rhind (1833–1863), who bought the two larger parts (EA10057–58) in Luxor in 1858. After his death, the papyrus was purchased by the British Museum in 1865.[109]

The papyrus was entitled 'Method of calculating for investigating into (all) things, knowing that, what all is, the obscurity […] every secret' and was a textbook used by scribes to learn how to solve particular mathematical problems by writing down examples. Writing during the Second Intermediate Period (1650–1550 BCE), the scribe Ahmose states that he copied the document from an older papyrus. The eighty-seven mathematical 'problems' are mostly calculations or tables for references.[110] Each one is introduced by a 'method of calculating', often written in red (underlined in the example below), and then sets out how to approach and solve the problem. For example, problem 65 is laid out as follows:[111]

> Method of dividing 100 loaves among 10 men: a sailor, a commander and a door keeper should receive double the portion of the remaining 7 men. The calculation: you shall add these three beneficiaries to the total number of men. 13 shall result. Divide by 13 these 100 loaves of bread. $7\ ^{2}/_{3}\ ^{1}/_{39}$ shall result. You shall say: This is the food for these men and the sailor, the commander and the door keeper who shall receive double the portion.

$7\ ^{2}/_{3}\ ^{1}/_{39}$	$7\ ^{2}/_{3}\ ^{1}/_{39}$	the sailor $15\ ^{1}/_{3}\ ^{1}/_{26}\ ^{1}/_{78}$	
$7\ ^{2}/_{3}\ ^{1}/_{39}$	$7\ ^{2}/_{3}\ ^{1}/_{39}$	the commander $15\ ^{1}/_{3}\ ^{1}/_{26}\ ^{1}/_{78}$	
$7\ ^{2}/_{3}\ ^{1}/_{39}$	$7\ ^{2}/_{3}\ ^{1}/_{39}$	the door keeper $15\ ^{1}/_{3}\ ^{1}/_{26}\ ^{1}/_{78}$;	sum: 100.
$7\ ^{2}/_{3}\ ^{1}/_{39}$			

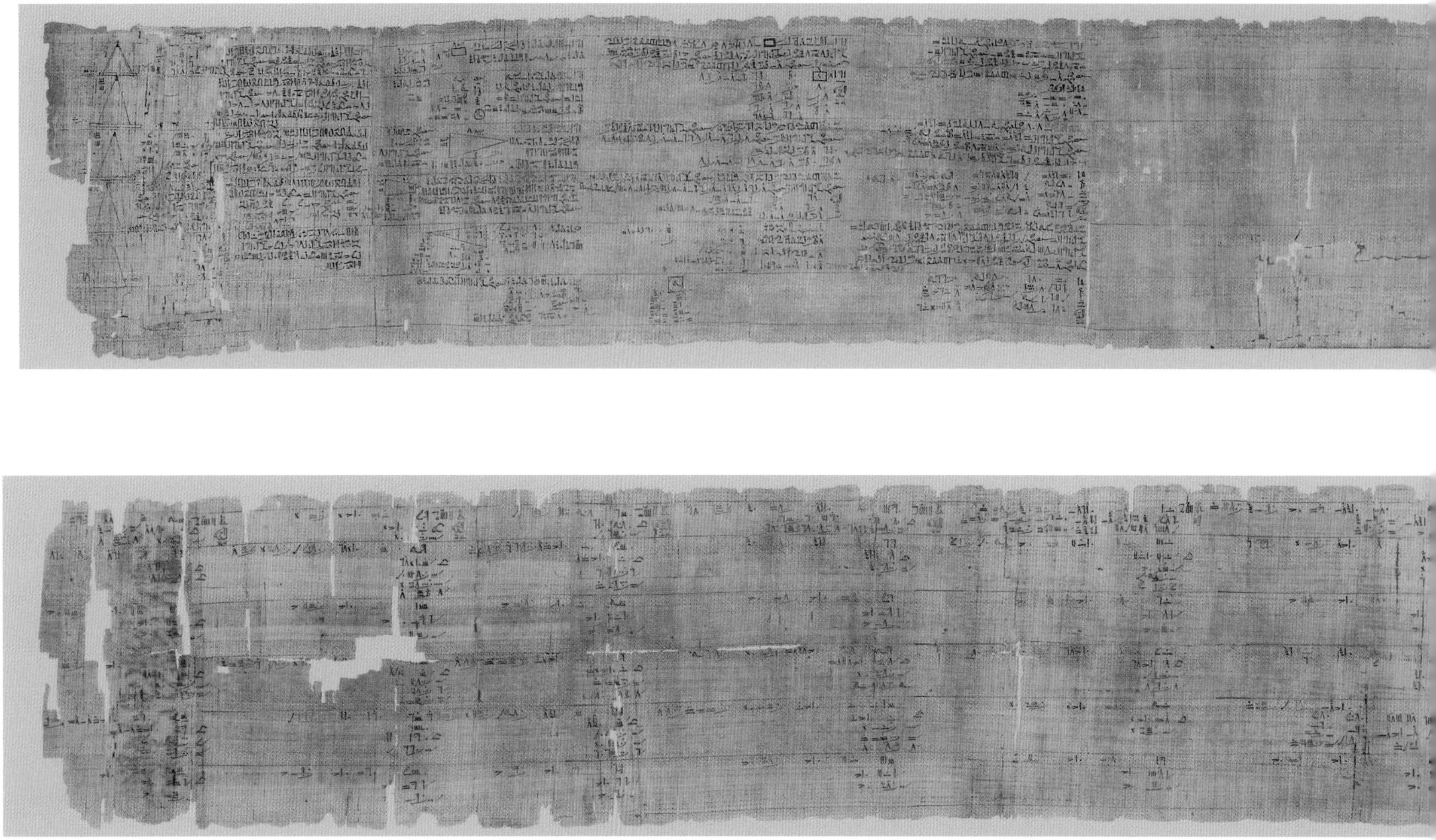

The approach to solving this problem is solution-oriented. One hundred loaves of bread are to be divided between 10 men, 3 of whom receive double rations: to simplify the task, the sailor, the commander and the door keeper are simply counted twice. Therefore, the 100 loaves of bread are divided by 13, which results in $7\ \frac{2}{3}\ \frac{1}{39}$ loaves of bread for each of the seven men, and twice that amount, or $15\ \frac{1}{3}\ \frac{1}{26}\ \frac{1}{78}$ loaves of bread, for each of the three exceptional beneficiaries. The total is 100 loaves of bread.

Obsessed with building large monuments and measuring the height of the annual Nile flood, the Egyptians used different units of measurement depending on their needs. Length units were mainly inspired by the human body. For example, the basic unit was the cubit (*mḥ*) (fig. 176), which is the length of a person's forearm from the elbow to the tip of the middle finger

175
The Rhind Mathematical Papyrus
Thebes, Second Intermediate Period, c. 1550 BCE
Papyrus, H. 33 cm, W. 296 cm, D. 0.2 cm (top), H. 32 cm, W. 198.5 cm, D. 0.2 cm (bottom)
British Museum, EA10057–58

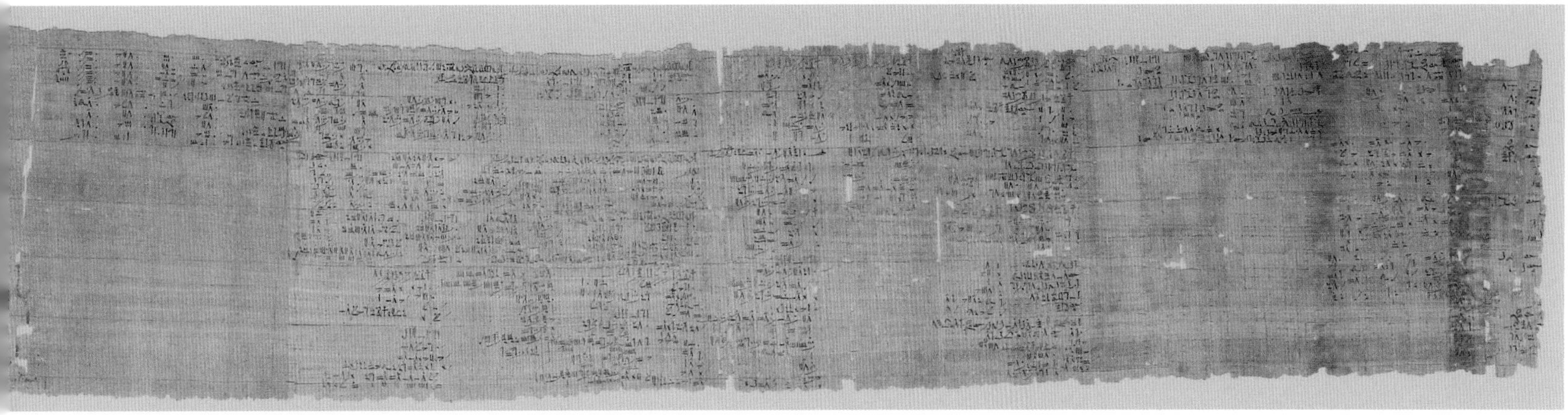

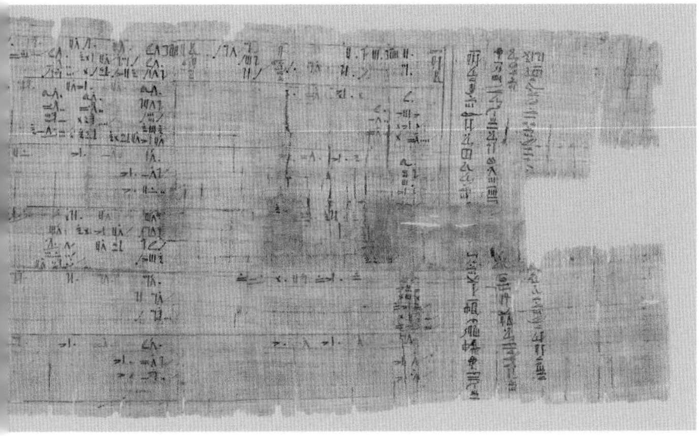

(approximately 45 cm). The cubit was subdivided into seven palms (7.5 cm), which were further separated into four fingers (1.875 cm). Longer distances were measured with the help of ropes and a unit of 100 cubits.[112] In the Rhind Mathematical Papyrus, the so-called royal measuring-rod or cubit is used, which is 52.2 cm long and therefore most likely longer than the cubit used in daily life (fig. 177).

The Rhind Mathematical Papyrus contains one of the oldest approximations to the constant π (3.14159), used to calculate the ratio of a circle's circumference to its diameter: 3.1605.[113] The only other ancient approximation of π was found in Babylon, where a clay tablet dated 1900–1600 BCE has a geometrical statement that, by implication, treats π as 25/8 = 3.1250.

For measurement of volume, the units *ḥḳ3.t* (about 4.8 litres) and *ẖ3r* ('sack') were used; 20 *ḥḳ3.t* fit into 1 *ẖ3r*, but this division changed over time. Such units were needed to measure grain or flour, the standard currency for salaries or other transactions where money, in the present-day sense, was not used. Small weights, mainly used for metal or gemstones, had *dbn* as the basic unit but, as with the *ẖ3r*, the weight significantly changed during pharaonic times and also depending on what kind of material was being measured (fig. 178). Over 3,000 years ago in Deir al-Medina, the price for a bed fluctuated between 12 and 25 *dbn*, which we know from other texts is between 6 and 12.5 *ẖ3r* of grain (fig. 179).[114]

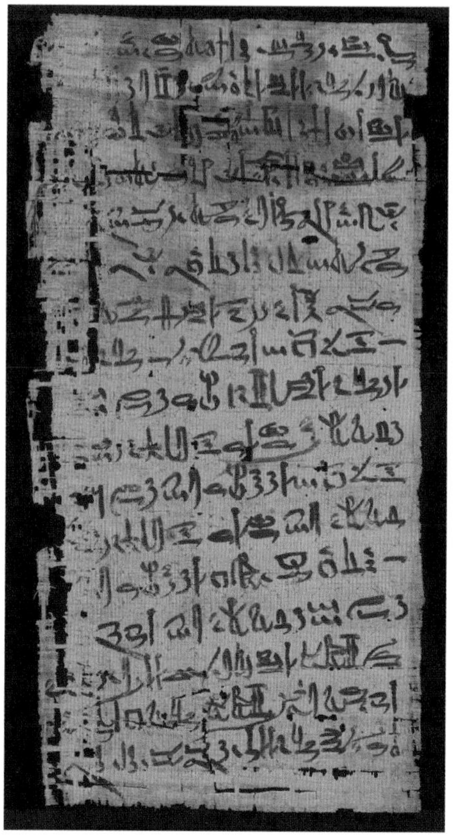

176
Letter by Mentuhotep to the scribe Ahmose of Peniat with instructions about the construction of a house, including the height of the walls in cubits. Ahmose is overseeing the project and is to pass this information to the builder, Amenmose.
Thebes, 18th Dynasty, 1550–1295 BCE
Papyrus, H. 23.2 cm, W. 12 cm, D. 0.2 cm
British Museum, EA10102

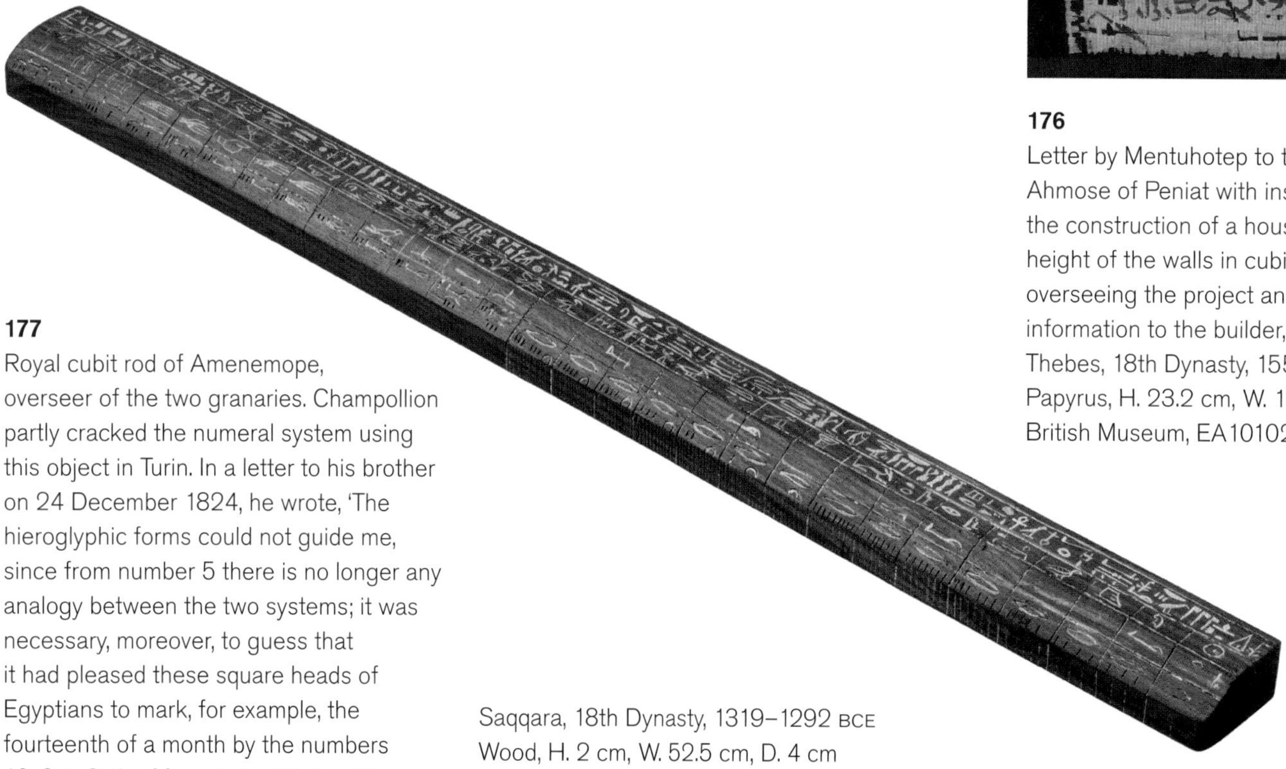

177
Royal cubit rod of Amenemope, overseer of the two granaries. Champollion partly cracked the numeral system using this object in Turin. In a letter to his brother on 24 December 1824, he wrote, 'The hieroglyphic forms could not guide me, since from number 5 there is no longer any analogy between the two systems; it was necessary, moreover, to guess that it had pleased these square heads of Egyptians to mark, for example, the fourteenth of a month by the numbers 10, 2 + 2, the fifteenth by 10, 3 + 2.'

Saqqara, 18th Dynasty, 1319–1292 BCE
Wood, H. 2 cm, W. 52.5 cm, D. 4 cm
Museo Egizio, Cat. 6347

CRIME IN ANTIQUITY

Ilona Regulski

The evidence for crime in ancient Egypt is diverse and can be found in royal decrees, administrative texts such as court proceedings and private writings.[115] Crimes against the state or the king comprised treason and desertion of military posts, while crimes against other human beings included murder, injury, adultery, robbery and theft. No formal Egyptian code of law has been preserved, although several pharaohs were known as lawgivers. In a legal proceeding, the plaintiff was required to bring the complaint against the defendant, who was then given the court order by a tribunal. The parties were not represented by lawyers but spoke for themselves and presented any relevant evidence. Witnesses were sometimes called, but the judge could rule on the grounds of the documents and the testimony of each party. The judgments included recommendations for preserving the written record of the trial – possibly the main reason why so many documents have survived.

A special problem that occurred widely was the plundering of tombs, those of ordinary people as well as kings (see fig. 4).[116] Looting royal tombs was punishable by death, but there seems to have been no such penalty for plundering private tombs. Instead, tombs were secured by threat formulas or temple oaths were sworn.

> Wording of the oath that Pelaias … should take for X (i.e. female name) … [on the dromos of Hathor in the year …]: 'as well as Hathor, who dwells here, lives, [and every god who dwells here] with her! As for this *ḳbꜣ.t* cloth and this … that were stolen from your tomb, I did not take them, nor did I cause [them to be taken]. I don't know anyone who has taken it.' If he takes the oath […] and …, his sister, takes it for his hand, saying: 'it is true', they are far from [him] …[117]

Theft of private property, especially items of daily life, is frequently mentioned. The penalty consisted of returning the stolen object and also paying the victim double or triple its value. The later years of the Twentieth Dynasty (1186–1069 BCE) yielded a lot of evidence, and several incidents can be ascribed to the same group of thieves.[118] A famous case concerned the theft of the copper fittings from a portable chest belonging to Ramessesnakht, High Priest of Amun, during the late part of the reign of Ramesses XI (1107–1077 BCE) (fig. 180). A porter and possible witness, Ahautinufer, was forced to give the names of all the men he had seen go into 'this place and do damage to the fittings of this portable chest'. He suggested that Pentehetnakht, who allegedly knew about the affair, should be questioned, and added quite incidentally that the culprits were the same group who had damaged the portable chest of Ramesses II and the *gs-pr* (probably also a chest) of Sety. Pentehetnakht was brought forward and described the attack in detail. Depositions were taken from the thieves in the temple by the scribe of the Necropolis Nesamenope, who is known from other similar cases.

Legal documents also described mortgages and moneylending. Accounts from private archives suggest that credit was readily available in Egypt. Panas, son of Espemetis, was a member of a well-known family of mortuary priests and moneylenders in Thebes in the early second century BCE.[119] Several papyri in his archive concern tombs, which was typical for such priests as their income came from the performance of mortuary rituals.

The other papyri attributed to Panas' archive concern sales or large loans secured by contracts.[120] In a demotic loan contract from 162 BCE (dated year 20, Phaophi 2 of Ptolemy VI Philometor and Cleopatra II, his sister), including, as was typical, a signature or short piece of writing in Greek at the end of the document, the herdsman Harsiesis acknowledged to the woman Ata that he had a debt of 690 silver *dbn*, due to be repaid in year 20, Pakhôn 30, eight months later (fig. 181). The loan was secured against his plot of high land in the temple endowment of Montu in the field of Tarkutis, which

PREVIOUS PAGE
178 (above left)
Sandstone weights using *dbn* as the basic unit, here marked with '60' (*c.* 948 g), '6' (*c.* 95 g) and the third with 'Sahura, beloved of the gods, unit 35' (*c.* 554 g).

(from top)
Gebelein, Middle Kingdom, 2055–1650 BCE. Sandstone, H. 2.7 cm, W. 5 cm, D. 3.4 cm. British Museum, EA15775

Gebelein, Middle Kingdom, 2055–1650 BCE. Sandstone, H. 6.9 cm, W. 9.4 cm, D. 6.4 cm. British Museum, EA23067

Egypt, 5th Dynasty, 2494–2345 BCE. Steatite, H. 4 cm, W. 4 cm, D. 2.9 cm. British Museum, EA65836

179 (above right)
Ostracon with part of a receipt for a bed and wooden furniture purchased by Amenemope from the carpenter Meryre
Deir el-Medina, late 19th Dynasty, 1200–1186 BCE
Ceramic, H. 13 cm, W. 15 cm, D. 2.7 cm
British Museum, EA5644

180 (facing page)
Papyrus with hieratic legal text concerning the trial of a group of men accused of stealing the copper fittings from the portable chest of Ramessesnakht
Egypt, 20th Dynasty, 1099–1069 BCE
Papyrus, H. 44 cm, W. 34 cm, D. 0.2 cm
British Museum, EA10403

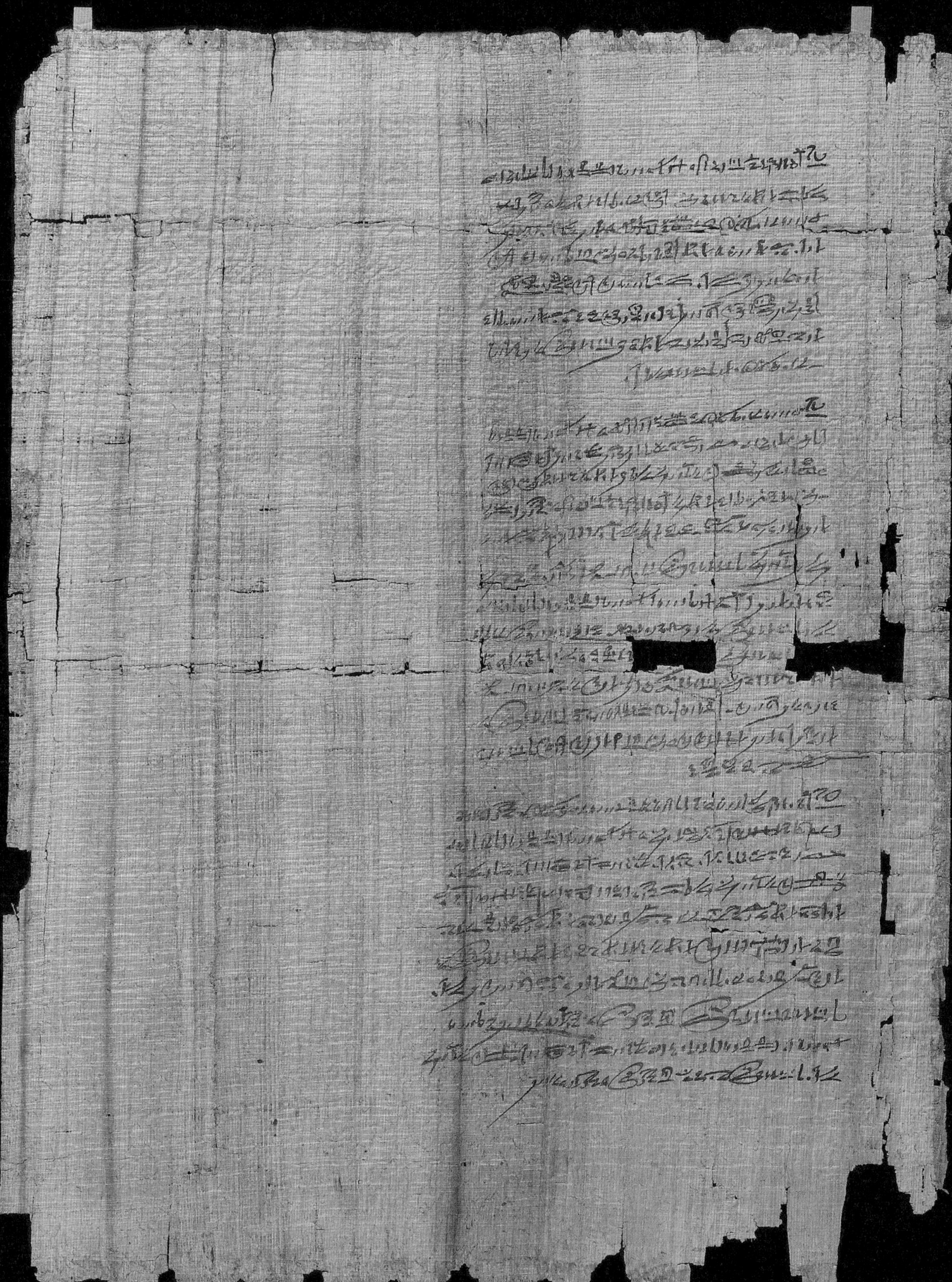

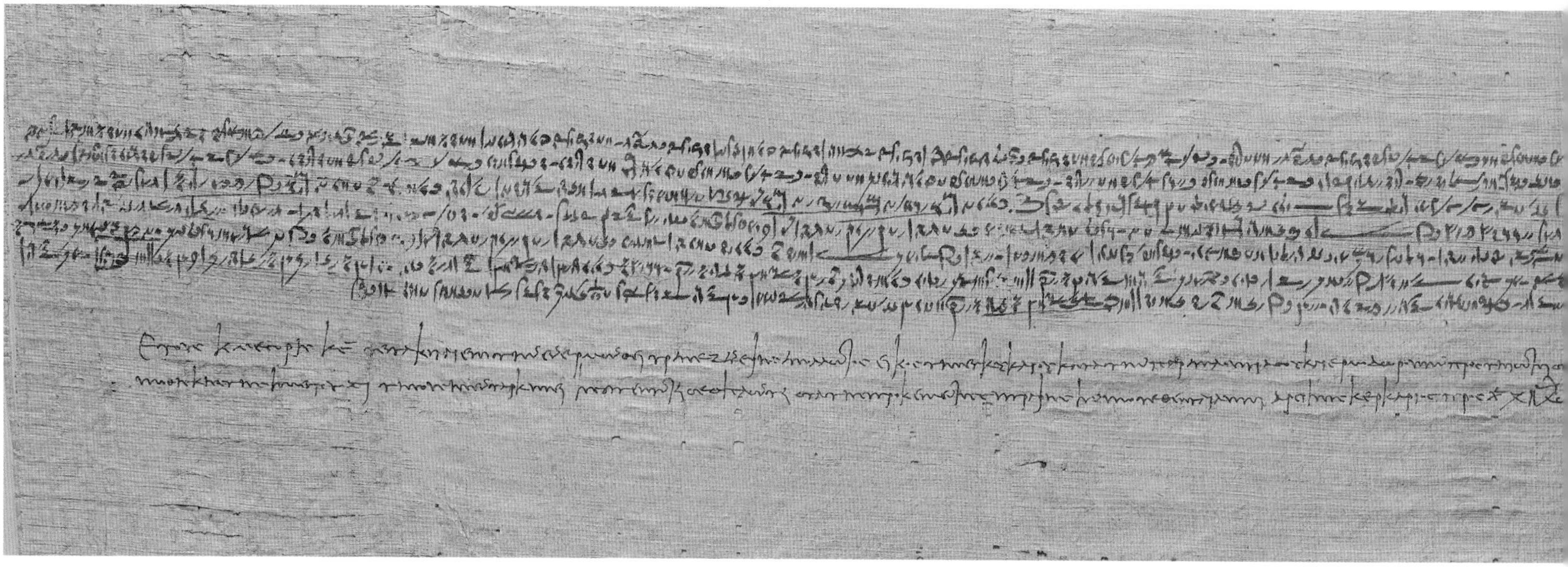

measured 10 *arourae* (about 6 acres). Harsiesis had repaid the debt and the document was returned to him. He evidently had money problems as he took out a new loan from Panas two years later. He failed to repay this loan and Panas took possession of the land. Harsiesis surrendered the contract to him as proof of Panas' entitlement to the plot of land (fig. 182).

Account summaries reveal that Panas also made many smaller loans, secured by objects or guarantors rather than a notarised contract, or in some cases apparently without security. Security for loans could consist of jewellery, jars, implements of metal or even cloth. Panas' archive suggests that he was a moneylender with a side business as a mortuary priest, rather than the other way around.

FAMILY, MARRIAGE AND DIVORCE

Susanne Beck

Family played an important role in Egyptian society. For many Egyptians, the main goal of life was to marry and have children.[121] The significance of family is expressed in Wisdom Texts and on stelae, where entire genealogies of extended families are immortalised. The Teaching of Ani says:

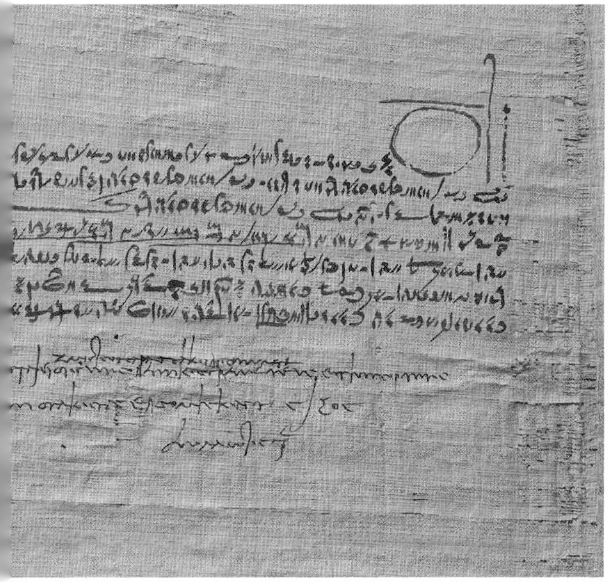

> Take a wife while you are a youth. Teach her so that she behaves as a human being. She will give birth to a son when you are still young, and offspring comes into being for you. A man exists while he is surrounded by humans – he is respected [literal translation: greeted] because of his children.[122]

Wisdom Texts suggest that a husband should cherish his wife even if she doesn't bear any children. If a wife was not able to conceive (which was how the Egyptians perceived it – that the woman, not the man, was the cause of infertility), a child could be adopted.[123] The family was often depicted with their parents on stelae to remember the deceased (see fig. 169). Respect for one's father and mother was a cornerstone of morality and the most fundamental duty of the eldest son (or occasionally daughter) was to care for the parents. In 1072 BCE Butehamen writes to the Troop-Commander Shedsuhor, expressing concerns about his father Tjaroy, who is about to go on a journey to Nubia with Shedsuhor (fig. 183):

181 (facing page, top)
Demotic loan contract from Panas' archive with phrases in Greek and demotic
Thebes, Ptolemaic Period, 162 BCE
Papyrus, H. 33 cm, W. 84.5 cm
British Museum, EA10823

182 (facing page, bottom)
Boundary stela incised with the words *pr-snt*, 'the house of Senet', marking his ownership of the estate
Egypt, Middle Kingdom, 2055–1650 BCE
Limestone, H. 23.4 cm, W. 9.6 cm, D. 5.7 cm
British Museum, EA59205

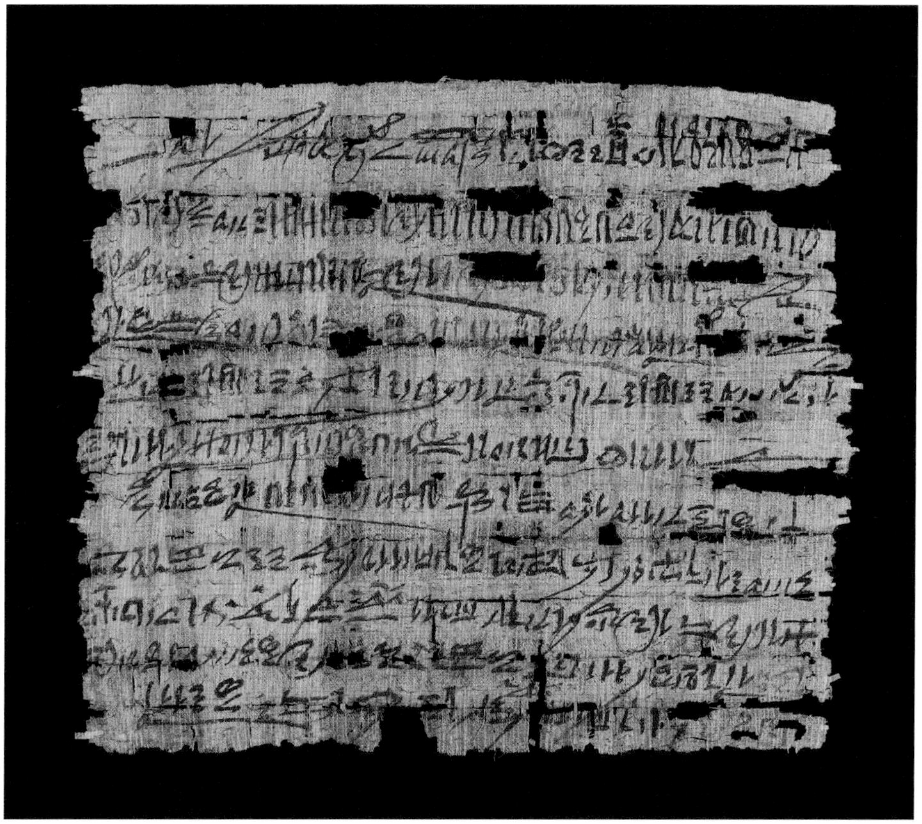

183 (right)
Letter from Butehamen expressing concerns about his elderly father, Tjaroy, who is about to go on a long journey, dated 'Year 10 of the "Renaissance Era" [Year 28 of Ramesses XI]'.
Thebes, 20th Dynasty, 1072 BCE
Papyrus, H. 32 cm, W. 53 cm, D. 0.2 cm
British Museum, EA10284

Indeed you are kind, and my father belongs to you. Be a pilot for the scribe of the (royal) tomb Tjaroy! You know he is a man who has no courage/experience of his own at all, since he has never before made such journeys as now. Help him in the boat. Look after (him) with vigilance in the evening as well, while he is in your hands, since you are journeying [...]. Now a man is childlike when he has become troubled, when he has never before seen the face of fear. Now your people are alive; no harm has come to them. I am writing to let you know. Farewell![124]

Intimacy between family members is especially revealed by the motif of the mother feeding her child. The striking representation of the mother goddess Isis holding and breastfeeding her son Horus was later adapted by Christians into the image of the nursing Virgin with child, known as Madonna Lactans (fig. 184). Depicted individually, children are often shown

184 (left)
Enthroned statue of Isis nursing Harpocrates, commissioned by Panebu, son of Wesirnakht, one of the king's teachers
Egypt, 26th Dynasty, *c.* 664–525 BCE
Feldspar, breccia and gold, H. 17.5 cm, W. 6.6 cm, D. 12 cm
British Museum, EA23050

185 (right)
Statue of Harpocrates, its base inscribed with hieroglyphs and Phoenician
Egypt, 6th–4th century BCE
Bronze, H. 26.8 cm, W. 14.9 cm, D. 6.4 cm
British Museum, 132908

186 (left)
Bes amulet with suspension ring
Egypt, date unknown
Glazed composition, H. 6.9 cm, W. 2.9 cm, D. 1.9 cm
British Museum, EA61218

187 (centre)
Heket good luck charm
Egypt, New Kingdom to Third Intermediate Period, 1550–747 BCE
Diorite/gneiss, H. 1 cm, W. 2 cm, D. 1.4 cm
British Museum, EA14758

188 (right)
Taweret amulet with suspension ring
Egypt, date unknown
Glazed composition, H. 3.7 cm, W. 1.3 cm, D. 1.7 cm
British Museum, EA11853

naked, suckling on their index fingers and wearing the side lock of youth (a special hairstyle worn by the young). The typical depiction of 'Horus the child' was adopted by the Greeks as Harpocrates and became popular in Egypt and beyond (fig. 185, see fig. 39).

As family was so significant for the Egyptians, it was essential to protect one's relatives from evil. Several gods and goddesses were known to protect the family, especially children, pregnant women, mother and baby during childbirth, and newborns. The most important ones were Bes, Heket and Taweret. Bes, depicted as a dwarf with a lion's mane and protruding tongue, was mostly a god of popular religion and was worshipped at home; one of his responsibilities was ensuring fertility (fig. 186). Heket was a goddess of fertility, associated with the goddess Hathor and represented in the form of a frog (fig. 187).[125] Taweret was shown as a hippopotamus with breasts, the paws of a lion and the tail of a crocodile, who walked on two legs like a human (fig. 188).

The legal and administrative organisation of families can be traced by large family archives, such as the one of necropolis workers and priests discovered at Asyut that covers almost ten years between the reigns of Ptolemy V and VI (between 181 and 170 BCE). These papyrus archives consist of court cases, petitions, leases, purchase orders, mummification contracts,

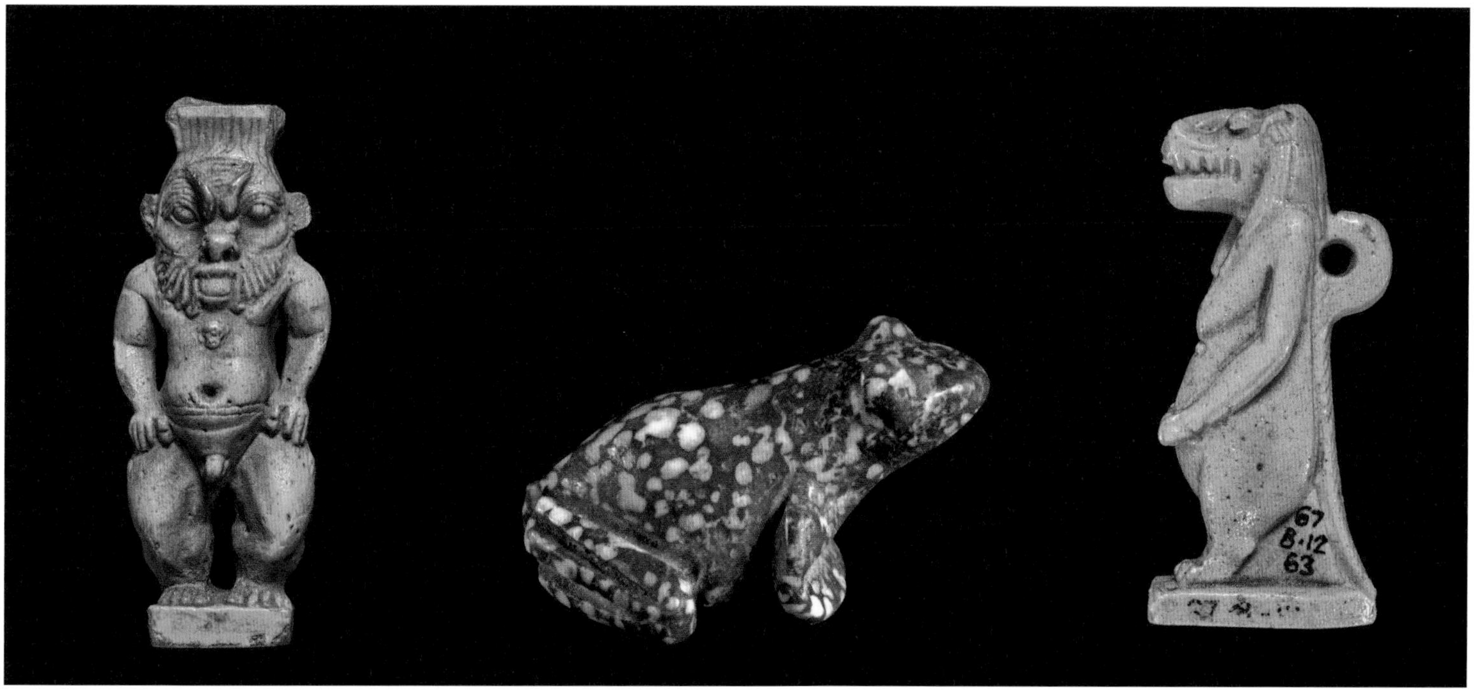

receipts and marriage contracts (fig. 189). Marriage contracts usually stated what would happen to the property of the wife and children in case of death or divorce.[126] When the father died, the son usually took his widowed mother, aunts and unmarried sisters into his household. Single men and women could have their own households.

Not all marriages turned out to be happy unions. An ostracon dating to *c.* 1186–1069 BCE reports the separation of Hessunebef from his wife Hener (fig. 190). According to the text he supported her for three years after the divorce.[127] In the case of a separation, which could be initiated by either party, the wife kept the possessions that she had brought to the marriage, and additionally had a partial claim to the properties she had acquired with her former husband.[128] The reason for the break-up between Hessunebef

189
Marriage document with the names of sixteen witnesses on the verso
Asyut, Ptolemaic Period, 172 BCE
Papyrus, H. 32 cm, W. 53 cm, D. 0.2 cm
British Museum, EA10593

190
Ostracon with a divorce document in hieratic, dated 'year 2, 3rd month of the summer, Setnakht'
Thebes, 20th Dynasty, 1186–1069 BCE
Limestone, W. 23 cm, D. 19 cm
Petrie Museum, UC 19614

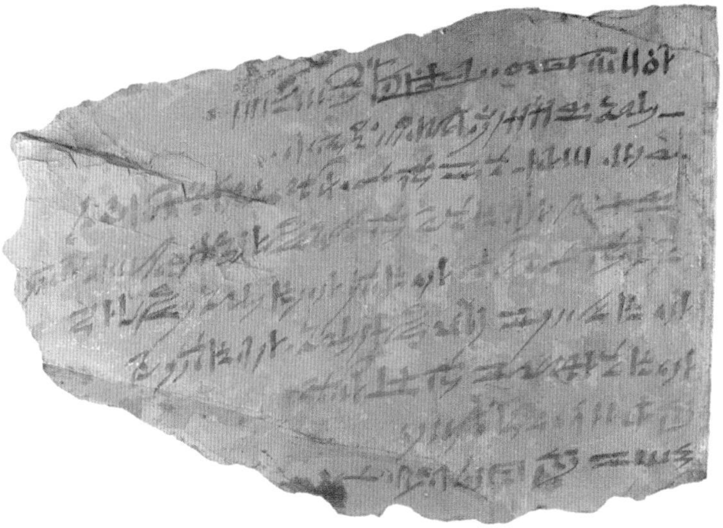

and Hener is not mentioned but, as today, several factors could have played a role; adultery was one. It was generally considered a bad deed, but the punishment for it was harsher for women.

SOCIAL SATIRE, SEXUAL SUBVERSION AND LOVE SONGS

Ilona Regulski

Social satire, in which the known world is turned upside-down and officials are mockingly portrayed as animals, is timeless. In ancient Egypt such depictions were not acts of overt rebellion, but expressed the human urge to criticise and ridicule social structures. As they have left little trace in the formal monumental record, it is difficult to reconstruct the original cultural context in which such concepts emerged.

The Tale of the Two Brothers, featuring two semi-divine protagonists and their adventures, has variously been interpreted as a fairy tale, a historical allegory and a political satire, among other readings (fig. 191, see p. 136). Highly entertaining and sophisticated, the tale is one of the most famous Egyptian compositions that became popular in New Kingdom Egypt (1550–1070 BCE).[129] The papyrus is unique in specifying the owner as the scribe Inena; it was unusual for this to be done in ancient Egypt. The text was written around 1215 BCE while Sety II was still crown prince. Inena is thus a near-contemporary of the famous Qenherkhepshef from Thebes (fig. 206).

191
The Tale of the Two Brothers, also known as Papyrus d'Orbiney
Memphis, 19th Dynasty, *c.* 1215 BCE
Papyrus, H. 28.7 cm, W. 49.8 cm
British Museum, EA10183,6

The story begins by presenting an idyllic household, consisting of Anubis, his wife and his brother, Bata.[130] Their pleasant lifestyle is disrupted when the wife of Anubis unsuccessfully tries to seduce her brother-in-law. Upset by the humiliation of his refusal, she claims that Bata attacked her. Believing his wife, Anubis initially turns against his brother and forces him to leave the family. Anubis later discovers his wife's disloyalty and kills her, and the brothers are reunited. Meanwhile the gods have fashioned a wife for Bata. Unfortunately she rejects him in favour of the king. To win her over Bata assumes a sequence of different forms, the last being a *persea* tree. Bata's wife orders the tree to be cut down. A splinter from the tree flies into her mouth, 'she swallowed it and in a moment she became pregnant'. Bata is reborn, now as her son, and becomes king of Egypt. He elevates his brother, Anubis, to succeed him, overcoming the catastrophes that had beset the pair.

Explicit depictions of erotic and sexual acts were uncommon in formal iconography, although nakedness was abundantly shown in Egyptian art. The purpose and context of explicitly erotic scenes, such as the ostracon showing two people having sex, is uncertain (fig. 192); sexual activity was associated with religious festivity, but the sketchy draughtsmanship of this and other examples suggests a frivolous, throw-away quality, like doodles on

192 (left)
Ostracon with sketchy black-painted erotic scene depicting two people having sex
Deir el-Medina, 19th to 20th Dynasty, 1295–1069 BCE
Limestone, H. 13.8 cm, W. 19 cm, D. 3.4 cm
British Museum, EA50714

193 (right)
Statuette of a squatting man with his phallus wrapped over his head
Egypt, Late Period to Ptolemaic Period, 400–50 BCE
Glazed composition, H. 4.2 cm, W. 3 cm, D. 1.5 cm
British Museum, EA90380

papyri.[131] There is a hieroglyphic caption in front of the woman that reads 'gentle is the charm of my skin'. The use of hieroglyphic instead of hieratic script may suggest that the maker was satirising more modest representations by mimicking the formal painting style.

Other erotic figures had apparently humorous aspects, such as the images of enormous phalli wrapped around the person's neck (fig. 193).[132] These objects could have been worn as amulets, as many have a hole for suspension at the back. Their purpose could have been to ensure potency, or perhaps to ward off evil: ithyphallic gods (gods depicted with erect penises) are often protective. They were also deposited in cultic areas as votive offerings.[133]

Love poems composed thousands of years ago may provide more intimate glimpses into ancient everyday life, as they are surprisingly direct about love and romance. Love poetry was part of an oral tradition and was probably sung, using the elements of the natural world – growing fruit, capturing birds, swimming in the Nile – as metaphors to talk about affection and desire (figs 194–198, see p. 219).[134]

194 (above)
Papyrus Harris 500, containing a collection of love songs (recto) and two Late Egyptian stories, *The Capture of Joppa* and *The Doomed Prince* (verso)
Egypt, 18th Dynasty, 1550–1295 BCE
Papyrus, H. 19.9 cm, W. 143.5 cm, D. 0.2 cm
British Museum, EA10060

195 (facing page, left)
Decorated and engraved sistrum, a musical instrument used in dances and religious ceremonies, especially in the worship of Hathor, goddess of love and music. Its sound had the power to appease the anger of gods and kings.
Egypt, Late Period, 747–332 BCE
Bronze, H. 38.4 cm, W. 10.8 cm, D. 6.7 cm
British Museum, EA36310

196 (facing page, right)
Cosmetic spoon in the form of a naked woman swimming with a duck
Egypt, New Kingdom, 1550–1069 BCE
Wood, H. 5 cm, W. 26.9 cm, D. 5.6 cm
British Museum, EA38186

197 (facing page, bottom centre)
Vase in the form of a pomegranate. In Papyrus Harris 500, sweet pomegranate wine is said to taste like bitter gall of birds if one suffers from love sickness.
Egypt, 18th Dynasty, 1550–1295 BCE
Glazed composition, H. 8.3 cm, W. 7.1 cm, D. 6.9 cm
British Museum, EA59398

198 (facing page, bottom right)
Ancient pomegranate
Egypt, date unknown
Organic, diam. 5 cm
British Museum, EA91062

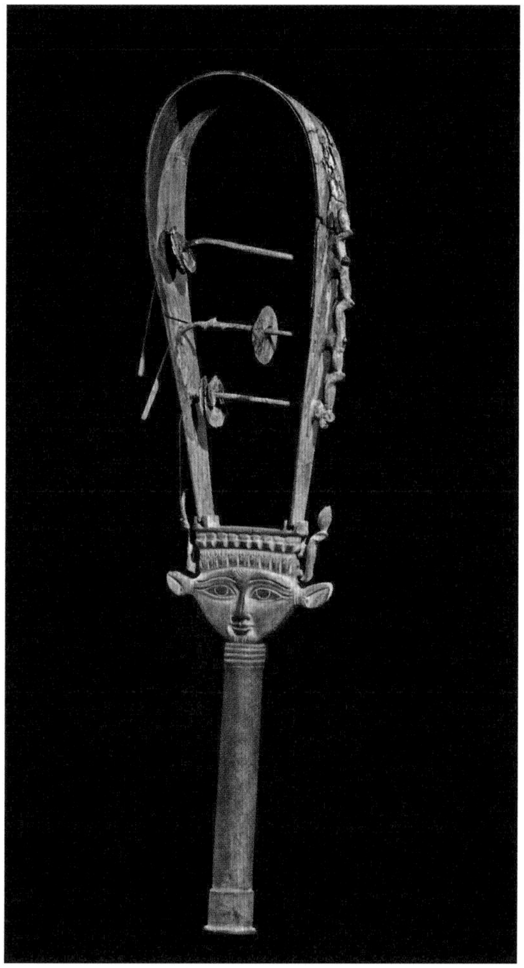

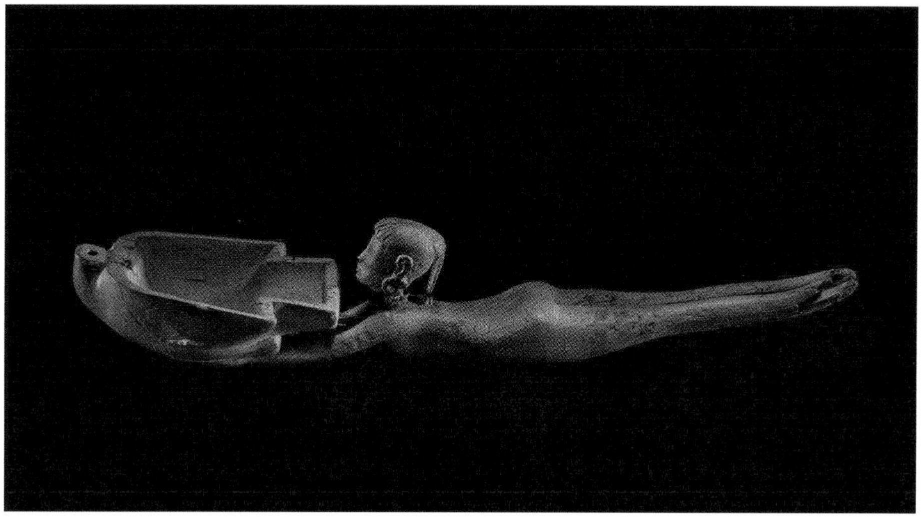

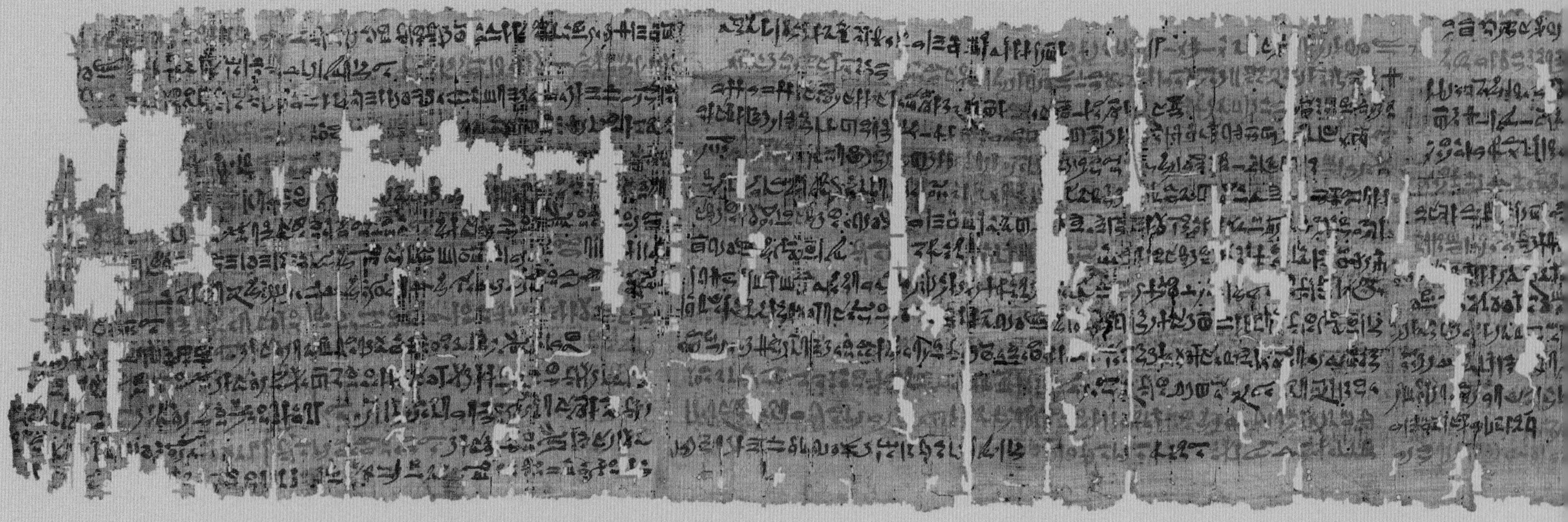

MEDICINE AND MAGIC

Susanne Beck

199 (above)
The London Medical Papyrus, with magical charms against infections and diseases
Egypt, 18th Dynasty, 1550–1295 BCE
Papyrus, H. 18.6 cm, W. 114.6 cm, D. 0.2 cm
British Museum, EA10059,1
Donated by the Royal Institution of Great Britain

Medicine in ancient Egypt was understood as a combination of practical technique and magical incantation and ritual. The London Medical Papyrus contains a broad range of charms and recipes against skin complaints, burns, eye diseases and miscarriages (fig. 199). Spell 7, for example, gives a remedy for the *tmj.t* disease, clearly a skin disease, using *psḏ* (an unidentified material), red ochre, Lower Egyptian salt, fruit of the *ḏ3js*-plant and barm (froth) of sweet beer (fig. 200). The papyrus also contains spells in a foreign language to repel contagious ailments.[135]

Spell 47 reads: 'Another [remedy against a burn]: incense, honey. [It] is anointed with it.' Honey is antimicrobial and incense has anti-inflammatory properties, so the remedy would have helped protect burns from infection.[136] The ancient Egyptians were plagued by plenty of eye ailments in daily life. More than ninety different recipes are known for the treatment of eyes; five are included in this medical papyrus.[137] One very common procedure was to apply eye-liner; preventative and cosmetic uses were not distinguishable from one other in ancient Egypt. Black (galena) and green (malachite) kohl powder, which has partial antibacterial properties, could be carried around in kohl-jars and painted around the eyes as necessary (fig. 201).[138]

200 (right)
Ingredients mentioned in magical and medical papyri for curing infections and diseases

(clockwise from top left)
Dish with fruits and textile remains. Egypt, New Kingdom, 1550–1069 BCE. Organics and ceramic, H. 4.7 cm, diam. 18.2 cm. British Museum, EA37254

Dates in a bowl. Egypt, New Kingdom, 1550–1069 BCE. Organics and ceramic, H. 4.3 cm, diam. 10.8 cm. British Museum, EA5369

Red ochre. Egypt, date unknown. H. 6.1 cm, W. 12.6 cm, D. 9.8 cm (in box). British Museum, EA91061

Salt in linen. Lower Egypt, Roman Period to Late Antique Period, 1st–8th century CE. Linen and mineral, H. 3.7 cm, diam. 8.3 cm (in container). British Museum, EA53927. Donated by the Egypt Exploration Fund

201 (left)
Kohl-jar with a band of gold foil around the rim
Egypt, Middle Kingdom, 2055–1650 BCE
Hematite and gold, H. 5.5 cm, diam. 5.6 cm
British Museum, EA32151

202 (below)
Head and upper body of the goddess Isis-Serqet with a scorpion on her head
Egypt, Late Period, 747–332 BCE
Green basalt, H. 10.5 cm, W. 7.1 cm, D. 6.6 cm
British Museum, EA57365

Incantations and hymns could also focus on repelling dangerous animals such as lions, crocodiles and venomous creatures.[139] These animals were a real threat in ancient Egypt and thus protective measures were a necessity. Perhaps for this reason, the scorpion goddess Serqet, or Selkis, was a patron for magical-medical healing of venomous bites and stings (fig. 202).

Other deities could also aid patients in need. In a famous myth, Thoth, the god of writing and wisdom, healed the eye of the god Horus after his battle with his uncle Seth; Isis healed her son Horus as a child when he was attacked by venomous animals; Horus the elder/Haoeris enjoyed a reputation as a physician; the moon and war god Khonsu and the ferocious lion goddess Sakhmet, both associated with plagues, could aid in overcoming diseases; and the procreation deity Min, as well as Imhotep, the architect of Djoser's step pyramid (*c.* 2720–2700 BCE), were both known as healers. Two thousand years after his death, Imhotep was deified and worshipped as a god of medicine and healing (fig. 203).[140] Because of his association with health, Imhotep was equated by the Greeks with Asklepios, their own god of health who was also a deified mortal.

Protective spells could either be recited when needed or written on long papyrus strips, rolled up and worn in amulet cases around the neck (fig. 204).[141] Evil could be warded off with good luck charms in the form of the *wedjat* (fig. 205), the eye of Horus, or by employing so-called Horus cippi, a specific kind of magical stela depicting the god Horus as a naked child standing on crocodiles and holding snakes, scorpions, a lion or an antelope. Often these stelae are topped by the face of the god Bes with inscriptions on the back (see fig. 39). The ritual consisted of pouring water over them to enhance the power of the inscriptions.[142]

203 (top left)
Solid-cast bronze seated figure of Imhotep with an unrolled papyrus on his lap
Egypt, Late Period, 747–332 BCE
Bronze, H. 15.5 cm, W. 4 cm, D. 7 cm
British Museum, EA64495
Donated by Marion Whiteford Acworth JP

204 (right)
Oracular amuletic decree of Buiharkhons, in hieratic. The text is a series of sentences starting with 'we shall keep her safe from …' For example, 'We shall keep her safe from Sakhmet and her son. We shall keep her safe from the collapse of a wall and from the fall of a thunderbolt. We shall keep her safe from leprosy, from blindness and from the Wedjat-eye'.
Thebes, 22nd Dynasty, *c.* 900 BCE
Papyrus, H. 64 cm, W. 5.8 cm, D. 0.3 cm
British Museum, EA10083

205 (bottom left)
Protection amulet in the shape of the *wedjat*, the eye of Horus
Egypt, date unknown
Steatite, H. 1.9 cm, W. 1.7 cm, D. 0.6 cm
British Museum, EA8069

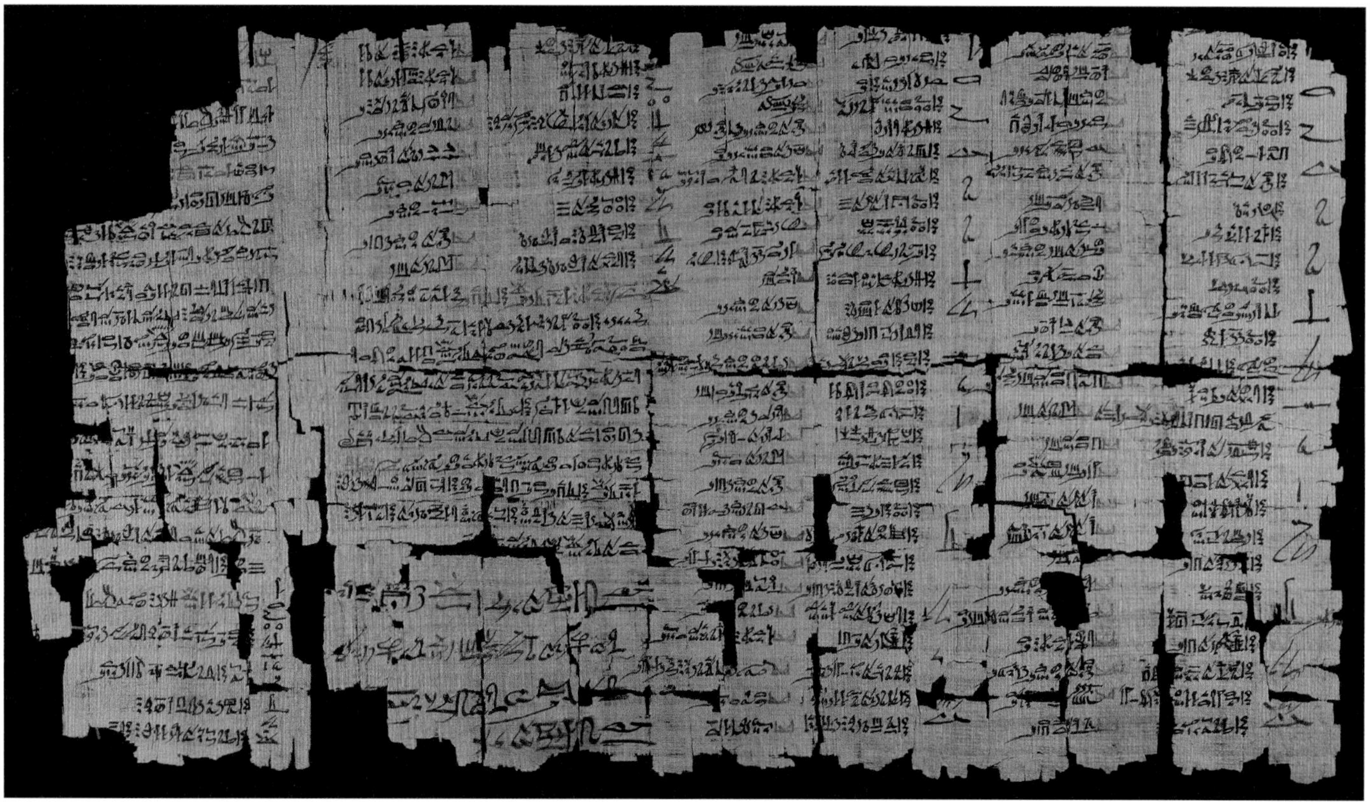

206
Papyrus Chester Beatty III, with a manual for interpreting dreams on the recto and Qenherkhepshef's bold handwriting on the verso. The latter reveals copies of the poem of the Battle of Qadesh and a letter to a high official.
Deir el-Medina, 19th Dynasty, *c.* 1220 BCE
Papyrus, H. 33.5 cm, W. 60.7 cm, D. 0.2 cm
British Museum, EA10683,3
Donated by Sir Alfred Chester Beatty and Lady Edith Chester Beatty

The outlook for an individual's day could be consulted in the calendar of lucky and unlucky days (see fig. 150) and it was believed that dreams could reveal the future. Papyrus Chester Beatty III contains parts of a dream book used to determine a person's fate (fig. 206).[143] The beginning and end of the manuscript are lost; the rest is divided into columns starting with 'If a man sees himself in a dream' followed by a list of actions. Then it is stated whether this is a good or bad omen and how the dreamer would benefit or suffer from it. Furthermore the dream book distinguishes different personalities, including a description of the most typical aspects of their nature. Treatises for female users are known from later dream books, but the preserved parts of this one are only applicable to well-behaved men:

> If a man sees himself in a dream fetching vessels from the water: good – the finding of increased life in his house.
> If a man sees himself in a dream, seeing his penis erect: <u>bad</u> – this means victory for his enemies.

Love song from Papyrus Harris 500, 1550–1295 BCE

'The voice of the goose calls,
It is trapped by its bait.
Your love restrains me,
I cannot let go of it.

I shall gather up my nets,
But what shall I say to my mother,
To whom I return every day
Burdened with my catch of birds?
I did not set my trap today, for love of you has trapped me.

The goose flies and alights;
It plunged into the trap,
While many birds are circling around.
I hasten [away] but turn back again,
Held fast by love when I am alone.
My heart inclines towards your heart,
And I shall never be distant from your beauty.

I shall go out [to seek my lover].
[I yearn] for our love,
And my heart stops within me.
To look at a sweet cake,
Is like looking at salt;
Sweet pomegranate wine in my mouth
Is like the bitter gall of birds.

The breath of your nostrils
Is the sole thing which can revive my heart,
And I am determined that Amun will grant you to me
For ever and eternity.'[144]

CREATING AND PRESERVING WRITING

Ilona Regulski

> I watched those seized for labour. There's nothing better than books![145]
>
> *The Teaching of Khety, or 'Satire of the Trades',*
> *1300–1200 BCE*

In ancient Egypt, being able to write was a key to success. That does not mean that all scribes mastered hieroglyphs, which were reserved for formal and religious monuments. Many of the literate were trained only in the cursive scripts (hieratic and demotic) that were used to produce everyday documents generated by the Egyptian bureaucracy. Estimating degrees of literacy in ancient Egypt is difficult, but it must have been restricted to a very low percentage of the population, perhaps 1 per cent.[146] Those unable to read or write themselves employed scribes to draw up contracts, letters and wills. Unsurprisingly, every parent hoped to see their son become a scribe: they were highly respected members of society. In Papyrus Lansing, we read:

> Befriend the scroll, the palette. It pleases more than wine. Writing for him who knows it is better than all other professions. It pleases more than bread and beer, more than clothing and ointment. It is worth more than an inheritance in Egypt, than a tomb in the West.
>
> British Museum, EA9994,2–4[147]

This is how scribes typically referred to the value of their own profession, addressing others who were to follow the same path. It is unclear to what extent this reflected the general perception of education among members of Egyptian society. Yet scribal tools became grave goods for those who wanted to stress their social status beyond the here and now (figs 207–208).

SCRIBAL TRAINING

Education and apprenticeship in ancient Egypt were profession-oriented, aimed at training scribes and specialist craftsmen to work in local and national institutions such as the palace and temples. The main term employed to denote 'education' in the ancient Egyptian language was *sbꜣ.jt*, meaning 'instruction'.[148] The same term features in the titles of Egyptian works of wisdom known as 'Instructions', which may suggest a pedagogical use of such literary works (see p. 172).

Ancient Egyptians referred to schools as *pr-ꜥnḫ*, 'house of life', or less commonly, *tꜣ-sbꜣ*, 'place of instruction'. The House of Life may also have been a 'scriptorium' or a space in which scribes worked, studied, produced

207 (facing page, right)
Scribal palette bearing an incised funerary text, with empty spaces to add the owner's name. The palette does not show traces of usage, suggesting it was specially made as part of the funerary equipment.
Egypt, 18th Dynasty, 1550–1295 BCE
Schist, H. 31.7 cm, W. 4.5 cm, D. 1.2 cm
British Museum, EA12779

208 (facing page, bottom left)
Knives for sharpening or cutting writing brushes
Thebes, 18th Dynasty, 1550–1295 BCE
Bronze, L. 17 cm (top), L. 22 cm (bottom)
British Museum, EA65636, EA65635

209 (right)
Statue of an anonymous scribe seated cross-legged with an unfolded papyrus on his lap. The statue entered the Louvre in 1827, when it was still called the Musée Charles X after the king. The year before, Champollion had become the first curator of the Egyptian collection.
Egypt, 5th Dynasty, 2494–2345 BCE
Limestone, H. 58 cm, W. 35 cm, D. 33 cm
Musée du Louvre, N 43-A 42

and copied texts (fig. 209). These institutions were closely connected to temples, which included libraries and archives where religious, magical, medical and scientific writings were composed, copied and stored.[149]

The patron deity of the scribal profession was Thoth, god of the moon, thinking, learning and writing. His name means 'the one of the ibis', and he could be depicted as an ibis, or a man with the head of an ibis, or a baboon, another animal sacred to him (figs 210–212). He was the creator of languages and an interpreter and adviser of the gods. The Greeks associated him with Hermes, and eventually with Hermes Trismegistus, the legendary inventor of writing (see p. 38).

Evidence for the training of draughtsmen and sculptors exists in the form of practice ostraca, wooden or stone tablets, small papyrus fragments and trial pieces (figs 213–214).[150] For easy reuse, tablets or writing boards were sometimes waxed and written upon with a stylus, or ink inscriptions could be effaced and later writing superimposed over them (objects known as palimpsests). In the latter case, remnants of the previous inscription can still be seen (fig. 215).

210 (facing page, top)
Statue of Thoth as a figure with the head of an ibis
Egypt, 26th Dynasty, 664–525 BCE
Glazed composition, H. 12.3 cm, W. 3.1 cm, D. 5 cm
British Museum, EA64606
Donated by Marion Whiteford Acworth JP

211 (facing page, bottom left)
Figure of an ibis, one of the animals sacred to Thoth
Egypt, Late Period to Ptolemaic Period, 747–30 BCE
Bronze, H. 24 cm, W. 8.7 cm, D. 34 cm
British Museum, EA64095
Donated by Thomas Edward Lawrence

212 (facing page, bottom right)
Statue of Thoth as a baboon wearing the lunar-disc and seated upon a plinth with a staircase
Egypt, date unknown
Black steatite, H. 18.5 cm, W. 6.6 cm, D. 9.1 cm
British Museum, EA24655

213 (top)
Drawing board with a red grid. The two cartouches next to the seated figure of the king contain the throne name Menkheperkare, used by Thutmose III during the time of his co-regency with Hatshepsut.
Egypt, 18th Dynasty, *c.* 1479–1425 BCE
Wood and plaster, H. 37 cm, W. 54 cm, D. 1 cm
British Museum, EA5601

214 (centre)
Tile with a trial-hieroglyph of a falcon
Memphis, 26th Dynasty, 664–525 BCE
Quartzite, H. 22.8 cm, W. 22.2 cm, D. 5.1 cm
British Museum, EA69159

215 (bottom)
Writing board inscribed with a school text in Coptic and a medical/magical spell against eye disease. Raised around the edges, the board was intended to be waxed and incised, but the present inscription is in ink.
Egypt, 7th century CE
Wood, H. 8.7 cm, W. 25.3 cm, D. 0.9 cm
British Museum, EA29528

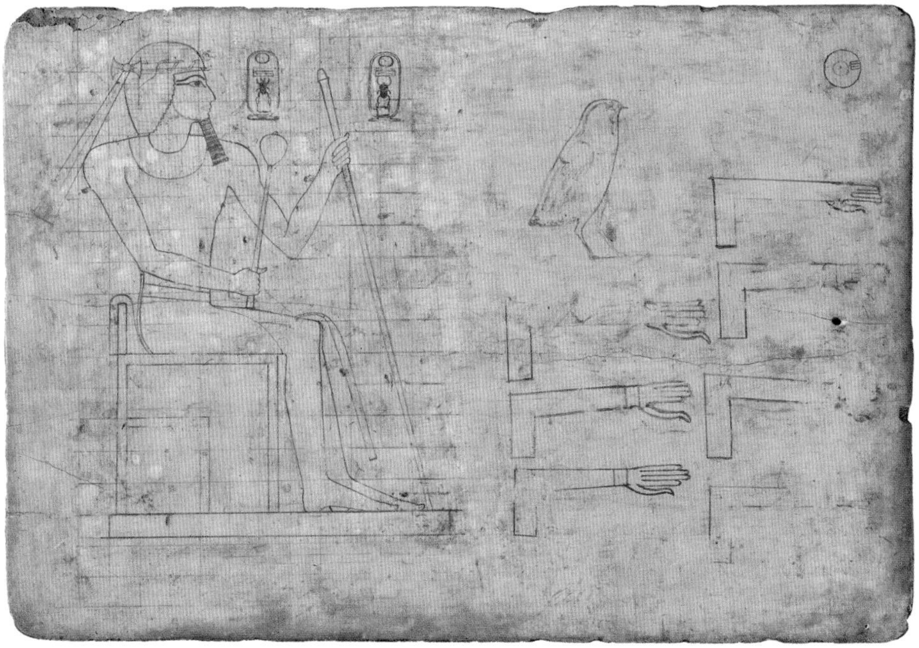

Exercises varied from basic spelling exercises to the copying of whole texts. Distinguishing between 'professional' copies produced by scribes and student copies can be difficult.[151] In most cases, the material used as a writing surface, the context of the artefact, the style of writing and the content determines whether a text is student-made.[152] Ostraca were cheap and easily available so were a good medium on which to practise lists of words or phrases (fig. 216). These writings were often crude, containing mistakes and corrections.

The first script an Egyptian pupil learned was probably hieratic, which was replaced by demotic in later periods. These cursive scripts were used to practise writing letters and various types of administrative documents (figs 217–220). Pupils were also exposed to literary works whose language and style differed from those used in documentary texts. They were taught to write by doing spelling and grammar exercises, recording passages dictated by the teacher and copying parts of real or model documentary and literary texts. In some cases, the pupils learned how to read and write hieroglyphs, the main script for monumental and archaising writing during most periods of Egyptian history.

When demotic replaced hieratic and Greek became the official language of the administration, those who wanted to climb the social ladder in Hellenistic and Roman Egypt had to master both languages. When Coptic became the vehicle for promoting Christian literature in Egypt, schooling relocated to Christian monasteries, which took over the task of maintaining and developing Coptic language and literature.[153]

216
Ostracon with hieratic text to which a sketch of a bull was added later. The red text is a eulogy on the scribal profession. The reverse is a list of villagers' personal marks, a kind of signature for people who could not write.
Deir el-Medina, 19th to 20th Dynasty, 1295–1069 BCE
Limestone, H. 11.5 cm, W. 19 cm, D. 3 cm
British Museum, EA50716

217 (below left)
Scribal palette inscribed with the titles and name of the owner. The inkwells at the end show remnants of black and red pigment, the most common colours used for writing.
Egypt, 13th Dynasty, 1795–1650 BCE
Wood, H. 0.9 cm, W. 3.1 cm, D. 24.6 cm (case only)
British Museum, EA5516

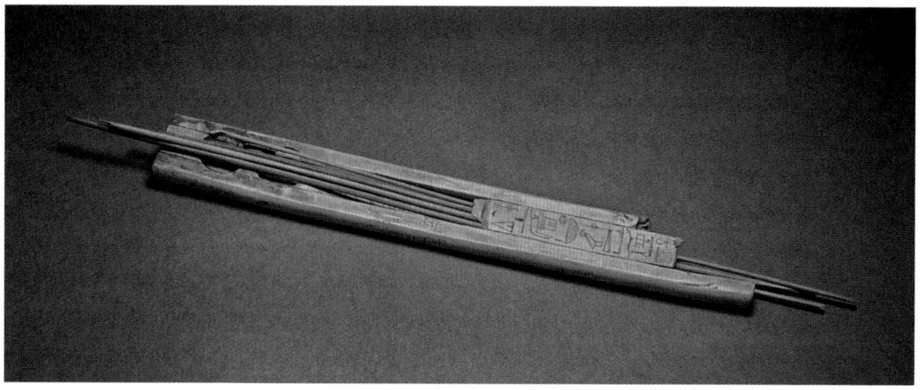

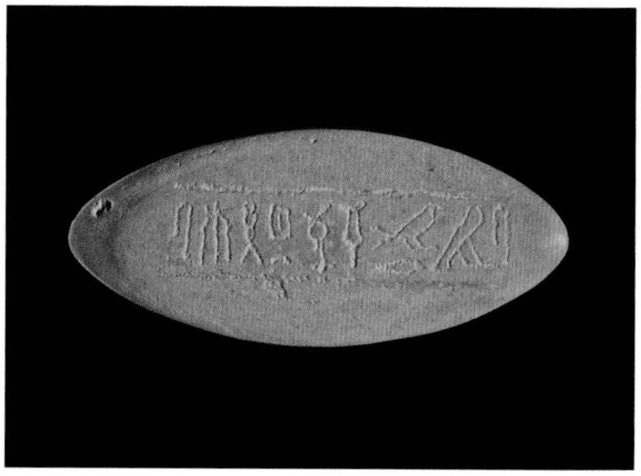

218 (facing page, bottom right)
Tool used to smooth papyrus, inscribed on one side with the titles and name of Ptahmose
Egypt, 18th Dynasty, 1550–1295 BCE
Stone, H. 8.4 cm, W. 3.6 cm, D. 1.1 cm
British Museum, EA66212
Donated by James Bomford

TEXT TRADITIONS

Being a professional scribe involved more than just producing writing; scribes preserved the written memory of Egypt by copying, reinterpreting and reworking esteemed pieces of literature or religious and mortuary texts. They were also responsible for standardising grammar and vocabulary and keeping the hieroglyphic corpus tidy and up to date.

From the New Kingdom onwards, older literary works written in Middle Egyptian were studied in schools. The Teaching of Khety, or the 'Satire of the Trades', for example, was produced in the Middle Kingdom but mostly preserved through later copies. In the tale, Khety escorts his son to the Twelfth Dynasty capital (probably near el-Lisht) where his son is to be admitted to the scribal school (fig. 221, see p. 228).

The preservation of written heritage became a political tool, as illustrated by the Shabaka Stone (fig. 222). The text on the stone records the 'Memphite Theology', an intellectualised version of the creation of the universe in which the god Ptah created the world by reading out loud the names of gods, people, cities and temples.[154] The most important organs of the creator god Ptah are his heart and tongue, because the heart thinks and the tongue speaks

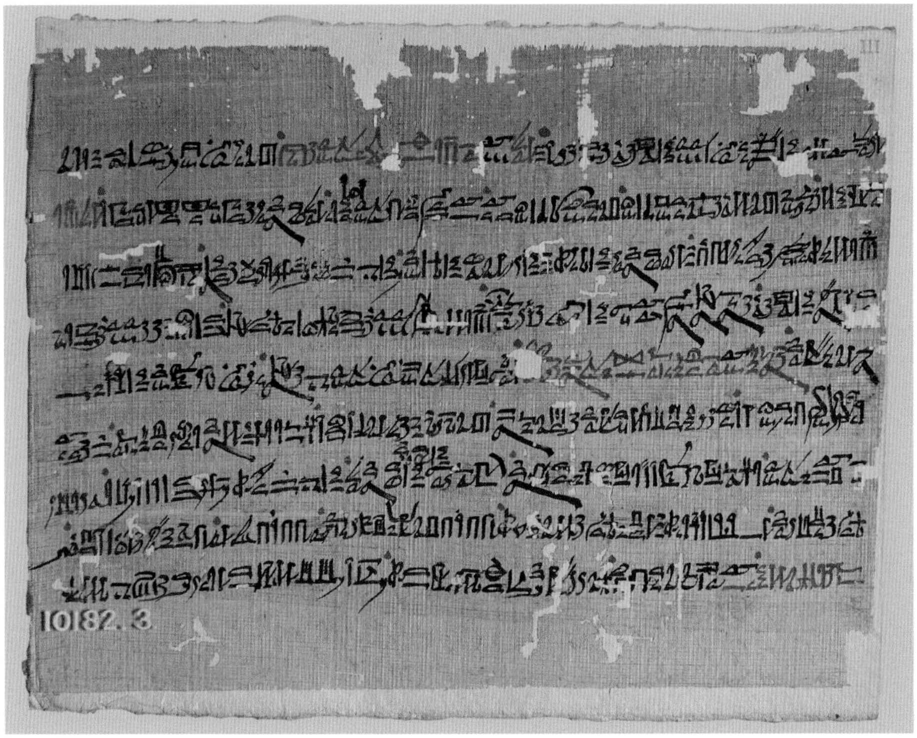

PREVIOUS PAGE
219
Materials for writing hieratic and painting grid lines for monumental writing

(clockwise from top left)
Ink-pot in the form of a cartouche. Egypt, 26th Dynasty, 664–525 BCE. Steatite, H. 2.4 cm, W. 6.7 cm, D. 3 cm. British Museum, EA59852
Inkwell. Tanis, 1 BCE–1 CE. Glazed composition, H. 5.2 cm, W. 6.3 cm, D. 6.2 cm. British Museum, EA22015. Donated by the Egypt Exploration Fund.
Pigment container. Egypt, Late Period, 747–332 BCE. Glazed composition, H. 2.6 cm, W. 8.6 cm, D. 7.5 cm. British Museum, EA5539
Reed. Egypt, date unknown. H. 0.2 cm, W. 15 cm, D. 0.2 cm. British Museum, EA27452. Donated by Reverend Greville John Chester
Reed pen cut into a nib at one end, inscribed in an unknown script. Egypt, date unknown. H. 0.6 cm, W. 16.1 cm, D. 0.9 cm. British Museum, EA5535

220
(bottom)
Lump of Egyptian blue. Egypt, date unknown. H. 2 cm, W. 3.6 cm, D. 3.6 cm. British Museum, EA5570.

221 (left)
The Teaching of Khety, also known as the 'Satire of the Trades'
Egypt, 19th Dynasty, 1295–1186 BCE
Papyrus, H. 30 cm, W. 21.6 cm, D. 0.7 cm
British Museum, EA10182,3

222
The Shabaka stone with vertical lines of hieroglyphs recording the 'Memphite Theology'. The text is retrograde, i.e. the birds look towards the end of the text rather than towards the beginning, and the individual signs are read from the back of the birds. This unusual reading direction is found in religious texts.
Memphis, 25th Dynasty, 700 BCE
Conglomerate stone, H. 95 cm, W. 137 cm, D. 20.5 cm
British Museum, EA498
Donated by George John Spencer, 2nd Earl Spencer

the thoughts, which by being spoken become reality. The text purports to be a copy of an ancient worm-eaten papyrus which pharaoh Shabaka ordered to be transcribed for posterity. The content recalls earlier texts in which Ptah is responsible for the creation of all things by means of the spoken word, but the current text was composed in Shabaka's own time (705–690 BCE). The story of its rescue is a rhetorical device well known in Egyptian inscriptions. The creator of the text introduced archaic spellings and grammatical usages to lend the piece a feeling of antiquity. Shabaka reigned during a period when Nubian rulers were trying to establish firm control over the whole of Egypt; Memphis, the first capital and one of Egypt's most important cities, had been a focal point for opposition and had only recently been conquered. By erecting an inscription which gave new prestige to the city's patron deity Ptah, Shabaka was probably seeking to conciliate the inhabitants and gain the support of the powerful Memphite priesthood.

The Teaching of Khety, or 'Satire of the Trades', 1300–1200 BCE

'I do not see a stoneworker on an (important) errand or a goldsmith in a place to which he has been sent, but I have seen a coppersmith at his work at the mouth of his furnace. His fingers were like the claws of the crocodile, and he stank more than fish eggs.

Every carpenter who bears the adze is wearier than a labourer. This field is his wood, his hoe is the axe. It is the night that will rescue him, for he must labour excessively in (his) activity. But at night-time he (still) must light (his lamp).

The jeweller pierces (stone) in stringing beads in all kinds of hard stone. When he has completed the inlaying of the eye amulets, his strength vanishes and he is tired out. He sits until the arrival of the sun, his knees and his back bent at the place called Aku-Re.

The barber shaves until the end of the evening. But he must be up early, crying out, his bowl upon his arm. He takes himself from street to street to seek out someone to shave. He wears out his arms to fill his belly, like bees who eat (only) according to their work.

The arrow maker goes north to the Delta to fetch himself arrows. He must work excessively in (his) activity. When the gnats sting him and the sand fleas bite him as well, then he is judged.

The potter is covered with earth, although his lifetime is still among the living. He burrows in the field more than swine to bake his cooking vessels. His clothes being stiff with mud, his headcloth consists (only) of rags, so that the air which comes forth from his burning furnace enters his nose. He operates a pestle with his feet, with which he himself is pounded, penetrating the courtyard of every house and driving (earth) into (every) open place.

I shall also describe to you the like of the mason-bricklayer. His kidneys are painful. When he must be outside in the wind, he lays bricks without a loin cloth. His belt is a cord for his back, a string for his buttocks. His strength has vanished through fatigue and stiffness, kneading all his excrement. He eats bread with his fingers, although he washes himself but once a day.

It is miserable for the carpenter when he planes the roofbeam. It is [the roof of] a chamber 10 by 6 cubits. A month goes by in laying the beams and spreading the matting. All the work is accomplished. But as for the food which should be given to his household (while he is away), there is no one who provides for his children.

But if you understand writings, then it will be better for you than the professions which I have set before you.'[155]

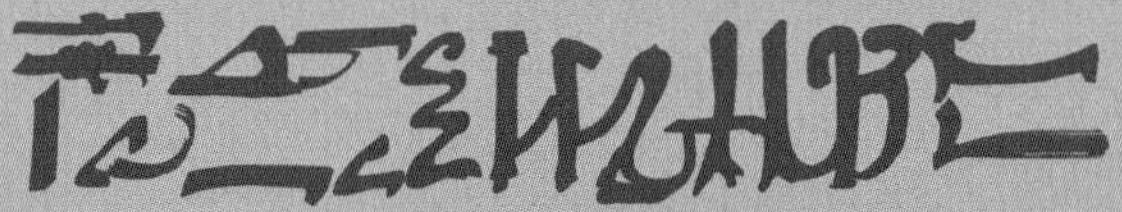

THE ROSETTA STONE AND THE MEMPHIS DECREE

Willy Clarysse

As has been described earlier, the Rosetta Stone contains a long decree in three scripts and three languages: hieroglyphic (the incomplete section), demotic and Greek (see p. 90). The decree was drawn up on 27 March 196 BCE by a council of the Egyptian priests of all the important temples in the country, who gathered for this occasion in the old capital Memphis. The king himself, who lived in Alexandria, the Greek mega-city on the coast, was also present.

The decree consists of two main parts, followed by directions for how it is to be published. The first part (ll. 1–37 in the Greek text) gives a detailed motivation for divine honours dedicated to the king: he has cancelled debts to the crown, given amnesty to prisoners and deserters, guaranteed the traditional yearly allowances to the temples, lowered taxes, apportioned justice to all, protected the country against invaders and rebels, bestowed large gifts for the cult of the sacred animals, repaired existing temples and founded new ones.

The second part (ll. 37–53) lists the honours given to the king.[156] These are introduced by the formula 'it has been decided by the priests of all the temples in the country', followed by a series of resolutions: an image of the king will be set up in every temple alongside that of the god and this image will be worshipped like the divine images; a statue of the king will be placed in the temples in a golden shrine adorned with uraei (sacred serpents emblematic of supreme power, worn on the headdresses of ancient Egyptian deities and kings) and carried in procession on festival days; the royal birthday and his date of accession will be celebrated in the temples every month with sacrifices of food and drink; the priests of all gods will add to their titles that they are also priests of the king and put his name on their signet rings; his name will be included in the dating formulas of all notarial documents; the five days of the new year festival will be dedicated to him.

The decree ends by stating how it is to be published: 'This decree shall be inscribed on a stela of hard stone in sacred, native and Greek characters and set up in each of the first, second and third rank temples alongside the image of the ever-living king.' If the priests followed their own instructions, hundreds of copies in hard stone (the Rosetta Stone is made of granodiorite) were set up in all Egyptian temples. And indeed three fragmentary copies of this same decree have been found so far: one in Elephantine (fragments in three languages; fig. 223), one near Leontopolis (the Greek section only) and a later copy in Nobaira (only the hieroglyphic part).

But the Memphis decree, of which the Rosetta Stone is just one copy, is not an isolated text. This type of decree by the Egyptian priests, honouring Ptolemaic kings, is first attested in 243 BCE, nearly a century after Alexander

the Great conquered Egypt, and continues to appear until the early second century BCE (see p. 247). One such example, known as the decree of Canopus, was issued in 238 BCE and six copies of it are preserved (fig. 224).[157] Figure 225 depicts all decrees known from Egyptian temples.[158]

The decrees all have the same structure as the one recorded on the Rosetta Stone:

> A date, given according to both the Macedonian and Egyptian calendars, also mentioning the Greek priest of the royal cult in Alexandria.
>
> A list of benefactions by the king, introduced by the conjunction 'because he …'.
>
> A short formula saying 'it has been decided by the priests of Egypt', followed by a list of honours conferred by the priests upon the king.
>
> Stipulations about the publication of the decree on stelae in the temples.

The extensive lists of benefactions and honours are described together in very long sentences: because the king did this and this and this, the priests decided to honour him in such and such a way. Both the motivations and the honours are stereotypes and the same sentences occur repeatedly in such decrees from 243 BCE onwards. Some decrees even state that the king maintained or augmented the benefactions of his predecessors. If the stone on which the text is inscribed is broken, it is sometimes difficult to identify which specific decree appears on the fragment. Only a few stipulations are original in each decree, such as the establishment of a new calendar and a fifth priestly clan (known as a phyle) in honour of the royal couple in 238 BCE, the celebration of the victory against the Seleucids in 217 BCE, or the suppression of a revolt in the Delta in 196 BCE.

This type of priestly decree is unknown in the Egyptian tradition, where the pharaoh is by his very nature an intermediary between the human and divine world and has no need to be honoured by his subjects. It was, however, extremely common in the Greek world from the fifth century BCE onwards to honour meritorious citizens this way. In the Hellenistic period, Greek cities used such decrees to attribute divine or semi-divine honours to the successors of Alexander the Great. King Lysimachos is honoured in Priene in almost the same way in 286 BCE:

> Since king Lysimachos has always taken care of the people of Priene, and now saved the city by sending troops, the people have decided to send ambassadors to him in order to thank him, to erect statues of the king on the market, to set up an altar for the king, to celebrate his anniversary by means of festivals and processions.[159]

223 (facing page)
Fragments of a copy of the Memphis Decree, of which the Rosetta Stone is also an example
Elephantine, Ptolemaic Period, 196 BCE
Sandstone, H. 17 cm, W. 16.5 cm, D. 6 cm (smallest piece), H. 32 cm, W. 49 cm, D. 14 cm (largest piece)
Musée du Louvre, E 12677, AF 10006, AF 10007

The Egyptian priests started acting in the same way as those in the Greek cities in Asia Minor and Greece, using the same formulas and attributing very similar honours. They add local colour by translating the Greek decree into demotic, and from demotic into hieroglyphs (by that time an artificial language, more or less like the Latin used on degree certificates in many of today's Western universities). The Egyptian priests also deviate from Greek examples by including the traditional Egyptian motifs of a winged sun disc and an offering scene above the text, and by giving the king a pharaonic title here and there. In the Greek tradition, the decrees are voted (*psephisma*) and the priests are even grouped by *phylai* ('tribes'), just like the citizens of the Greek cities. In the past there has been a lot of discussion about the authorship of these texts, with some scholars suggesting that they must have been composed at the royal court. It is now accepted that some Egyptian priests copied the ways Greek citizens honoured their kings and sometimes played the same roles as them in Egypt, a country without independent city-states of the Greek type.[160]

The earliest priestly decree was issued in 243 BCE; a complete copy, without the Greek, found in 1999 in Akhmim, allows us to attribute several unidentified fragments to this same text. This is followed by the so-called Canopus decree of 238 BCE, the Raphia decree of 217, the Memphis decree of 196 (of which the Rosetta Stone is one copy) and the two Philae decrees of 186–185 BCE (preserved on the wall of the temple, not on a stela). Several stelae also celebrate military victories against the Seleucid kings in 243 and 217 BCE and against Egyptian rebels in 196 and 186 BCE. Though the Rosetta Stone describes in detail how a rebel city in the Delta was conquered, it does not mention the great revolt in Upper Egypt, where at that very moment native pharaohs were opposing Ptolemy V. Their defeat in 186 BCE was celebrated in the Philae decree.

The tradition of priestly decrees lasted for just over a century: there are no certain examples after 182 BCE. Perhaps by that time the royal cult was generally implemented in the temples and the priestly families were a fully integrated part of the Ptolemaic state. There was no longer any perceived need to organise assemblies in which the priests voted in new honours for the royal family.[161]

224 (above)
The Canopic decree, also called the Caristie stela, was found in 1800, where it was being used as the threshold of a mosque. Muhammed Ali presented the object to the French king and it was acquired by the Louvre in 1837.
Cairo, Ptolemaic Period, 238 BCE
Basalt, H. 194 cm, W. 45 cm, D. 30.5 cm
Musée du Louvre, C 122

225 (facing page)
Family tree showing the relationship between all known copies of the decree also written on the Rosetta Stone

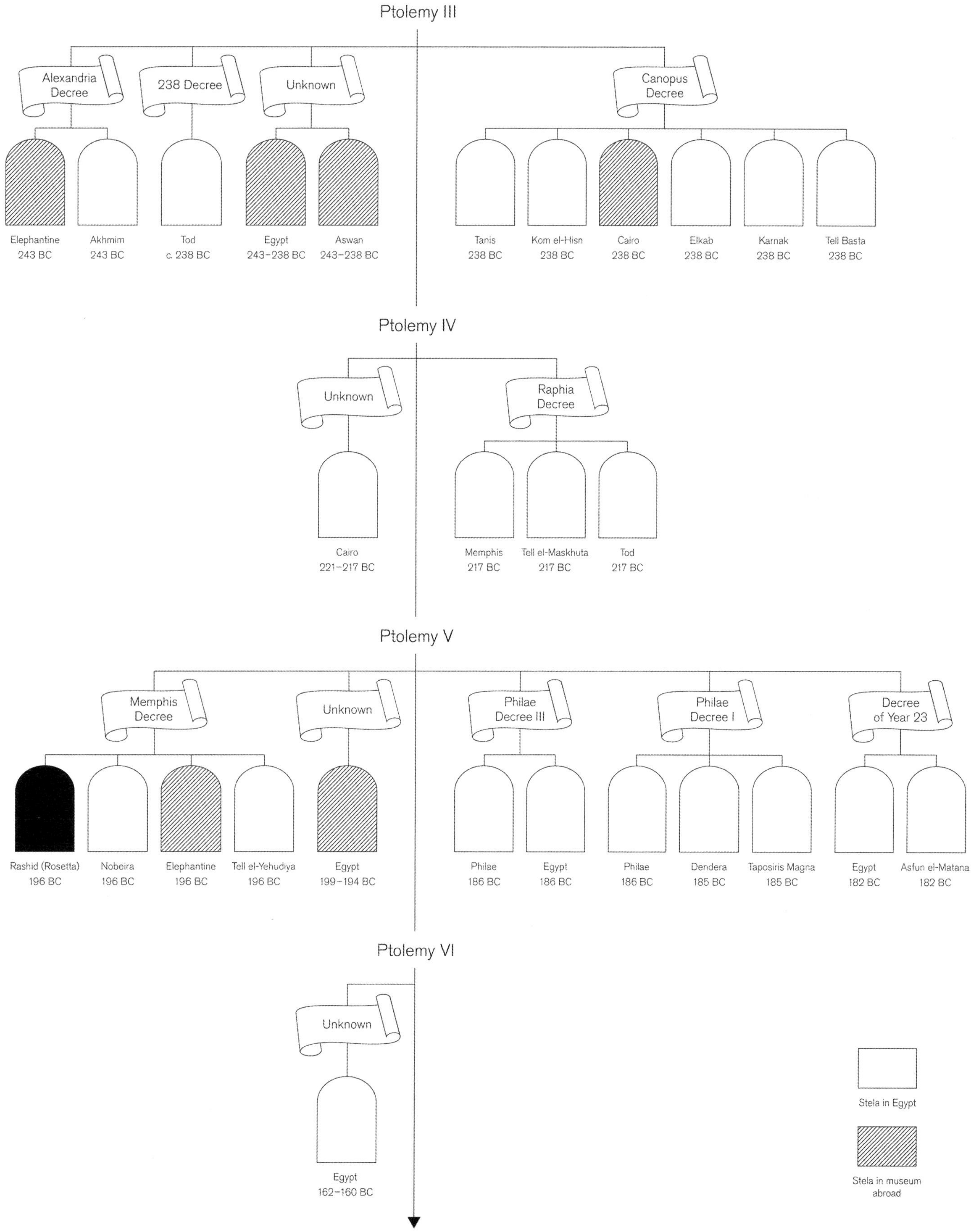
Ptolemy III
Alexandria Decree
238 Decree
Unknown
Canopus Decree
Elephantine 243 BC
Akhmim 243 BC
Tod c. 238 BC
Egypt 243–238 BC
Aswan 243–238 BC
Tanis 238 BC
Kom el-Hisn 238 BC
Cairo 238 BC
Elkab 238 BC
Karnak 238 BC
Tell Basta 238 BC
Ptolemy IV
Unknown
Raphia Decree
Cairo 221–217 BC
Memphis 217 BC
Tell el-Maskhuta 217 BC
Tod 217 BC
Ptolemy V
Memphis Decree
Unknown
Philae Decree III
Philae Decree I
Decree of Year 23
Rashid (Rosetta) 196 BC
Nobeira 196 BC
Elephantine 196 BC
Tell el-Yehudiya 196 BC
Egypt 199–194 BC
Philae 186 BC
Egypt 186 BC
Philae 186 BC
Dendera 185 BC
Taposiris Magna 185 BC
Egypt 182 BC
Asfun el-Matana 182 BC
Ptolemy VI
Unknown
Egypt 162–160 BC
Stela in Egypt
Stela in museum abroad

CHAPTER 5 New approaches

NEW APPROACHES

Ilona Regulski

At a time when our global society grows increasingly conscious of existential threats, the field of Egyptology reflects on its history and relevance for the future. Retrieving information across vast cultural divides and immense stretches of time is difficult, but preserving it for the future may be even more so. For all the millennia it spent plotting immortality, Egypt's resurrection was a happy accident.

What began as the endeavour of an exclusive group of scholars in 1822 is now often seen as the most important event in the history of Egyptology, a wide-ranging field that incorporates history, language, literature, religion, art and architecture in Egypt from the fifth millennium BCE until the fourth century CE.

Modern Egyptology is a developing field of research and is defined by innovative collaboration with colleagues in Egypt and around the world (fig. 226). Building on 200 years of research, philologists are still fine-tuning their understanding of ancient grammar and vocabulary while interpreting texts more holistically and embracing social context and materiality (fig. 227). The field of Egyptology has been conservative in making written sources available to all, and since the time of Champollion, scholars have encountered difficulties accessing ancient texts. These challenges are now being addressed through the development of digital tools and online museum collections.

THE DIGITAL ROSETTA STONE

Monica Berti and Franziska Naether

Since the 1990s all academic disciplines have undergone a digital transformation, and Egyptology is no exception. Collections and research institutions such as the British Museum are now publishing their objects online. Thanks to these initiatives, visitors, students and scholars alike are able to access websites and databases where they can find information about, and images of, millions of archaeological remains preserved from the past.

Online collections and high-resolution photographs are now of fundamental importance to our understanding and enjoyment of ancient

226
A team from Leipzig University and the University of Florida created a 3D scan of the Rosetta Stone in June 2018

artefacts. They help scholars advance their knowledge and make new scientific discoveries; they offer students dynamic and up-to-date resources to help them accomplish their learning goals; and they are wonderful companions that enhance the experience of visitors to museums, both online and in person.

The 'Digital Rosetta Stone', a project launched in 2017 at Leipzig University, Germany, in collaboration with the British Museum, has made major contributions to these aims. The project was originally developed to explore how digital technologies could help students improve their understanding of the past and their reading of ancient languages. The Rosetta Stone was chosen for its extraordinary qualities, not only because it is the most famous 'piece of rock' in the world, but also because it is a trilingual text produced by one of the most vibrant and multicultural of all ancient societies; namely, Egypt in the second century BCE.

The project was intended to test tools and methods in undergraduate and graduate classes, producing an environment for collaboration between institutions in Germany, the United Kingdom and the USA. The aim was to facilitate the teaching and learning of the three languages of the Rosetta Stone, especially for students who had no training in one of the three scripts: hieroglyphs, demotic and ancient Greek. Teaching was also adapted for students of Computational Linguistics and Computer Science, who are increasingly involved in digital humanities projects and therefore benefit from familiarity with complex research questions about languages. Three main techniques were used to achieve these goals: textual alignment, linguistic annotation and 3D imaging.

227
A 2021 reconstruction of the Rosetta Stone, demonstrating the latest research about the Stone's missing pieces

TEXTUAL ALIGNMENT

'Textual alignment' here refers to the critical matching of words or sections of text that have equivalent meanings, from different documents, in different languages. The three versions of the text of the Rosetta Stone were aligned using a digital editing tool that Leipzig University has developed to create both manual and computer-aided alignments of texts written in ancient languages. The experiment generated two types of alignment: one comparing the three versions of the text inscribed on the Rosetta Stone (figs 228–229), and another comparing each version with its English and German translations. Current computational standards allow the Greek script of the Rosetta Stone to be read by the machine, but hieroglyphs and demotic still have to be represented using transliteration, in which the signs are converted into letters mainly from the modern alphabet (see p. 23).[1]

Students successfully employed the alignment technique and also aligned texts similar to the Rosetta Stone, such as the Canopus decree (see p. 231) and the text inscribed on the Gallus stela. They found the experience to be more intuitive than with traditional methods and provided valuable feedback to the developers for future versions of the program.

LINGUISTIC ANNOTATION

Using the second method, the grammar and syntax of the Greek text of the Rosetta Stone was annotated using a collaborative online linguistic editor developed by Leipzig University in collaboration with the Perseus Project at Tufts University in Boston, USA. This editor has been specifically designed

228 (facing page)
Alignment between the text and the image of the Rosetta Stone

[ḫt.tw] sḫꜣ.w pn ḥr ꜥḥꜥ.w n ꜥꜣ.t rwḏ.t m sḫ n
mdw.w-nṯr (m) sḫ šꜥy (m) sḫꜣ.y n Ḥꜣ.w-nb.w(t)
rdi.t ꜥḥꜥ=f m gs.w-pr.w m rꜣ.w-pr.w nb(.w) ḥr
rn=f m mḥ-1 mḥ-2 mḥ-3 r-gs ḫnty n nsw-bjtj
(Ptlwmys ꜥnḫ(.w) ḏ.t mr.y Ptḥ)| nṯr pri(.w) nb
nfr.w

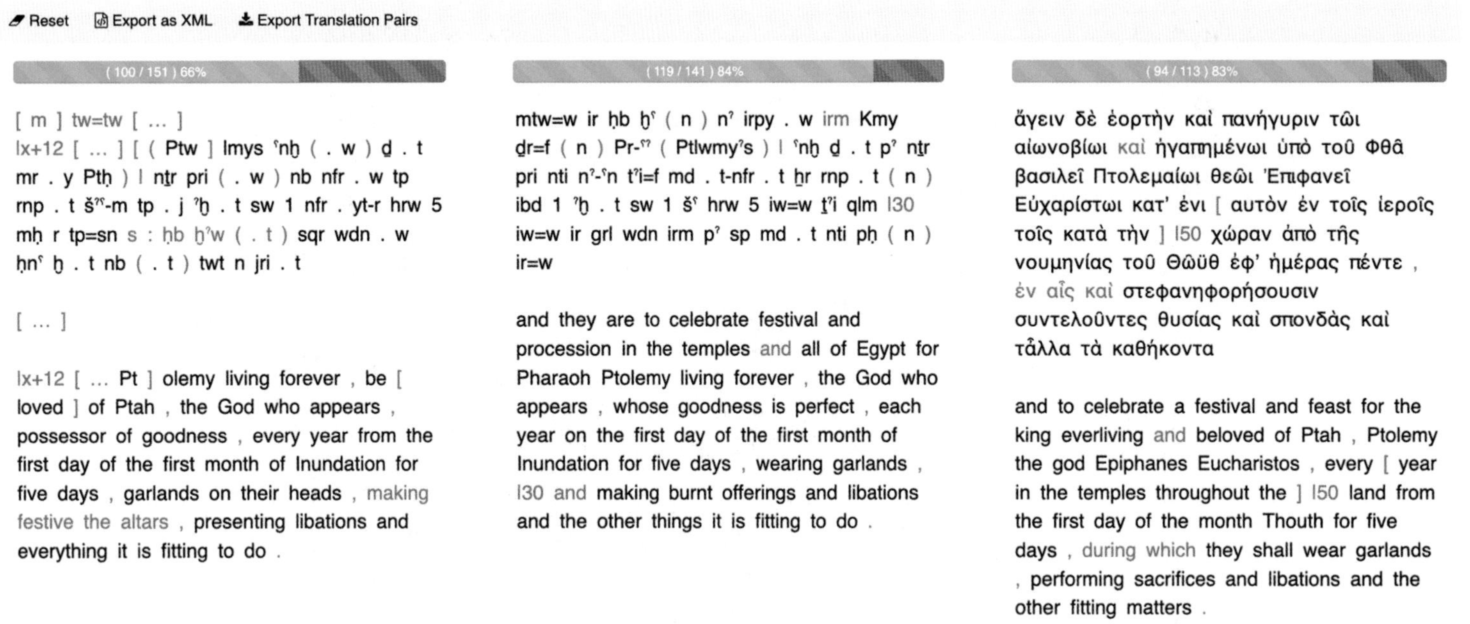
Reset
Export as XML
Export Translation Pairs
(100 / 151) 66%
[m] tw=tw […]
lx+12 […] [(Ptw] lmys ʿnḫ (. w) ḏ . t mr . y Ptḥ) l nṯr pri (. w) nb nfr . w tp rnp . t šʾʿ-m tp . j ʾḫ . t sw 1 nfr . yt-r hrw 5 mḥ r tp=sn s : ḥb ḫʾw (. t) sqr wdn . w ḥnʿ ḫ . t nb (. t) twt n jri . t
[…]
lx+12 [… Pt] olemy living forever , be [loved] of Ptah , the God who appears , possessor of goodness , every year from the first day of the first month of Inundation for five days , garlands on their heads , making festive the altars , presenting libations and everything it is fitting to do .
(119 / 141) 84%
mtw=w ir ḥb ḫʿ (n) nʾ irpy . w irm Kmy ḏr=f (n) Pr-ʿʾ (Ptlwmyʾs) l ʿnḫ ḏ . t pʾ nṯr pri nti nʾ-ʿn tʾi=f md . t-nfr . t ẖr rnp . t (n) ibd 1 ʾḫ . t sw 1 šʿ hrw 5 iw=w ṯʾi qlm l30 iw=w ir grl wdn irm pʾ sp md . t nti pḥ (n) ir=w
and they are to celebrate festival and procession in the temples and all of Egypt for Pharaoh Ptolemy living forever , the God who appears , whose goodness is perfect , each year on the first day of the first month of Inundation for five days , wearing garlands , l30 and making burnt offerings and libations and the other things it is fitting to do .
(94 / 113) 83%
ἄγειν δὲ ἑορτὴν καὶ πανήγυριν τῶι αἰωνοβίωι καὶ ἠγαπημένωι ὑπὸ τοῦ Φθᾶ βασιλεῖ Πτολεμαίωι θεῶι Ἐπιφανεῖ Εὐχαρίστωι κατ' ἐνι [αυτὸν ἐν τοῖς ἱεροῖς τοῖς κατὰ τὴν] l50 χώραν ἀπὸ τῆς νουμηνίας τοῦ Θῶϋθ ἐφ' ἡμέρας πέντε , ἐν αἷς καὶ στεφανηφορήσουσιν συντελοῦντες θυσίας καὶ σπονδὰς καὶ τἆλλα τὰ καθήκοντα
and to celebrate a festival and feast for the king everliving and beloved of Ptah , Ptolemy the god Epiphanes Eucharistos , every [year in the temples throughout the] l50 land from the first day of the month Thouth for five days , during which they shall wear garlands , performing sacrifices and libations and the other fitting matters .

229
Textual alignment of the three versions of the Rosetta Stone with an English translation of passage 44 using the tool 'Ugarit'

and equipped with guidelines for manual annotations of the morphology (the internal structure of words and phrases), syntax and semantics of ancient Greek and Latin texts.[2] One method of annotation is the creation of trees representing the parts of a sentence (usually verbs, subjects, objects and subordinate clauses) and their dependencies. Linguistic guidelines for Middle Egyptian and demotic are presently lacking; this is a work in progress and the project has increased the interest of the scholarly community in advancing the use of such linguistic methods for annotating ancient texts.

3D IMAGING

The third technique was 3D imaging. In order to increase the readability and accessibility of the Rosetta Stone inscriptions, the Digital Rosetta Stone project has produced new high-resolution pictures of the inscription thanks to a collaboration with the Digital Epigraphy and Archaeology Project at the University of Florida, USA (see fig. 226). Photographs were taken with lighting coming from four directions and were then processed to compose 3D representations of the surface of the Stone (fig. 230). The 3D details of the inscribed surface were captured in a depth map, which is an image only in shades of grey: parts of the object closer to the camera (such as

230
Detail of the 3D depth map of the Rosetta Stone

the surface of the Stone) are lighter, while more distant parts (such as the script) appear darker. The depth map is accessible online[3] and users can manipulate it by moving, scaling and rotating the Rosetta Stone under different virtual lighting orientations and shading methods.

ACCESS NOW AND IN THE FUTURE

The combination of digital images, machine-readable textual data and aligned translations has improved access to the text of the Rosetta Stone for those with scholarly, educational and general interests. There are still challenges to overcome, such as the proper encoding of hieroglyphs and the linguistic annotation of ancient Egyptian. However, the data produced by the Digital Rosetta Stone project is currently being used in a range of real-life contexts and there is great potential for more studies, especially on other multilingual texts.

DECIPHERMENT AND THE REVELATION OF EGYPTIAN IDENTITY

Fayza Haikal

> As an Arabic-speaking Egyptian Egyptologist myself, cultural continuity in Egypt through transmission and adaptation has always fascinated me because I constantly see the impact of ancient Egyptian culture on our daily life, despite the changes in language, religion and circumstance that the country has undergone during its very long history. This continuity makes me recall an Arabic saying meaning that what you learn as a child remains engraved in your mind forever (*al-ʿilm fi al-seghar misl al-naqsh ʿal-sakhr*) … In the case of Egypt, childhood would be the first stage of its civilisation.

Before the decipherment of hieroglyphs, the only sources of insight into ancient Egyptian daily life were tomb murals depicting the customs of high officials. In the centuries that followed, modern archaeologists developed new tools and methodologies that were applied to mummies and the food found in tombs, opening the door to more information about the health and diet of ancient Egyptians. But what about the less tangible elements that made up ancient Egyptian cultural identity? What about science, technology, literature, magic and religion? Imagine for a moment that decipherment had never happened and that the Egyptian objects in museums had no explanatory labels, and the texts written on stone and papyri could not be understood. Many intangible aspects of ancient Egyptian cultural identity would still be locked away and our relationship with ancient Egypt would be completely different from what it is today.

UNDERSTANDING EGYPTIAN IDENTITY: CULTURAL MEMORY AND THE DEPTHS OF CIVILISATION

After Champollion's breakthrough in 1822, Egyptology became a rapidly progressing science, with Western scholars teaming up to create dictionaries and grammar books. Their research confirmed the theory that ancient Egyptian belonged to the Afro-Asiatic group of languages. Even in Egypt, the field of Egyptology was appropriated by Western scholars,[4] and about a century after the publication of Champollion's *Lettre à M. Dacier,* when the first generation of Egyptian Egyptologists wanted to join the field, they were

231
Alaa Shams (left) and Rehab Sabry Shazly (right) record hieroglyphs on tomb walls with the Theban Tomb 110 Epigraphy & Research Field School, organised by the American Research Center in Egypt. Projects like this one help to shed new light on ancient texts.

pushed aside. Another two to three generations would pass before ancient texts began to resonate with a new wave of young Egyptian students, who recognised in them the roots of their own culture.[5] Unfortunately, there are still strikingly few Egyptian contributions to ancient Egyptian language studies, as many Egyptians cannot write fluently in a foreign language and most people globally cannot read Arabic. Even today, only a limited number of international research teams include Arabic speakers (fig. 231). As a result, despite two hundred years of reading and research, problems of translation persist.

It is time to seriously consider a new approach based on ethno-Egyptology, exploring how modern Egyptian folklore and the study of Egyptian Arabic dialect can help us understand history. We must embrace the idea that today is an extension of the past and that cultural memory and transmission are, in fact, prerequisites for the development of cultures and preservation of identities. These theories are generally accepted by Arabic-speaking Egyptologists but supported by only a small number of Western scholars.[6] Very few of the latter compare ancient Egyptian and Arabic texts, in which authors use similar rhetorical devices natural to both languages as a matter of stylistic choice. These devices are either totally unfamiliar to, or not to the taste of, many Western readers.

Among these devices is the repetition of specific words for emphasis or exaggeration. In the following example, the king writes to one of his attendants: 'My majesty saw this beautiful, beautiful writing that you caused to be brought to the palace on this beautiful day of making happy the heart of the king Isesi, justified, justified.'[7] Writers in ancient Egypt also used metaphors that were translated into Arabic when it became Egypt's official language after the Arab conquest (640 CE). In a famous literary text, we read 'his talk causes the face to be covered for him', meaning in both Egyptian and Arabic 'his talk will protect him from shame', as the context requires.[8] When translated into Western languages, the individual words are often understandable, but their combination does not make sense, which has led to frequent mistranslations. By contrast, the meaning becomes clear when the expressions are translated into Arabic.[9]

There are also typically Egyptian gestures that appear in texts since the New Kingdom, such as this example from a love poem of the Ramesside period: 'to kiss one's hand four times', meaning 'to thank God'.[10] This expression has not been encountered elsewhere, so foreign readers lack the frame of reference needed to understand it. Unless it is compared with the same expression in Arabic, it remains untranslatable.

Other rhetorical devices include *Jinas*, which is widely appreciated in Arabic literature but relatively unknown in the West.[11] It consists of echoing a word's sounds or composition in another word within the same verse or sentence, drawing attention to the skill of the author and enriching the power of the verse. This device is also found in ancient Egyptian discourse but renders passages mostly untranslatable in Western languages. *Jinas* is used visually as well as phonetically in a eulogy engraved on one of Hatshepsut's famous obelisks in the temple of Karnak, and its effect becomes most evident when read aloud (fig. 232). A grammatical form almost unknown to Western languages but common to Arabic and Egyptian is also used here to further emphasise the verbs: that is, an intransitive verb (such as 'to happen', or 'to rise') is given an object:

232
Hatshepsut's obelisk in the temple of Karnak. The hieroglyphs inscribed on it demonstrate *Jinas*, a rhetorical device that later became popular in Arabic literature.

Kheperet Kheperw mi Kheperi, Kha'et kha'w mi Akhti[12]
'[Hatshepsut] … who happened a happening like (the god) Khepry and who rose a rising like He of the Horizon.'

Note the repetition of the sound kh in this line and the added objects after the intransitive verbs.

The ancient Egyptians' deep belief in the power and creative capability of words affected their speech and continues to shape their descendants' speech to this day. This made them reluctant to mention by name things they did not want to happen. Instead of stating directly that someone was ill, they magically diverted the illness by saying that it affected the enemies of the person. In the same spirit, the bier on which the deceased is carried to the cemetery is called 'possessor of life' (nb ankh) in ancient Egyptian, and 'the one that gives life/resurrects' (naAsh) in Egyptian Arabic. Both names include the idea of *ʿnkh*, meaning 'life', in order to repel death. Likewise, the Egyptian word *ḥtpw*, translated into English as 'offerings', is translated into Arabic as 'forgiveness' or 'compassion', dematerialising it and adding a moral or religious value to offerings that are today distributed to the poor and clearly not given to nourish the dead.

The ancient Egyptian belief in the judgement of the soul after death, which probably lay at the root of their day-to-day ethics, and the deep piety expressed in marvellous hymns to their gods, whose mere invocation satisfies all the needs of the supplicants and protects them from evil, is so similar to subsequent texts of the Fathers of the Coptic orthodox Church and the Muslim Sufi that they immediately call to mind these essentially Eastern compositions.[13]

It seems clear, therefore, that colloquial Egyptian Arabic should be taught in all Egyptology programmes to allow members of diverse archaeological and research teams to truly benefit from one other's knowledge. Engaging deeply with the contemporary language and customs of this country allows us to decipher and better understand the culture of ancient Egypt, its real soul and identity.

APPENDIX

DECREES	No.	DATE (BCE)	PROVENANCE	CURRENT LOCATION	MATERIAL	PRESERVATION	Date found	TM No.
	Ptolemy III (Ptolemy Euergetes I)[1]							
Alexandria decree[2]	1a[3]	243, 3 Dec	Elephantine, Khnum temple	Louvre E 33071 + Uppsala 1757+1758	Red granite	Demotic + Greek (fragm.)	Before 1908	www.trismegistos.org/text/6079
	1b[4]	243, 3 Dec	El-Khazindariya (Panopolis)	Akhmim magazine	Limestone	Hieroglyphic + demotic	1999	www.trismegistos.org/text/129851
	2[5]	Before 238?	Tod	Egypt, Tod, no. 1862; now lost	Granite	Greek (fragm.)	1934–6	www.trismegistos.org/text/6080
	1 or 2[6]	243–238?	Unknown	Durham, Oriental Museum DUROM.1982.4	Limestone	Hieroglyphic (fragm.)		www.trismegistos.org/text/754921
	1 or 2[7]	Before 238?	Aswan	Louvre MG 23093 / E 33065	Diorite	Demotic (fragm.)	1906–11	www.trismegistos.org/text/703189
Canopus decree[8]	3a[9]	238, 7 Mar	Tanis, temple	Cairo CG 22187	Limestone	Hieroglyphic + Greek Demotic on edge	1866	www.trismegistos.org/text/55659
	3b[10]	238, 7 Mar	Kom el-Hisn	Cairo CG 22186	Limestone	Hieroglyphic + demotic + Greek	1881	www.trismegistos.org/text/6378
	3c[11]	238, 7 Mar	Cairo, Emir Kour mosque	Louvre C 122	Basalt	Hieroglyphic + demotic + Greek (damaged)	1800	www.trismegistos.org/text/7221
	3d[12]	238, 7 Mar	Elkab, temple	Cairo Museum TR 17/3/46/1	Sandstone	Hieroglyphic + demotic + Greek (fragm.)	Before 1946	www.trismegistos.org/text/88492
	3e[13]	238, 7 Mar	Karnak, under hypostyle hall floor	3rd pylon, Karnak	Red granite	Hieroglyphic + demotic (damaged)	1929	www.trismegistos.org/text/290106
	3f[14]	238, 7 Mar	Tell Basta	Museum Port Said 493	Black granite	Hieroglyphic	1923	www.trismegistos.org/text/107245
	3g[15]	238, 7 Mar	Tell Basta	Magazine, IF TB XV 001	Black granite	Hieroglyphic + Demotic + Greek	2003	www.trismegistos.org/text/107245
	Ptolemy IV (Ptolemy Philopator)							
	4[16]	221–217	Cairo	Cairo TR 3/5/33/1	Granite	Greek (fragm.)	Before 1933	www.trismegistos.org/text/6081
Raphia decree[17] (Decree of Memphis 217 BCE)	5a[18]	217, 15 Nov	Memphis (Mit Rahina)	Cairo CG 31088	Basalt	Hieroglyphic + demotic + Greek	Before 1902	www.trismegistos.org/text/2985
	5b[19]	217, 15 Nov	Tell el-Maskhuta (Pithom)	Cairo CG 50048	Limestone	Hieroglyphic + demotic + Greek	1923	www.trismegistos.org/text/2984
	5c[20]	217, 15 Nov	Tod	Egypt, Tod, inv. no. 257; now lost?	Limestone?	Hieroglyphic + demotic + Greek	1934–6	www.trismegistos.org/text/6082
	Ptolemy V (Ptolemy Epiphanes Eucharistos)							
Memphis decree (Decree of Memphis 196 BCE)	6a[21]	196, 27 Mar	Rosetta (Sais?)	British Museum EA24	Granodiorite	Hieroglyphic + demotic + Greek	1799	www.trismegistos.org/text/8809
	6b[22]	186, 29 Apr[23]	Nobaira	Cairo CG 22188	Sandstone	Hieroglyphic	1884	www.trismegistos.org/text/2979
	6c[24]	196, 27 Mar	Elephantine	Louvre AF 10006 + AF 10007 + E 12677	Sandstone	Hieroglyphic + demotic + Greek (fragm.)	1907–8	www.trismegistos.org/text/6311
	6d[25]	196, 27 Mar	Noub Taha, near Leontopolis	Alexandria, Graeco-Roman Museum 21352	Basalt	Greek	1923 (purchased)	www.trismegistos.org/text/5958
	7[26]	199–194	Unknown	Louvre AF 10077 + AF 10078	Sandstone	Hieroglyphic (fragm.)	Before WWII	www.trismegistos.org/text/290107
Second decree of Philae (Philensis II)	8a[27]	186, 6 Sept	Philae	Philae *in situ* – Mammisi wall	Sandstone	Hieroglyphic + demotic	1820s	www.trismegistos.org/text/48339
	8b[28]	186, 6 Sept	Unknown	Cairo TR 27/11/58/4	Limestone	Hieroglyphic	Before 1952	www.trismegistos.org/text/97833
First decree of Philae (Philensis I)	9a[29]	185, Oct–Nov	Philae	Philae *in situ* – Mammisi wall	Sandstone	Hieroglyphic + demotic	1820s	www.trismegistos.org/text/48335
	9b[30]	185	Dendera	Unknown (Cairo?)	Sandstone	Hieroglyphic	1950	www.trismegistos.org/text/943024
	9c[31]	185	Taposiris Magna	Borg el-Arab magazine, GEM(?)	Limestone	Hieroglyphic + demotic (fragm.)	2011	
Decree of Year 23[32]	10a	182, 19 Apr?	Unknown (probably En-Nobaireh)	Cairo TR 2/3/25/7	Limestone	Hieroglyphic	Before 1911	www.trismegistos.org/text/2986
	10b	182, 26 July	Asfoun al-Matana	Cairo JdE 44901	Nubian sandstone	Hieroglyphic	Before 1914	www.trismegistos.org/text/2987
	Ptolemy VI (Ptolemy Philometor)?							
	11[33]	162/160	Unknown (Delta?)	Cairo CG 22184	Limestone	Hieroglyphic (fragm.)	Before 1904	www.trismegistos.org/text/89794

GLOSSARY

alchemy A medieval chemical science and speculative philosophy that aimed to achieve the transmutation of the base metals into gold, and to discover a universal cure for disease and a means of indefinitely prolonging life.

cartonnage Layers of linen or papyrus covered with plaster to encase the deceased body or parts of it. This type of material was used in ancient Egyptian funerary masks and mummy covers from the First Intermediate Period to the Roman era.

humanism A philosophical stance that considers human beings the starting point for all serious moral debate and which favours rationalism and scientific method over superstition.

ideograms A written or pictorial symbol intended to represent an idea.

logograms A written or pictorial symbol intended to represent a whole word.

Neoplatonism A strand of Platonic philosophy that emerged in the third century CE. Rather than a set of ideas, the term encapsulates a series of thinkers starting with Ammonius Saccas (175–242 CE) and his student Plotinus (204/5–271 CE). Some ideas are common to Neoplatonic systems; for example, that all of reality can be derived from a single simple principle, 'the One', which is both the creative source of the universe and determines the purpose of all existing things.

ostracon (pl. ostraca) A pottery or stone flake used to write or draw on.

philology A discipline that studies the structure, historical development and relationships of languages.

phonetic Representing spoken language or speech sound.

phonographic Spelling more directly based on pronunciation.

Platonism (adj. Platonic) The philosophy of Plato (428/7–348/7 BCE), which stresses that actual things are copies of transcendent ideas and that these ideas are the objects of true knowledge.

Ptah-Sokar-Osiris statuettes Mummiform statuettes on rectangular bases, understood by Egyptologists as aids for the rebirth of the deceased. They usually take the form of the deity Osiris merged with the Memphite funerary gods Ptah and Sokar.

shabti Mummiform statuettes inscribed with spells and deposited in tombs. According to their magical formulae, shabtis could be called upon to carry out any work or unpleasant duties their owners wished to avoid in the afterlife.

stela (pl. stelae) A slab of stone or wood, usually bearing inscriptions, reliefs or paintings, erected most frequently as tombstones and boundary markers, but also as votive and commemorative monuments.

squeeze (or paper squeeze) A reverse copy of an inscription, made by applying and pushing moist filter paper into the depressions by percussive use of a stiff brush. The paper is allowed to dry and then removed. The image is reversed from the inscription and protrudes from the squeeze paper.

NOTES

All translations are the authors' own, unless otherwise stated below.

Introduction, pp. 16–29

1 Regulski, I. 2016, *The Origins and Early Development of Writing in Egypt.* Oxford Handbooks online: www.oxfordhandbooks.com/view/10.1093/oxfordhb/9780199935413.001.0001/oxfordhb-9780199935413-e-61 (last accessed 17 May 2022).

2 Depauw, M. 1997, *A Companion to Demotic Studies.* Papyrologica Bruxellensia 28. Brussels, 25.

3 For an annotated bibliography on Jean-François Champollion and his work on decipherment until 1989, see Kettel, J. 1990, *Jean-François Champollion le Jeune: Répertoire de bibliographie analytique 1806–1989.* Mémoires de l'Académie des inscriptions et belles-lettres, nouvelle série 10. Paris.

4 Regulski, I. 2009, The Beginning of Hieratic Writing in Egypt, *Studien zur altägyptischen Kultur* 38, 259–74.

5 Hoffmann, F. and Pfeiffer, S. 2021, *Der Stein von Rosetta.* Stuttgart, 49.

6 Quack, J.F. 2017, How the Coptic Script Came About, in: Eitan, G., Dils, P., Richter, T.S. and Schenkel, W. (eds), *Greek Influence on Egyptian-Coptic: Contact-induced Change in an Ancient African Language*, 27–96. Lingua Aegyptia, Studia Monographica 17. Hamburg.

7 von Lieven, A. 2016, Sounds of Power: The Concept of Sound in Ancient Egyptian Religion, in: Reichling, Ph. and Strothmann, M. (eds), *Religion für die Sinne/Religion for the Senses*, 25–35. Oberhausen.

8 Hamilton, A. 2006, *The Copts and the West 1439–1822: The European Discovery of the Egyptian Church.* Oxford, 196.

Chapter 1: The truth in translation, pp. 32–89

1 Horapollo, 1993, *The Hieroglyphics of Horapollo*, trans. George Boas. Bollingen Series 23. New York, 66 (52).

2 Burnett, Ch. 2003, Images of Ancient Egypt in the Latin Middle Ages, in: Ucko, P. and Champion, T. (eds), *The Wisdom of Egypt: Changing Visions Through the Ages*, 65–99. London, 77.

3 Iversen, E. 1993. *The Myth of Egypt and Its Hieroglyphs in European Tradition*, 2nd edn. Princeton, 45–6.

4 Ibn Fatik, A. 1048–9, *Kitāb mukhtār al-ḥikam wa-maḥāsin al-kalim* ('Book of Selected Maxims and Aphorisms'). Cairo, 54; el-Daly, O. 2005, *Egyptology: The Missing Millennium; Ancient Egypt in Medieval Arabic Writings.* London, 57–73.

5 al-Muqaddasī, S. 2014, *Aḥsan al-taqāsīm fī maʿrifat al-aqālīm*, Bibliotheca Geographorum Arabicorum 2–2. Leiden, 193, 203; el-Daly 2005, 22.

6 Diethart, J.M. and Satzinger, H. 1983. Eine griechisch-koptische Wörterliste, in: *Festschrift zum 100-jährigen Bestehen der Papyrussammlung der österreichischen Nationalbibliothek: Papyrus Erzherzog Rainer (P. Rainer Cent.) 1*, 206–13. Vienna (= Papyrus Vindob. G26018, 7th century BCE); Sidarus, A.Y. 2000, Onomastica aegyptiaca: The Tradition of Thematic Lexicography in Egypt through the Ages and Languages, *Bulletin de la Société d'Archéologie Copte* 39, 11–22.

7 el-Daly 2005, 66.

8 el-Daly 2005, 54–5.

9 Sundermeyer, A. 2020, Interpretations and Reuse of Ancient Egyptian Hieroglyphs in the Arabic Period (Tenth–Sixteenth Centuries CE), in: Davies, V. and D. Laboury (eds), *The Oxford Handbook of Egyptian Epigraphy and Paleography*, 176–92. New York.

10 Ibn Waḥshīyah, A. ibn 'Alī; Hammer-Purgstall, Joseph von. 1806, *Ancient Alphabets and Hieroglyphic Characters Explained; With an Account of the Egyptian Priests, Their Classes, Initiation, and Sacrifices.* London.

11 Hallum, B. and Marée, M. 2016, A medieval alchemical book reveals new secrets, https://blog.britishmuseum.org/a-medieval-alchemical-book-reveals-new-secrets; el-Daly 2005, 72, fig. 24. The 'climes' (from which the English word 'climate' is derived) are the seven latitudinal zones into which astronomer and geographer Claudius Ptolemy (2nd century CE) divided the inhabited world.

12 Fowden, G. 1993, *The Egyptian Hermes: A Historical Approach to the Late Pagan Mind.* Princeton, 216–17. The writings attributed to Hermes Trismegistus were probably written by a number of different authors at different dates.

13 Van Bladel, K.T. 2009, *The Arabic Hermes: From Pagan Sage to Prophet of Science.* New York, Oxford, 3.

14 el-Daly 2005, 117; Van Bladel 2009.

15 el-Daly 2005, 58.

16 Curran, B.A. 2007, *The Egyptian Renaissance: The Afterlife of Ancient Egypt in Early Modern Italy.* Chicago; Jirásková, L. 2020, The Reception of Ancient Egypt and Its Script in Renaissance Europe, in: Davies, V. and Laboury, D. (eds), *The Oxford Handbook of Egyptian Epigraphy and Palaeography*, 193–204. New York.

17 Curran, B.A. and Grafton, A. 1995, A Fifteenth-Century Site Report on the Vatican Obelisk, *Journal of the Warburg and Courtauld Institutes* 58, 234–48.

18 Fowden, G. 1982, The Pagan Holy Man in Late Antique Society, *Journal of Hellenic Studies* 102, 33–59; von Lieven, A. 2010, Wie töricht war Horapollo? Zur Ausdeutung von Schriftzeichen im Alten Ägypten, in: Knuf, H., Leitz, Ch. and von Recklinghausen, D. (eds), *Honi soit qui mal y pense: Studien zum pharaonischen, griechisch-römischen und spätantiken Ägypten zu Ehren von Heinz-Josef Thissen.* Orientalia Lovaniensia Analecta 194, 567–74. Leuven, Paris.

19 The oldest surviving manuscript was acquired by the Florentine traveller and manuscript hunter Christoforo Buondelmonti on the island of Andros in 1419 and was presented to the great antiquarian Niccolò Niccoli around 1422 (Giehlow, K. 1915, *Die Hieroglyphenkunde des Humanismus in der Allegorie der Renaissance*, Jahrbuch der kunsthistorischen Sammlungen 32, 12–18); Allen, D.C. 1960, The Predecessors of Champollion, *Proceedings of the American Philosophical Society*, 104, no. 5, 527.

20 Horapollo 1993, 59 (26); Thissen, H.J. 2001, *Des Niloten Horapollon Hieroglyphenbuch, I: Text und Übersetzung.* Archiv für Papyrusforschung und verwandte Gebiete, Beiheft 6. Munich, Leipzig, 21 (26); Winand, J. 2018, Un Frankenstein sémiotique: Les hiéroglyphes d'Athanase Kircher, *Signata: Annales des sémiotiques / Annals of Semiotics* 9, 213–51.

21 Curran 2007, 23; Fowden 1993.

22 Giehlow 1915, 12–18.

23 Curran, B.A. 2003, The Renaissance Afterlife of Ancient Egypt (1400–1650), in: Ucko and Champion (eds), 101–31, 106; Winand 2018, 217.

24 Morenz, L. 2003, Neohieroglyphs of the Italian Renaissance – Tradition and Its Invention, in: Morra L. and Bazzanella, C. (eds), *Philosophers and Hieroglyphs*, 50–73. Turin, 62; Jirásková 2020, 196–9.

25 Curran 2003, 114.

26 Stolzenberg, D. 2013, *Egyptian Oedipus: Athanasius Kircher and the Secrets of Antiquity*. Chicago, London, 45.

27 See collezioni.museoegizio.it/it-IT/material/Cat_7155 for digital images of the Mensa Isiaca.

28 Dewachter, M. 1986, L'Egypte ancienne dans les 'Cabinetz de raretez' du Sud-Est de la France aux XVIIe et XVIIIe siècles, in: Université Paul Valéry, Institut d'égyptologie (ed.), *Hommages à François Daumas*. Montpellier, volume 1, 181–206.

29 de Maillet, B. 1740, *Description de l'Égypte, contenant plusieurs remarques … sur la géographie … de ce Païs, sur ses monumens anciens, sur les mœurs … des habitans … &c. Composée sur les mémoires de M. de Maillet … par M. l'Abbé Le Mascrier*. La Haye; Lüscher, B. 2018, *Der sogenannte 'Calendrier égyptien' oder die Mumienbinden der Aberuai (BN 89 + BN 229 / Louvre N. 3059 u.a.): zur frühen Rezeptionsgeschichte eines späten Totenbuches*. Beiträge zum Alten Ägypten 8. Basel.

30 Haskell, F. and McBurney, H. 2018, The Paper Museum of Cassiano dal Pozzo: General Introduction, in: Vaiani, E., Prosperi Valenti Rodinò, S. and Whitehouse, H. (eds), *Egyptian and Roman Antiquities and Renaissance Decorative Arts: The Paper Museum of Cassiano Dal Pozzo* 8. London, 1–3.

31 Lo Sardo, E. 2001, *Athanasius Kircher: Il museo del mondo: macchine, esoterismo, arte*, Rome; Mayer-Deutsch, A. 2010, *Das Musaeum Kircherianum: Kontemplative Momente, historische Rekonstruktion. Bildrethorik*. Zurich.

32 Stolzenberg 2013 provides a comprehensive account of Kircher's life, with an extensive bibliography and generous assessment of his work. For a critical analysis of Kircher's work on Coptic, see Hamilton 2006, 203–28.

33 Iversen 1993, 92–9; Stolzenberg 2013, 198.

34 Stolzenberg 2013, 71, 85, 156. On Kircher more generally, see Findlen, P. 2004, *Athanasius Kircher: The Last Man Who Knew Everything*, New York, London.

35 Allen 1960, 527–47; Curran 2003, 127.

36 Stolzenberg 2013, 115–39.

37 The obelisk received its name because it was re-erected on the Piazza Navona in front of the Palazzo Pamphili.

38 Kircher A. 1650, *Obeliscus Pamphilius*. Rome, 557; Allen 1960, 531–2.

39 Kircher A. 1636, *Prodromus Coptus sive Ægyptiacus*. Rome, 5–16, 238–77; Stolzenberg 2013, 143.

40 Stolzenberg, D. 2003, Lectio idealis: Theory and Practice in Athanasius Kircher's Translations of the Hieroglyphs, in: Morra and Bazzanella (eds), 74–99, 95.

41 Kircher, A. 1652–4, *Oedipus Aegyptiacus*. 3 vols. Rome.

42 These examples have been taken by Beinlich, H. 2002, Athanasius Kircher und die Kenntnis vom Alten Ägypten, in: Beinlich, H., Daxelmüller, C., Vollrath, H.-J. and Wittstadt, K. (eds), *Magie des Wissens: Athanasius Kircher 1602–1680. Universalgelehrter, Sammler, Visionär*, 85–98. Dettelbach.

43 Stolzenberg 2013, 245.

44 Graczyk, A. 2015. *Die Hieroglyphe im 18. Jahrhundert: Theorien zwischen Aufklärung und Esoterik*. Hallesche Beiträge zur Europäischen Aufklärung 51. Berlin, Munich, 58.

45 Christiansen, T. 2020, The Reliefs from Obelisks in Rome (L204–L255): Thorvaldsen, His Collection of Egyptian Antiquities and the Egyptologist Milieu, in: Zahle, J. (ed.), *Thorvaldsen: Collector of Plaster Casts from Antiquity and the Early Modern Period II, The Roman Plaster Cast Market, 1750–1840*. Copenhagen, 16.

46 Ciampini, E.M. 2004, *Gli obelischi iscritti di Roma*. Rome, 142–9; Bøggild Johannsen, K. 2015, Relics of a Friendship: Objects from Georg Zoëga's Estate in Thorvaldsens Museum, Copenhagen, in: Ascani, K., Buzi, P. and Picchi, D. (eds), *The Forgotten Scholar: Georg Zoëga (1755–1809): At the Dawn of Egyptology and Coptic Studies*, 25–35. Leiden. After Zoëga's death a considerable number of objects from the estate ended up in Thorvaldsen's possession and later entered into the collections of Thorvaldsens Museum in Copenhagen: www.thorvaldsensmuseum.dk/en.

47 Zoëga, G. 1797, *De origine et usu obeliscorum*. Rome, pl. 6; Ciampini 2004, 148–9; Christiansen 2020, 18.

48 Olmi, G. and Simoni, F. 2018, *Ulisse Aldrovandi: Libri e immagini di Storia naturale nella prima Età moderna*. Bologna.

49 Haxhiraj, M. 2016, *Ulisse Aldrovandi: Il museografo*. Bologna.

50 Pomian, K. 1990, *Collectors & Curiosities: Paris and Venice 1500–1800*. Cambridge, 35.

51 Aldrovandi, U. 1648, *Musaeum metallicum in libros 4 distributum Bartholomaeus Ambrosinus … labore, et studio composuit cum indice copiosissimo*. Bononiae, 542, 750.

52 Cf. Lollio Barberi, O., Parola, G. and Toti, P. 1995, *Le antichità egiziane di Roma Imperiale*. Rome.

53 Invernizzi, A. 2001, *In viaggio per l'Oriente. Le mummie, Babilonia, Persepoli*. Turin, in particular 99–120.

54 Kircher 1652–4, 405–10, 432–5; Bartola, A. 2004, Alle origini del Museo del Collegio Romano, *NUNCIUS. Annali di Storia della Scienza* 19, no. 1, 297–356.

55 The area around the ancient capital city of Memphis, south of present-day Cairo, including its burial places of Giza, Saqqara and Dahshur.

56 Blount, H. 1636, *Voyage into the Levant*. London, 45; Coppin, J. 1686, *Le Bouclier de l'Europe, ou La Guerre sainte, contenant des avis politiques, et chrêtiens … avec une Relation de voyages faits dans la Turquie, la Thébaïde et la Barbarie*. Puy, 179–82.

57 Mummiform statuettes on rectangular bases showing Osiris merged with the Memphite funerary gods Ptah and Sokar and understood by Egyptologists as aids for the rebirth of the deceased.

58 Picchi, D. 2004, Le antichità egiziane del Museo Cospiano, *Ricerche di Egittologia e di Antichità Copte* 6, 51–86.

59 Picchi, D. 2014, Il generale Luigi Ferdinando Marsili e le prime antichità egizie dell'Instituto delle Scienze di Bologna, in: Ciampini, E.M. and Zanovello, P. (eds), *Antichità egizie e Italia: Prospettive di ricerca e indagini sul campo*. Antichristica 6, Serie di Studi Orientali 2. Venice.

60 Germano, A. and Nocca, M. 2001, *La collezione Borgia: Curiosità e tesori da ogni parte del mondo*. Naples; Nocca, M. 2001, *Le quattro voci del mondo: Arte, culture e saperi nella collezione di Stefano Borgia 1731–1804*. Naples.

61 *Catalogo dei monumenti egiziani esistenti in Velletri composto ed ordinato dal Sig. Giorgio Zoëga nel mese di Ottobre 1784*; cf. Ascani, K., Buzi, P. and Picchi, D. 2015, *The Forgotten Scholar: Georg Zoëga (1755–1809): At the Dawn of Egyptology and Coptic Studies*. Culture and History of the Ancient Near East 74. Leiden.

62 Picchi, D. 2022, Un rilievo dalla tomba menfita di Ptahmes e le trattative fallite per la vendita a Leopoldo II della terza collezione Nizzoli, *CADMO. Revista de História Antiga* 30, 11–37.

63 Picchi, D. and Chilò, L. 2021, Pelagio Palagi and the Belzoni Family Collection of Egyptian Antiquities, in: Rocheleau, C.M. and Hardwick, T. (eds), *Offerings to Maat: Essays in Honour of Emily Teeter*, CIPEG Journal 5, 129–48. Heidelberg.

64 Stolzenberg 2013, 233.

65 See individual contributions in Ascani, Buzi, Picchi, 2015.

66 Zoëga 1797, viii, 178–82.

67 *Numi Aegyptii Imperatorii in Museo Borgiano Veletris*. Engravings and sketches for this catalogue are today housed in the Thorvaldsens Museum and the Royal Library in Copenhagen; Johannsen 2015; Christiansen 2020, 17.

68 Allen 1960, 527–47.

69 Such as the statue of Wahibre (EA111), the Nectanebo slab (EA22), the basalt block of Psamtek I (EA20) and a tomb relief (EA430).

70 Hamilton 2006, 248.

71 Dalrymple, W. 2020, *The Anarchy: The Relentless Rise of the East India Company*, London, 332–3.

72 Bret, P. 1998, *L'expédition d'Égypte, une entreprise des Lumières 1798–1801: Actes du colloque international organisé par l'Académie des inscriptions et belles-lettres et l'Académie des sciences, sous les auspices de l'Institut de France et du Muséum national d'histoire naturelle, 8–10 juin*, 359–64. Paris.

73 Denon, V. 1802, *Voyage dans la Basse et la Haute Égypte, pendant les campagnes du Général Bonaparte*. 3 vols. Paris.

74 Denon 1802, vol. 1, 109.

75 Reybaud, L., Fortia d'Urban, A., Marcel, J.-J. and Vaulabelle, A. de. 1830–6, *Histoire scientifique et militaire de l'expedition française en Égypte, Tome IV.6*. Paris, 434. For the discovery and reception at the Institut: 434–44.

76 Clarke, E.D. 1817, *Travels in Various Countries of Europe, Asia and Africa. Part II, 2: Greece, Egypt and the Holy Land. Volume V*, London, 71. He describes seeing a large, scarcely legible trilingual stone.

77 Now British Museum EA10.

78 For these events, see Reybaud et al. 1830–6, 395–422.

79 Scurr, R. 2021, *Napoleon: A Life in Gardens and Shadows*. London, 228–32.

80 Étienne, M. 2008, La collection d'antiquités égyptiennes de Malmaison, in: Descamps-Lequime, S. and Denoyelle, M. (eds), *De Pompéi à Malmaison, les antiques de Joséphine*, 41–5. Paris, 42.

81 Clarke 1817, 340–5.

82 Clarke to W. Otter, quoted in: Downs, J. 2008, *Discovery at Rosetta: The Stone that Unlocked the Mysteries of Egypt*. London, 156.

83 Clarke 1817, 40.

84 Hamilton, W. 1809, *Remarks on Several Parts of Turkey: Part I. Aegyptiaca*. London, 403.

85 Clarke 1817, 27.

86 Clarke 1817, 366–8.

87 Clarke 1817, 372.

88 Clarke 1817, 373.

89 Clarke 1817, 373.

90 Clarke 1817, 376.

91 Raper, M. 1812. An Account of the Rosetta Stone, in three languages, which was brought to England in the year 1802, *Archaeologia, or Miscellaneous Tracts Relating to Antiquity, published by The Society of Antiquaries of London* 16, no. 27, 208–14. London.

92 Bierbrier, M.L. 1999, The Acquisition by the British Museum of Antiquities Discovered during the French Invasion of Egypt, in: Davies, W.V. (ed.), *Studies in Egyptian Antiquities: A Tribute to T.G.H. James*, 111–13. London.

93 Parkinson, R.B. 2005, *The Rosetta Stone*. London, 32.

94 Thomas Young, letter to Henry Bankes, AES Ar. 387, Archive of the Department of Egypt and Sudan, the British Museum.

95 Denon 1802; Belzoni, G. 1820, *Narrative of the Operations and Recent Discoveries within the Pyramids, Temples, Tombs, and Excavations in Egypt and Nubia*. London.

96 Bednarski, A. 2005, *Holding Egypt: Tracing the Reception of the* Description de l'Égypte *in Nineteenth-Century Great Britain*. Golden House Publications Egyptology 3. London.

97 Reid, D.M. 2002, *Whose Pharaohs? Archaeology, Museums, and Egyptian National Identity from Napoleon to World War I*. Berkeley, Los Angeles, London, 54.

98 Colla, E. 2007, *Conflicted Antiquities: Egyptology, Egyptomania, Egyptian Modernity*. Durham, London, 40–1.

99 Bierbrier, M.L. 2019, *Who Was Who in Egyptology*, 5th revised edn. London, 136; Ridley, R.T. 1998, *Napoleon's Proconsul in Egypt: The Life and Times of Bernardino Drovetti*. London.

100 Bierbrier 2019, 409–10; Manley, D. and Rée, P. 2001, *Henry Salt: Artist, Traveller, Diplomat, Egyptologist*. London.

101 Thompson, J. 2015, *Wonderful Things: A History of Egyptology 1: From Antiquity to 1881*. Cairo, New York, 132–4.

102 Henniker, Sir F. 1823, *Notes During a Visit to Egypt, Nubia, the Oasis, Mount Sinai and Jerusalem*. London, 139.

103 Bierbrier 2019, 394–5; Fiechter, J.J. 1994, *La moisson des dieux: La constitution des grandes collections égyptiennes 1815–1830*. Paris, 40–9, 63–5, 94–105, 114, 144–6, 148–53, 229–48; Bruwier, M.-C., Claes, W. and Quertinmont, A. 2014, *La description de l'Égypte de Jean-Jacques Rifaud (1813–1826)*. Brussels, 11–29.

104 Bierbrier 2019, 16.

105 Reid 2002, 39, 46.

106 Schmidt, H.C. 2011, *Westcar on the Nile: A Journey through Egypt in the 1820s*. Wiesbaden, 160. For d'Athanasi, see Taylor, J.H. 2020, The Collecting Activities of Giovanni d'Athanasi: Recovering Object Provenances and Associations from Archival Sources, in: Perrot, A.-H., Pietri, R. and Tanré-Szewczyk, J. (eds), *L'Objet Égyptien: Source de la Recherche. Actes du colloque École du Louvre 17, 18, 19 juin 2015*, 249–74. Paris. For Passalacqua: Bierbrier 2019, 355.

107 Thompson 2015, 147.

108 Thompson, J. 1992, *Sir Gardner Wilkinson and His Circle*. Austin, 102.

109 Sherer, M. 1824, *Scenes and Impressions in Egypt and in Italy*. London, 116–17. See also Madden, R.R. 1829, *Travels in Turkey, Egypt, Nubia and Palestine in 1824, 1825, 1826 and 1827*. London, vol. 2, 78ff.

110 Sherer 1824, 111–12.

111 Steegmuller, F. 1996, *Flaubert in Egypt: A Sensibility on Tour*. London, 54.

112 Bierbrier 2019, 263.

113 Bierbrier 2019, 491–3 and 81–2.

114 Bierbrier 2019, 211.

115 Thompson 2015, 182–9.

116 Thompson 1992, 75–81; Reid 2002, 40–1.

117 Colla 2007, 97–100.

118 Reid 2002, 54–8.

119 Colla 2007, 118–20. For al-Tahtawi: Bierbrier 2019, 451.

120 Barker and Mimaut: Bierbrier 2019, 35, 319.

121 al-Jabarti, A. al-R. 1993, *Napoleon in Egypt: Al-Jabarti's Chronicle of the French Occupation, 1798*. Translation by Shmuel Moreh, introduction by Robert L.Tignor. Princeton, New York, 43, 64. With permission of Markus Wiener Publishers, Princeton, NJ, USA.

Chapter 2: The race to decipherment, pp. 92–125

1 Gillispie, Ch. C. and Dewachter, M. 1987, *Monuments of Egypt: The Napoleonic Expedition. The Complete Archaeological Plates from* La Description de l'Égypte. Princeton, 21–2; Iversen 1993, 127; Parkinson, R.B. 1999, *Cracking Codes: The Rosetta Stone and Decipherment*. London, 20; Regulski, I. 2020b, The Rosetta Stone: Copying an Ancient Copy, in: Davies, V. and Laboury, D. (eds), *The Oxford Handbook of Egyptian Epigraphy and Palaeography*. Oxford, with further references. In this section, the word 'cast' refers to a thin cast of the top layer of the Stone (usually between 5 and 10 cm thick) made in a mould, rather than full-sized replicas.

2 Palin, N.G. 1804, *Analyse de l'inscription en hiéroglyphiques du Monument trouvé à Rosette contenant un décret des Prêtres de l'Égypte en l'honneur de Ptolémée Épiphane*, Dresden; Iversen 1993, 128.

3 E.-F. Jomard, 1809, *Description de l'Égypte: Antiquités; descriptions.* Volume 1. Paris, 372.

4 Hamilton 2006, 248.

5 Thompson 2015, 109.

6 Åkerblad, J.D. 1802, *Lettre sur l'inscription égyptienne de Rosette: Adressée au citoyen Silvestre de Sacy, Professeur de langue arabe à l'École spéciale des langues orientales vivantes, etc.; Réponse du citoyen Silvestre de Sacy*. Paris, 40; Thomasson, F. 2013,

The Life of J.D. Åkerblad: Egyptian Decipherment and Orientalism in Revolutionary Times. Leiden, Boston.

7 Young's answer to Åkerblad's second letter, August 1815.

8 Robinson, A. 2006, *The Last Man Who Knew Everything: Thomas Young, the Anonymous Genius Who Proved Newton Wrong and Deciphered the Rosetta Stone, among Other Surprising Feats.* London.

9 Young, T. 1823. *An Account of Some Recent Discoveries in Hieroglyphical Literature and Egyptian Antiquities.* London, xiv.

10 Hoffmann and Pfeiffer 2021.

11 Robinson, A. 2012, *Cracking the Egyptian Code: The Revolutionary Life of Jean-François Champollion.* London, 99.

12 Young, T. 1816, Extracts of Letters and Papers Relating to the Egyptian Inscription on Rosetta, *Museum Criticum* or *Cambridge Classical Researches* 6, 157. Cambridge.

13 Young 1816; Young, T. 1824, *Egypt*, Supplement to the Fourth, Fifth, and Sixth Editions of the *Encyclopaedia Britannica*: With Preliminary Dissertations on the History of the Sciences 4, 38–74. Edinburgh, London. Fourth edition of the 1819 original.

14 Robinson 2012, 95.

15 For example, fragments of a papyrus roll collected in 1811 from a mummy found near a Theban tomb by his friend, British antiquarian and traveller William Edward Rouse Boughton (1788–1856): Boughton, W. 1817, A Letter from W.E. Rouse Boughton, Esq. F.R.S. to the Rev. Stephen Weston, B.D. respecting some Egyptian Antiquities, *Archaeologia* 18, 59–72. It has not been possible to locate the Boughton papyrus. One of the manuscripts was published in Denon, V. 1802, *Voyage dans la Basse et la Haute Égypte, pendant les campagnes du Général Bonaparte*, vol. 2, pl. 137. Young tried to make sense of the texts using the demotic alphabet compiled by Åkerblad in 1802 (see p. 94) but was unable to retrieve any meaning: Robinson 2012, 95.

16 Buchwald, J.Z. and Josefowicz, D.G. 2020, *The Riddle of the Rosetta: How an English Polymath and a French Polyglot Discovered the Meaning of Egyptian Hieroglyphs.* Princeton, 268.

17 Young 1824, 60.

18 For Bankes's account of the discovery see Bankes's Manuscripts, vol. I, 92 at the British Museum; Usick, P. 2002, *Adventures in Egypt and Nubia: The Travels of William John Bankes (1786-1855).* London.

19 Bednarski, A. 2015, Beyond Traveler's Accounts and Reproductions: Unpublished Nineteenth-Century Works as Histories of Egyptology, in: Carruthers, W. (ed.), *Histories of Egyptology: Interdisciplinary Measures*, Routledge Studies in Egyptology 2, 81–95. New York, London; Mainterot, Ph. 2011, *Aux origines de l'égyptologie: Voyages et collections de Frédéric Cailliaud (1787–1869).* Rennes.

20 Schenkel, W. 2006, Ramses, Thutmosis und Henry Salt, *Göttinger Miszellen* 208, 89–94; Salt, H. 2007, *The Sphinx Revealed: A Forgotten Record of Pioneering Excavations*, ed. P. Usick and D. Manley. British Museum Research Publications 164. London.

21 Buchwald and Josefowicz 2020, 345.

22 Iversen, E. 1972, *Obelisks in Exile. Volume 2: The Obelisks of Istanbul and England*, Copenhagen, 62; James, T.G.H. 1993–4, Egyptian Antiquities at Kingston Lacy, Dorset, *KMT* 4, no. 4, 27.

23 A translation was distributed by Letronne in 1821, and an edition of the Greek text, based on Cailliaud's copy, appeared in 1823.

24 Champollion, J.F. 1822a, De l'obélisque égyptien de l'Îsle de Philae, *Revue Encyclopédique* 13, 512–21, 512; Schenkel, W. 2014/15, Champollion's Kleopatra, *Mitteilungen des Deutschen Archäologischen Instituts, Abteilung Kairo* 70/71, 398.

25 Buchwald and Josefowicz 2020, fig. 20.1.

26 Coenen, M. 1985, The So-Called Denon Papyri, *Journal of Egyptian Archaeology* 81, 237–41; Boddens Hosang, F.J.E. 1989, *De Egyptische verzameling van Baron van Westreenen.* The Hague, 68–70, inventory no. 42/88, pl. 34; De Meulenaere, H. 1989, Notes de prosopographie thébaine: quatrième série, *Chronique d'Égypte* 64, no. 127–8, 55–73. The papyrus was purchased at the auction of Denon's collection on 18 January 1827, by Baron van Westreenen, the founder of the present Meermanno-Westreenianum Museum; Dubois, L.J.J. 1826, *Description des objets d'arts qui composent le cabinet de feu M. le baron V. Denon.* Paris, 29, no. 230.

27 Vaillant, P. 1984, *Jean-François Champollion: Lettres à son frère, 1804–1818.* Champollion et son temps 2. Paris, 5.

28 Champollion, J.F. 1808–10, *L'Égypte sous les Pharaons: Description geographique; Introduction.* Paris, xii–xvi; Champollion, J.F. 1836. *Grammaire égyptienne.* Paris, ix–xix. Hartleben, H. 1906, *Champollion: Sein Leben und sein Werk*, 2 vols. Berlin, vol. I, 374–87, 421–97. Buchwald and Josefowicz 2020, 152.

29 Robinson 2012, 68.

30 Faure, A. 2004, *Champollion: Le savant déchiffré.* Paris, 135–6; Hamilton 2006, 249. On Champollion's Coptic studies, see Bourguet, P. du, 1982, Champollion et les études coptes, *Bulletin de la Société française d'Égyptologie* 95, 62–75. Another prominent member of the Coptic community was Yuhanna Chiftichi, an Egyptian priest and a member of the Coptic legion: Buchwald and Josefowicz 2020, 143; Madrigal, K. 2021, *Jean-François & Jacques-Joseph Champollion: L'aventure du déchiffrement des hiéroglyphes. Correspondance.* Paris, 47, 57.

31 In a letter to his brother dated 2 April 1809 (ADI, 185 J 10, pièce 51, fols 90–1); Vaillant 1984, 25; Madrigal 2021, 47, 58.

32 In an 1811 review of Zoëga's catalogue: Champollion, J.F. 1811, *Observations sur le catalogue des manuscrits coptes du musée Borgia à Velletri, ouvrage posthume de George Zoëga.* Paris, 5–6. Comprehensive Egyptological training at universities teaches Sahidic first and introduces other dialects by way of comparison.

33 Buchwald and Josefowicz 2020, 153, 218.

34 Devauchelle, D. 1990, D'une pierre deux écritures, in: Anonymous (ed.), *Mémoires d'Égypte: Hommage de l'Europe a Champollion*, 110–17. Strasbourg; Valbelle, D. 1999, *Le décret de Memphis: Colloque de la Fondation Singer-Polignac à l'occasion de la célébration du bicentenaire de la découverte de la pierre de Rosette.* Paris. The influence of his brother must have been significant here, as in a letter dated 26 May 1809, Jacques-Joseph Champollion suggests translating the Greek text into Coptic to approach the Egyptian text: Madrigal 2021, 78.

35 Robinson 2012, 73.

36 Champollion's 1811 *L'Égypte sous les Pharaons* was conceived, organised and promoted as a geography. The work's originality lay in the way Champollion used contemporary ideas to unearth the ancient Egyptian language, employing early nineteenth-century French linguistics coupled with a sympathetic effort to inhabit another point of view: Buchwald and Josefowicz 2020, 151, 160.

37 Champollion, J.F. 1811–14, *L'Égypte sous les Pharaons, ou Recherches sur la géographie, la religion, la langue, les écritures et l'histoire de l'Égypte avant l'invasion de Cambyse*, 2 vols. Paris.

38 Robinson 2012, 81.

39 Vaillant 1984, 41–2. According to some (Hartleben 1906, 299), the members of the *Description* commission were not forthcoming because Jomard, the editor-in-chief, was himself busy with hieroglyphs and was not a fan of Champollion. Letter held at the Archives départementales de l'Isère à Grenoble.

40 Faure 2004, 418.

41 Although only sixty-six different hieroglyphs, as many signs are repeated: Hoffmann and Pfeiffer 2021, 147.

42 Champollion, J.F. 1821, *De l'écriture hiératique des anciens Égyptiens: Explication des Planches.* Grenoble.

43 Buchwald and Josefowicz 2020, 338.

44 Robinson 2012, 137.

45 For an image of the papyrus: https://gallica.bnf.fr/ark:/12148/btv1b8304634x.r=Casatipapyrus?rk=42918;4; Schenkel 2014/15, 395–6.
46 Hoffmann and Pfeiffer 2021, 148.
47 For Champollion's note on the demotic papyrus Grey: Bibliothèque nationale de France, NAF 20314, fol. 141: https://gallica.bnf.fr/ark:/12148/btv1b10085297g/f280.item.
48 Buchwald and Josefowicz 2020, 408.
49 NAF (Nouvelles acquisitions françaises) 20352, fol. 45.
50 Usick 2002, 79. The original lithograph seems to have disappeared.
51 Under the title 'l'alphabet des hieroglyphs phonétiques employés par les Egyptiens pour inscrire sur leurs monumens les titres, les noms et les surnoms des souverains grecs et romains'.
52 Robinson 2012, 143–4.
53 Buchwald and Josefowicz 2020, 376.
54 Champollion, J.F. 1822b, *Lettre à M. Dacier, … relative à l'alphabet des hiéroglyphes phonétiques employés par les Égyptiens pour inscrire sur leurs monuments les titres, les noms et les surnoms des souverains Grecs et Romains.* Paris, 41–2.
55 And not the vertical s-sign as often repeated by scholars: Schenkel, W. 2002, Ramses: Die Erfindung einer Graphie in der Nacherzählung der Entzifferungsgeschichte der Hieroglyphen, *Göttinger Miszellen* 191, 85–8.
56 This was to be discovered in 1837 by the father of German Egyptology, Karl Richard Lepsius (1810–1884): Hoffmann and Pfeiffer 2021, 155.
57 Buchwald and Josefowicz 2020, 389.
58 Champollion, J.-F. 1824, *Précis du système hiéroglyphique des anciens Égyptiens, ou, Recherches sur le éléments premiers de cette écriture sacrée.* Paris, 175–9.
59 Buchwald and Josefowicz 2020, fig. 31.2 on p. 425.
60 The reprint in 1828 incorporated an amended version of the Dacier letter with alterations reflecting his change of mind on phonetism.
61 Buchwald and Josefowicz 2020, 246.
62 Usick 2002, 78.
63 Faure 2004, 431. See also Devauchelle, D. 1999, De la pierre de Rosette à Champollion, in: Bret, P. (ed.), *L'expédition d'Égypte, une entreprise des Lumières 1798–1801: Actes du colloque international organisé par l'Académie des inscriptions et belles-lettres et l'Académie des sciences, sous les auspices de l'Institut de France et du Muséum national d'histoire naturelle, 8–10 juin 1998*, 359–64. Paris.
64 Robinson 2012, 188.
65 Leitch, J. 1855, *Miscellaneous Works of the Late Thomas Young, M.D., F.R.S., &c., Vol. III Hieroglyphical Essays and Correspondence.* London, 79.

Chapter 3: The impact of decipherment, pp. 128–43

1 Robinson 2012, 176.
2 Museo Egizio Collection online at: https://collezioni.museoegizio.it/en-GB/material/Cat_1874/?description=royal+canon&inventoryNumber=&title=&cgt=&yearFrom=&yearTo=&materials=&provenance=&acquisition=&epoch=&dynasty=&pharaoh= (last accessed 17 May 2022).
3 Salt, H. 2007, *The Sphinx Revealed: A Forgotten Record of Pioneering Excavations*, ed. Patricia Usick and Deborah Manley. British Museum Research Publications 164. London; Usick 2002, 199; Usick, P. 1998, The Egyptian Drawings of Alessandro Ricci in Florence: A List of Drawings from a Portfolio in the Museo Egizio di Firenze, *Göttinger Miszellen* 162, 73–92. As with so many private collections, most of Ricci's objects had no secure provenance. Part of the collection later went to the königlichen Antikensammlung, now Staatliche Kunstsammlungen Dresden, in 1831: Elsner, G. 1993, *Ägyptische Altertümer der Skulpturensammlung, Ausstellung im Albertinum zu Dresden, 30 July 1993–24 July 1994.* Dresden.
4 Champollion, J.F. 1909, *Lettres de Champollion le Jeune. I: Lettres écrites d'Italie*, ed. H. Hartleben. Bibliothèque Égyptologique 30. Paris, 79ff.
5 Regulski, I. 2019, *Abydos: The Sacred Land of the Western Horizon: Proceedings of the Annual Egyptological Colloquium at the British Museum 'Abydos: The Sacred Land at the Western Horizon', on 9–10 July, 2015.* British Museum Publication on Egypt and Sudan 8. Leuven.
6 Usick 2002, 193.
7 Redford, D.B. 1986, *Pharaonic King-Lists, Annals and Day-Books: A Contribution to the Study of the Egyptian Sense of History.* SSEA Publications 4. Missisauga, 20–1.
8 It is unclear whether Champollion was aware of the later reception of Manetho's work by medieval Arab scholars, some of whom had already composed king lists of Egyptian dynasties: el-Daly 2005, 129.
9 Buchwald and Josefowicz 2010, 305–7, for the challenge it posed religious orthodoxy.
10 Bresciani, E. 1972, L'expédition franco-toscane en Égypte et en Nubie (1828–1829) et les antiquités égyptiennes d'Italie, *Bulletin de la Société Française d'Égyptologie* 64, 5–29.
11 For the inventory of the 102 objects brought to the Louvre: Archives des musées nationaux 7 DD*7; Ziegler, C. 1993, Champollion en Égypte: Inventaire des antiquités rapportées au Musée du Louvre, in: Strybol, J. and Limme, L. (eds), *Aegyptus Museis Rediviva: Miscellanea in Honorem Hermanni De Meulenaere.* 197–213, Brussels; Jagot, H. 2013, Le Musée Charles X: Un écrin pour les collections égyptiennes du Louvre, in: Mainterot, Ph. and Jagot, H. (eds), *Du haut de ces pyramides . . : l'expédition d'Égypte et la naissance de l'égyptologie (1798–1850)*, 206–39. Roche-sur-Yon.
12 Salvoldi, D. 2018, *From Siena to Nubia: Alessandro Ricci in Egypt and Sudan, 1817–22.* Cairo, New York, 52.
13 The collection of fifteen fine watercolours by Salt, Beechey and Ricci were published (without photographs) by Bierbrier, M.L. 1983, The Salt Watercolours, *Göttinger Miszellen* 61, 9–12. See also Salt 2007; Usick 2002, 199.
14 Guichard, S. 2013, D'une expedition à l'autre, de Bonaparte à Champollion (1798–1828), in: Mainterot and Jagot (eds), 192–203.
15 Betrò, M. 2010, *Ippolito Rosellini and the Dawn of Egyptology: Original Drawings and Manuscripts of the Franco-Tuscan Expedition to Egypt (1828–29) from the Biblioteca Universitaria di Pisa.* Cairo, 22–5.
16 Textor de Ravisi, A.A. 1878. Recherches et conjectures sur la poésie pharaonique, in: Textor de Ravisi, A. A. (ed.), *Congrès Provincial des Orientalistes Français: Compte-rendu de la première session, Saint-Étienne, 1875 2*, 473–554. Paris, 475.
17 Champollion, J.-F. 1868, *Lettres écrites d'Egypte et de Nubie en 1828 et 1829.* Paris, 18; see also Sallier, F. 1828, *Sur une découverte de Champollion dans des papyrus égyptiens.* Aix.
18 Rougé, E. de. 1908, Notice sur un manuscript égyptien en écriture hiératique …, in: *Oeuvres Diverses* 2. Bibliothèque d'étude 22. Cairo, 303–19, quotes from 306, 319.
19 Chabas, F. 1899, 'Note sur la littérature des anciens égyptiens', unpublished but dated 1859, printed in *Oeuvres diverses* 1. Bibliothèque d'étude 9. Cairo, 317.
20 Maspero, G. 1911 [1882], *Les contes populaires de l'Égypte ancienne.* Paris, vi.
21 Birch, S. 1857, Introduction to the Study of the Egyptian Hieroglyphs, in: J. Gardiner Wilkinson, *The Egyptians in the Time of the Pharaohs: Being a Companion to the Crystal Palace Egyptian Collections*, 175–282. London, quotes from 211, 279.
22 Maspero, G. 1872, *Du genre épistolaire chez les anciens égyptiens (doctoral thesis).* Paris, iii.
23 Textor de Ravisi, 1878.
24 Goodwin, C.W. 1866, *The Story of Saneha, an Egyptian Tale of Four Thousand Years Ago.* London [reprinted from *Fraser's Magazine for Town and Country* 71, no. 422, 131–50], quotes from 11, 44, 44–5.

25 *The Caledonian Mercury*, 4 February 1865, 6; *The London Review*, 4 February 1865, 155.

26 Minute of 1835 on Indian Education, quoted in e.g. Said, E. 1984, *The World, the Text and the Critic*. London, 12.

27 Griffith, F. Ll. and Griffith, K.B. 1896–7, Egyptian Literature, in: C.D. Warner et al. (ed.), *Library of the World's Best Literature, Ancient and Modern* [30 vols], 5225–344. New York, quote from 5225.

28 Erman, A. 1894, *Life in Ancient Egypt*, trans. H.M. Tirard. London, 385; Griffith and Griffith 1896–7, 5225; Gardiner, A.H. 1916, *Notes on the Story of Sinuhe*. Paris, 56.

29 Erman, A. 1927, *The Literature of the Ancient Egyptians: Poems, Narratives, and Manuals of Instruction, From the Third and Second Millennia B.C.*, trans. A.M. Blackman. London, xliii.

30 Peet, T.E. 1931, *A Comparative Study of the Literature of Egypt, Palestine and Mesopotamia: Egypt's Contribution to the Literature of the Ancient World* [Schweich Lectures 1929]. London, 131–2, 135.

31 Peet 1931, 6.

32 Most recently: Hagen, F. 2019, New Copies of Old Classics: Early Manuscripts of Khakheperreseneb and The Instruction of a Man for his Son, *Journal of Egyptian Archaeology* 105, 177–208.

33 Williams, R. 2006 [1960], *Border Country*. Cardigan, 99. Study of reception; Parkinson, R.B. 2009, *Reading Ancient Egyptian Poetry: Among Other Histories*. Chichester, Malden, MA.

34 E.g. Barbara Ewing, The Life of Sinuhe: podcasts.ox.ac.uk/life-sinuhe 2016; Talking with the Soul: A Dialogue about Life and Death: podcasts.ox.ac.uk/talking-soul-dialogue-about-life-and-death 2019.

35 Mahfouz, N. 2002, *Voices from the Other World: Ancient Egyptian Tales*, trans. R. Stock. Cairo, 47–56; `Abd al-Salam, S. 1970, *Shakawa al-fallah al-fasih* [The Complaints of the Eloquent Peasant]. Cairo: Ministry of Culture's National Centre for Documentary Films.

36 P. Chester Beatty IV (P. BM EA10684) vso 2.7: see e.g. McDowell, A. 1999, *Village Life in Ancient Egypt: Laundry Lists and Love Songs*. Oxford, 137–8. The Teaching of Ptahhotep v. 519: see e.g. Parkinson, R.B. (trans.), 1997, *The Tale of Sinuhe and Other Ancient Egyptian Poems 1940–1640 BC*, Oxford World's Classics. Oxford, 262.

37 Iser, W. 1989, *Prospecting: From Reader Response to Literary Anthropology*. Baltimore, London, 208.

38 E.g. Parkinson, R.B. 2012. The Tale of Sinuhe, in: Puchner, M. (ed.), *The Norton Anthology of World Literature*, vol. A. New York and London.

39 Textor de Ravisi 1878, 554.

40 From Parkinson (trans.), *The Tale of Sinuhe*, 34–5.

Chapter 4: Rediscovering ancient Egypt, pp. 146–232

1 Spalinger, A.J. 2002, *The Transformation of an Ancient Egyptian Narrative: P.Sallier III and the Battle of Kadesh*. Göttinger Orientforschungen, 4. Series: Ägypten 40. Wiesbaden.

2 Morris, E. 2018, *Ancient Egyptian Imperialism*. Hoboken, 67–88.

3 Champollion le jeune, J.F. 1827. *Notice descriptive des monuments égyptiens du musée Charles X*. Paris, 1:35.

4 Salvoldi 2018, 58.

5 Morris 2018, 89–116.

6 Bietak, M. and Forstner-Müller, I. 2009, Der Hyksos-Palast bei Tell el-Dab'a: zweite und dritte Grabungskampagne (Frühling 2008 und Frühling 2009), *Ägypten und Levante* 19, 115–18; Mourad, A.L. 2015, *Rise of the Hyksos: Egypt and the Levant from the Middle Kingdom to the early Second Intermediate Period*. Archaeopress Egyptology 11. Oxford.

7 Morenz, L.D. and Popko, L. 2010, The Second Intermediate Period and the New Kingdom, in: Lloyd, A.B. (ed.), *A Companion to Ancient Egypt*, vol. 1, 101–19. Chichester, Malden, MA.

8 Letters to his brother on 25 August and 4 September 1824: Champollion 1909, 42, 51.

9 Ryholt, K.S.B. 1997, *The Political Situation in Egypt during the Second Intermediate Period c. 1800–1550 BCE*. With an appendix by Adam Bülow-Jacobsen. CNI Publications 20. Copenhagen.

10 Davies, W.V. 2003, Sobeknakht of Elkab and the Coming of Kush, *Egyptian Archaeology* 23, 3–6; Davies, W.V. 2003, Kush in Egypt: A New Historical Inscription, *Sudan and Nubia* 7, 52–4.

11 For example at the southern border at Kurgus in present-day Sudan: Davies, W.V. 1998, New Fieldwork at Kurgus: The Pharaonic Inscriptions, *Sudan and Nubia* 2, 26–30; Davies, W.V. 2001, Kurgus 2000: The Egyptian Inscriptions, *Sudan and Nubia* 5, 46–58.

12 Török, L. 1998, *The Kingdom of Kush: Handbook of the Napatan-Meroitic Civilization*. Leiden, 132–3, 153–84; Welsby, D.A. 1996, *The Kingdom of Kush: The Napatan and Meroitic Empires*, London.

13 Donker van Heel, K. 2020, Some Issues in and Perhaps a New Methodology for Abnormal Hieratic, in: Davies, V. and Laboury, D. (eds), *The Oxford Handbook of Egyptian Epigraphy and Paleography*. Oxford. DOI: 10.1093/oxfordhb/9780190604653.013.45 (last accessed 30 December 2021).

14 Martin, C.J. 2007, The Saite 'Demoticisation' of Southern Egypt, in: Lomas, K., Whitehouse, R.D. and Wilkins, J.B. (eds), *Literacy and the State in the Ancient Mediterranean*, 26. Specialist Studies on the Mediterranean 7. London.

15 Champollion 1909, 38.

16 Vleeming, S.P. 1981, La phase initiale du démotique ancien, *Chronique d'Égypte* 56, 31–48. The difference between abnormal hieratic and early demotic is determined not only by geography but also by the level of standardisation in both scribal traditions. Demotic is more advanced, which could suggest that it may have been subjected to a conscious standardisation process, whereas abnormal hieratic developed organically: Donker van Heel 2020, 5.

17 Ray, J.D. 1986, Psammuthis and Hakoris, *Journal of Egyptian Archaeology* 72, 150.

18 Lichtheim, M. 2006, *Ancient Egyptian Literature: A Book of Readings II: The New Kingdom*. Berkeley, 65–6. Reproduced with permission of University of California Press Books and Copyright Clearance Center.

19 Moran, W.L. 1992, *The Amarna Letters*. Baltimore, London; Rainey, A.F. 2015, *The El-Amarna Correspondence: A New Edition of the Cuneiform Letters from the Site of El-Amarna Based on Collations of All Extant Tablets*, 2 vols. Handbook of Oriental Studies, section 1: The Near and Middle East 110. Leiden, Boston.

20 Porten, B. 1968, *Archives from Elephantine: The Life of an Ancient Jewish Military Colony*. Los Angeles.

21 Quack, J. 2005, Zu den vorarabischen semitischen Lehnwörtern des Koptischen, in: Burtea, B., Tropper, J. and Younansardaroud, H. (eds), *Studia Semitica et Semitohamitica: Festschrift für Rainer Voigt anläßlich seines 60. Geburtstages am 17. Januar 2004*, 307–38. AOAT 317, Münster.

22 Vittmann, G. 2003, *Ägypten und die Fremden im ersten vorchristlichen Jahrtausend*. Kulturgeschichte der Antiken Welt 97. Mainz am Rhein, 180–93.

23 Quack 2017, 30, with further references in n. 28.

24 Tropper, J. 2003, Die Erfindung des Alphabets und seine Ausbreitung im nordwestsemitischen Raum, in: Seipel, W. (ed.), *Der Turmbau zu Babel: Ursprung und Vielfalt von Sprache und Schrift. Eine Ausstellung des Kunsthistorischen Museums Wien für die Europäische Kulturhauptstadt Graz 2003*, 173–81. Vienna.

25 Kammerzell, F. 2001, Die Entstehung der Alphabetreihe: zum ägyptischen Ursprung der semitischen und westlichen Schriften, in: Borchers, D., Kammerzell, F. and Weninger, S. (eds), *Hieroglyphen, Alphabete, Schriftreformen:*

Studien zu Multiliteralismus, Schriftwechsel und Orthographieneuregelungen, 117–58. Göttingen. However, see Quack, J.F. 2003, Die spätägyptische Alphabetreihenfolge und das 'südsemitische Alphabet', *Lingua Aegyptia* 11, 178–81.

26 Kahl, 1991, 33–47; Quack, J.F. 1993. Ägyptisches und südarabisches Alphabet, *Revue d'égyptologie* 44, 141–51; Quack 2003, 163–84; Darnell, J.C.F., Dobbs-Allsopp, W., Lundberg, M.J., McCarter, P.K., Zuckerman, B. and Manassa, C. 2005, Two Early Alphabetic Inscriptions from the Wadi el-Hôl: New Evidence for the Origin of the Alphabet from the Western Desert of Egypt, *The Annual of the American Schools of Oriental Research* 59, 79–80 (l. 7), 82 (l. 14), 124 (table); Strudwick, N. 2005, Theban Tomb 99 (Senneferi): University of Cambridge Theban Mission 2002, *Annales du Service des Antiquités de l'Égypte* 79, 157–64; Haring, B. 2015, Halaḥam on an Ostracon of the Early New Kingdom?, *Journal of Near Eastern Studies* 74, no. 2, 189–96.

27 Daniels, P.T. and Bright, W. 1996, *The World's Writing Systems*. New York, 788–90; Gzella, H., Abecedaries, in: Khan, G. (ed.), *Encyclopedia of Hebrew Language and Linguistics*. Leiden. http://dx.doi.org/10.1163/2212-4241_ehll_EHLL_COM_00000228 (last accessed 14 January 2022).

28 Healey, J.F. 1990, The Early Alphabet, in: Hooker, J.T. (ed.), *Reading the Past: Ancient Writing from Cuneiform to the Alphabet*, 221–35. London.

29 Wilson, P. 2015, Baltim, Parallos, and Mutubis: Late Period and Ptolemaic Antecedents for Late Antique Ports and Settlements in Northern Egypt, in: Robinson, D. and Franck G. (eds), *Thonis-Heracleion in Context*, 297–314. Oxford, 300.

30 Thomas, R. and Higgs, P. 2017, Greek and Roman Sculpture, in: Villing, A., Bergeron, M., Bourogiannis, G., Johnston, A., Leclère, F., Masson, A. and Thomas, R.I. (eds), 2013–19, *Naukratis: Greeks in Egypt*, 8. British Museum Online Research Catalogue: www.britishmuseum.org/naukratis.

31 Vittmann 2003, 200.

32 See Quack 2017, 34, for more examples.

33 UPZ I 148. English translation in Bagnall, R.S. and Cribiore, R. 2006, *Women's Letters from Ancient Egypt, 300 BCE–AD 800*. Ann Arbor, 113. A recent study of the papyrus has identified its provenance as Memphis, its date as around 168 BCE, and the probable sender and recipient to be Isias and her husband Hephaistion: Ricciardetto, A. 2020, Nouvelles données sur un papyrus relatif au bilinguisme gréco-égyptien: Réexamen et mise en contexte de l'UPZ I 148, *Papyrologica Lupiensia* 29, 93–125.

34 On the high esteem in which Egyptian medicine was held in antiquity, see Aufrère, S.H. and Marganne, M.-H. 2019, Encounters between Greek and Egyptian Science, in: Vandorpe, K. (ed.), *A Companion to Greco-Roman and Late Antique Egypt*, 507–8. Hoboken. For the medical papyri written in demotic, see Jacobs, A. 2018, Demotic Pharmacology: An Overview of the Demotic Medical Manuscripts in the Papyrus Carlsberg Collection, in: Reggiani, N. and Bertonazzi, F. (eds), *Parlare la medicina: Fra lingue e culture, nello spazio e nel tempo. Atti del Convegno Internazionale, Università di Parma, 5–7 Settembre 2016*, 52–79. Studi sul Mondo Antico 7. Milan.

35 For the early history of the Greeks in Egypt, see Vittmann 2003, 194–235.

36 Other groups that had settled in Egypt included Carians, Jews, Phoenicians and Idumaeans; see Thompson, D.J. 2012, *Memphis under the Ptolemies*, 2nd edn. Princeton, Oxford, 76–98.

37 These soldiers who were settled on the land in Ptolemaic Egypt were called cleruchs. Fischer-Bovet, C. 2014, *Army and Society in Ptolemaic Egypt*. Cambridge, 199–237.

38 This had also been the situation during the Persian occupation when Aramaic was the language of the central administration at the higher levels. Schütze, A. 2017, Local Administration in Persian Period Egypt According to Aramaic and Demotic Sources, in: Jacobs, B., Henkelman, W.F.M. and Stolper, M.W. (eds), *Die Verwaltung im Achämenidenreich*, 489–515. Classica et Orientalia 17, Wiesbaden; Fried, L.S. 2020, Aramaic Texts and the Achaemenid Administration of Egypt, in: Tuplin, C.J. and Ma, J. (eds), *Aršāma and His World: The Bodleian Letters in Context*, vol. 3, 278–90. Oxford.

39 On the founding of Ptolemais by Ptolemy I as a Greek counterweight to Thebes, see Thompson, D.J. 2018, Ptolemy I in Egypt: Continuity and Change, in: McKechnie, P. and Cromwell, J.A. (eds), *Ptolemy I and the Transformation of Egypt, 404–282 BCE*, 11–12. Mnemosyne Supplements 415. Leiden, Boston.

40 For example, in the more than 1,600 filiations in the census lists there is not a single instance of a double name: see Clarysse, W. and Thompson, D.J. 2006, *Counting the People in Hellenistic Egypt*. Volume 2; *Historical Studies*. Cambridge, 323–8. In the third century a Greek name can be taken to be an indication of Greek origin, but later on it becomes very common for Egyptians also to use Greek names, so a name is no longer indicative of a person's ethnicity. Coussement, S. 2016, *'Because I am Greek': Polyonymy as an Expression of Ethnicity in Ptolemaic Egypt*. Studia Hellenistica 55. Leuven, Paris, Bristol, CT, 209–13.

41 Boswinkel, E. and Pestman, P.W. 1982, *Les archives privées de Dionysios, fils de Kephalas: Textes grecs et démotiques*. Papyrologica Lugduno-Batava 22. Leiden, 3–8; Fischer-Bovet 2014, 277–8. There is also one Greek text (no. 10) in which he appears under his Egyptian name.

42 Boswinkel and Pestman 1982, text no. 25.

43 Intermarriage is only rarely attested in the third century BCE, but becomes more common in the second. Greek integration into Egyptian society is discussed by Clarysse, W. 1992, Some Greeks in Egypt, in: Johnson, J.H. (ed.), *Life in a Multi-Cultural Society: Egypt from Cambyses to Constantine and Beyond*, 51–6. Studies in Ancient Oriental Civilization 51. Chicago, Fischer-Bovet 2014, 246–55.

44 The archive is published and discussed by Vandorpe, K. 2002, *The Bilingual Family Archive of Dryton, His Wife Apollonia and Their Daughter Senmouthis*. Collectanea Hellenistica 4. Brussels.

45 His first wife was Sarapias, citizen of the Greek city of Ptolemais; Vandorpe 2002, 13.

46 Fischer-Bovet 2014, 275–6.

47 She sometimes also referred to herself as a 'Cyrenaean woman', as her grandparents or great-grandparents had emigrated from Cyrene in the third century. Vandorpe, K. 2002, Apollonia, a Businesswoman in a Multicultural Society (Pathyris, 2nd–1st Centuries B.C.), in: Melaerts, H. and Mooren, L. (eds), 2002, *Le rôle et le statut de la femme en Égypte hellénistique, romaine et byzantine: Actes du colloque international, Bruxelles – Leuven 27–29 novembre 1997*, 325–36. Paris, Leuven, Sterling, VA; Scheuble-Reiter, S. and Bussi, S. 2019, Social Identity and Upward Mobility: Elite Groups, Lower Classes, and Slaves, in: Vandorpe (ed.), 284–5.

48 Klotz, D. 2009, The Statue of the *dioikêtês* Harchebi/Archibios (Nelson-Atkins Museum of Art 47-12), *Bulletin de l'Institut français d'archéologie orientale* 109, 281–310.

49 Collombert, P. 2000, Religion égyptienne et culture grecque: L'exemple de Διοσκουρίδης, *Chronique d'Égypte* 75, 47–63.

50 Clarysse, this volume, pp. 229–32.

51 For exceptions – Greek texts on Egyptian monuments, see Clarysse, W. 2020a, Greek Texts on Egyptian Monuments, in: Bowman, A. and Crowther, C. (eds), *The Epigraphy of Ptolemaic Egypt*, 35–58. Oxford.

52 Scheuble-Reiter and Bussi 2019, 286–7. For images of the stelae, see Clarysse 2020a, 36–7.

53 Clarysse, W. 2020b, Inscriptions and Papyri: Two Intersecting Worlds, in: Bowman and Crowther (eds), 174–5.

54 Modrzejewski, J. 1975, Chrématistes et laocrites, in: Bingen, J., Cambier, G. and Nachtergael, G. (eds), 1975, *Le monde grec: Pensée, littérature, histoire, documents. Hommages à Claire Préaux*. Université Libre de Bruxelles, Faculté

de Philosophie et Lettres 52. Brussels, 699–708; Pestman, P.W. 1985a, The Competence of Greek and Egyptian Tribunals According to the Decree of 118 B.C., *Bulletin of the American Society of Papyrologists* 22, 265–9.

55 Pestman, P.W. 1993, *The Archive of the Theban Choachytes (Second Century B.C.): A Survey of the Demotic and Greek Papyri Contained in the Archive*. Studia Demotica 2. Leuven, 361–84.

56 Pestman 1993, 56–63 texts 7–8, 69–71 text 11.

57 Pestman 1993, 180–2 text 54.

58 Pestman 1993, 191–2 text 58.

59 Pestman, P.W. 1985b, Registration of Demotic Contracts in Egypt: P. Par. 65; 2nd cent. B.C., in: Ankum, J.A., Spruit, J.E. and Wubbe, F.B.J. (eds), *Satura Roberto Feenstra sexagesimum quintum annum aetatis complenti ab alumnis collegis amicis oblata*, 17–25. Freiburg; Jördens, A. 2020, Griechische Texte aus Ägypten, in: Janowski, B. and Schwemer, D. (eds), *Texte zur Wissenskultur*, 594–5. Texte aus der Umwelt des Alten Testaments, Neue Folge 9. Gütersloh.

60 For example, EA10823 and EA10824. Muhs, B. 2014/15, More Papyri from the Archive of Panas Son of Espemetis, *Enchoria* 34, 89–103.

61 This can be seen in the decline in the number of personal letters written in demotic, only a handful of which can be assigned to the Roman period: Depauw, M. 2006, *The Demotic Letter: A Study of Epistolographic Scribal Traditions against their Intra- and Intercultural Background*. Demotische Studien 14. Sommerhausen, 91–2; Quack, J.F. 2020, Zwei demotische Briefs in hieratischer Schrift, in: Ryholt, K. (ed.), *Hieratic Texts from Tebtunis, Including a Survey of Illustrated Papyri*, 148–9. The Carlsberg Papyri 15 = CNI Publications 45. Copenhagen.

62 Herodotus, *Histories* II, 77.1, 100; Moyer, I.S. 2002, Herodotus and an Egyptian Mirage: The Genealogies of the Theban Priests, *Journal of Hellenic Studies* 122, 70–90.

63 Sist, L. 2008, The Sense of History in Ancient Egypt, in: Tiradritti, F. (ed.), *Pharaonic Renaissance: Archaism and the Sense of History. Cankarjev dom, Ljubljana 4th March–20th July 2008*, 21–35. Ljubljana.

64 For an overview, see the contributions in Tiradritti 2008.

65 Morkot, R. 2003, Archaism and Innovation in Art from the New Kingdom to the Twenty-sixth Dynasty, in: Tait, J. (ed.), *'Never Had the Like Occurred': Egypt's View of its Past*, 79–99. London; Kahl, J. 2010, Archaism, in: Wendrich, W. (ed.), *UCLA Encyclopedia of Egyptology*. Los Angeles. https://digital2.library.ucla.edu/viewItem.do?ark=21198/zz0025qh2v (last accessed 14 March 2022).

66 Redford 1986, 151.

67 See examples throughout Tiradritti 2008.

68 Schulz, R. 1992, *Die Entwicklung und Bedeutung des kuboiden Statuentypus*. 2 vols, Hildesheimer Ägyptologische Beiträge 33–4. Hildesheim, 33: 372–3 (EA570) and 381–2 (EA1210); Schulz, R. 2011, Block Statue, *UCLA Encyclopedia of Egyptology*, 1, no. 1. https://escholarship.org/uc/item/3f23c0q9 (last accessed 22 December 2021).

69 Parkinson, R.B. 1991. *Voices from Ancient Egypt: an Anthology of Middle Kingdom Writings*. London, 149–50.

70 Posener, G. 1976, *L'Enseignement loyaliste: Sagesse égyptien du Moyen Empire*. Centre de Recherches d'Histoire et de Philologie II. Hautes Études Orientales 5. Geneva; Verhoeven, U. 2009, Von der 'Loyalistischen Lehre' zur 'Lehre des Kairsu': Eine neue Textquelle aus Assiut und deren Auswirkungen, *Zeitschrift für ägyptische Sprache und Altertumskunde* 136, 92.

71 Parkinson 1997, 235–45.

72 Verhoeven 2009, 87–98.

73 Brand, P. 2010, Usurpation of Monuments, *UCLA Encyclopedia of Egyptology*, 1, no. 1. https://escholarship.org/uc/item/5gj996k5 (last accessed 23 December 2021).

74 Examples in Brand, P. 2010, Reuse and Restoration, *UCLA Encyclopedia of Egyptology*, 1, no. 1. https://escholarship.org/uc/item/2vp6065d (last accessed 23 December 2021).

75 Varner, E.R. 2004, *Mutilation and Transformation: Damnatio Memoriae and Roman Imperial Portraiture*. Monumenta Graeca et Romana 10. Leiden.

76 Spalinger, A.J. 1995, The Lunar System in Festival Calendars: From the New Kingdom Onwards, *Bulletin de la Société d'Égyptologie de Genève* 19, 25–40; Spalinger, A.J. 2002, Ancient Egyptian Calendars: How Many Were There? *Journal of the American Research Center in Egypt* 39, 241–50.

77 Spalinger, A.J. 1996, *The Private Feast Lists of Ancient Egypt*. Ägyptologische Abhandlungen 57. Wiesbaden, 81.

78 Leitz, C. 1994, *Tagewählerei: Das Buch ḥ3t nḥḥ pḥ.wy ḏt und verwandte Texte*, I–II. Ägyptologische Abhandlungen 53. Wiesbaden, 66–7.

79 Depuydt, L. 1998, Ancient Egyptian Star Clocks and Their Theory, *Bibliotheca Orientalis* 55, nos 1–2, 5–44.

80 Robinson 2012, 203.

81 Parkinson 1991, 149–50.

82 Hartleben, H. 1983, *Jean-François Champollion: Sa vie et son œuvre 1790–1832*, trans. Denise Meunier and Ruth Schumann Antelme. Paris, 121; Faure, A. 2004, *Champollion: Le savant déchiffré*. Paris, 165.

83 Montfaucon, B. de. 1724, *L'antiquité expliquée et représentée en figures. Supplement II: Le culte des Grecs, des Romains, des Egyptiens, et des Gaulois*, Paris, pl. xlix and p. 169; Moss, R. 1968, By-Products of Bibliography, *Journal of Egyptian Archaeology* 54, 173–5.

84 Kemp, B.J. 1968, Canopic Jars in the Lady Lever Art Gallery, *Orientalia Nova Series* 37, no. 1, 63–74.

85 Cavalier, O. 2013, Un ciel brillant d'images: Un recueil de dessins d'antiquités du XVIIIe siècle, *Monuments et Mémoires de la Fondation Eugène Piot* 92, 93–175.

86 Maitland, M. 2015, Hieroglyphs from the North: Newcastle's Early Travellers in Egypt and Their Correspondence with Jean-François Champollion, in: Cooke, N. and Daubney, V. (eds), *Every Traveller Needs a Compass: Travel and Collecting in Egypt and the Near East*, 113–30. Oxford, Philadelphia, 116.

87 Maitland 2015, 117.

88 A translation of the letter by Mr J. Bruce was published as 'The Hieroglyphics on the Egyptian Mummy, Belonging to the Literary and Philosophical Society of Newcastle, Deciphered', *The Newcastle Magazine*, February 1824, 92–3; Maitland 2015, 122.

89 Champollion, J.F. 1936, *Grammaire égyptienne*, Paris, 128–9.

90 Maitland 2015, 124.

91 Taylor, J.H. 2003, Theban Coffins from the Twenty-Second to the Twenty-Sixth Dynasty: Dating and the Synthesis of Development, in: Strudwick, N. and Taylor, J.H. (eds), *The Theban Necropolis: Past Present and Future*, 95–121. London, 101, 106–7.

92 Gray, P. 1967, Two Mummies of Ancient Egyptians in the Hancock Museum, Newcastle, *Journal of Egyptian Archaeology* 53, 77–8, pls 15–16.

93 Watson, E.J. and Myers, M. 1993, The Mummy of Baket-en-Her-Nakht in the Hancock Museum: A Radiological Update, *Journal of Egyptian Archaeology* 79, 179–87.

94 *Description de l'Égypte, Antiquités* 2, pls 72–5; Cadet, M. 1805, *Copie figurée d'un rouleau de papyrus trouvé à Thèbes dans un tombeau des rois*. Paris.

95 Lenzo, G. 2020, Un papyrus funéraire de la Troisième Période intermédiaire de l'ancienne collection Passalacqua, *Revue d'égyptologie* 70, 37–56.

96 Mehlitz, H. 2011, *Richard Lepsius: Ägypten und die Ordnung der Wissenschaft*. Berlin; Lepper, V.M. and Hafemann, I. (eds) 2012, *Karl Richard Lepsius: Der Begründer der deutschen Ägyptologie*. Berlin.

97 Taylor, J.H. 2010, *Journey through the Afterlife: Ancient Egyptian Book of the Dead*. London, 234–7. The right-hand end of this papyrus is in the Louvre (E 6258) and the central section was formerly in Munich but is now lost.

98 Berlin P. 10489; Lüddeckens, E. 1994, *Ägyptische Handschriften, Teil 4, beschrieben von Günter Burkard und Hans-Werner Fischer-Elfert*. Verzeichnis der Orientalischen Handschriften in Deutschland. Wiesbaden, 65 (no. 90); Hue-Arcé, Ch. 2020, *La violence interpersonnelle en Égypte au Nouvel Empire et a l'époque gréco-romaine*. Wallasey, 188.

99 Seidlmayer, S.J. 2006, Ushebti, in: *Brill's New Pauly*, Antiquity volumes, ed. Cancik, H. and Schneider, H. English edition. http://dx.doi.org/10.1163/1574-9347_bnp_e1226300 (last accessed 27 December 2021).

100 Gardiner, A.H. and Sethe, K. 1928, *Egyptian Letters to the Dead, Mainly from the Old and Middle Kingdoms*. London, 3–5; Wente, E.F. 1990, *Letters from Ancient Egypt*. Society of Biblical Literature Writings from the Ancient World 1. Atlanta, 211–19.

101 Ritner, R.K. 1993, *The Mechanics of Ancient Egyptian Magical Practice*. Studies in Ancient Oriental Civilization 54. Chicago, 180–2; Regulski, I. 2020a, *Repurposing Ritual. Pap. Berlin P. 10480–82: A Case Study from Middle Kingdom Asyut*. Ägyptische und Orientalische Papyri und Handschriften des Ägyptischen Museums und Papyrussammlung Berlin 5. Berlin, 297–333.

102 Friedman, F. 1985, On the Meaning of Some Anthropoid Busts from Deir el-Medîna, *Journal of Egyptian Archaeology* 71, 82–97.

103 Now in Luxor Museum, accession number J.147. A statue of Amenmose, also found within his tomb space, is now in the British Museum collection (EA137); Taylor 2021, 102.

104 Shubert, S.B. 2007, *Those Who (Still) Live on Earth: A Study of the Ancient Egyptian Appeal to the Living Texts*. Toronto, Ottawa. For a reassessment of their locations, see Salvador, Ch. 2013, From the Realm of the Dead to the House of the God: The New Kingdom Appeals to the Living in Context at Thebes, in: Accetta, K., Fellinger, R. and Gonçalves, M.P.L. (eds), *Current Research in Egyptology 2013: Proceedings of the Fourteenth Annual Symposium, University of Cambridge 2013*, 153–67. Oxford.

105 Pestman 1993, 7–8.

106 Shore, A.F. and Smith, H.S. 1960, A Demotic Embalmers' Agreement (Pap. dem. B. M. 10561), *Acta Orientalia* 25, 277–94.

107 One of them is called Psenmonthes but it is not certain whether he was the writer or the recipient, as the beginning of the text is broken off: Almásy-Martin, A. and Martin, C.J. 2020, Always Remember to Check the Back: A Closer Look at Some Published Ostraca in the British Museum and British Library, in: Stolk, J.V. and Van Loon, G.A.J.C. (eds), *Text Editions of (Abnormal) Hieratic, Demotic, Greek, Latin and Coptic Papyri and Ostraca: Some People Love Their Friends Even When They Are Far Away. Festschrift in Honour of Francisca A. J. Hoogendijk*, 33–7. Papyrologica Lugduno-Batava 37. Leiden, Boston.

108 Petrie Museum, UCL – UC.16163. Translation after Wente 1990, 211–12.

109 Additional fragments were purchased by the American dealer and collector Edwin Smith (1822–1906) in 1862/3 and have been kept in the Brooklyn Museum (37.1784Ea–b) since 1949.

110 Robins, G. and Shute, C. 1987, *The Rhind Mathematical Papyrus: An Ancient Egyptian Text*. London, 9–11; Clagett, M. 1999, *Ancient Egyptian Science: A Source Book. Volume 3: Ancient Egyptian Mathematics*. Memoirs of the American Philosophical Society 232. Philadelphia, 113–20; Imhausen, A. 2016, *Mathematics in Ancient Egypt: A Contextual History*. Princeton, 65–7.

111 Robins and Shute 1987, pls 19–20; Clagett 1999, 171, pl. 87; Imhausen 2016, 107–8.

112 Robins and Shute 1987, 12–13; Imhausen 2016, 41–5.

113 Robins and Shute 1987, 44–6; Clagett 1999, 162–3; Imhausen 2016, 118–21.

114 Janssen, J.J. 1975, *Commodity Prices from the Ramessid Period*. Leiden, 123, 180.

115 Müller-Wollermann, R. 2015, Crime and Punishment in Pharaonic Egypt, *Near Eastern Archaeology* 78, no. 4, 228–35. https://doi.org/10.5615/neareastarch.78.4.0228 (last accessed 27 December 2021).

116 Peet, Th. E. 1930, *The Great Tomb-Robberies of the Twentieth Egyptian Dynasty: Being a Critical Study, with Translations and Commentaries, of the Papyri in Which These Are Recorded*, Oxford.

117 Translation after Kaplony-Heckel, U. 1963, *Die demotischen Tempeleide I: Text*. Ägyptologische Abhandlungen 6. Wiesbaden, 315, with updates from Cary Martin (pers. comm.).

118 Mentioned in the dockets on the verso of P. Abbott (EA10221) and P. Mayer A in Liverpool (Peet 1930, 128–9); Peet 1930, 169–75.

119 Muhs, B. 2005, The Girls Next Door. Marriage Patterns among the Mortuary Priests in Early Ptolemaic Thebes, *Journal of Juristic Papyrology* 35, 169–94, esp. fig. 4, 184–5. EA10612 may belong to the same archive because it mentions Tathotes, who could have been his wife; Muhs, B. 2014/2015, More Papyri from the Archive of Panas Son of Espemetis, *Enchoria* 34, 91.

120 The other papyri in the British Museum collection, not featured here, are EA10532A–B; EA10556; EA10612–15; EA10670; EA10823. For the identification of documents that do not mention Panas, see Muhs 2014/2015.

121 Robins, G. 1993, *Women in Ancient Egypt*. London, 92–9; Feucht, E. 1995, *Das Kind im alten Ägypten: Die Stellung des Kindes in Familie und Gesellschaft nach altägyptischen Texten und Darstellungen*. Frankfurt, New York, 22–51, 89, 222, 558.

122 16,1–3. The translation follows version L (= pChester Beatty V/pBM EA10685 V:II6–7) of the Wisdom Text of Ani; Gardiner, A.H. 1935, *Hieratic Papyri in the British Museum: Third Series: The Chester Beatty Gift*, I–II. London, I, 50, II, pl. 27; Quack, J.F. 1994, *Die Lehren des Ani. Ein neuägyptischer Weisheitstext in seinem kulturellen Umfeld*. Orbis Biblicus et Orientalis 141. Fribourg/Göttingen, 146–7, 284–5.

123 Feucht 1995, 36.

124 Parkinson 1999, 160, with some tweaks from the author.

125 For amulets in ancient Egypt see Andrews, C. 1994, *Amulets of Ancient Egypt*. London.

126 Pestman, P.W. 1961, *Marriage and Matrimonial Property in Ancient Egypt: A Contribution to Establishing the Legal Position of the Woman*. Papyrologica Lugduno-Batava 9. Leiden; Baetens, G. and Depauw, M. 2015, The Legal Advice of Totoes in the Siut Archive (P. BM 10591, verso, col. I–III), *Journal of Egyptian Archaeology* 104, 85–104.

127 Allam, S. 1973, *Hieratische Ostraka und Papyri aus der Ramessidenzeit*. Tübingen, 253 [no. 256].

128 For more general information on divorce, see Robins 1993, 62–74; Feucht 1995, 40–4, 182, 558.

129 Hollis, S.T. 1990, *The Ancient Egyptian 'Tale of the Two Brothers': The Oldest Fairy Tale in the World*. Oklahoma Series In Classical Culture 7. London.

130 Simpson, W.K. 2003, *The Literature of Ancient Egypt: An Anthology of Stories, Instructions, Stelae, Autobiographies, and Poetry*. New Haven, London, 80–90. Reproduced with permission of the Licensor through PLSclear.

131 Parkinson 1999, 171 (82); Johns, C. 1997, *Erotica*. British Museum Pocket Treasury. London, 12–13.

132 Johns 1997, 20–1; Parkinson, R.B. 2013, *A Little Gay History: Desire and Diversity across the World*, London, 87.

133 Parkinson 1999, 173 (86); Derchain, Ph. 1981, Observations sur les erotica, in: Martin, G.T. (ed.), *The Sacred Animal Necropolis at North Saqqâra: The Southern Dependencies of the Main Temple Complex*, 166–70. Excavation Memoir 50. London.

134 McDowell 1999; Parkinson, R.B. 2009, *Reading Ancient Egyptian Poetry: Among Other Histories*, Chichester, Malden, MA.

135 Leitz, C. 1999, *Magical and Medical Papyri of the New Kingdom*. Hieratic Papyri in the British Museum 7. London, 51–84.

136 Beck, S. 2018, *Exorcism, Illness and Demons in an Ancient Near Eastern Context: The Egyptian Magical Papyrus Leiden I 343+ 345*. PALMA 18. Leiden, 31 with further literature.

137 Leitz 1999, 64–6, 79.

138 Grapow, H. 1955, *Grundriss der Medizin der alten Ägypter.* Volume 2: *Von den medizinischen Texten.* Berlin, 122–4; Grapow, H. 1956, *Grundriss der Medizin der alten Ägypter.* Volume 3: *Kranker, Krankheiten und Arzt.* Berlin, 53–5; Nunn, J.F. 1996, *Ancient Egyptian Medicine.* London, 146, 197–202; Westendorf, W. 1999, *Handbuch der altägyptischen Medizin*, 2 vols. Leiden, Boston, Cologne, 146–7.

139 Leitz 1999, 31–50.

140 Wildung, D. 1977, *Imhotep und Amenhotep: Gottwerdung im alten Ägypten.* Münchner Ägyptologische Studien 36. Munich; Nunn 1996, 121–4.

141 Edwards, I.E.S. 1960, *Oracular Amuletic Decrees of the Late New Kingdom.* Hieratic Papyri in the British Museum IV, I–II. London, I, 1–12, II, pls I–III.

142 Sternberg-el Hotabi, H. 1999, *Untersuchungen zur Überlieferungsgeschichte der Horusstelen: Ein Beitrag zur Religionsgeschichte Ägyptens im 1. Jahrtausend v. Chr.*, 2 vols. Wiesbaden, vol. 1, 148–50; vol. 2, 180–1 /pls XLIII–XLIV.

143 Szpakowska, K. 2011, Dream Interpretation in the Ramesside Age, in: Collier, M. and Snape, S. (eds), *Ramesside Studies in Honour of K.A. Kitchen*, 509–17. Bolton.

144 Combined translation from Simpson 2003, 313 and Langráfová, R. and Navrátilová, H. 2009. *Sex and the Golden Goddess.* Volume 1: *Ancient Egyptian Love Songs in Context.* Prague, 176–7. Reproduced with permission of the Licensor through PLSclear.

145 Translation by Simpson 2003, 432–5.

146 Baines, J. 1983, Literacy and Ancient Egyptian Society, *Man* 18, 572–99; Baines, J. 1984, Schreiben, in: Wolfgang, H. and Westendorf, W. (eds), *Lexikon der Ägyptologie V: Pyramidenbau-Steingefäße*, 693–8. Wiesbaden; Szpakowska, K. 2008, *Daily Life in Ancient Egypt: Recreating Lahun.* Malden, Oxford.

147 Lichtheim 2006, 168; Moers, G. 2001, Der Papyrus Lansing: Der Lob des Schreiberberufes in einer ägyptischen Schülerhandschrift aus dem ausgehenden Neuen Reich, in: Kaiser, O. (ed.), *Ergänzungslieferung*, 109–42. Texte aus der Umwelt des Alten Testaments. Gütersloh.

148 Fischer-Elfert, H.-W., 2001, Kindheit im Alten Ägypten, in: Forster, J. and Krebs, U. (eds), *Kindheit zwischen Pharao und Internet: 4000 Jahre in interdisziplinärer Perspektive*, 21–39. Bad Heilbrunn/Obb, 439.

149 Ryholt, K. and Barjamovic, G. 2019. *Libraries before Alexandria: Ancient Near Eastern Traditions.* Oxford.

150 Brunner, H. 1991, *Altägyptische Erziehung.* Wiesbaden.

151 Hagen, F. 2006, Literature, Transmission, and the Late Egyptian Miscellanies, in: Dahn, R. (ed.), *Current Research in Egyptology 2004: Proceedings of the Fifth Annual Symposium, University of Durham, January 2004*, 84–99. Oxford; Hagen, F. 2007, Ostraca, Literature and Teaching at Deir el-Medina, in: Mairs, R. and Stevenson, A. (eds), *Current Research in Egyptology 2005: Proceedings of the Sixth Annual Symposium, University of Cambridge, 6–8 January 2005*, 38–51. Oxford.

152 Lazaridis, N. 2010, Education and Apprenticeship, in: Wendrich (ed), https://digital2.library.ucla.edu/viewItem.do?ark=21198/zz0025jxjn (last accessed 9 March 2022).

153 Nassim, S. 1991, Education, Coptic, in: Atiya, A.S. (ed.), *The Coptic Encyclopedia.* New York, Toronto, Oxford.

154 Hawary, Amr El, 2010, *Wortschöpfung: die Memphitische Theologie und die Siegesstele des Pije – zwei Zeugen kultureller Repräsentation in der 25. Dynastie.* Orbis Biblicus et Orientalis 243. Fribourg, Göttingen.

155 Translation by Simpson 2003, 432–5. Reproduced with permission of the Licensor through PLSclear.

156 Bowman, A.K., Crowther, Ch.V., Hornblower, S., Mairs, R. and Savvopoulos, K. 2021, *Corpus of Ptolemaic Inscriptions, Part I: Greek, Bilingual, and Trilingual Inscriptions from Egypt.* Volume 1: *Alexandria and the Delta (nos 1–206).* Oxford Studies in Ancient Documents. Oxford, 292–5.

157 The Canopic decree of Ptolemy III (238 BCE) (3a) was discovered in 1866 by Lepsius. The well-preserved stela, 220 cm high, has the hieroglyphic text and the Greek on the front face and the demotic on the left side of the stela, where it remained unnoticed at first: Bowman et al. 2021, 241–64. With this discovery, Champollion's hypotheses could be checked using a hieroglyphic text that had a certainly identified ancient translation. The Tanis stela is thus another important milestone; only now did Champollion's decipherment become certainty, not hypothesis: Hoffmann and Pfeiffer, 2021.

158 Several texts in the list have been published and translated many times. See the Trismegistos website (www.trismegistos.org/tm), where readers can find the relevant bibliography by entering the TM number. A recent list of sacerdotal decrees is given by Nespoulous-Phalippou, A. 2015. *Ptolémée Épiphane, Aristonikos et les prêtres d'Égypte: le Décret de Memphis (182 a.C.). Édition commentée des stèles Caire RT 2/3/25/7 et JE 44901.* CÉNIM 12 (I-II). Montpellier.

159 Dittenberger, W. 1903–5. *Orientis graeci inscriptiones selectae*: supplementum sylloges inscriptionum graecarum. Leipzig, vol. 1, 11.

160 Clarysse, W. 1999. Ptolémées et temples, in: Valbelle, D. and J. Leclant (ed.), *Le décret de Memphis*, 41–65. Paris.

161 Gorre, G. and Veisse, A.-E. 2020, Birth and Disappearance of the Priestly Synods in the Time of the Ptolemies, in: Gorre, G. and Wackenier, S. (eds), *Quand la fortune du royaume ne dépend pas de la vertu du prince: Un renforcement de la monarchie lagide de Ptolémée VI à Ptolémée X (169–88 av. J.-C.)?*, 113–39. Studia Hellenistica 59. Leuven.

Chapter 5: New approaches, pp. 236–45

1 Alignments were produced by Josephine Hensel. Results are accessible online: Amin, M., Barmpoutis, A., Berti, M., Bozia, E., Hensel, J. and Naether, F. 2022,The Digital Rosetta Stone Project, in: Lucarelli, R., Roberson, J.A. and Vinson, S. (eds), *Ancient Egypt – New Technology.* Harvard Egyptological Studies, Leiden, Boston, and the Project website: https://rosetta-stone.dh.uni-leipzig.de/rs/the-digital-rosetta-stone (last accessed 21 March 2022).

2 Polina Yordanova generated the annotation of the Greek text of the Rosetta Stone, which is available online; see Amin et al. 2022 and the project website: https://rosetta-stone.dh.uni-leipzig.de/rs/the-digital-rosetta-stone (last accessed 21 March 2022).

3 Amin, M., Barmpoutis, A., Berti, M., Bozia, E., Hensel, J. and Naether, F. 2018, Depth Map of the Rosetta Stone. http://dx.doi.org/10.17613/t1e2-0w02 (last accessed 21 March 2022).

4 In those days Egyptians were too busy decolonising their country to truly engage with researching the past.

5 Egyptological teaching was conducted in English, as most references on the subject were written by Westerners. Students 'felt' and understood the texts better when they began translating into Arabic. They even recognised ancient Egyptian words as words they used in their daily life at home.

6 See, for example, Quirke, S. 2004, *Egyptian Literature 1800 BC: Questions and Readings*, Golden House Publications 2. London, 28.

7 Sethe, K. 1933, *Urkunden des Alten Reichs* I, 1–4. Leipzig.

8 Blackman, A.M. 1972, *Middle Egyptian Stories.* Bibliotheca Aegyptiaca II. Brussels, 42 (The Shipwrecked Sailor), line 19.

9 In addition to their shared taste for endless metaphors, Egyptian Arabic and Ancient Egyptian share many words which may be derived from Semitic common roots. Space constraints prevent me from further developing these analogies and other rhetorical devices typical to non-Western languages.

10 Haikal, F. 1998, A Gesture of Thanksgiving in Ancient Egypt, in: Guksch, H. and Polz, D. (eds) 1998, *Stationen: Beiträge zur Kulturgeschichte Ägyptens, Rainer Stadelmann gewidmet*, 291–2. Mainz.

11 For new comparative research on similarities between Arabic and Ancient Egyptian languages see Hany Rashwan's seminal research; Rashwan, H. 2020. Arabic Jinās is not Pun, Wortspiel, Calembour, or Paronomasia: A Post-Eurocentric Approach to the Conceptual Untranslatability of Literary Terms in Arabic and Ancient Egyptian Cultures, *Rhetorica* 38, no. 4, 335–70.

12 Sethe, K. 1906, *Urkunden der 18 Dynastie, Abteilung IV*, 13–16. Leipzig, 361.

13 Haikal, F. 2009, Performativité du nom divin en Egypte de l'Antiquité a nos jours, in: Piacentini, P. and Orsenigo, Ch. (eds), *Egyptian Archives*, 197–217. Universita degli Studi di Milano, Faccolta di Lettere e Filosofia, Quaderni III, Cisalpino.

Appendix, p. 246

1 Schwartz, J. 1992, Décrets de prêtres sous Ptolemée III Evergète, *Zeitschrift für Papyrologie und Epigraphik* 91, 83–4.

2 El-Masry, Y., Altenmüller, H. and Thissen, H.-J. 2012, *Das Synodaldekret von Alexandria aus dem Jahre 243 v. Chr, Studien zur Altägyptischen Kultur*, 11.

3 https://collections.louvre.fr/en/ark:/53355/cl010034787. Bernand, É. 1992, *Inscriptions grecques d'Égypte et de Nubie au Musée du Louvre*. Paris; Bingen, J. 1992, Le décret du synode sacerdotal de 243 avant notre ère, *Chronique d'Égypte* 67, no. 134, 319–27.

4 El-Masry, Altenmüller and Thissen 2012.

5 Schwartz, J. and Malinine, M. 1960, Pierres d'Égypte, *Revue archéologique*), 77–90, esp. 82–6.

6 Tait, W.J. 1984, A New Fragment of a Ptolemaic Priestly Decree at Durham, *Journal of Egyptian Archaeology* 70, 149–50.

7 https://collections.louvre.fr/en/ark:/53355/cl010035034. Devauchelle, D. 1986, Fragments de décrets ptolémaïques en langue égyptienne conservés au musée du Louvre, *Revue d'égyptologie* 37, 45–51.

8 Pfeiffer, S. 2004, *Das Dekret von Kanopos (238 v. Chr.): Kommentar und historische Auswertung eines dreisprachigen Synodaldekretes der ägyptischen Priester zu Ehren Ptolemaios' III. und seiner Familie. Archiv für Papyrusforschung und verwandte Gebiete*, 18. Munich.

9 http://cpi.csad.ox.ac.uk/CPI-I/CPI-119.html. Spiegelberg, W. 1922, *Der demotische Text der Priesterdekrete von Kanopus und Memphis (Rosettana): mit den hieroglyphischen und griechischen Fassungen und deutscher Übersetzung nebst demotischem Glossar.* Heidelberg, 3–37. https://archive.org/details/derdemotischetexoospie/page/n3/mode/2up.

10 http://cpi.csad.ox.ac.uk/CPI-I/CPI-129.html. Spiegelberg 1922, 3–37.

11 https://collections.louvre.fr/en/ark:/53355/cl010027713. Bernand, É. 1992, *Inscriptions grecques d'Égypte et de Nubie au Musée du Louvre*. Paris.

12 Bayoumi, A. and Guéraud, O. 1947, Un nouvel exemplaire du décret de Canope, *Annales du Service des antiquités de l'Égypte* 46, 373–82.

13 Lauffray, J., Sauneron, S., Ramadan Sa'ad and Anus, P. 1970, Rapport sur les travaux de Karnak: Activités du Centre franco-égyptien en 1968–1969, *Kêmi* 20, 57–99, esp. 74–5.

14 http://cpi.csad.ox.ac.uk/CPI-I/CPI-176.html. Sauneron, S. 1957, Un cinquième exemplaire du décret de Canope: La Stèle de Boubastis, *Bulletin de l'Institut français d'archéologie orientale* 56, 67–75. See also works under 39.

15 http://cpi.csad.ox.ac.uk/CPI-I/CPI-176.html. Tietze, C., Lange, E.R. and Hallof, K. 2005, Ein neues Exemplar des Kanopus-Dekrets aus Bubastis, *Archiv für Papyrusforschung und verwandte Gebiete* 51, no. 1, 1–29; Tietze, C., Maksoud, M. and Lange, E. 2004a, Das Kanopus-Dekret von Tell Basta, *Kemet* 3, 65–6; Tietze, C., Maksoud, M. and Lange, E. 2004b, Zeichen setzen: spektakulärer Fund; das Kanopus-Dekret von Tell Basta im östlichen Nildelta, *Antike Welt*, 35, no. 3, 75–6.

16 Raphael, M. 1935–8, Un nouveau décret ptolémaïque, in: Anonymous (ed.), *Mélanges Maspero I: Orient ancien*, vol. 2, 509–12. Cairo: l'Institut français d'archéologie orientale.

17 Thissen, H.-J. 1966, *Studien zum Raphiadekret*. Beiträge zur klassischen Philologie 23. Meisenheim am Glan.

18 http://cpi.csad.ox.ac.uk/CPI-I/CPI-190.html. Sottas, H. 1927, Notes complémentaires sur le décret en l'honneur de Ptolémée IV, *Revue de l'Égypte ancienne* 1, 230–42.

19 http://cpi.csad.ox.ac.uk/CPI-I/CPI-144.html. Gauthier, H. 1923, Un nouveau décret trilingue ptolémaïque, *Comptes rendus des séances de l'Académie des Inscriptions & Belles-Lettres* 67, no. 5, 376–83.

20 Schwartz and Malinine 1960, 82–6.

21 http://cpi.csad.ox.ac.uk/CPI-I/CPI-126.html. Hoffmann and Pfeiffer 2021. Reclams Universal-Bibliothek 14200. Ditzingen.

22 Spiegelberg, W. 1922, *Der demotische Text der Priesterdekrete von Kanopus und Memphis (Rosettana): mit den hieroglyphischen und griechischen Fassungen und deutscher Übersetzung nebst demotischem Glossar.* Heidelberg, 38–65.

23 See Appendix 2 in: Nespoulous-Phalippou, A. 2015, *Ptolémée Épiphane, Aristonikos et les prêtres d'Égypte: Le Décret de Memphis (182 a.C.). Édition commentée des stèles Caire RT 2/3/25/7 et JE 44901*. Cahiers 'Égypte Nilotique et Méditerranéenne' 12 (I–II). Montpellier: Université Paul Valéry – Montpellier III.

24 Devauchelle 1986, 45–51. https://collections.louvre.fr/en/ark:/53355/cl010029521; https://collections.louvre.fr/en/ark:/53355/cl010030343.

25 http://cpi.csad.ox.ac.uk/CPI-I/CPI-122.html. Lanciers, E. 1986, Die Ägyptischen Tempelbauten zur Zeit des Ptolemaios V. Epiphanes (204–180 v.Chr.): Part 1, *Mitteilungen des Deutschen Archäologischen Instituts, Abteilung Kairo* 42, 81–98; Lanciers, E. 1987a, Die ägyptischen Tempelbauten zur Zeit des Ptolemaios V. Epiphanes (204–180 v. Chr.). Part 2: Irrtümlich Ptolemaios V. zugeschriebene Denkmäler, *Mitteilungen des Deutschen Archäologischen Instituts, Abteilung Kairo* 43, 173–80; Fraser, P.M. 1956, An Unpublished Fragment of the Memphian Decree of 196 B.C., *Bulletin de la Société archéologique d'Alexandrie* 41, 57–62.

26 Devauchelle 1986, 45–51. https://collections.louvre.fr/en/ark:/53355/cl010035035; https://collections.louvre.fr/en/ark:/53355/cl010035036; https://collections.louvre.fr/en/ark:/53355/cl010035037; https://collections.louvre.fr/en/ark:/53355/cl010035038; https://collections.louvre.fr/en/ark:/53355/cl010035039.

27 Recklinghausen, D. von 2018, *Die Philensis-Dekrete: Untersuchungen über zwei Synodaldekrete aus der Zeit Ptolemaios' V. und ihre geschichtliche und religiöse Bedeutung*, 2 vols. Ägyptologische Abhandlungen 73. Wiesbaden.

28 Eldamaty, M.M. 2005, Ein ptolemäisches Priesterdekret aus dem Jahr 186 v. *Chr: eine neue Version von Philensis II in Kairo, Archiv für Papyrusforschung und verwandte Gebiete*, 20. Munich.

29 Recklinghausen 2018.

30 Daumas, F. 1958, Un duplicata du premier décret ptolémaique de Philae, *Mitteilungen des Deutschen Archäologischen Instituts, Abteilung Kairo* 16, 73–82.

31 Recklinghausen, D. von and Martinez, K. 2021, A New Version of 'Philensis I' from Taposiris Magna, in: Robinson, D. and Goddio, F. (eds), *Constructing, Remaking, and Dismantling Sacred Landscapes in Lower Egypt: Late Dynastic–Early Medieval Period*, 133–73. Oxford.

32 Nespoulous-Phalippou 2015.

33 Lanciers, E. 1987b, Die Stele CG22184: ein Priesterdekret aus der Regierungszeit des Ptolemaios VI. Philometor, *Göttinger Miszellen* 95, 53–61.

FURTHER READING

Allen, J.P. 2010, *Middle Egyptian: An Introduction to the Language and Culture of Hieroglyphs*. Cambridge

Bednarski, A. 2005, *Holding Egypt: Tracing the Reception of the Description de l'Égypte in Nineteenth-Century Great Britain*. Golden House Publications Egyptology 3. London

Bierbrier, M.L. 2019, *Who Was Who in Egyptology*, 5th revised edn. London

Buchwald, J.Z. and Josefowicz, D.G. 2020, *The Riddle of the Rosetta: How an English Polymath and a French Polyglot Discovered the Meaning of Egyptian Hieroglyphs*. Princeton

Clagett, M. 1999, *Ancient Egyptian Science: A Source Book*. Volume 3: *Ancient Egyptian Mathematics*. Memoirs of the American Philosophical Society 232. Philadelphia

Colla, E. 2007, *Conflicted Antiquities: Egyptology, Egyptomania, Egyptian Modernity*. Durham, WC, London

Curran, B. A. 2007, *The Egyptian Renaissance: The Afterlife of Ancient Egypt in Early Modern Italy*. Chicago

Davies, V. and Laboury, D. (eds) 2020, *The Oxford Handbook of Egyptian Epigraphy and Paleography*. New York

el-Daly, O. 2005, *Egyptology: The Missing Millennium: Ancient Egypt in Medieval Arabic Writings*. London

Fischer-Bovet, C. 2014, *Army and Society in Ptolemaic Egypt*. Cambridge

Hamilton, A. 2006, *The Copts and the West 1439–1822: The European Discovery of the Egyptian Church*. Oxford

Hoffmann, F. and Pfeiffer, S. 2021, *Der Stein von Rosetta*. Stuttgart

Horapollo, 1993, *The Hieroglyphics of Horapollo*, trans. George Boas, Bollingen Series 23. New York

Imhausen, A. 2016, *Mathematics in Ancient Egypt: A Contextual History*. Princeton

Iversen, E. 1993, *The Myth of Egypt and Its Hieroglyphs in European Tradition*, 2nd edn. Princeton

Leitz, C. 1999, *Magical and Medical Papyri of the New Kingdom*. Hieratic Papyri in the British Museum 7. London

Moran, W. L. 1992, *The Amarna Letters*. Baltimore, London

Morris, E. 2018, *Ancient Egyptian Imperialism*. Hoboken

Parkinson, R.B. 1997, *The Tale of Sinuhe and Other Ancient Egyptian Poems 1940–1649 BC*. Oxford

Parkinson, R.B. 1999, *Cracking Codes: The Rosetta Stone and Decipherment*. London

Pomian, K. 1990, *Collectors & Curiosities: Paris and Venice 1500–1800*. Cambridge

Reid, D.M. 2002, *Whose Pharaohs? Archaeology, Museums, and Egyptian National Identity from Napoleon to World War I*. Berkeley, Los Angeles, London

Robinson, A. 2006, *The Last Man Who Knew Everything: Thomas Young, the Anonymous Genius who Proved Newton Wrong and Deciphered the Rosetta Stone, among Other Surprising Feats*. London

Robinson, A. 2012, *Cracking the Egyptian Code: The Revolutionary Life of Jean-François Champollion*. London

Stolzenberg, D. 2013, *Egyptian Oedipus: Athanasius Kircher and the Secrets of Antiquity*. Chicago, London

Taylor, J.H. 2010, *Journey Through the Afterlife: Ancient Egyptian Book of the Dead*. London

Thompson, J. 2015, *Wonderful Things: A History of Egyptology 1: From Antiquity to 1881*. Cairo, New York

Tiradritti, F. (ed.) 2008, *Pharaonic Renaissance: Archaism and the Sense of History. Cankarjev dom, Ljubljana 4th March–20th July 2008*. Ljubljana

Ucko, P. and Champion, T. (eds) 2003, *The Wisdom of Egypt: Changing Visions through the Ages*. London

Usick, P. 2002, *Adventures in Egypt and Nubia: The Travels of William John Bankes (1786–1855)*. London

Vandorpe, K. (ed.) 2019, *A Companion to Greco-Roman and Late Antique Egypt*. Hoboken

Wendrich, W. (ed.) 2016, *UCLA Encyclopedia of Egyptology*. Los Angeles

MAP AND CHAPTER OPENERS

Page 8
This map uses the most widely known place names, either the ancient name, a transposition of the ancient name, or the modern Arabic name of the nearest town, village or even hill. For example, the ancient city of Herakleopolis can be called any of the following: Ihnasya, Ehnâsya, Ahnas, Ahnassia, Ehnas, Ehnasya el-Medina, Ehnâsija el-Medîna, Ihnasiah elMédinèh, Ihnasya el-Madina, Ihnasya el-Medina or Ihnasya el Medina.

Page 14
Detail of the Book of the Dead of Nedjmet; see figs 1 and 163

Page 30
Watercolour of the stela of Nestjerenmaat; see fig. 51

Page 90
The Rosetta Stone, a priestly decree in hieroglyphs, demotic and Greek
Rashid, Ptolemaic period, 196 BCE
Granodiorite, H. 112.3 cm, W. 75.7 cm, D. 28.4 cm
British Museum, EA24
Donated by King George III

Page 126
Watercolour of a scene in the tomb of Sety I showing the king seated before a table of bread, by Henry William Beechey (1788/89–1862)
Thebes, 19th century CE
Paper, H. 73 cm, W. 55.3 cm, D. 2.5 cm (framed)
British Museum, AESAr.278

Page 144
Statue of Sety II; see fig. 116

Page 234
Different scripts on the outer wall of the Bibliotheca Alexandrina, 2002. © Bibliotheca Alexandrina 2022

ILLUSTRATION CREDITS

The publisher would like to thank the copyright holders for granting permission to reproduce the images illustrated. Every attempt has been made to trace accurate ownership of copyrighted images in this book. Any errors or omissions will be corrected in subsequent editions provided notification is sent to the publisher.

Further information about the Museum and its collection can be found at britishmuseum.org. Registration numbers for British Museum objects are included in the image captions. Unless otherwise stated, copyright in photographs belongs to the institution mentioned in the caption. All images of British Museum objects are © 2022 The Trustees of the British Museum, courtesy the Department of Photography and Imaging. All illustrations are by Claire Thorne, unless otherwise stated below. The map and timeline on pp. 8 and 12–13 are by Martin Brown.

6 Adapted from Allen, J.P. 2010, *Middle Egyptian: An Introduction to the Language and Culture of Hieroglyphs*. Cambridge, p. 18. Reproduced with permission of the Licensor through PLSclear.
8 The Bodleian Libraries, University of Oxford, MS. Copt. a.2
10 Bibliothèque nationale de France
11 © British Library Board, 66.b.24 pp. 82–3
12 The Bodleian Libraries, University of Oxford, MS. Arab. d. 221, fol. 48b and 49a
13 British Library, London, UK © British Library Board. All Rights Reserved/Bridgeman Images
15 Thorvaldsens Museum, inv. no. ThM E1327, Photographer: Helle Nanny Brendstrup
16 Florence, The Biblioteca Medicea Laurenziana, ms. Plut.69.27, f. 69v. Reproduced with permission of MiC. Further reproduction by any means is prohibited.
19 Torino, Museo Egizio
20 Photo © Musée du Louvre, Dist. RMN-Grand Palais / Georges Poncet
21 Bibliothèque nationale de France
26 © British Library Board, G.2083, Tome IV, Volume 3, pp. 502–3
27 Thorvaldsens Museum, inv. no. ThM L214, Photographer: Ole Haupt
28 Thorvaldsens Museum, inv. no. ThM L206, Photographer: Ole Haupt
29 Thorvaldsens Museum, inv. no. ThM D1161, Photographer: Helle Nanny Brendstrup
31 Courtesy Museo Civico Archeologico Bologna
32 Courtesy Museo Civico Archeologico Bologna
33 Courtesy Museo Civico Archeologico Bologna
34 Courtesy Ministero della Cultura – Museo Archeologico Nazionale di Napoli. Photo by Giorgio Albano
35 Thorvaldsens Museum, inv. no. ThM E1416, E1418, Photographer: Helle Nanny Brendstrup
36 Det Kgl. Bibliotek – Royal Danish Library, NKS 357b folio, XIII, 1c (XIII, 3, 3, 6)
37 Courtesy Museo Civico Archeologico Bologna
38 Thorvaldsens Museum, inv. no. ThM D1167r+v, Photographer: Jakob Faurvig
40 Thorvaldsens Museum, inv. no. ThM E1394, Photographer: Helle Nanny Brendstrup
42 Photo: Ahmed Mostafa
43 The National Archives, UK
49 National Trust Images
53 © H. Neveu-Dérotrie / Musée Dobrée – Grand Patrimoine de Loire-Atlantique
57 © British Library Board, ADD 27281, f92
60 © British Library Board, ADD 27282, f77
63 National Trust Images

66 Musée Champollion – Les Écritures du Monde | Figeac
67 The Hague, Huis van het boek
68 © British Library Board, MS Or 1325, fol. 117a
69 © British Library Board, ADD MS 5114, foo2r
70 Bibliothèque nationale de France
72 © British Library Board, ADD 21026, f16
74 Bibliothèque nationale de France
76 The Bodleian Libraries, University of Oxford, MS. Egypt a.4
77 Bibliothèque nationale de France
79 Bibliothèque nationale de France
84 Archives départementales de l'Isère, 185 J 18
86 Bibliothèque nationale de France
87 Bibliothèque nationale de France
90 National Trust Images
91 © Fitzwilliam Museum, Cambridge
92 Photo © Musée du Louvre, Dist. RMN-Grand Palais / Hervé Lewandowski
94 Biblioteca Universitaria di Pisa – Ministero della Cultura-Italia
95 Biblioteca Universitaria di Pisa – Ministero della Cultura-Italia
98 © Staatliche Museen zu Berlin – Ägyptisches Museum und Papyrussammlung, Inv. Nr. P. Berlin 3024, photo: S. Steiß
102 © Staatliche Museen zu Berlin – Vorderasiatisches Museum, Photo: Olaf M. Teßmer
103 Biblioteca Universitaria di Pisa – Ministero della Cultura-Italia
106 National Trust Images
110 Archives départementales de l'Isère, 185 J 18
119 © Antiquariat Inlibris, Vienna
124 Carpentras, bibliothèque-musée Inguimbertine, Stele de Taba, inv. 2007.0.16, photographer: Chaline Photo
140 Photo © Musée du Louvre, Dist. RMN-Grand Palais / Georges Poncet
154 © courtesy of NML
155 © courtesy of NML
156 Photo © Musée du Louvre, Dist. RMN-Grand Palais / Christian Décamps
157 © Fondation Calvet-Avignon France
158 Courtesy of the Natural History Society of Northumbria. Image © Tyne & Wear Archives & Museums
159 Courtesy of the Natural History Society of Northumbria. Image © Tyne & Wear Archives & Museums
160 Bibliothèque nationale de France
161 Bibliothèque nationale de France
162 Private collection of David and Molly Lowell Borthwick
167 Courtesy of the Petrie Museum, UCL
177 Torino, Museo Egizio
190 Courtesy of the Petrie Museum, UCL
209 Photo © Musée du Louvre, Dist. RMN-Grand Palais / Georges Poncet
223 Photo © Musée du Louvre, Dist. RMN-Grand Palais / Christian Décamps
224 Photo © Musée du Louvre, Dist. RMN-Grand Palais / Christian Décamps
225 OPERA Amsterdam
226 The Digital Rosetta Stone Project
227 Friedhelm Hoffmann / Stefan Pfeiffer : *Der Stein von Rosetta* © 2021 Philipp Reclam jun. Verlag GmbH, Ditzingen/Germany
228 The Digital Rosetta Stone Project
229 The Digital Rosetta Stone Project
230 The Digital Rosetta Stone Project
231 Photo by JJ Shirley, Director, TT110 Epigraphy & Research Field School
232 Photo: Marcel Marée

LIST OF LENDERS

Biblioteca Medicea Laurenziana
Bibliothèque Inguimbertine, Carpentras
Bibliothèque nationale de France
The Bodleian Libraries
The British Library
The Fitzwilliam Museum
Great North Museum: Hancock
Huis van het boek, The Hague
Musée du Louvre
Musée Champollion – Les Écritures du Monde
Musée Dobrée – Grand patrimoine de Loire-Atlantique
Musée Calvet
Museo Archeologico Nazionale di Napoli
Museo Civico Archeologico, Bologna
Museo Egizio
The National Archives, UK
National Museums Liverpool, Lady Lever Art Gallery
National Trust
Natural History Society of Northumbria
The Petrie Museum of Egyptian and Sudanese Archaeology, UCL
Pisa University Library
Private Collection of David and Molly Lowell Borthwick
Thorvaldsens Museum

ACKNOWLEDGEMENTS

Much of the research and some of the writing for this publication took place in Cairo during the Covid-19 pandemic. We are grateful to the French Archaeological Institute and the Dutch-Flemish Institute in Cairo for providing unlimited access to their libraries during this challenging time.

Many colleagues made the book and exhibition possible, sharing their novel work and expertise on the history of Egyptology and Egyptian collections worldwide. Several scholars have generously contributed their time to the publication: Susanne Beck, Monica Berti, Willy Clarysse, Fayza Haikal, Cary Martin, Franziska Naether, Richard Bruce Parkinson, Daniela Picchi, John Taylor, Patricia Usick and Pascal Vernus. Many others provided information on objects featured in the publication or provided technical assistance with hieroglyphic and hieratic signs: Alexandra Ault, Gert Baetens, Colin Baker, Jean-Yves Baudouy, Odile Cavalier, Yves Champollion, Thomas Christiansen, Helen Copping, Luke Dady, Vanessa Descaux, Juliane Eule, Azza Ezzat, Anna Garnett, Christian Greco, Paul Guermond, Hélène Guichard, Svenja Gülden, Bink Hallum, Kristine Bøggild Johannsen, Fatma Keshk, Philippe Mainterot, Ahmed Mansour, Francesca Marini, Caroline McDonald, Floriana Miele, Gianluca Miniaci, Rosanna Pirelli, Alyson Pollard, Federico Poole, Luigi Prada, Chrystelle Quebriac, Céline Ramio, Vincent Rondot, Ishwant Sahota, Silvia Scipioni, Hazel Shorland, Helen Strudwick, Ilana Tahan, Rickey Tax, Steen Søndergaard Thomsen and Alasdair Watson.

At the British Museum, an expert team has made this book and exhibition possible. The excellent core project team consisted of: David Agar, Guy Carr, Hennah Khan, Ann Lumley, Sean McParland, Charis Millett, Lauren Papworth, Paul Richards, Stephanie Vasiliou, Victoria Ward, William Westwood, Philip Woods, Sam Wyles and Evan York. A special thanks must go to Project Curator, Kelly Accetta Crowe, for her admirable dedication and hard work, and especially for managing images and other visual resources that appear in the book; and to Holly Wright for her excellent project management. We are grateful to the entire conservation, photography and collection management teams for facilitating state-of-the-art presentation of the objects in the British Museum collection, and to the loans department for assistance with objects borrowed from international partners. We also wish to thank the Department of Egypt and Sudan, its Keeper, Daniel Antoine, and especially Patricia Usick and John Taylor for advising on the content of both the exhibition and this publication, to which they also contributed. Thanks to colleagues in other departments who advised on specific content. We would like to thank senior management and Director of Public Engagement, Jill Maggs, Head of Interpretation and Volunteers, Stuart Frost and Corporate Relations Officer, Samuel Waizeneker for their positive spirit when championing the project.

Last but not least, we are very grateful to the Publishing team at the British Museum for bringing this book to completion: Head of Publishing, Claudia Bloch; Project Editor, Yvonne Thouroude; Production Manager, Beata Kibil; and Sales and Marketing Manager, Toni Allum. Thank you to designer, Catherine Bankhurst, copy-editor, Carolyn Jones, proofreader, Hilary Hammond, indexer, Nicola King and Julia Bettinson and Harry King at Altaimage.

Personal gratitude is owed to Maria Golia and Jeff Allen for inspiration and critical feedback on content and language.

INDEX

Numbers in *italic* denote pages with figures.